D0847527

WITHDRAWN
FROM THE COLLECTION
CARNEGIE LIBRARY OF PITTSBURGH

Carnegie
Library of
Pittsburgh
Main

The Operas of Maurice Ravel

Maurice Ravel's operas *L'Heure espagnole* (1907/1911) and *L'Enfant et les sortilèges* (1919–25) are pivotal works in the composer's relatively small œuvre. Emerging from periods shaped by very distinct musical concerns and historical circumstances, these two vastly different works nevertheless share qualities that reveal the heart of Ravel's compositional aesthetic. In this comprehensive study, Emily Kilpatrick unites musical, literary, biographical and cultural perspectives to shed new light on Ravel's operas. In documenting the operas' history, setting them within the cultural canvas of their creation and pursuing diverse strands of analytical and thematic exploration, Kilpatrick reveals crucial aspects of the composer's working life: his approach to creative collaboration; his responsiveness to cultural, aesthetic and musical debate; and the centrality of language and literature in his compositional practice. The first study of its kind, this book is an invaluable resource for students, specialists, opera-goers and devotees of French music.

EMILY KILPATRICK's fascination with Ravel's operas dates from a memorable summer spent helping to restore the composer's former home in Montfort l'Amaury. With a Ph.D. in Musicology from the University of Adelaide, she has published widely on the music of Ravel and Fauré and is co-editor, with Roy Howat, of the new Peters critical edition of Fauré's complete songs, a project based at the Royal Academy of Music in London. Emily also maintains an active performing career as a pianist and vocal accompanist, and regularly gives recitals, radio broadcasts, master classes and lectures on French opera and song. She holds a lectureship at the Royal Northern College of Music (Manchester).

MUSIC IN CONTEXT

Series editors:

J. P. E. Harper-Scott
Royal Holloway, University of London

Julian Rushton
University of Leeds

The aim of Music in Context is to illuminate specific musical works, repertoires or practices in historical, critical, socio-economic or other contexts; or to illuminate particular cultural and critical contexts in which music operates, through the study of specific musical works, repertoires or practices. A specific musical focus is essential, while avoiding the decontextualisation of traditional aesthetics and music analysis. The series title invites engagement with both its main terms; the aim is to challenge notions of what contexts are appropriate or necessary in studies of music, and to extend the conceptual framework of musicology into other disciplines or into new theoretical directions.

Books in the series

Simon P. Keefe, *Mozart's Requiem: Reception, Work, Completion*

J. P. E. Harper-Scott, *The Quilting Points of Musical Modernism: Revolution, Reaction, and William Walton*

Nancy November, *Beethoven's Theatrical Quartets: Opp. 59, 74, and 95*

Rufus Hallmark, *'Frauenliebe und Leben': Chamisso's Poems and Schumann's Songs*

Anna Zayaruznaya, *The Monstrous New Art: Divided Forms in the Late Medieval Motet*

Helen Deeming and Elizabeth Eva Leach, *Manuscripts and Medieval Song: Inscription, Performance, Context*

Emily Kilpatrick, *The Operas of Maurice Ravel*

The Operas of Maurice Ravel

EMILY KILPATRICK

ML410.R23 K55 2015
Kilpatrick, Emily, author.
The operas of Maurice Ravel
Cambridge : Cambridge
University Press, 2015.

CAMBRIDGE
UNIVERSITY PRESS

CAMBRIDGE
UNIVERSITY PRESS

University Printing House, Cambridge CB2 8BS, United Kingdom

Cambridge University Press is part of the University of Cambridge.

It furthers the University's mission by disseminating knowledge in the pursuit of education, learning and research at the highest international levels of excellence.

www.cambridge.org
Information on this title: www.cambridge.org/9781107118126

© Emily Kilpatrick 2015

This publication is in copyright. Subject to statutory exception
and to the provisions of relevant collective licensing agreements,
no reproduction of any part may take place without the written
permission of Cambridge University Press.

First published 2015

Printed in the United Kingdom by TJ International Ltd. Padstow Cornwall

A catalogue record for this publication is available from the British Library

Library of Congress Cataloguing in Publication data
Kilpatrick, Emily.
The operas of Maurice Ravel / Emily Kilpatrick.
    pages   cm. – (Music in context)
Includes bibliographical references and index.
ISBN 978-1-107-11812-6
1. Ravel, Maurice, 1875–1937. Operas.   2. Opera – France – 20th century.   I. Title.
ML410.R23K55   2015
782.1092–dc23

                                                                    2015014695

ISBN 978-1-107-11812-6 Hardback

Cambridge University Press has no responsibility for the persistence or accuracy of
URLs for external or third-party internet websites referred to in this publication,
and does not guarantee that any content on such websites is, or will remain,
accurate or appropriate.

for Roy, Rosie and Felix

Contents

List of figures   *page* [viii]
Preface   [ix]
Acknowledgements   [xiii]
List of abbreviations   [xv]
Opera synopses   [xvi]

PART I   MAKING OPERAS   [1]

1 Introduction: 'A single act at the Opéra-Comique'   [3]
2 Ravel's hour   [16]
3 The Child and the impresarios   [34]

PART II   WORDS AND MUSIC   [53]

4 The collaborative process   [55]
5 Songs into operas   [75]
6 'This archaic attempt at a modern fantasy'   [99]
7 A portrait of an opera-ballet   [121]

PART III   THE COMPOSITIONAL WEB   [143]

8 The 'calling cards' of *L'Heure espagnole*   [145]
9 From Carmen to Concepcion   [172]
10 The 'big, small world' of *L'Enfant et les sortilèges*   [197]
11 A Child of his time   [217]

Afterword   [236]
Bibliography   [243]
Index   [261]

Figures

0.1   Set designs by Alphonse Visconti for the première
of *L'Enfant et les sortilèges*, Monte Carlo, 1925. © Archives
Monte-Carlo SBM.   [*page* xii]

2.1   The *livre de bord* of the Opéra-Comique records the première of
L'Heure espagnole, 19 May 1911. Bibliothèque-musée de l'Opéra,
micr. 3453.   [25]

7.1   Libretto draft for Cup and Teapot scene of *L'Enfant et les
sortilèges*, given by Colette to Hélène Jourdan-Morhange.
Jourdan-Morhange, *Ravel et nous* (Geneva: Milieu du monde, 1945),
plate IX.   [125]

9.1   Gonzalve's extravagant exit from his clock (Fig. 68^{+10}), as
depicted in the 1911 production score of *L'Heure espagnole* (coll.
Roy Howat).   [182]

9.2   (a) Francisco Goya, *Portrait of the Duchess of Alba* (1797).   [190]

(b) Célestine Galli-Marié as Carmen, painted by Henri-Lucien
Doucet (1884). Reproduced in *Carmen, by Georges Bizet*, trans.
and introduction by Ellen H. Bleiler, Dover Opera Guide and
Libretto Series (New York: Dover, 1970); reproduced by kind
permission of Dover Publications.

(c) Costume design for Concepcion, from the 1911 production
material. Bibliothèque historique de la ville de Paris, coll. ART
(4-TMS-03777); reproduced by kind permission.

(d) Geneviève Vix as Concepcion, *Musica* 106 (July 1911), p. 132.
Bibliothèque des Arts décoratifs, Paris.

9.3   1912 photo-montage showing the Opéra-Comique's
Carmens, *Musica* 117 (June 1912). Bibliothèque des Arts
décoratifs, Paris.   [190]

9.4   Opéra-Comique memo detailing stage-walkers' costumes for
L'Heure espagnole, dated 11 May 1911 and tipped into the 1911
production score (coll. Roy Howat).   [191]

Preface

I first listened to *L'Enfant et les sortilèges* sitting on the living-room floor of Ravel's house, Le Belvédère in Montfort l'Amaury. The big French windows were open, and as I listened my gaze shifted between the long, sweeping curve of the facing hill, green and blue and gold on a summer afternoon, and the perfectly arranged and intricately detailed surroundings of the house itself.

Over the decade that has passed since I first visited Montfort l'Amaury that memory has remained vivid, for the juxtaposition of concentrated interiors and sunlit panorama seems an apt metaphor for Ravel's œuvre as a whole. It is an analogy, indeed, that echoes even in the sets for the 1925 première of *L'Enfant*: glimpses of tree and garden beckon beyond the cluttered and constricting nursery interior, while a spacious and enticing vista opens behind the garden itself (see Fig. 0.1 below).

Both of Ravel's operas, *L'Enfant et les sortilèges* (1919–25) and the earlier *L'Heure espagnole* (1907/1911), offer us windows through which we can shift our focus between the minutiae of a compositional world and a wider landscape of cultural and historical perspectives, biographical circumstances, and dramaturgical, literary and musical exploration. In many respects, the two works could hardly be more different. One was composed in the last years of the Belle Époque, the other in the *Années folles*; between them lies the great barrier of the First World War. One is a light-hearted, Spanish-themed bedroom farce, the other a magical evocation of childhood and fairytale. The libretto of *L'Heure* was drawn from a successful play; that of *L'Enfant* was purpose-written. *L'Heure* tells its story in rapid exchanges of dialogue; *L'Enfant* in description, dance and reflection. *L'Heure* was composed within the space of three or four months; the gestation of *L'Enfant* spanned twice that many years. *L'Heure* is the work of a young man claiming his place in the musical limelight, but by the time Ravel, within the space of a few weeks, celebrated his fiftieth birthday and the première of *L'Enfant*, he was widely acclaimed as the leading composer of his generation.

Given this wealth of material and perspective, it is perhaps surprising that, although Ravel has been the focus of unprecedented critical attention in recent years (particularly in the Anglophone literature), the present book is the first to be devoted to his operas.[1] One of its aims, therefore, is to extend and refine certain of the themes and theories presented in the more expansive canvases of recent major publications.[2] Relative to its more limited subject matter, this study takes up some of the dialogues initiated by Steven Huebner's many probing chapters on Ravel's operas and compositional philosophy, and by Jessie Fillerup's recent writings, which masterfully draw together many of the threads running through the rich cultural fabric of the composer's time and place. Deborah Mawer's *The Ballets of Maurice Ravel*, one of the few books to focus on a single genre within Ravel's output, was one of my points of departure; Roger Nichols's monumental 2011 biography was an indispensable resource. More broadly, the cultural and operatic landscape revealed in the writings of (*inter alia*) Barbara Kelly, Richard Langham Smith, Jann Pasler and Annegret Fauser provided invaluable context.

The present study falls into three parts. Its first chapters set *L'Heure* and *L'Enfant* in historical context; the central chapters explore the interplay of text and music; and the latter chapters are devoted to thematic and analytical aspects of the operas. The book is supplemented by a *Compendium of Sources* (www.cambridge.org/9781107118126), comprising early reviews, correspondence and other relevant documentation; readers seeking the original French texts of the archival sources quoted here in translation will find them in the *Compendium*.

It is perhaps natural to devote particular attention to the periods that bookend a work's development: on one hand the compositional background and process, and on the other early performances and critical reception. The study of opera, however, necessitates a third element: the passage – often long and rarely straightforward – from score to stage. Years elapsed between the initial conception and the theatrical realisation of both of Ravel's operas. Retracing these periods, as in the present Chapters 1, 2 and 3, throws new light on the composer's professional practice, as a correspondent, negotiator, self-publicist and man of the theatre.

Reaching beyond the operas themselves, this book has at its core the exchange of music and words, in the tug and rasp of a language that Ravel

---

[1] Schillmöller's *Maurice Ravels Schlüsselwerk* L'Enfant et les sortilèges (1999) is the only monograph to date on *L'Enfant* alone. Roland-Manuel's *Maurice Ravel et son œuvre dramatique* (1928) encompasses operas and ballets.

[2] See for example Zank's *Irony and Sound* and Puri's *Ravel the Decadent*, together with the edited collections *Ravel Studies* (ed. Mawer) and *Unmasking Ravel* (ed. Kaminsky). Mawer's 'Introduction' to *Ravel Studies* summarises the significant trends in Ravel scholarship up to 2010; Fillerup surveys these publications and contemporary Ravel scholarship in her 2014 review article 'Ravel's lost time'. See also Zank, *Maurice Ravel: A Guide to Research*.

once suggested was 'not designed for poetry'.[3] One of my primary aims is thus to highlight, more thoroughly than has yet been attempted, the centrality of language and literature in his compositional practice. Chapter 4 re-examines the dialogues, direct and oblique, between the composer and his librettists, Franc-Nohain and Colette. Setting new documentary evidence alongside sources from the composer's lifetime and more recent scholarly appraisals, the book draws out not just aesthetic concerns but practical insights into Ravel as a collaborator and colleague. Chapter 5 outlines Ravel's explorations of text and text-setting, viewing the operas through the prism of his songs. Special attention is given here to the development, through the *mélodie*, of the meticulously naturalistic recitative that he realised most completely in *L'Heure espagnole*. Riding the historical and philosophical currents that flow through the interplay of French speech and song, this chapter and those that follow build on the recent researches of Katherine Bergeron and Michel Gribenski, and extend studies of Ravel's text-setting by Kaminsky, James Hurd and Marie-Pierre Lassus, as well as literary analyses by scholars including Michel Mercier and Henry Bouillier, and Ravel's own reflections on language and text-setting. This chapter forms the point of departure for Chapters 6 and 7, which focus on Ravel's two libretti and the manner in which, at every level of the compositional process, he integrated his texts into his musical design.

Chapters 8–11 pursue text-driven musical and thematic analyses within the frame of the operas' central subjects, or settings: Spain and Spanishness, and children and childhood. Weaving a tapestry of sources literary, musical, philosophical, cultural and theatrical, they aim to nuance and hone our understanding of these themes relative to Ravel's compositional method, his aesthetic and his personal experience and perceptions.

Having established, in Chapter 8, the manner in which *L'Heure espagnole* uses an outwardly comic leitmotif technique to establish a large-scale musical logic, Chapter 9 explores the opera's conceptual, musical and theatrical 'Spanishness'. Drawing on the writings of Langham Smith, Hervé Lacombe, Samuel Llano and Kerry Murphy, it locates *L'Heure* within the turn-of-the-century Parisian culture of *espagnolade*. In probing the opera's typically Ravelian blend of irony and homage, the chapter draws new connections with the greatest of 'Spanish' operas, Bizet's *Carmen*. Turning to *L'Enfant*, Chapter 10 demonstrates how the musical characterisation of the eponymous Child – an onlooker rather

---

[3] Olin Downes, 'Maurice Ravel, man and musician', *New York Times*, 7 August 1927; in Orenstein (ed.), *A Ravel Reader*, 450.

than an active participant for much of the opera – imparts a compelling large-scale musical coherence, while Chapter 11 looks to conceptions and representations of childhood. Moving from cultural and political perspectives to notions of memory and nostalgia, from Jung to Klein and back to Colette herself, it illuminates the myriad interpretative paths traceable through this most mutable and most entrancing of operas.

Figure 0.1 Set designs by Alphonse Visconti for the première of *L'Enfant et les sortilèges*, Monte Carlo, 1925.

Acknowledgements

In the summer of 2004, Arnaud and Henriette de Vitry generously welcomed into their home in Montfort l'Amaury a young Australian on her first trip to Europe; this marvellous introduction to French culture, manners and humour remains a treasured memory. Claude Moreau, of the Musée Ravel, took me under her wing that summer, and her affectionate intimacy with the composer and his music has profoundly shaped my own relationship with both.

The generosity and goodwill of the international community of Ravelian and French music scholars makes working in this field a pleasure: I thank in particular Philippe Cathé, Michael Christoforidis, Keith Clifton, Manuel Cornejo, Katharine Ellis, Nina Gubisch-Viñes, Denis Herlin, Steven Huebner, Barbara Kelly, Elizabeth Kertesz, Richard Langham Smith, Eric van Lauwe, Heath Lees, Marcel Marnat, Deborah Mawer, Kerry Murphy, Michela Niccolai, Arbie Orenstein, Robert Orledge and Lesley Wright. I offer special thanks to Roger Nichols, who shared many sources with me and read this book in draft form, offering much valuable feedback; and to the late Philippe Rodriguez, whose gentle erudition illuminated so many issues of the *Cahiers Maurice Ravel*. I also thank David Lockett, Mark Carroll, Charles Bodman Rae and Kimi Coaldrake at the University of Adelaide; Timothy Jones, Nicole Tibbels and Neil Heyde at the Royal Academy of Music; and Joanna Drimatis, Edwina Farrall and Joshua van Konkelenberg, who shared this long journey with me. I am grateful for the assistance so generously provided by librarians and archivists at various institutions, and thank in particular Marie-Odile Gigou of the BIbliothèque historique de la ville de Paris, Charlotte Lubert of the Société des Bains de Mer, Monte-Carlo, and the unfailingly patient and helpful staff of the Bibliothèque nationale de France (in particular the BIbliothèque-musée de l'Opéra).

While I was still embroiled in my doctoral research Vicki Cooper, commissioning editor at Cambridge University Press, encouraged me to write this book; I thank her for her unwavering commitment to the project. Julian Rushton gently prodded me back into writing at a time when, as a sleep-deprived new parent, I might have put it to one side. I am grateful for his steadfast encouragement and his invaluable guidance, as well as that of his fellow series editor Paul Harper-Scott.

Finally, I thank my family: my parents David and Nancy, who gave me the gifts of music and words; my sisters Hannah and Fleur, singers, scholars and artists; my husband Roy Howat, whose generous musicianship is my constant inspiration, and without whom I could never have written this book; and our daughter Rosalind, whose arrival, midway through the writing process, rather delayed its completion but brought us joy beyond measure.

Last of all, I am inexpressibly grateful for the gift of the tiny being whose kicks and squirms are distracting me as I read these proofs, reminding me that a new era of mingled chaos and enchantment is imminent.

Emily Kilpatrick
June 2015

Abbreviations

BHVP   Bibliothèque historique de la ville de Paris

BnF   Bibliothèque nationale de France. Specific departments cited: Mus. (Département de la Musique); AdS (Département des Arts du spectacle); Bm-O (Bibliothèque-musée de l'Opéra)

CMR   *Cahiers Maurice Ravel*

OL   Arbie Orenstein (ed.), *Maurice Ravel: lettres, écrits, entretiens* (Paris: Flammarion, 1989), published in English (with some additional content) as *A Ravel Reader: Correspondence, Articles, Interviews* (New York: Columbia University Press, 1990). The present volume generally adopts the English translations presented in *A Ravel Reader*, with some minor adjustments for clarity and emphasis. Letters are cited by letter number (French and English editions are numbered equivalently); page numbers (for articles and interviews) refer to the French edition unless otherwise indicated. (Articles and interviews originally published in languages other than French are cited from *A Ravel Reader*.) Interviews and articles cited from this collection are not listed separately in the Bibliography.

SBM   Société des Bains de Mer, Monte-Carlo

*   Original French text given in *The Operas of Maurice Ravel: A Compendium of Sources* (www.cambridge.org/9781107118126)

Unless otherwise acknowledged, all translations are my own.

Musical examples are reproduced by kind permission of Éditions Durand. Examples from *L'Heure espagnole* and *L'Enfant et les sortilèges* are derived from the piano-vocal scores, supplemented by reference to the orchestral scores (see Bibliography).

Opera synopses

L'Heure espagnole

In a clockmaker's shop in Toledo, Concepcion eagerly awaits the weekly departure of her husband Torquemada to wind the municipal clocks, leaving her free to entertain her suitors. But this morning, her plans are upset by the arrival of the muleteer Ramiro, with a watch for Torquemada to fix. She has the ingenious idea of hiding her two swains, the poet Gonzalve and the banker Don Inigo, in large clocks, and employing Ramiro to carry them up to the bedroom for her. As Concepcion becomes frustrated by Gonzalve's self-absorption and Inigo's incompetence, however, Ramiro's great strength, compliance and unassuming manner become increasingly attractive: eventually, she invites the muleteer upstairs 'without a clock'. Torquemada returns, delighted to find his shop so busy, and sells the two clocks to their discomfited former occupants. The final quintet acknowledges the dubious 'morale de Boccace': that 'there comes a time when the muleteer has his turn!'

L'Enfant et les sortilèges

A bored and restless Child is seated at his desk, listening to the purr of the cat and the kettle boiling on the fire. His mother reproaches him for his laziness; his only response is to stick out his tongue. In punishment, she condemns him to stay by himself until dinner, with dry bread to eat and no sugar in his tea. After she leaves, the furious Child shrieks and stamps, destroying and injuring everything within reach. One by one the injured objects come to life, condemning the Child for his destructive acts. He finds himself in the Garden, where, amidst the birds, insects and little creatures there are more reminders of the havoc he has wrought. Lonely and afraid, he calls for his mother, rousing the fury of the Animals, who unite against him. In their frenzy a little squirrel is injured and the Child binds up the wounded paw before falling back weakly. Suddenly, there is a 'profound silence, stupor' among the Animals: the Child has finally atoned for his wrongdoing. Repenting of their own violence, the Animals try, hesitantly at first and then with confidence, to repeat the word the Child had sobbed: 'Maman!'

PART I

Making operas

1 | Introduction: 'A single act at the Opéra-Comique'

> I cannot forget that they were damning Faust the day of my first excursion with Renaud... Ignorant little provincial that I was, I asked, 'Is it a première?' He responded without malice, 'No, my little shepherdess, a two-hundred-and-seventy-seventh.'
>
> – Colette[1]

In the first decade of the twentieth century, success on the lyric stage was still regarded as the ultimate accolade for a young Parisian composer. Careers were kick-started, shaped and remembered by a composer's operas – or, sometimes, a lack of them. *Pelléas et Mélisande* made Debussy's name, the posthumous success of *Carmen* retrospectively redefined Bizet's compositional status, and the unflagging popularity of *Faust, Manon* and their companions assured the standing of Gounod and Massenet – and the coffers of their publishers. Chabrier's run of abysmal misfortune in the opera houses of Paris and Brussels left him long uncelebrated by the general public; and after the 1913 première of *Pénélope* almost all of the reviews noted the musical world's (appropriately) long wait for this, the 67-year-old Fauré's first opera, with many observing that there had been doubts as to whether he would ever be capable of the task.[2] Even Chopin, newly arrived in Paris in the early 1830s, had been exhorted by his erstwhile teacher Joseph Elsner to get on with *his* opera because 'only an opera can show your talent in a true light and win for it eternal life';[3] eighty years later Émile Vuillermoz, reviewing the première of *L'Heure espagnole*, was not being entirely facetious when he wrote 'It is well understood, in our twentieth century, that a single act at the Opéra-Comique is of more musical importance than three symphonies, ten quartets, twenty sonatas and a hundred songs.'*[4]

By the spring of 1907 Maurice Ravel had announced himself to the musical world with major contributions to the repositories of contemporary piano and chamber music and song. With four Prix de Rome cantatas

---

[1] 'Claudine au concert', *Gil Blas*, 12 January 1903, recalling a scene in *Claudine à Paris*.
[2] See the many reviews cited in Phillips, *Gabriel Fauré: A Guide to Research*, 358–79.
[3] Chopin, *Selected Correspondence*, 124.   [4] Vuillermoz, 'Les Théâtres: *L'Heure espagnole*', 67.

under his belt as well as the orchestral *Shéhérazade* songs, he had developed considerable expertise in writing for voices and orchestra, and with the *Histoires naturelles* he had pioneered a manner of vocal writing that was highly individual, technically daring and impeccably crafted. Although the *scandale* of the 1905 Prix de Rome (in which he had been disqualified in the preliminary round) had died down, the controversy surrounding the January 1907 première of *Histoires naturelles* was keeping Ravel's name in the press and the public eye. His friends and colleagues must have been encouraging him to try his hand at a work for the lyric stage, and he could not have been hard to convince. Ravel had for several years been acknowledged as one of the most gifted of the younger generation, but he had not yet won recognition as a composer of the first rank. A successful opera would be the most tangible evidence of his 'arrival'.

With his final spectacular failure in the Prix de Rome, Ravel had left his student days behind him. Buoyed by a contract with the prestigious publisher Durand, he was soon enjoying the most prolific compositional period of his life, riding a tide of works that carried him from the *Introduction et Allegro*, *Sonatine* and *Miroirs* (1905), *Histoires naturelles* (1906), *L'Heure espagnole* and *Rapsodie espagnole* (1907) to *Gaspard de la nuit* (1908) and the beginnings of *Daphnis et Chloé* (1909). Photos of Ravel around 1907 show him still sporting the jaunty moustache of his student days, plus the soft beard that he had grown around 1905 (by 1909 he would have shaved off both for good). Thirty-two years old that spring, the composer was living with his parents and brother Édouard near the Ravel family workshop in the Parisian suburb of Levallois. He was surrounded by a circle of close friends and staunch supporters, in the band of musicians, writers and artists who called themselves the 'Apaches'. Alongside the composers Florent Schmitt, Maurice Delage, Paul Ladmirault, Marcel Chadeigne and Déodat de Séverac, the pianist Ricardo Viñes, the painter Paul Sordes, the writers Léon-Paul Fargue and Tristan Klingsor (Léon Leclère) and the salon host Cipa Godebski,[5] the Apaches also included the critics Vuillermoz and Michel-Dimitri Calvocoressi, both of whom gave enormous practical assistance to Ravel by championing his music in the press. Besides the Apaches, Romain Rolland, Louis Laloy, Jean Marnold and Georges Jean-Aubry were also more-than-useful allies.

The support of these enlightened critics was essential to Ravel in the first half of 1907, a period undoubtedly satisfying in some respects but highly

---

[5] Haine, 'Cipa Godebski et les Apaches', argues convincingly that Godebski was a member of 'la bande', but see also Pasler, 'A sociology of the Apaches'.

uncomfortable in others. The year opened with a clutch of premières: after the rowdy first performance of *Histoires naturelles* on 12 January came the less turbulent debuts of the orchestrated *Une barque sur l'océan* (3 February) and *Introduction et Allegro* (22 February), then on 6 June the songs *Sainte* and *Les grands vents venus d'outremer* were premiered by soprano Hélène Luquiens with Ravel at the piano.

Whatever pleasure these performances brought Ravel, however, would have been undermined by the vicious campaign waged against him that spring by the critic Pierre Lalo. Lalo had responded to the première of *Histoires naturelles* with a vituperative article in *Le Temps*, in which a scathing critique of Ravel's cycle served as the point of departure for broader reflections on the mediocre *debussysme* of the younger generation of composers 'with Maurice Ravel at their head'.[6] It was not Lalo's first attempt thus to discredit Ravel. A year earlier he had greeted the appearance of the *Miroirs* with similar cries of *debussysme*:

The most striking of [Ravel's] faults is a strange resemblance to M. Claude Debussy; a resemblance so pronounced and so astonishing that often, when listening to a piece of Ravel's, it seems as if one is hearing a fragment of *Pelléas et Mélisande* [...] After Chopin, after Schumann, after Liszt, M. Debussy has created a new manner of writing for the piano, a special style, a distinctive virtuosity [...] all the young composers are immediately mirroring him, employing the same methods, writing in the same style.*[7]

At the time Ravel had replied to Lalo privately by letter, pointing out that his own *Jeux d'eau* had been published at the beginning of 1902, when *Pour le piano* was Debussy's only major published piano work: 'I don't have to tell you of my deep admiration for these pieces, but from a <u>purely pianistic</u> point of view, they contained nothing new.'[8] In 1907, effectively accused once again of plagiarism, Ravel responded publicly in a forthright missive to *Le Temps*, which was published on 9 April:

Lalo attributes to 'certain musicians' some unusual remarks concerning an artist of genius, Claude Debussy. According to current practice, M. Lalo does not name the 'young musicians' that he accuses so lightly. However, my name being cited rather

---

[6] Lalo, 'La Musique', Feuilleton du *Temps*, 19 March 1907; see Cornejo and Diamantopoulou, 'Maurice Ravel et Pierre Lalo', 28.

[7] *Le Temps*, 30 January 1906.　　[8] *OL*, letter 29.

frequently in the course of the article could give rise to a regrettable confusion, and unsuspecting readers might think that it is about me [...] I do not care whether those who know my works only through reviews think me a shameless plagiarist. I will not, however, even by those sorts of people, be taken for an imbecile.*[9]

Lalo's response, printed in the same column, was malevolent. 'M. Ravel defends himself without having been accused', he wrote. Without seeking the composer's permission to publish what had been a private communication, he reproduced Ravel's 1906 letter, an act that contributed substantially to the permanent rupture between Ravel and Debussy. A final fiery exchange of letters appeared in the columns of *Le Temps* a month later. Ravel furiously repudiated Lalo's 'ridiculous accusations'; Lalo in response bluntly accused Ravel of dishonesty and concluded: 'I have often spoken of him as an artist endowed with very great gifts. But I have also regretted that the most obvious of these gifts is that of imitation. I have no reason to alter that opinion.'*[10]

This personal attack distressed and angered Ravel, for whom professional and personal integrity was paramount. In a letter to Jean-Aubry in March he wrote, 'I wanted to tell you how touched I was by your interest in my works. People are endeavouring, especially in recent times, to prove to me that I'm deceiving myself, or better, that I'm trying to deceive others. I cannot prevent myself from feeling a certain annoyance about this.'[11] Two months later Romain Rolland recorded in his journal, '[Ravel's] rift with Debussy seems to distress him.'[12]

The impact upon Ravel of Lalo's malicious campaign must have been intensified by his distress over the failing health of his father. The Ravel family was close-knit and Pierre-Joseph, a master engineer, inventor and musician *manqué*, had wholeheartedly supported his son's musical career. As Marcel Marnat writes, Pierre-Joseph also shared the general opinion that 'real success for a musician would be conferred in the theatre'.[13] This explains in part why Ravel worked so feverishly, that spring and summer, on his setting of Franc-Nohain's one-act play *L'Heure espagnole*. In a letter to his Basque relative Jane Courteault in mid-August he wrote, 'This is how I'm relaxing from the fatigue caused by a crazy amount of work: in less than three months, I've put together a comic opera in one act, *L'Heure*

---

[9] 'La Musique', Feuilleton du *Temps*, 19 April 1907; *OL*, letter 41.

[10] 'La Musique', Feuilleton du *Temps*, 7 May 1907. See Cornejo and Diamantopoulou, 'Maurice Ravel et Pierre Lalo', 32–5.

[11] *OL*, letter 40.   [12] Strauss and Rolland, *Correspondance*, 158.

[13] Marnat, *Maurice Ravel*, 261.

Ex. 1.1a Debussy, 'Clair de lune' (*Suite bergamasque*), bars 29–30

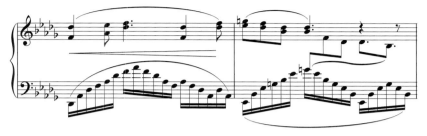

Ex. 1.1b Ravel, *Sur l'herbe*, bar 21

espagnole, on a libretto by Franc-Nohain. This work will probably be mounted at the Opéra-Comique this winter.'[14] But on 15 November he would write to Ida Godebska, 'Things are not well at home. My father is weakening continually. His mental capacity is at its very lowest: he mixes up everything and no longer knows where he is at times. I no longer have any hope that he will see my work on stage: he is already too far gone to understand it.'[15] In the end, more than three years would pass before *L'Heure espagnole* went into rehearsal. Pierre-Joseph Ravel died in October 1908.

These personal and professional traumas did not prevent the year 1907 from being one of Ravel's most productive. In March he completed his *Vocalise-Étude en forme de Habanera*, in April *Les grands vents venus d'outremer*, and in June *Sur l'herbe*. The last of these arguably contains a pointed riposte to Lalo: its final line ('Hé! bonsoir la Lune') unmistakeably quotes Debussy's 'Clair de lune' from the *Suite bergamasque*, published just two years earlier (Ex. 1.1). The rhythm, texture and modality – where every note in the bar contradicts the four-sharp key signature – are so different

[14] *OL*, letter 43.   [15] Orenstein, *Ravel, Man and Musician*, 54n15.

from the surrounding bars that the citation stands out as if in quotation marks.

By October Ravel was able to sign off on both the piano duet score of *Rapsodie espagnole* and the vocal score of *L'Heure espagnole*, although the latter must have been well advanced by July, when he first showed it to Albert Carré, the director of the Opéra-Comique (see p. 17). It is impossible not to wonder whether his decision to undertake the opera, and the speed with which he drafted it – he had begun work only in April – were due not just to his father's failing health but also to his desire to respond to Pierre Lalo's intemperate attacks. An opera would prove his capacity to write a major work and demonstrate that he, Maurice Ravel, had a unique compositional voice. He would choose a text set not in the misty 'Allemonde' of *Pelléas et Mélisande* but in earthy Spain, no Symbolist drama but a rollicking farce.

From *L'Heure* to *L'Enfant*, and a 'sunken' opera

L'Heure espagnole was written and first performed in an era that saw a number of significant French operatic premières, from *Louise* in 1900 and *Pelléas et Mélisande* in 1902 to *Ariane et Barbe bleue* in 1907 and *Pénélope* in 1913. In many respects, *L'Heure* is a reactive work, deliberately provocative in its subject matter and its text-setting. Via the French fascination with *espagnolade*, it makes game of both the frivolity of *opéra comique* and the self-conscious seriousness of grand opera. Although by no means the work of a composer who felt himself obliged to make obeisance to any operatic shrines, *L'Heure* nevertheless gestures more, and more directly, to its musical and cultural circumstances than does *L'Enfant et les sortilèges*.

In 1907 Ravel was still a young man. A decade later he was entering middle age, hastened into it by the War that had deprived him of energy, health, inspiration and the solitude that was so necessary to him. He had lost friends and relatives at the front, and in January 1917 his beloved mother died too. 'I think that this terrible period has crushed me, and I will not be able to pick myself up again', he wrote to Hélène Kahn-Casella in the autumn of 1919.[16] But he was trying: sometime in the spring of 1917 he had accepted a commission from Jacques Rouché, the director of the Opéra Garnier, to set to music a 'petit poème' by Colette. Perhaps Ravel was thus

---

[16] Roy (ed.), 'Lettres de Maurice Ravel à Hélène et Alfredo Casella', 77.

forcibly attempting to apply himself to composition, although the long gestation of the opera – which he would finish just weeks before its 1925 première – suggests that the task was more than he could manage immediately, at that low ebb in his life. The works Ravel did complete during the six-year period 1919–25 (*La Valse*, the Sonata for Violin and Cello, *Tzigane* and a few short pieces) total fewer minutes of music than he had composed during that single fruitful year of 1907. Even in August 1924, as he was at last throwing himself into the completion of *L'Enfant*, he would write to his house-editor Lucien Garban, 'I'm slogging away but with no success, the magneto is worn out.'[17]

In 1917 Ravel had been trying to recover his *métier* by resuscitating several projects that the war had forced him to put aside. In January 1917 he wrote to Sergei Diaghilev, formally giving his commitment to a new work for the Ballets russes.[18] Although the specified project (based on a scenario by the Italian Futurist poet Francesco Cangiullo) was never even partially sketched, what Ravel did eventually present to Diaghilev was *La Valse*. This was his realisation of a work he had been tinkering with intermittently since as early as 1906 but abandoned after the outbreak of war in 1914, in part because of its working title, 'Wien': it was, he admitted, inescapably unfortunate.[19] In June 1917 Ravel also returned to another project he had put aside three years earlier, *Le Tombeau de Couperin* (eventually completed in November 1917). Then there was a third work, which, like 'Wien', had been on Ravel's mind for more than a decade: *La Cloche engloutie*.

Based on Gerhardt Hauptmann's play *Die versunkene Glocke*, *La Cloche engloutie* had been translated and transformed into a libretto by Ferdinand Hérold, to whom Ravel was introduced by his old counterpoint and orchestration teacher André Gedalge. The story was, as Arbie Orenstein writes, 'a spiritual descendant of *Der Freischütz*, with a generous supply of forest scenes, elves, nymphs, prayers, incantations, and dances, as well as human and supernatural beings'.[20] When he began work on *La Cloche* in the summer of 1906, Ravel was excited and optimistic:

[12 June]
For two weeks I've had my nose to the grindstone [je ne quitte pas le turbin]. I've never worked with such intensity. [...] It's thrilling to write a work for the theatre! I won't say that it comes all by itself, but that's precisely what's best of all.

---

[17] Orenstein (ed.), 'La Correspondance de Maurice Ravel à Lucien Garban (1919–1934)', 56.
[18] *OL*, letter 143. [19] *OL*, letters 121–2. [20] Orenstein, *Ravel, Man and Musician*, 50.

[20 August]

Think of what there is already: in addition to what already existed of the first act, a large part of the 2nd as well. (You want an opera in 5 acts? You'll have it in 1 week!)[21]

Less than a year later, however, Ravel would set *La Cloche engloutie* aside. The knowledge that he had to work quickly for his father's sake was undoubtedly a factor in the decision to abandon the grand opera in favour of a one-act farce. But he must also have been prompted by potent aesthetic concerns. In *La Cloche* he was contemplating an opera whose scale, narrative and continuous musical discourse would inevitably prompt critics to think of *Pelléas*, and indeed of Wagner. With Pierre Lalo's censure ringing in his ears, to offer the musical world a five-act opera on a mythical subject by a writer associated with the Symbolist movement was simply asking for trouble.

By 1908, however, with the vocal score of *L'Heure* in press, the orchestration to complete and *Gaspard de la nuit* on his work table, Ravel was still eager to resume work on *La Cloche engloutie*: 'I'm going to get back to it', he wrote to Theodor Szántó on 4 June.[22] Two weeks later, he wrote to Ida Godebska, 'I re-examined what was written of *La Cloche engloutie*. Lord! how it has aged! It has to be redone! Dog of a profession, but it has its charms . . .'[23] He was to return to the opera periodically over the next few years, even signing a contract for it with Hérold and Hauptmann in 1909.[24] In an interview in 1912, he seems pre-emptively to have announced that it was 'on the point of being finished' – though either the composer or the journalist (who claimed in the same article that Ravel was also about to write an opera on *Don Quichotte*) was certainly exaggerating.[25] But by 1914 the opera seemed to have stalled for good: 'Working at *La Cloche engloutie* is delicate [because of its German origins] – I think it really is [sunk] this time', he wrote to Roland-Manuel in October.[26]

It is difficult to ascertain how much of *La Cloche engloutie* Ravel had actually sketched; Orenstein suggests parts of Acts 1 and 2 only.[27] He points out, however, that the opening material of *L'Enfant et les sortilèges* is strikingly similar to the start of Act 2 of *La Cloche*, while Roland-Manuel claimed that the 'Nocturne' that opens the second part of *L'Enfant* was likewise drawn from the sketches for the second act.[28] It seems probable,

---

[21] *OL*, letters 32 and 35.   [22] *OL*, letter 52.   [23] *OL*, letter 53.

[24] Orenstein, 'Some unpublished music and letters', 320.

[25] Max-Harry, 'M. Maurice Ravel écrit à son tour un "Don Quichotte".'   [26] *OL*, letter 122.

[27] See Orenstein, 'Some unpublished music and letters', 317–22.

[28] Orenstein, *Ravel, Man and Musician*, 210; Roland-Manuel, *Maurice Ravel et son œuvre dramatique*, 149.

therefore, that when Ravel agreed to consider the libretto that Jacques Rouché offered to him in the spring of 1917, he was thinking of the drafted chunks of his abandoned opera. The fairytale atmosphere of Colette's text was not unlike that of *La Cloche engloutie*, and both narratives set fantasy against a background of everyday realism. Ravel seems to have recognised in Colette's words not just a settable text, but one that offered him a compositional head start.

The decision to undertake *L'Enfant et les sortilèges* was thus made, at least in part, on a more prosaic basis than the complex set of personal and professional circumstances that lay behind the genesis of *L'Heure*. In the spring of 1917 Ravel needed a new project, and Rouché presented him with one that fitted his plans particularly well. At once opera and ballet, at one time titled 'divertissement', and its orchestration frequently that of a chamber opera, *L'Enfant et les sortilèges* would look to the number-operas of the late nineteenth century and the opera-ballets of the mid eighteenth, as well as to the musical comedies and music halls of the 1920s. Its mutability showcases the diversity of musical style that characterised the *Années folles*. Alongside musical techniques including bitonality, wind- and percussion-dominated orchestral timbres, pastiche, economy of means and the incorporation of the vernacular, *L'Enfant* unites many of the era's cultural preoccupations: the symbolic or psychological implications of the Child protagonist, dialogues between modernism and nostalgia, and themes of destruction and reparation. If *L'Heure espagnole* was in part a reaction against the operatic and cultural conventions of its time, *L'Enfant et les sortilèges*, the work of a more mature and confident composer, defined its own terms, and in so doing captured a Zeitgeist.

Ravel's libretti

L'Heure espagnole, L'Enfant et les sortilèges and *La Cloche engloutie* were not the only operas Ravel attempted or meditated. His correspondence reveals various fleeting inspirations for lyric works, and late in life he seriously contemplated an opera/oratorio based on the life of Jeanne d'Arc, as well as an Arabian Nights-inspired creation titled *Morgiane*. External factors aside, what was it that prompted Ravel not just to choose but, more tellingly, to complete *L'Heure* and *L'Enfant*?

In his 1913 review of Chabrier's *Une éducation manquée*, Ravel wrote: 'How many "light" works, even among the most recent, will not seem outmoded compared with this one, although it is already thirty-four years old? Sadly, the libretto has not retained a comparable freshness, and the poverty of the text stands in painful contrast to the originality, the character and the delicate orchestration of this delightful score.'[29]

His review – of a work by a composer he cited again and again as 'the one musician who has influenced me above all others'[30] – shows him acutely aware of the importance of finding a libretto that would last, one that would sustain and enrich a musical score. He needed a text in which he could be confident, both as a libretto and as literature in its own right.

Given this, plus the literary 'poverty' of many purpose-written nineteenth-century libretti, it is perhaps unsurprising that neither *L'Heure espagnole* nor *L'Enfant et les sortilèges* was conceived as an 'opera' *per se*: *L'Heure* began life as a play; *L'Enfant*, in Colette's original conception, as a ballet, 'féerie-ballet' or 'ballet-opéra'. The published scores bear the respective subtitles 'comédie musicale' and 'fantaisie lyrique',[31] though Ravel himself treated these appellations flexibly. He often referred to *L'Heure* as an *opéra comique* (which it technically isn't, since it has no spoken dialogue), but his 'Autobiographical Sketch' of 1928 describes it as a 'comédie lyrique'; a letter that appeared in *Le Figaro* just before the première refers to his 'opérette'; and another interview announces 'I have written an *opéra bouffe*'.[32] *L'Enfant*, which took several years to assume its final title, appears in Ravel's correspondence before 1924 as 'opéra-dansé', 'opéra' and, more laconically, 'la machine lyrique' (he seems never to have used Colette's title *Divertissement* himself). Late in 1924, the work became 'ma fantaisie lyrique', but in interviews given shortly before and after the première he refers to it both as 'opéra' and 'opéra fantastique', and links it specifically with 'opérette' and 'opérette américaine'.[33]

If Ravel's libretti had unusual provenances, they were nevertheless the creations of two of the most accomplished writers of their generation. Franc-Nohain (Maurice Étienne Legrand) was a fine poet and experienced librettist as well as a playwright: he collaborated with the composers Émile Jaques-Dalcroze (*Le Bonhomme jadis*, 1906) and Claude Terrasse, a close friend with whom he wrote many *opéras bouffes* (and who introduced him to Ravel, in 1906). However, *L'Heure espagnole* represented the first

[29] Ravel, 'Au Théâtre des Arts', *Comœdia illustré* 5/9 (5 February 1913); *OL*, 308.
[30] *OL*, letter 312.
[31] Explanatory or expressive subtitles of this type were standard for French operas of this period: among innumerable examples, *Pelléas et Mélisande* is subtitled 'drame lyrique'; Massenet's *Le Jongleur de Notre Dame*, 'miracle en trois actes'; and Charpentier's *Louise*, 'roman musical'.
[32] *OL*, 45, 339 and letter 84.   [33] *OL*, 363, 349.

occasion that Franc-Nohain had had a published play transformed into a libretto. In its original form, his *L'Heure espagnole* had opened on 28 October 1904 at the Théâtre de l'Odéon, where it enjoyed a fairly successful run of more than a hundred performances. Reviews were limited (it was a curtain-raiser, not the main event), but Émile Faguet placed it 'among the best of this genre',[34] and two of the reviewers of the 1921 production of Ravel's *L'Heure espagnole* specifically drew attention to the success of that 1904 season: Adolphe Boschot – admittedly Franc-Nohain's brother-in-law – wrote that the literati and the public had hailed *L'Heure espagnole* as 'a triumph', and Henri Duvernois called the initial success of this *acte en vers* 'tremendous'.[35]

Notwithstanding this 'triumph', when Ravel turned his play into a libretto in 1907 Franc-Nohain was still relatively little-known; it was only with the creation of the character and novel *Jaboune* (1910) that he would win widespread recognition. His stature would later be cemented by his post as editor of *L'Écho de Paris*, the publication of his popular fables in the 1920s, and the bestowal of a Grand Prix de Littérature by the Académie française in 1932. By contrast, by the time Ravel received her libretto in 1917, Colette was a household name. Already notorious as a performer and a creator of *scandales*, she was also beginning to win acclaim as one of the greatest of France's literary figures: in 1926 Raymond Charpentier, reviewing the Opéra-Comique première of *L'Enfant*, could write that 'the authors of *L'Enfant et les sortilèges* are, the one just as much as the other, at the summit of the current phalanx of French art'*.[36] Although she had considerable theatrical experience, however, Colette had never before written directly for the stage, nor would she ever do so again.

One of Ravel's reasons for accepting the libretto of *L'Enfant* was undoubtedly how far removed its content, characters and setting were from those of his first opera. A much-discussed characteristic of Ravel's œuvre is his determination never to repeat himself: each work deliberately sets out to achieve something new, in its means, its form and its self-imposed limitations. If the creator of one string quartet, one piano trio and one *symphonie chorégraphique* set out to write a second one-act opera, it was because he knew it would be cast in a very different mould from his first. *L'Heure* had demanded a continuously evolving structure, each scene running into the next; *L'Enfant*, a more segmented music. *L'Heure*

---

[34] Faguet, 'La Semaine dramatique'.

[35] Boschot, 'À l'Opéra – *L'Heure espagnole*'; Duvernois, 'Franc-Nohain'.

[36] Charpentier, '*L'Enfant et les sortilèges*'.

suggested one broad musical character – Spanish idioms – whereas *L'Enfant* suggested many. *L'Heure* offered a subversive moral ('there comes a time when the muleteer has his turn!'); *L'Enfant*, a good fairytale one (the naughty Child repents).

Beyond the subject matter, perhaps the most important structural difference between *L'Heure espagnole* and *L'Enfant et les sortilèges* – the difference that impacted most profoundly upon the music – lies in the way they tell their stories. The narrative of *L'Heure espagnole* advances primarily through conversation. Only in the closing scene do the *dramatis personae* step out of character and reflect on the piece; otherwise, the story advances quickly, sentence by sentence, in dialogue and direct exchange. *L'Enfant*, by contrast, can be reduced to a single key action – the Child's destructive rage – followed by a single reaction – the response, diverse though it is, of the injured creatures and objects. The text is thus primarily descriptive: the furniture, objects and animals tell about themselves and their state, but their words do little to advance the narrative. The different origins of the two libretti largely determined this distinction: *L'Heure* was written to be spoken, but Colette seems to have imagined from the outset that her story would be told through dance. Her words, written to be sung, embellish but, for the most part, do not define the narrative.

This contrast – dialogue versus description – determines the musical and dramatic form, focus, and manner of communication of Ravel's two operas. It necessitated two entirely different ways of treating the text, the meticulously realised speech of *L'Heure* and the more expansive lyricism of *L'Enfant*. As Ravel himself put it: 'More than ever [. . .] I am for melody, yes, melody, *bel canto*, vocalises, vocal virtuosity – this is for me a point of departure. If, in *L'Heure espagnole*, the theatrical action itself demanded that the music be only the commentary on each word and gesture, here, by contrast, this lyric fantasy calls for melody, nothing but melody.'[37]

But despite these disparate operatic designs, settings and foci, *L'Heure* and *L'Enfant* also share some important qualities. They both develop subjects that had long been sources of inspiration for the composer. In *L'Heure*, Ravel had a tale set in what he felt was partly his own territory, for he always thought of his heritage as Spanish as well as Basque. Imagery of childhood and fantasy similarly drew him again and again, underlying works including *Ma mère l'Oye*, the wartime *Trois chansons pour chœur mixte* and the 1905 song *Noël des jouets*, as well as *L'Enfant*. In literary and structural terms, more direct affinities may be traced between the two

---

[37] [Anon.], 'Avant-première: *L'Enfant et les sortilèges*', *Le Gaulois*, 20 March 1925; *OL*, 349.

libretti. Both, for example, are focussed and economical in style. Franc-Nohain uses Inigo's occasional prolixity and Gonzalve's extravagant poeticism as deliberately comic qualities in themselves, set in relief by the more straightforward language of the other characters. Although *L'Enfant* is descriptive where *L'Heure* is conversational, it is nevertheless concise: even in the longer passages of text, every line has a distinct point to make. Viewed against the traditional operatic format, in which arias are primarily designed to express and embroider a single emotion (or two contrasted ones), this economy of means would certainly have appealed to Ravel.

Although Ravel was one of many composers then turning increasingly to more 'literary' operatic libretti, the careful structures of his chosen texts, by writers noted for their professionalism and craft, are noteworthy. Both operas, too, are self-contained and unpretentious, making no grand statements and not attempting to portray or reflect on anything beyond their own particular and very localised worlds. (A director or an audience may read broader messages or portrayals into them, but they are not intrinsic to the text.) Neither do they hinge, as Tony Aubin pointed out, upon the two great dramatic staples, romantic love and death, although both themes are evoked in *L'Enfant*, and the former at least is satirised in *L'Heure*.[38] Humour is never far away in either work; grandiosity, so often encountered in opera, never appealed to Ravel. Beneath their surface directness, *L'Heure* and *L'Enfant* also share a subtlety of wit and humour that contrasts with their more 'bouffish' passages and is often matched with great beauty of expression. Both are layered with all sorts of wordplay, employing evocative or onomatopoeic patterns of rhymes and rhythms, whose variety and flexibility suggest similarly varied patterns of musical realisation. As Chapter 5 explores, these are qualities to which Ravel was consistently drawn in the song texts he chose, so it is not surprising to see them working under the surface of his operas.

Ravel, then, was surely drawn to his texts *as* texts, not simply as stories or settings or scenarios. If, as a composer and seasoned professional, Ravel knew that *L'Enfant* would draw from him an opera quite unlike the one he had written a decade earlier, as a craftsman and a writer himself he would have recognised some innate similarities in the way Colette and Franc-Nohain went about the business of creating a text. These qualities – focus and economy, wordplay and assonance, carefully judged structures – were ones that he could work with. At the level of *métier*, Ravel's two libretti are related.

---

[38] Aubin, 'L'Œuvre lyrique', 24.

2 | Ravel's hour

Convincing Albert Carré: 1907–1911

Perhaps the best evidence of just how rapidly Ravel composed *L'Heure espagnole* is its late appearance in his correspondence. On 15 May 1907 he wrote to Jean-Aubry, 'For nearly a month I've been working like a horse: the piece with Franc-Nohain. It's almost half done. But I'm spending whole days on it, hardly taking time for meals and going out to sniff the air a little in the evenings.'[*1] Less than two months later, the opera had reached a sufficiently advanced state to be given an 'audition' before Albert Carré; at the same time *Le Courrier musical* announced that Ravel 'is working in collaboration with M. Franc-Nohain on a *comédie lyrique* called *L'Heure espagnole*. This work, in one act, involves five comic roles. Its authors intend it for the Opéra-Comique.'[*2]

Writing an opera was one thing, getting it staged was – as most composers will testify – quite another. The Opéra-Comique was the obvious venue for *L'Heure espagnole*. A smaller theatre than the Opéra Garnier, it better suited the proportions of the work (five performers, one set, one act), and its patrons were accustomed to *opéra comique* and operetta. It was also the livelier and, in terms of repertoire, the more innovative of the two opera houses. In May 1911, for example, the theatre staged sixteen operas, of which four were new or almost-new: alongside *L'Heure espagnole* was Massenet's *Thérèse* (receiving its Parisian though not its world première), together with Raoul Laparra's *La Jota* and Charles Pons's *Le Voile du bonheur*, which had both opened the previous month. Carré seems to have prided himself on his theatre's commitment to new music, at least in retrospect:

---

[1] Letter sold at auction on 6 December 2011 (Salle Drouot), catalogue *Piasa: lettres et manuscrits autographes*, no. 286.

[2] *Le Courrier musical* 10/13 (1 July 1907), 427.

After Debussy, after Paul Dukas, after Gabriel Fauré [...] I was granted the opportunity to preside over the stage début of that other representative of the modern French school: Maurice Ravel. That was in 1911, the very year that musicians had so bitterly reproached me for neglecting French operas. Was not the delicious jewel that is *L'Heure espagnole* the best response that I could make to them?*[3]

There is more than a hint of disingenuousness in this reflection. If Carré was later able to congratulate himself on recognising the worth of this 'delicious jewel', it would take him three and a half years of prevarication to stage it, and his first reaction was equivocal at best.[4]

Ravel presented *L'Heure espagnole* to Carré on 6 July 1907, letting off steam afterwards by giving an 'aperçu' of the work *chez* Jean Marnold (Ricardo Viñes described it as 'très amusante'[5]). A few days later he wrote to Ida Godebska:

You are doubtless waiting for the result of Saturday's play-through. There isn't one, or at least hardly anything! Carré began by finding the subject a bit risqué; that won't surprise you, given the strict morals of our severe director. [Ravel has his tongue firmly in his cheek here.] But in the end he'd let that pass. The action begins a bit slowly etc. Tidy that up a bit. Of course I agreed, with no intention of doing anything about it. Once it's finished I'll come back and see him. I've heard from several sources that there's enough there to give me good hope. It seems that Séverac obtained more formal promises [for his *Le Cœur du moulin*] but given the outcome I feel I'm justified in thinking the best of this reserve.*[6]

If Carré held some reservations about *L'Heure*, the result of that first 'audition' still seemed hopeful. To Jane Courteault, Ravel wrote, 'This work will probably be performed at the Opéra-Comique this winter, the director having declared that we won't have to wait a long time.'[7] Three weeks later, on 9 September, he wrote to Marnold, 'What, didn't I give you any news of *L'Heure espagnole*? [...] Carré listened to it, and his terms seemed so good that Durand closed with him straight away, convinced that this work will be given later in the current season.'*[8]

But Carré was not to be hurried into a commitment. Although Ravel had signed off on the vocal score by the middle of October, on 15 November he

---

[3] Carré, *Souvenirs du théâtre*, 339–40.

[4] Fauré's *Pénélope* in fact made its Parisian debut in 1913 at Gabriel Astruc's Théâtre des Champs-Élysées; it was not until 1919 that it entered the repertoire of the Opéra-Comique.

[5] Rodriguez, '*L'Heure espagnole*: chronologie critique', 11.

[6] Chalupt and Gerar, *Ravel au miroir de ses lettres*, 61–2.   [7] *OL*, letter 43.

[8] Letter in the collection of Eric van Lauwe.

wrote to Ida Godebska, 'Carré has still not responded to me'.[9] Hearing nothing further by the end of the year, Ravel enlisted a powerful new supporter: Louise Cruppi, wife of the leftist politician Jean Cruppi. In late December or early January, Carré attended a private performance of *L'Heure espagnole* at the home of the Droz family, at which Mme Cruppi herself sang the role of Concepcion (Alfred Droz, a lawyer, was a specialist in literary and artistic affairs, and a professional connection of Jean Cruppi).[10] As a result, it seems, Ravel was invited to present the opera to Carré again, on 14 January 1908. He wrote to Ida Godebska on 20 January:

I'm going to tell you the full story of the adventures of *L'Heure espagnole*: last Tuesday, I display my best Toledo voice and present myself to Carré with Bathori alone (Engel[11] detained at the last minute). I hum more off-key than ever, begin by breaking three strings on a dance-hall piano, let Bathori attack the bravura passages, and then we await the supreme decision: Refused... It is impossible to impose such a subject on the naïve ears of the subscribers of the Opéra-Comique. Just think of it: these lovers enclosed in clocks that are carried up to the bedroom! We know very well what they are going to do there!! [...] Perverted no doubt by unwholesome reading, when I see lovers disappear 'into the shade', I had always imagined dishonourable intentions. I realise now, thanks to that severe moralist who is the director of the Opéra-Comique, that my interpretation was shameful, and that the least innocent foible of Carmen, Manon, Chrysis or Queen Fiamette was picking their nose too much.

Jane Bathori recalled that Carré 'said to Ravel, word-for-word, "But Monsieur Ravel, you don't realise! What will those mothers who only bring their daughters to the Opéra-Comique so that they can catch themselves a husband say to me?"'*[12] His words would later be echoed by critic Jean Chantavoine, who suggested that 'Bourgeois families short of betrothals will abstain from visiting the Opéra-Comique on the evenings that *L'Heure espagnole* is playing: they would do well to wait until marriage, at least.'*[13] As Bathori pointed out, however, most of the operas in the theatre's repertoire could hardly be said to offer better morality tales. *Carmen*? *Manon*?

Although Carré's objections to the opera may have been framed as a light-hearted moral quibble, in fact the director was almost certainly more disconcerted by its style, particularly its naturalistic text-setting. The *scandale* provoked by the *Histoires naturelles* just six months earlier was probably

[9] Clifton, 'Maurice Ravel's *L'Heure espagnole*', 93. See also Nichols, *Ravel*, 392.
[10] Rodriguez, '*L'Heure espagnole*: chronologie critique', 20. It seems that another private performance also took place around this time at the home of the Cruppis (*ibid.*, 17–20).
[11] Bathori's husband, the singer and choral director Émile Engel.
[12] Bathori, 'Quelques mots sur Maurice Ravel'.   [13] Chantavoine, 'Chronique musicale', 579.

fresh in his memory: although Debussy had made a success of an opera in which 'characters speak like ordinary people', as Marnat notes, 'what might be acceptable in a drama seemed pointlessly audacious in a comedy'.[14]

Ravel's letter to Ida Godebska continues:

[Mme Cruppi] was shocked [by Carré's refusal], and her first impulse was to write to Carré. After mature consideration, she decided nevertheless to follow her impulse, and the most pungent exchange of correspondence followed. I'll tell you all about it on Friday. For the moment, I'm keeping my foot light on the fury pedal [je modère le gaz de mon fureur], having need of all my *sang-froid* to hold the critics in first gear – I'm scared of skids.[15]

Carré's side of this 'pungent exchange' couched his failure to appreciate the potential of *L'Heure espagnole* as an almost avuncular concern for the reputation of the composer. On 17 January he wrote to Mme Cruppi:

It's precisely because we expect great things of M. Ravel that his debut must be unequivocal. I've introduced to the theatre musicians such as Gustave Charpentier, Debussy [and] Dukas, but their operas were *Louise*, *Pelléas et Mélisande*, *Ariane et Barbe Bleue*. The public was with them from the beginning, because of the significance of their efforts. M. Ravel who, in the musical world, enjoys a reputation equal to that of his predecessors, is not well known to the general public. What does he offer us, in order to assume his place in his turn? A short work, rather amusing, but whose risqué subject would need to be treated with the wit and gaiety of an Offenbach disciple. Perhaps a picturesque music, vivid, nimble and straightforward, would make this subject acceptable. M. Ravel's music is original and witty, but it is also very melancholy and very slight. This is not the impression I received of it at the home of our friends the Droz, no doubt thanks to the outstanding performance that I heard there, but I felt it fully the other night, and my clear feeling is that were I to mount M. Ravel's *L'Heure espagnole* I would be leading M. Ravel into a failure that would do the gravest damage to his future [. . .] This is not a responsibility I wish to accept. I leave it to you, Madame, to decide.*[16]

Despite his flattery, it seems that even Mme Cruppi's 'outstanding' performance had failed to sway Carré: some weeks after this exchange Ravel wrote to Cipa Godebski that Mme Droz had told him that Carré had told *her* that *L'Heure espagnole* wouldn't be understood. 'I'm well aware that it's a bit abstruse', he added acerbically.[17] Mme Cruppi's response to Carré, however, was unequivocal: 'You will stage *L'Heure espagnole*', she wrote, 'for [the sake of] music, and not for the Republic'.[18] Thus, on 15 February,

---

[14] Marnat, *Maurice Ravel*, 304.   [15] *OL*, letter 46.
[16] Rodriguez, '*L'Heure espagnole*: chronologie critique', 19–20.   [17] *OL*, letter 49.
[18] Rodriguez, '*L'Heure espagnole*: chronologie critique', 20.

an announcement appeared in the *Courrier musical*: 'M. Carré has just accepted, to be produced at the Opéra-Comique, *L'Heure espagnole*, a one-act work by Maurice Ravel.'

Although Carré had officially given his consent, Ravel's letters to Marnold and the Godebskis throughout 1908 and 1909 show that the director was keeping his composer on a string, encouraging him to believe that *L'Heure espagnole* would soon be mounted in the Salle Favart:

[to Marnold, 23 September 1908]
Durand's had me sent the Op-Com's poster, which Carré had sent him. *Le Coeur du moulin* and *L'Heure espagnole* share a rather singular billing there! Besides, it's these 'singularities' that will work, have no fear!*[19]

[to Ida Godeska, 24 September 1908]
L'Heure espagnole is going to be joined with *Le Coeur du moulin* in the repertory of the Op. Com. The good M. Carré has concluded, most rightly, that several years' worth of publicity can only be profitable for a young composer.*[20]

[to Marnold, 22 December 1908]
Carré has just advised Séverac that *Le Cœur du moulin* will be staged in March. In the expectation of a similar result for *L'Heure*, I'm finishing the orchestration. The piano-vocal score that has just appeared will perhaps decide the matter.*[21]

[to Marnold, 27 January 1909]
Carré called us in yesterday to talk about the staging of *L'Heure*, which should be mounted with *Feuersnot* in May.*[22]

By early 1909, the newly published vocal score was making its way around the critics, composers and salons of Paris. 'We read through Ravel's *L'Heure espagnole*', noted Marguerite de Saint-Marceaux on 17 February – 'it's bewildering, this music'.[23] On 26 February she wrote: 'Ravel sang and played *L'Heure espagnole* to us. It's a bizarre musical play, without much musicality but with a certain rhythmic sense that will benefit from being orchestrated, doubtless with affectation.' Then, on 19 March, 'Ravel played us his *L'Heure espagnole* again. This emotionless music is nevertheless interesting. It is an art without a heart.'*[24] Her summation echoes the trope of 'heartlessness' so often applied to Ravel's music and epitomised in Pierre Lalo's 1911 review of

[19] Chalupt and Gerar, *Ravel au miroir de ses lettres*, 75.   [20] *Ibid.*, 75–6.
[21] *Ibid.*, 77; *OL*, letter 58. *Le Cœur du moulin* would première on 8 December 1909.
[22] Chalupt and Gerar, *Ravel au miroir de ses lettres*, 78.   [23] Saint-Marceaux, *Journal*, 533.
[24] *Ibid.*, 534, 537.

L'Heure (see p. 27 and *Compendium of Sources*), which would again contrast Debussy – 'tout sensibilité' – with Ravel – 'tout insensibilité'.[25]

Ravel's meeting with Carré on 26 January 1909 (mentioned in his letter above to Marnold) had undoubtedly been prompted by the publication of the vocal score, and perhaps also by an article devoted to *L'Heure espagnole* that had appeared in *Le Guide musical* two days before.[26] Henri de Curzon pointed out that the opera

has been heralded several times as among the new works in preparation at the Opéra-Comique, and even been advertised as if it were to be performed this year. But the season is so full, and the obligations of M. Albert Carré so numerous and so pressing, that everything suggests that this little score will be postponed to a later date. Nevertheless, such is the confidence of the publisher and the authors in this work that they have taken the decision – very unusually – to publish it straight away and allow enthusiasts to judge it in advance. [. . .] Everything suggests that this experiment is a happy one. The orchestration of M. Ravel's score remains to be heard, but the manner in which the dialogue is treated, according to the characters, according to the unexpected turns of the action, according to the piquant turns of the poetry; then the way in which, through orchestral coloration and the choices of instruments, he has exploited this atmosphere of a clockmaker's workshop, and the 'bouffish' nature of these various caricatured figures; finally, the prevailing suppleness of this little masterpiece of musical transposition of a literary work, [all] seem to have succeeded absolutely, and make it eminently to be wished that M. Albert Carré will not postpone its dramatic realisation too much longer.*[27]

Le Guide musical kept the pressure on Carré throughout 1909. '*L'Heure espagnole* seems to have been put off', noted Charles Cornet (who reviewed for *Comœdia* as Charles Tenroc) on 2 May, and in July the journal announced that 'M. Gatti-Casazza, the director of the Metropolitan [Opera House] and the New York Opéra-Comique [*sic*] intends next year to mount no fewer than forty-seven operas' – including, it seemed, *L'Heure espagnole* (nothing came of this). In September, *Le Guide* again

---

[25] Lalo, 'La Musique [. . .] *L'Heure espagnole*' (1911). Roland-Manuel later teased out this theme, writing that 'Far from humanising his characters, far from softening the passions that he saw animating them, [Ravel] pitilessly stripped bare the elemental mechanisms of their instincts. [. . .] But, in a strange substitution, the heart that he tore from them beats tenderly in the breasts of the clocks and automatons, lending their small steel frames an illusory soul and the sweet warmth of life' (*Maurice Ravel et son œuvre dramatique*, 55).

[26] Rodriguez ('*L'Heure espagnole*: chronologie critique', 22) suggests that the vigorous support of Henri de Curzon and *Le Guide musical* had been prompted by Marnold.

[27] Curzon, '*L'Heure espagnole* de Maurice Ravel', 70–1.

suggested that *L'Heure* would be among 'the most immediate projects' planned for the 1909–10 Opéra-Comique season.[28]

Meanwhile, on 14 March 1909 Ravel wrote to Cipa Godebski, 'I'm finishing [the orchestration of] *L'Heure*. Tomorrow Durand will have the last pages of the score.'[29] The orchestral score would not be published until 1911, but on 9 June 1910 Gonzalve's little aria 'Adieu, cellule' was featured at the fifth concert of the newly formed Société musicale indépendante, performed by Henri Fabert and accompanied by the Hasselmans Orchestra, conducted by Désiré-Émile Inghelbrecht.[30] 'M. Fabert sang Gonzalve's aria with great authority', wrote Cornet, 'the fragment of this *comédie musicale* is full of humour, of ornaments, of grotesque glissandos underlined by the funniest of serenade rhythms.'*[31] And René Chalupt wrote bluntly, 'the work manifests a glittering orchestration and unbelievable mastery of style. Why has it not yet been mounted on the stage?'[32] At last, in early September, *Le Guide musical* announced that the details of the 1910–11 Opéra-Comique season had been released, and among the new works was *L'Heure espagnole*, 'the short work by Maurice Ravel that we have already discussed in these pages'.[33]

For all his vaunted commitment to mounting new operas, when it came to unusual or potentially controversial works Carré clearly needed to be pushed. Despite his later self-declared sagacity in mounting *Pelléas et Mélisande*, Debussy's opera had similarly taken four years to reach the stage of the Salle Favart: as Robert Orledge notes, it had been accepted 'in principle' by the theatre as early as May 1898, but not until 3 May 1901 was it confirmed for the 1901–2 season.[34] Carré's eventual decision to stage *L'Heure espagnole* was undoubtedly due in part to the pressure brought to bear by the influential Mme Cruppi, to whom Ravel would dedicate the opera in gratitude. Perhaps more important, however, was the momentum that by then had gathered around *L'Heure espagnole*. The three years that had already passed since its composition had consolidated Ravel's status as one of the most significant musical figures of the day. His last major work, *Gaspard de la nuit*, had won an enthusiastic public response, and by the middle of 1910 it would also have been generally known that Ravel had

---

[28] *Le Guide musical* 55/18 (2 May 1909), 371; 55/27–8 (4/11 July 1909), 503; 55/37–8 (12/19 September 1909), 582.

[29] *OL*, letter 60.   [30] Duchesneau, *L'Avant-garde musicale*, 306.

[31] Cornet, 'Société musicale indépendante', 492.   [32] Chalupt, 'Le Mois du musicien'.

[33] 'Nouvelles', *Le Guide musical* 56/31–2 (31 July/7 August 1910), 561; and 56/37–8 (11/18 September 1910), 617.

[34] Orledge, *Debussy and the Theatre*, 59–60.

been commissioned by Diaghilev's Ballets russes – who had just given the hugely successful première of Stravinsky's *Firebird* – to provide them with a major new work (see Chapter 4).[35] The personal and professional respect in which Ravel was held by his colleagues had also been demonstrated through his active leadership in the foundation of the new Société musicale indépendante. By the summer of 1910, everyone knew that Ravel had an opera ready to perform, and everyone knew who was meant to be staging it. If he did not give way, Albert Carré was going to look extremely foolish.

Casting and rehearsals

Although *L'Heure espagnole* had at last been confirmed for the 1910–11 season, no date had been set for the première: 'Nor do I hear anything more of *L'Heure espagnole*', Ravel wrote to Ida Godebska on 27 September; 'If it's going ahead in November, it's time to get moving.'[36] He would have to wait five more months, but on 20 February 1911 his opera finally appeared in the *livre de bord*, or *registre*, of the Opéra-Comique, the theatre's official record of all rehearsals and performances.[37] At 4 o'clock that afternoon, Geneviève Vix (Concepcion), Jean Périer (Ramiro), Edmond Tirmont (Gonzalve), Maurice Cazeneuve (Torquemada), Louis Hasselmans (conductor) and Fernand Masson (vocal coach and chorus master) gathered with Ravel and Franc-Nohain to read the opera through. Absent from this first call was Don Inigo, M. Delvoye, who appears to have been cast a little later.

Ravel found himself with an extremely good cast, comprising two of the theatre's leading lights, two of its most experienced and versatile performers, and a bright new star in Edmond Tirmont. Jean Périer was the most senior performer of the five: he had joined the Opéra-Comique in 1892, and of his many roles the most important had undoubtedly been that of the first Pelléas. Geneviève Vix, who had made her Opéra-Comique debut in *Louise* in 1906, was a leading soprano, her roles including Carmen and the Puccini heroines. Delvoye, who had made his debut in 1898, had sung roles including Bartolo and Figaro in *Il Barbiere di Siviglia*, Escamillo in *Carmen* and Alfio in *Cavalleria Rusticana*, while Maurice Cazeneuve (debuted 1900) was one of the theatre's busiest and most reliable performers, playing

---

[35] The piano score of *Daphnis et Chloé* is dated 1 May 1910; Durand published a first version of it later that year.

[36] *OL*, letter 78.   [37] Bm-O, Micr. 3453.

a host of supporting roles (Monostatos in *Die Zauberflöte*, Goro in *Madama Butterfly*). Tirmont was a very new arrival to the company, having made his debut only in November 1910, but he would go on to an illustrious career, playing all the big tenor roles at the Salle Favart and later appearing on many audio recordings.[38]

Within a few weeks of that first read-through, however, Louis Hasselmans had been replaced as conductor, and Ravel, in a letter to Cipa Godebski of 22 March, was discussing possible alterations to the casting: 'We're working at the Op-Com, but my presence isn't necessary yet [because the singers were having individual coaching sessions]. Carré has written to me that H[asselmans] would be incapable of conducting a work of this difficulty, so [François] Ruhlmann will take over. He has also suggested a small casting change to me. We'll see.'[39] This proposed change may have been for Don Inigo or Torquemada: a M. Belhomme attended two calls for the former role in late March, and M. Donval rehearsed the latter for some weeks (including ensemble rehearsals), though in the event Delvoye and Cazeneuve resumed their roles.[40]

One casting change did take place, however, late in the rehearsal process: on the afternoon of 20 April, four of the singers attended a rehearsal but the tenor Tirmont was absent, making his debut as Gérald in a matinée performance of *Lakmé*. Later that afternoon, M. Coulomb was called to a coaching session, the indication '*L'Heure* (Gonzalve) urg[t] [urgent]' appended to his name in the *livre de bord*. Coulomb had perhaps been drafted to give Tirmont some relief from an increasingly hectic workload: among the latter's other roles that spring were Alfredo (*La traviata*) and Wilhelm Meister (*Mignon*). (Tirmont's schedule possibly got the better of him: on 6 May he failed to show up to one of the theatre's 'Concerts historiques' and the next day, the *livre de bord* records, he was fined 50 francs. On 25 May he didn't appear at a rehearsal of *Mignon* and was fined again.)

Closer examination of the performers' schedules reveals the commitment, stamina and flexibility the theatre demanded of them. Delvoye sang in *La Bohème* and Massenet's *Manon* all through February and March, then again in May and June (during the run of *L'Heure*), while rehearsing another five operas as well. Périer was headlining in *Pelléas* and *Le Voile du bonheur* and Geneviève Vix was regularly appearing in the title role of *Manon* (and rehearsing at least three other roles) in this period, while Cazeneuve played in six other operas while rehearsing *L'Heure*.

---

[38] Information from Wolff, *Un demi-siècle d'Opéra-Comique.*   [39] *OL*, letter 82.
[40] See Kilpatrick, 'The Carbonne copy', 108–11.

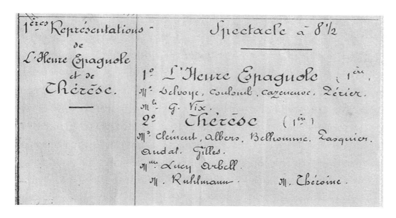

Figure 2.1 The *livre de bord* of the Opéra-Comique, 19 May 1911

Following that first read-through of 20 February, the singers were called daily for six weeks for individual coachings, mostly under the direction of coach Masson. Ensemble rehearsals began in early April, and on 25 April the production moved into the theatre. Orchestral rehearsals began on 28 and 29 April with calls for winds and strings respectively; Ravel attended both of these. The first full orchestral rehearsal took place on 1 May, and later that afternoon the singers and orchestra rehearsed together for the first time, 'à l'Italienne' (Sitzprobe). From this date the set and props were in place and the *livre de bord* indicates the presence of technical staff. A second Sitzprobe took place four days later, and a call for the orchestra alone on the morning of 8 May. Five rehearsals were called for cast and orchestra, including two full dress rehearsals on 12 and 15 May, followed by the 'répétition générale devant la presse' on 17 May. Finally, on 19 May 1911, the *livre de bord* announces the '1ères Représentations' of *L'Heure espagnole* and *Thérèse* (Fig. 2.1).

Three further points about the rehearsal process are noteworthy. First, while all four of the new works in preparation that spring (*L'Heure, La Jota, Le Voile du bonheur* and *Thérèse*) had one or two full orchestral calls before the first combined rehearsal for orchestra and singers, *L'Heure* was the only one to precede these calls with orchestral sectionals. Second, during the first two months of rehearsals, the individual coaching sessions for *L'Heure* were unusually focussed: the performers were usually called one after each other, to rehearse not eight or ten roles (as was standard) but one alone. The years between the work's composition and its première had presumably given Carré and his staff ample opportunity to recognise the score's technical challenges, and Ravel had probably made his wishes clear too.

The *livre de bord* demonstrates that singers and orchestra were prepared with thoroughness and care, by the theatre staff and by the composer himself. No matter what reservations they held about the work, many of the reviewers were to note that the performances of the cast, the orchestra and conductor Ruhlmann were musically and dramatically outstanding: as no less a critic than Gabriel Fauré summed up, 'The performance of *L'Heure espagnole* is perfection itself. Nothing funnier than M. Périer as the muleteer-remover could be imagined: this outstanding artist does not imitate types, he creates them. Mlle Vix is charming, she could not be more alluring. M. Coulomb, M. Delvoye and M. Cazeneuve are all three excellent.'*[41]

Finally, the most important single piece of information offered by the *livre de bord* is its record of the composer's presence during the rehearsal period for his opera, demonstrating that he was involved at every stage of the production process. Ravel attended the initial read-through and took control of the first two ensemble rehearsals. He was present at Ruhlmann's first rehearsal with the ensemble on 15 April and the first rehearsal on the theatre's main stage ten days later. He attended the two orchestral sectionals, and from the end of April he was at the Salle Favart almost every day. The Opéra-Comique had a tradition of close collaboration with its authors:[42] among the works being prepared at the same time as *L'Heure*, the *livre de bord* notes the presence of Massenet at rehearsals for *Thérèse*, Raoul Laparra at almost every call for his *La Jota*, and Franc-Nohain, as well as Ravel, attending rehearsals for *L'Heure espagnole*. Ravel and Franc-Nohain's engagement with the production would be equally thorough in the 1921 Opéra reprise of *L'Heure espagnole*, of which Louis Laloy wrote that the staging was 'fine-tuned in rehearsal after rehearsal' by Jacques Rouché 'in the presence of the authors', with all the 'care, assurance, lightness of touch and feeling for the work that one could imagine'*.[43]

Critical reception

The nine performances that comprised the first season of *L'Heure espagnole* (19, 23, 25, 27 and 30 May, then 1, 3, 7 and 28 June) elicited a critical response which unsurprisingly ranged from lavish praise to sweeping

[41] Fauré, '*L'Heure espagnole*'.

[42] See Bartlet, 'Archival sources for the Opéra-Comique and its "Registres"', which explores many aspects of the theatre's functioning, its dealings with composers and librettists and the role of the *livres de bord*.

[43] Laloy, 'À l'Opéra: *L'Heure espagnole*'.

disparagement. A few reviews noted, with varying degrees of disapproval, that the subject matter was rather unusual and its text ill suited to musical realisation, but most of the objections raised in this regard were sardonic rather than serious (Jean Marnold was a notable exception, deploring the text while vigorously praising the music*[44]). The music, however, drew a few malicious responses. Camille Bellaigue, in the *Revue des deux mondes*, began by conceding that

M. Ravel's score contains a few passages that aren't unbearable. [...] Pages 12 and 13, page 20, pages 88 and 98 – two, three and as many as nine bars together which, by their rhythm or melody, offer a sense or a semblance of form, the appearance of being something almost like music, or what we generally used to understand by that word.*[45]

But, he went, on, 'of melody, there cannot properly be said to be any. Of harmonies, there are hardly any, except those that one wishes weren't there at all.' Without dealing in detail with the libretto and the score, and with no mention at all of the production or the performers, Bellaigue went on to attack Ravel's entire musical aesthetic, and that of his generation: 'The "young masters" of our time [...] strip back [music], on the pretext of liberating it; thinking to make it more supple, they pull it apart and break it. So-called workers for progress, they advance nothing but decadence. They stand not for life, but for nothingness.'*[46]

Pierre Lalo, although offering a few words of faint praise for the orchestration, lambasted the music with the same adjectives that figure over and over again in his reviews of Ravel: 'His characters are as bereft in life and soul as they could possibly be. [...] Everything about them is icy, frozen; everything is small, thin, narrow, limited.'*[47] Reynaldo Hahn famously described Ravel's technique as 'a sort of transcendent ju-jitsu'*,[48] while the anonymous reviewer of *Le petit journal* was one of several who, perhaps suspecting that Ravel was poking covert fun at his audience and critics, responded in kind: 'M. Ravel is one of the most progressive musicians of today, and nobody expected that his characters would be singing melodies. [...] M. Ravel has a good deal of talent. His stated aim is to

---

[44] Although he had pushed hard for the première, Marnold called the libretto 'this coarse and ungainly farce', declaring that it had 'absolutely nothing in common' with 'the exquisite art that accompanies it. [...] In musical terms, *L'Heure espagnole* is, since *Pelléas*, the most forcibly original and accomplished work that our French school has bestowed upon the lyric stage'* (Marnold, 'Musique' (June 1911), 869–70).

[45] Bellaigue, 'Revue musicale', 218–19.   [46] *Ibid.*, 220.

[47] Lalo, 'La Musique [...] *L'Heure espagnole*' (1911).   [48] Hahn, '*L'Heure espagnole*'.

modernise the old "opera buffa" tradition, and he has achieved it, but next time he should really allocate a larger role to his singers.'*[49]

Ravel would probably have been pleased, however, to see that several reviewers drew connections between his opera and those of his beloved Chabrier: Paul Souday suggested that Ravel 'stems in part from Chabrier'*, and Louis Vuillemin particularly cited Chabrier's orchestration, his use of orchestral colour and humorous instrumental effects, as directly related to Ravel's, while delighting in the opera's 'charming and spontaneous ingenuity'*.[50] Albert Bertelin, in *Comœdia illustré*, was one of the few wholeheartedly enthusiastic reviewers, declaring that *L'Heure* revealed 'the very rare qualities of the spirit of observation united with a fine and distinguished musical nature: the most unexpected orchestral combinations are familiar to [Ravel] and he employs them with a surety of touch that is absolutely remarkable'*.[51]

Beyond this familiar blend of potshots, dismissals and a few glowing encomiums, however, we may also note a shifting balance in the critical response to Ravel's music. With the extra column inches accorded to opera reviews, and prompted by the broader canvas offered by the composer's first lyric work, critics other than Ravel's staunch supporters Laloy and Marnold seemed prepared to probe, with a greater degree of appreciation and open-mindedness, both his aesthetic and his method. Gabriel Fauré's lifelong championship of his former student in no way impinged on the clear-headedness of his musical criticism: although he had been disconcerted by the *Histoires naturelles* (see p. 89), Fauré praised *L'Heure* warmly, extolling its 'many delightful pages, marvellous harmonic and orchestral discoveries and subtle ingenuity'. He also noted, half-seriously, a certain 'irreverence towards the rules of music. [. . .] Never has the chance to cultivate the *fausse note* been so generously offered to M. Ravel, and he has joyously availed himself of it.'*[52] But Fauré also remarked perceptively on Ravel's faithfulness to his text. Countering the complaint of Paul Souday, who suggested that 'M. Ravel's score [. . .] is at once too exclusively picturesque and too meticulous: it loses itself in the detail. It abounds in amusing and delicious trinkets [menuailles]; it lacks a coherent structure, breadth and movement'*,[53] Fauré highlighted the interplay of small- and large-scale musical architecture:

[49] [Anon.], 'Premières représentations: Gaité-Lyrique [*sic*] – *L'Heure espagnole*'.
[50] Vuillemin, '*L'Heure espagnole*'; Souday, 'Les Premières'.
[51] Bertelin, "*Thérèse* [. . .] *L'Heure espagnole*'.   [52] Fauré, '*L'Heure espagnole*'.
[53] Souday, 'Les Premières'.

[Ravel's music] translates faithfully and continuously the least whim of the text as well as the greatest, the simplest and the most extravagant impulses of the action, just as it allies itself with the general shape as well as the smallest details of a *mise-en-scène* where the chiming of clocks, carillons, music boxes and mechanical dolls cannot help but hold an important place.*

The sense of a turning critical tide emerges still more profoundly from the anonymous reviewer of *La Revue musicale*. While his critique recycles some well-worn tropes – Ravel's seeming dryness and lack of emotion – here we also see the reviewer genuinely seeking to understand the composer's aesthetic:

The music reconciled me to M. Maurice Ravel, who has an original style. It is often bizarre, strange, aiming for the commonplace, but he is without doubt an artist who writes solely in accordance with his own methods, and with complete awareness [à bien escient]. [. . .] M. Ravel's aesthetic has its dangers; the first of these is vulgarity, and I knew some works by M. Ravel that have disappointed me with their incontestable banality. But yesterday I finished by finding myself very appreciative of the courageous endeavour of the musician. Although his clear intention is to conceal himself behind the things of which he speaks, and while he may appear from time to time as a *pince-sans-rire*, one recognises in him a highly gifted artist.*[54]

Also noteworthy here is the highlighting of Ravel's musical integrity and self-awareness, and the emphasis, albeit in veiled terms, of his independence from the aesthetic and compositional method of Debussy. These qualities would come to play an important role in post-war music criticism: in 1926 Henry Prunières placed Ravel alongside Fauré, declaring that 'Ravel is a revolutionary, but in his own manner, which is that of his teacher Gabriel Fauré, and in no way akin to Berlioz and Debussy. The latter two were essentially intuitive composers. Ravel is always aware [toujours conscient].'[55]

---

[54] 'G.', '*L'Heure espagnole*', 238–9.

[55] Prunières, 'Trois silhouettes de musiciens', 235. Prunières's appraisal must be read in the context of his key role in shaping Debussy's legacy, as established in Barbara Kelly's *Music and Ultra-Modernism* (see Chapter 1, 'Remembering Debussy'), as well as the changing post-war perceptions of Fauré and Ravel. Here he echoes Roland-Manuel who, as Kelly notes, in a 1921 essay in *La Revue musicale*, 'sought to re-launch [Ravel] in the context of the post-war musical scene', situating him 'as a successor of Chabrier and Fauré' (*Music and Ultra-Modernism*, 58). Ravel himself would emphasise the notion of 'un artiste conscient', contrasting *conscience* with *sincérité*, in the 1931 article 'Mes souvenirs d'enfant paresseux' (*La Petite Gironde*, 12 July 1931; Orenstein (ed.), *A Ravel Reader*, 395).

From the Opéra-Comique to the Opéra

By mid-July 1911, Ravel was on his way to the Basque coast. He was still there when the 1911–12 Opéra-Comique season opened on 1 September, and still there when, on 19 September, *L'Heure espagnole* was given one last time, featuring rather incongruously as the curtain-raiser to *La bohème*. Cazeneuve and Coulomb (neither of whom appears to have been contracted to the theatre for the 1911–12 season[56]) were replaced by MM. Dumoutier (Torquemada) and Pasquier (Gonzalve); the other three performers were the same. Since the late spring, however, a M. Gilles had been studying the role of Inigo and Nelly Martyl that of Concepcion; both rehearsed the opera intensively during September 1911. On the morning of 18 September, Jean Périer joined the new ensemble for a Sitzprobe, followed by a full dress rehearsal that afternoon. Pasquier and Dumoutier played, but Gilles did not (Delvoye resumed his role), and Mme Martyl, although she was 'also in the room', attended only to watch Vix sing Concepcion.[57]

During those first weeks of the new season it was not Carré but his *régisseur* Ernest Carbonne who was in charge of the Opéra-Comique. On 27 May, Carré and a sizeable portion of the company – 127 people in all, including singers, dancers, production, musical and administrative staff – had left Paris for Buenos Aires, where they mounted twenty operas in a two-month season.[58] The touring party returned to Paris on the evening of 17 September (their arrival at the Gare d'Orsay reported in gushing detail by *Le Temps*), and on the 18th Carré was back in the theatre. On 10 October, he announced the definitive programme for the 1911–12 season; the announcement, which would normally have been made in early September, had been delayed because of the tour. The list of planned operas did not include *L'Heure espagnole*.

The success of the tour had been well canvassed in the daily press, and Carré undoubtedly wanted to capitalise on it by featuring the artists and

[56] Cazeneuve returned to the Opéra-Comique in the 1912–13 season but Coulomb did not, playing at the Théâtre de l'Apollo in 1911–12 and the Théâtre des Arts in 1912–13; the 1913 issue of *Les Annales du théâtre et de la musique* describes him as a *transfuge* (defector) from the Opéra-Comique (Stoullig, *Les Annales du théâtre et de la musique* 39 (1913), 426).

[57] During all these months no alternative (or understudy) Ramiro appears in the registers, except, very briefly, a M. Laure, who had just two calls for the part (12 and 16 May). The role seems to have been very much Périer's, and had he fallen ill *L'Heure* would have undoubtedly been replaced at the last minute with another opera – not an uncommon practice in this busy repertory company.

[58] Stoullig, *Les Annales du théâtre et de la musique* 37 (1911), 128–9; Carré, *Souvenirs du théâtre*, 346; *Le Temps*, 21 September 1911.

productions that had starred in Buenos Aires. It is hard not to suspect that this gave him an excuse to pull the plug on Ravel's opera. Ernest Carbonne, rehearsing *L'Heure* intensively with a new cast during the first weeks of the new season, must have foreseen more than a single performance. Carré, however, had discharged his responsibilities by putting Ravel's opera on stage, and – as he seems to have expected – its reviews had been mixed and its receipts low.[59] He had never been enthusiastic about the work – it seems entirely possible that putting it off until so late in the 1910–11 season was a backhanded turn, leaving it insufficient time to establish itself before the season closed – and having at last fulfilled his obligations, he was under no obligation to keep it in the repertoire. *L'Heure* would not be seen again in the Salle Favart until 1945, thirty-four years after its creation and eight years after Ravel's death. In the meantime it would be staged at Covent Garden (1919), in New York and Chicago (1920) and, in January 1921, at the Théâtre de la Monnaie in Brussels.

In June 1921, Jacques Rouché mounted a production of *Daphnis et Chloé* at the Opéra Garnier. During the run he approached its composer about transferring *L'Heure espagnole* to the larger theatre. Ravel responded enthusiastically on 30 June: 'Of course I would be delighted to see you put on *L'Heure espagnole*. I have only one concern: the proportions of the theatre... and of the work. But you have doubtless already considered these inconveniences. So, it's settled.'*[60]

The second Parisian season of *L'Heure espagnole* opened on 5 December 1921 under the baton of Philippe Gaubert, with Fanny Heldy as Concepcion, M. Couzinou as Ramiro, Albert Huberty as Inigo, Henri Fabert as Torquemada and M. Dubois as Gonzalve. If 1911 had won the opera an uncertain response, this time it was almost universally admired. Ravel had been ordained by the critics and the public as the new figurehead of French music, assuming the place left vacant by Debussy's death in 1918: notwithstanding the proclamations of Les Six and their advocates (see p. 49), it was now more politic to praise Ravel than to revile him.[61] Perhaps more generously, critics and public had by this time arrived at an understanding with Ravel's language and aesthetic, and through familiarity were more prepared to accept a work like *L'Heure espagnole*, whose dryness of wit and sonority seemed in any case to accord more naturally with the Zeitgeist of the 1920s. 'Ravel's music', wrote 'L.S.' in *Le Gaulois*,

---

[59] See Marnat, *Maurice Ravel*, 308, 313.   [60] BnF Mus., LAS Ravel 164.
[61] See Kelly, *Music and Ultra-Modernism*, 56–61.

completely captures the caricature and comic spirit that this very funny play by M. Franc-Nohain demands; it moulds itself upon the text like a silken vest upon the body; it is ironic, comical, earthy; it is descriptive and picturesque, it follows the finest details of the action, with an obedience that seems mechanical, and which derives from the most perceptive wit; it photographs in sound the smallest events and gestures of the characters.*[62]

In *Opinion*, Henry Bidou discussed the work's detail of characterisation and underlined the role of the music in creating an effective 'comédie psychologique', rare in the realm of operetta or *opéra bouffe*.[63] Maurice Brillant devoted an extended piece to the opera in *Le Correspondant*, concluding with the claim that 'the pairing of this poet and this musician has produced what might have appeared to be one of the slightest, but is in reality one of the most perfect works of recent years'*.[64] Even Pierre Lalo had moderated his tone: if his review reapplies the familiar labels of 'irony', 'pinched smiles', 'coolness', 'lack of sensibility' and so on, they are now situated in the context of 'a music in perfect accord with its subject, and an art extraordinarily sure of itself, [which] attains a perfection of style and effect. [...] Never has [Ravel] succeeded so completely.'*[65] *Toujours conscient*, Ravel would have as little time for this new gushing Lalo as he had had for his vituperative predecessor.[66]

This time, too, *L'Heure* plainly delighted audiences as well as critics. 'L.S.' described the 'long ovation' for singers, orchestra and conductor alike, in which the 'whole theatre' united.* Louis Laloy's summation is perhaps the most evocative, coming as it does from a critic who had championed Ravel's music for almost two decades: 'What we hadn't dared to expect were the endless curtain calls [...] Never in all the time I have been attending the Opéra, that is for twenty years or so, have I ever witnessed such an ovation, except for Ballets russes performances. M. Ravel, however, refused to appear onstage: "It's not", he said, "a French practice".'*[67]

But the final word comes from Ravel himself, who wrote to Rouché after the première:

---

[62] 'L.S.', 'Opéra – *L'Heure espagnole*'.   [63] Bidou, '*L'Heure espagnole*'.

[64] Brillant, '*L'Heure espagnole*'.

[65] Lalo, 'La Musique [...] *L'Heure espagnole*' (1922). Zank briefly summarises the changing reception to *L'Heure*, noting the difference in pre- and post-war responses to its essentially ironic nature; see *Irony and Sound*, 10–14 (although he mistranslates Chalupt's 1925 description of the score's 'spirituelle ironie' as 'spiritual irony' (*recte* 'witty irony'), 12).

[66] Ravel would finally dismiss Lalo, comprehensively and in print, in 1927; see *OL*, 351–4.

[67] Laloy, 'A l'Opéra: *L'Heure espagnole*'.

You knew that, until Monday, I wasn't certain that this adventure would end happily. You were right. In truth, to your audacity in granting my *opéra bouffe* entry into the Académie Nationale de Musique [the Opéra Garnier], you have added that of endowing it with the performers and the production that best suited it. It is this perfect combination that earned the success for which I am doubly grateful to you.*[68]

On 26 January 1924, *L'Heure espagnole* would open the winter opera season at the Opéra de Monte-Carlo, enjoying a success that almost certainly prompted the theatre's director, Raoul Gunsbourg, to approach Ravel about the possibility of staging his still-unfinished new opera, *L'Enfant et les sortilèges*. Perhaps Jacques Rouché had had something similar in mind when he mounted *L'Heure* in 1921: when Rouché and Ravel met that June to talk about its staging, did they also discuss the progress of Colette's *féerie-ballet*?

[68] BnF Mus., LAS Ravel 165.

3 | The Child and the impresarios

1916–1923: Jacques Rouché and the Opéra Garnier

On 10 March 1916, 'Conducteur Ravel' of the 'Convois automobiles' drove out of Paris, bound for the Western Front.[1] Twelve days after his departure, a *pneumatique* arrived in Jacques Rouché's office: 'Cher Monsieur, I've finished. I've sorted out the last third – changed it, rather – and I'd like to know if you share Sidi's [Henry de Jouvenel's] good opinion of the *Ballet pour ma fille*. Would you telephone me? Believe me amicably yours, Colette de Jouvenel.'*[2]

Rouché (1862–1957) was one of the most significant figures in French cultural life during the first half of the twentieth century. A brilliant graduate of the École Polytechnique and Sciences Politiques, he held the post of *chef du commissariat* at the 1889 Exposition Universelle, succeeding so well as to be awarded the Légion d'honneur at the youthful age of twenty-seven. Rouché owned and managed *La grande revue* from 1907 until its closure in 1939, wrote an important treatise on theatre décor and production (*L'Art théâtral moderne*, 1910) and directed three highly successful seasons at the Théâtre des Arts from 1910 to 1913. 'I had long dreamed of offering a work to the Théâtre des Arts', Ravel wrote to Rouché after the 1912 première of his ballet *Ma mère l'Oye* – 'it is the only theatre in France that is currently bringing us anything new'.[3]

On 25 November 1913, Rouché was appointed to the directorship of the Opéra Garnier. He took over full responsibility in September 1914 and remained in the post until 1945.[4] As normal programming was suspended during the First World War, and Rouché's appointment was only provisional during that period,[5] it was not until 1919 that he was able to run the

---

[1] Roy (ed.), *Lettres à Roland-Manuel*, 32.
[2] Bm-O, Fonds Rouché 406, LAS Colette de Jouvenel 1. On 10 March Colette wrote to Rouché putting off a meeting to read over the libretto together; see Mercier, 'L'Enfant et les sortilèges: genèse', 70–1.
[3] *OL*, letter 92.   [4] Garban, *Jacques Rouché*, 182.   [5] Nichols, *The Harlequin Years*, 62.

theatre at full throttle. But from the earliest days of his new role Rouché was planning for the future: one of his first acts on his appointment seems to have been to communicate with Colette about a possible scenario or libretto for his new theatre. Michel Mercier has traced a letter from Colette to Rouché, seemingly written shortly before Christmas 1913, which concludes 'Je pense au *Divertissement. . .*'[6] No *Divertissement* eventuated, however, so it appears that Rouché approached Colette again sometime in late 1915 or early 1916. Rouché himself recalled in 1939:

I had long been persuaded of the necessity of creating a new form of opera libretto, one capable of engaging, touching and moving our younger audience. Some years ago, as I recall (I'm not sure quite how many), encountering Mme Colette in a friend's salon, I asked her to apply her imaginative talents to a scenario for a ballet or a lyric work. Some months later she brought me the delightful poem of *L'Enfant et les sortilèges*, and I asked Maurice Ravel to set it to music.*[7]

Colette enshrined a rather more compressed version of the opera's genesis in her own 1939 reflection on her collaboration with Ravel, the essay 'Un salon en 1900':

I still cannot explain how I, who work slowly and painfully, was able to give [Rouché] *L'Enfant et les sortilèges* in less than eight days. . . He liked my little poem, and suggested several composers whose names I accepted as politely as I could.

'But', said Rouché after a silence, 'if I suggested Ravel to you?'

I was startled out of my politeness and the expression of my enthusiasm left nothing to be desired.

'We mustn't kid ourselves,' said Rouché, 'it could take a long time, even assuming Ravel accepts. . .'

He accepted. It took a long time. He disappeared with my libretto and we heard nothing more of Ravel, nor of *L'Enfant*. . . Where did Ravel work? *Was* he working? I was not then familiar with what the creation of a new work demanded of him, the slow frenzy that possessed him and held him isolate, careless of the days and hours. The war took Ravel, consigning his name to impervious silence, and I fell out of the habit of thinking of *L'Enfant*. Five years passed. The completed work and its author emerged from silence, escaping from the blue, nyctalopic gaze of his confidants, his Siamese cats. But Ravel did not treat me with any privilege, explaining nothing nor granting me an early hearing. He seemed to concern himself only with the duo of the two Cats, asking gravely if I minded if he replaced 'mouâu' with 'mouain', or perhaps it was the other way around. . .[8]

---

[6] Mercier, '*L'Enfant et les sortilèges*: genèse', 69.   [7] Rouché, '*L'Enfant et les sortilèges*'.

[8] Colette, 'Un salon en 1900', *Journal à rebours, Œuvres*, vol. IV, 166–7. Chapter 4 returns to Colette's essay; see also Kilpatrick, 'Enchantments and illusions', for a full discussion of the circumstances surrounding the composition of *L'Enfant*.

Whether it had taken days, months or even years to draft, Rouché certainly received a preliminary version of Colette's libretto in mid-March 1916; a final version followed later that month (as attested to by the *pneumatique* quoted above).

While Colette's enthusiasm at the prospect of a collaboration with Ravel, as recorded in 'Un salon en 1900', was certainly genuine, neither her nor Rouché's account mentions that Ravel was not in fact the first or even the second composer approached about the then *Ballet pour ma fille*. Rather, 'here is the *Ballet pour ma fille* – have you found Dukas?' wrote Colette to Rouché in late March 1916.[9] The director duly approached the composer of *L'Apprenti sorcier* and *La Péri* in a letter of 14 April: 'Cher Maître et ami, Colette de Jouvenel has brought me a delightful libretto for a ballet-opera. Her wish is to read it to you so you can understand what she has in mind; you can also understand how happy I am to be the intermediary.'[*10]

Dukas, however, refused the project by return post. He was 'certain that a Ballet by [Colette] could not do otherwise than refresh the genre. It would give me great pleasure to hear her reading [it].' But he nevertheless declared himself unwilling to participate in any sort of collaborative venture: 'You know my views on collaborations. They have not changed', he wrote firmly.[*11]

The next composer on the shortlist seems to have been Igor Stravinsky:

Monsieur Jacques Rouché is sending you the scenario of my ballet. And this little creature would become, if you consented to set it to music, a marvel. And Thévenaz will dance the Fire (we'll take out the words wherever they get in the way) the Fire [*sic*], the Squirrel, everything that's wanted.

Please take this as a tribute of my admiration. I miss *Le Rossignol* terribly.[*12]

If a response was forthcoming, it must have been negative (no trace survives), and by the summer of 1916, Colette was writing once more to Rouché: 'Are you keeping the ballet, or will you send it back to me? If you're keeping it, have you any thoughts about a composer with plenty of talent – and also haste?'[*13]

---

[9] Bm-O, LAS Colette 3. This and the other five letters under the catalogue reference 'LAS Colette' are undated. Their sequence and approximate dates have been deduced from their context and provenance; see *Compendium of Sources*.

[10] Nichols, *The Harlequin Years*, 91.   [11] Bm-O, LAS Dukas 10.

[12] Delahaye, 'L'Enfant et les sortilèges', 33 (Fondation Paul-Sacher (Basel), micr. 401294). Although Delahaye ascribes this letter to late 1918 or early 1919, it was addressed from Colette's apartment in rue Cortambert, which she left in October 1916 for a new apartment in Boulevard Suchet. 1916 – before the approach to Ravel – therefore seems a more probable dating.

[13] Bm-O, LAS Colette 1.

Although the practical Rouché may initially have been reluctant to commission a composer then serving at Verdun, it was at this juncture that he posted a libretto of Colette's 'fairy-ballet' to Ravel. But 'I had changed stations', Ravel said later, and the letter went astray.[14] Even if the libretto had arrived at that time, Ravel, on active service, distant, miserable and ill (with dysentery and then a hernia), was in no state to undertake a major project. He returned to Paris to recuperate in late October, only to find his beloved mother seriously ill. Marie Ravel died on 5 January 1917. 'Physically, I'm still alright', he wrote to his wartime 'godmother' Mme Dreyfus on 9 February, 'Spiritually, it's dreadful. . . so little time has passed since I was writing to her, since I was receiving her poor letters, which saddened me. . . and yet which gave me such joy. [. . .] I didn't know that it would come so quickly.'[15]

Ravel returned briefly to army service in February, but by 1 June his continuing ill health had earned him a temporary discharge.[16] And some-time that spring he accepted the libretto that he had at last received from Rouché: 'it grabbed me straight away', he said later.[17] His acceptance, however, appears to have been conditional upon a few alterations. Colette's next letter to Rouché reveals that her 'fantasy-ballet' was changing shape – and that the prospect of a collaboration with Ravel (although his name is not mentioned) was an attractive one: 'You have put fairies into my head. It's much more fun than a play or a novel. I'd like both to talk with you and to offer you two or three ideas. Where? When?'*[18] A subsequent letter (20 June 1917) from Ravel to Lucien Garban, his friend and house-editor at Durand, also hints at the composer's role in determining the work's final form: 'I have several things to ask of you: firstly, the address of Colette Willy, which you will be able to find easily. I charged Rouché with a task for her and have not yet had any response.'*[19] It seems that another letter had gone astray: somewhere around this period Colette wrote to Rouché, 'Thankyou for having passed Ravel's letter to me; it arrived, rather late, with the annotation "addressee deceased". Alas, alas! With my friend-ship from beyond the grave / Colette de Jouvenel / I will write immediately and explain the above to Ravel.'*[20]

---

[14] Méry, 'Avant-première'. Ravel arrived in Châlons-sur-Marne on 6 September but was in hospital by the 24th (*Archives Roland-Manuel*, 51–2).

[15] *OL*, letter 144.   [16] Roy (ed.), *Lettres à Roland-Manuel*, 108.

[17] Arnoux, 'Avant-première'. In March 1917, Ravel and Rouché were communicating about a performance of *Adélaïde* at the Opéra (*Archives Roland-Manuel*, 56).

[18] Bm-O, LAS Colette 6.

[19] Orenstein (ed.), 'La Correspondance de Maurice Ravel à Lucien Garban (1901–1918)', 66.

[20] Bm-O, LAS Rouché 239.

After this, however, silence fell. In the autumn of 1917, Colette wrote to Rouché again: 'What is happening with the *Divertissement pour ma fille*? And with Ravel? I would love to hear any news about it.'*[21] It seems that little was forthcoming until early 1919, when she addressed the same question to Rouché once more. This time she got a response: Rouché duly passed a message to Ravel, who replied first to him, from Mégève, on 20 February 1919:

You see how timely your letter was: for days I have wanted to write to Colette de Jouvenel – I've just lost my address book, it's a disaster – to ask her if she still wants to have me as a collaborator. [...] I hope to return [to Paris] in April and the first thing I intend to work on is Colette's 'opéra dansé'. [...] Would you be good enough to write to her, and to give me her address? I should like to write to her about our planned work.*[22]

There followed the first known direct communication between the collaborators:

[Ravel to Colette, 27 February 1919]

Chère Madame,

Just as you were expressing in Rouché's presence your regret at my silence, I was contemplating, from the depths of my snow, asking whether you still wanted such an inefficient collaborator. In truth, I am already working on [our opera]: I'm taking notes – without writing any – I'm even thinking of some modifications... Don't be afraid, they're not cuts – on the contrary. For example, couldn't the squirrel's tale be developed? Imagine all that a squirrel could say of the forest, and how that could be expressed in music!

Another thing: what would you think of the cup and the teapot, in old Wedgwood – black – singing a ragtime? I confess that the idea of having a ragtime sung by two Negroes at the Académie Nationale de Musique fills me with delight. You'll observe that the form – a single couplet, with refrain – is perfectly suited to the action in this scene: reproaches, recriminations, fury, pursuit. Perhaps you will object that you don't usually write Negro slang. I, who know not a word of English, would do the same as you – I'd wangle it somehow [je me débrouillerais].

I would be most grateful if you would give me your opinion on these two points, and please trust, dear Madame, in the lively artistic sympathy of yours sincerely,

Maurice Ravel*[23]

[21] Bm-O, LAS Colette 4.   [22] *OL*, letter 153.
[23] *OL*, letter 154 (facsimile reproduced in Delahaye, '*L'Enfant et les sortilèges*', 37).

[Colette to Ravel, 5 March 1919]

Cher Monsieur,

But certainly a ragtime! But of course Negroes in Wedgwood! May a terrific gust from the music hall stir up the dust of the Opéra! Go for it! I'm happy to learn that you are still thinking about 'Divertissement pour ma fille', I despaired of you, and I had heard that you were ill. Do you know that cinema orchestras are playing your charming 'Contes de Ma mère l'Oye' while they show Westerns? If I were a composer and Ravel, I believe that I would derive much pleasure from learning that.

And the squirrel will say all that you wish. Does the 'cat' duo, exclusively miaowed, please you? We'll have acrobats. Isn't the Arithmetic business a polka?

I wish you good health, and I shake your hand impatiently.

Colette de Jouvenel*[24]

Despite this exchange, Ravel continued 'not writing any notes' for some time. Perhaps in order to hurry him up a little, in December 1919 Colette gave a newspaper interview, which appeared under the headline 'Mme Colette, librettiste d'un ballet de Maurice Ravel':

A piece of news that promises a delicate pleasure: Mme Colette has written the libretto for a ballet, with music by Ravel, which we will applaud, next season, at the Opéra. We asked the author of *La Vagabonde* for some details of this new work, created, we know, on the entreaties of M. Jacques Rouché. 'In truth', Mme Colette replies, 'my ballet will be more of a *divertissement* that will be danced, sung and mimed. It is called *Divertissement pour ma fille*, and I had enormous pleasure putting it together. We will see in it dancers who sing, acrobats who dance, cats who miaow. The objects themselves, the table and the sofa, the teapot and the cup will take part in the action and will be mimed. The heroine will have to know how to sing, dance and mime. Since there is so much opera with dancing, why should we not have ballets with singing?' Of course. We ask Mme Colette if she has written a libretto before. 'No. The *Divertissement pour ma fille* is the first, but it will probably not be the last. The great composer Ravel is, at this moment, putting the finishing touches to his work, in which you will recognise his tone-colours, so varied, so original, so expressive.'*[25]

But Ravel, far from 'putting the finishing touches' to the work, had barely begun, and his health and morale remained fragile. To Georgette Marnold on 15 January 1920, he wrote, 'I didn't know that the designs had been commissioned [...] for my opera, of which the first note is not yet written'*;[26] and to an unknown correspondent in May, 'I've hardly started a

---

[24] *OL*, letter 155.   [25] [Anon.], 'Mme Colette, librettiste d'un ballet de Maurice Ravel'.
[26] BnF Mus., LAS Ravel 213.

work that the Opéra has been waiting for since 1916.'[27] By the summer of 1920, *La Valse* complete, he had at last begun work on *L'Enfant*, which he mentions in letters to Roland-Manuel and Garban; Roland-Manuel claimed that he had sketched the opera as far as the Arithmetic scene, but in a letter of July 1921 Ravel describes it merely as 'commencé'.[28] Other projects took over: the Sonata for Violin and Cello, correcting proofs of *La Valse*, buying and renovating Le Belvédère in Montfort l'Amaury, overseeing the Brussels and then the Opéra premières of *L'Heure espagnole* . . . and *L'Enfant et les sortilèges* disappeared from his correspondence entirely. 'Oh! *cher ami*, when, oh when, the *Divertissement pour ma. . . petite-fille*? Is it true, that it is going to be finished? With hope and friendship', wrote Colette to Ravel, probably in the summer of 1923.*[29] *Divertissement pour ma. . . petite-fille* was a pun and a prod: Colette's small daughter (*fille*), born in 1913, was growing up rapidly, and if Ravel didn't hurry up, she might find herself with a granddaughter (*petite-fille*) instead.

1924–1925: Raoul Gunsbourg and the Opéra de Monte-Carlo

'I began working on [*L'Enfant*] in the spring of 1920', Ravel said, in an interview given just before the opera's première,

And then. . . I stopped. Was it the challenges of the scenario, or was it my poor health that prompted this interruption? In short, I gave up on it, though this did not prevent me from thinking about it all the time. Then suddenly, last spring, Gunsbourg burst upon me like a bomb; bombs no longer astonish me, but Gunsbourg did: 'Your *L'Heure espagnole*', he told me, 'has been a triumph in Monte Carlo. Give me something else fast!'*[30]

Raoul Gunsbourg (1860–1955) headed the Opéra de Monte-Carlo from 1892 until 1951. Born in Bucharest, in 1880 he travelled to Russia, where he

---

[27] *OL*, letter 169.

[28] *OL*, letter 172; Orenstein, 'La Correspondance de Ravel à Garban (1919–1934), 29; Roland-Manuel, *Maurice Ravel et son œuvre dramatique*, 134; unpublished letter to Claude Roger-Marx, 2 July 1921, kindly communicated by Manuel Cornejo (*Édition (la plus complète possible) des correspondances, articles et entretiens de Maurice Ravel*, in preparation).

[29] Orenstein, '*L'Enfant et les sortilèges*: correspondance inédite', 216, but see also Kilpatrick, 'Enchantments and illusions', 39n28.

[30] Méry, 'Avant-première'. Although Druilhe and Orenstein suggest that Gunsbourg's approach was made in the summer of 1923 (Druilhe, 'Les grandes créations de l'Opéra de Monte-Carlo', 9; Orenstein, '*L'Enfant et les sortilèges*: correspondance inédite', 218), the successful 1924 season of *L'Heure espagnole* suggests that Ravel's 'last spring' is accurate.

established the first French opera theatre in Moscow before taking over the management of the Théâtre des Variétés in Moscow (in winter) and the Théâtre populaire in St Petersburg (in summer).[31] In 1892, according to the impresario's memoirs, the Tsar wrote personally to Prince Albert of Monaco, requesting that he appoint Gunsbourg as the new director of the Opéra de Monte-Carlo.[32] A composer *manqué*, Gunsbourg wrote and staged eight operas in Monte Carlo, but it was as a director that he became famous: he was the first to stage Berlioz's *La Damnation de Faust* as an opera (1893), the first to present the complete *Ring* cycle within the cultural ambit of France (1909), and he oversaw the premières of Saint-Saëns's *Hélène* (1904) and *Déjanire* (1911), Fauré's *Pénélope* (1913) and most of Massenet's late operas (*Le Jongleur de Notre Dame, Thérèse, Don Quichotte, Chérubin*). 'If I finished this opera', said Ravel in another *avant-première* interview,

it was because M. Raoul Gunsbourg pestered me for it, demanding, double-quick, a work [. . .] for the Opéra de Monte-Carlo. Even though I had ceased to work at it, I was thinking of *L'Enfant* constantly [. . .] – and, when M. Gunsbourg set his spurs to my belly, I harnessed myself to the task: he said to me, so persuasively, that my *L'Heure espagnole* had been such a great success in Monte-Carlo the previous year (he said: 'a triumph!' – excuse me!) – and I was unable to resist this devil of a man, who is the salvation of French musicians.*[33]

Absent from these interviews is all mention of Jacques Rouché and the Opéra Garnier. How had Rouché lost not only the première of the opera he had originally commissioned, but also its first Parisian performance, which would take place not at the Opéra Garnier but at the Opéra-Comique, on 1 February 1926? Unfortunately, no documentation can be traced: a brief note from Colette to Ravel arranging a meeting with Gunsbourg in late October 1924 offers one of the only glimpses of the contractual negotiations that must have been involved.[34] Meanwhile, a letter of November 1924 suggests that, while no communication had passed between Ravel and Rouché on the subject for quite some time, their relations had remained cordial. Ravel, addressing the director as 'Mon cher Rouché', felt the need to explain what his opera was, and, rather remarkably, offered no concession for any proprietary rights Rouché and the Opéra might have claimed:

[31] Kelly, 'Raoul Gunsbourg'; Gunsbourg, *Cent ans de souvenirs*, 1, 27, 33.
[32] Gunsbourg, *Cent ans de souvenirs*, 91.   [33] Arnoux, 'Avant-première'.
[34] BnF Mus., LAS Colette 2; Delahaye, '*L'Enfant et les sortilèges*', 45.

I am working to complete *L'Enfant et les sortilèges*, the *fantaisie lyrique* for which Colette has written the libretto, and which will be given in Monte Carlo at the beginning of March. Soon after that date, we will be able to offer the work elsewhere, and my collaborator and I would be happy to give you the first refusal. We would ask for a guarantee of a minimum fifteen performances per year during the next three years, in addition to what may be offered us elsewhere.[*35]

However, hints of disagreement between theatres and impresarios later emerged from Henry Prunières's review of the Opéra-Comique production, which laments an unspecified 'misunderstanding' that 'deprived' the Opéra of the chance to stage *L'Enfant*,[36] while Roland-Manuel would write to Ravel after the première that Jean Marnold 'had slapped Rouché's face for the hidden reason that Rouché had refused to stage *L'Enfant*' – but added '(*sic*)'.[37]

Whatever the contractual circumstances, by the spring of 1924 Ravel found himself obliged to finish in less than twelve months a major work that existed, at best, only in portions of draft. As Delahaye observes, Ravel's schedule only increased the pressure, as he travelled in April and May to London, Madrid, Barcelona and Brussels, conducting and accompanying his music.[38] By the summer, however, his correspondence shows him in a flurry of belated compositional activity. A letter of 6 June begs Marcelle Gerar to 'please excuse me, both of you: an opera and a sonata to get done by the end of the year: I'm not shifting anymore.'[*39] On 27 September, he wrote to Theodor Szántó, 'I'm only leaving the job to take some food, or to walk a few kilometres in the forest when I feel like my head's going to explode. Of course, I haven't left Montfort all summer.'[*40]

In early October, Colette sent him a revised version of the Cup and Teapot scene – '*Cher ami*, here are two pretty morsels of poetic artistry! Tell me if they'll do, or if we should find something else?'[*41] – and Ravel responded on 13 October: 'Perfect, *chère amie*, the two pretty morsels of poetic artistry! And so well-suited to the musician [. . .] It's understood, one would pronounce "Tchi-nô-hâ", I even want to write it thus: mistrust of singers.'[*42] The same day he wrote to Ida Godebska: 'Still hard at work. . . I'm up to the "Wedgwood tea-pot and Chinese cup", to lines Colette has

[35] Bm-O, LAS Ravel 10.
[36] Prunières, '*L'Enfant et les sortilèges* de Maurice Ravel à l'Opéra-Comique', 260.
[37] OL, letter 264.
[38] Delahaye, '*L'Enfant et les sortilèges*', 43; his engagements are detailed in Nichols, *Ravel*, 260–2.
[39] BnF Mus., LAS Ravel 158.   [40] OL, letter 244.
[41] BnF Mus., LAS Colette 1; Delahaye, '*L'Enfant et les sortilèges*', 44.
[42] Delahaye, '*L'Enfant et les sortilèges*', 45.

just sent me'.[43] Then he fell ill: to Charles Koechlin he wrote, on 21 October, 'I'm still a bit bleary: I'm emerging from a flu that seemed fairly serious and which has disappeared all of a sudden. But it's still made me lose 4 days. And the composition of my *fantaisie lyrique*, which is far from being finished, has to be done by the end of the year!'[44]

The illness lingered: on 14 November he wrote to Roland-Manuel, 'I fear that I won't be able to come and hear your ballet: this damned flu has made me lose more than three weeks, and I get vertigo calculating how much remains for me to do to finish *L'Enfant et les sortilèges* in a month and a half!'*[45] To Gerar on 21 November, Ravel claimed, 'I'm seeing nobody but my frogs, my Negroes, my shepherds and other insects.'[46] 'What irony! My work finished?', he wrote to Hélène Kahn-Casella three days later; 'In any case, I'm doing what I can [...] I'm hoping for nothing less than a miracle: for example, that the gift of being able to dash something off [bâcler] will be granted me all of a sudden.'*[47] On the 26th, he sent a note to Hélène Jourdan-Morhange: 'I'm not leaving my work, seeing nobody, going out only just enough so as not to wear myself out completely: if *L'Enfant et les sortilèges* doesn't come to term it won't be my fault...'[48] By Christmas he was getting desperate: 'I still have a little hope, but so little!', he wrote to Lucien Garban at Durand on 17 December, and three days after Christmas he asked Roland-Manuel to 'please excuse me [from joining the end-of-year festivities], and [I beg you] to forget neither Gunsbourg nor myself in your prayers'*.[49]

In the meantime, Ravel and Colette were still trying to negotiate a Paris première for their opera. In late 1924 or early 1925, Colette wrote to Ravel, 'in all haste',

Henri de Rotschild [*sic*] would take *L'Enfant et les sortilèges* for the opening of his new theatre, pairing it with *La Princesse d'Élide*, and would stage it magnificently, 1 March 1926. What do you feel about that? I don't know if you already have plans for after Monte Carlo. The staging, the orchestra and the performances would be beautiful, and everything would be conditional on the approval of the authors. But it requires a prompt response from you. The Baron de R[othschild] demands exclusive rights for Paris.*[50]

---

[43] Orenstein, '*L'Enfant et les sortilèges*: correspondance inédite', 218.   [44] *OL*, letter 245.

[45] Roy (ed.), *Lettres à Roland-Manuel*, 144   [46] *OL*, letter 247.

[47] Roy (ed.), 'Lettres de Maurice Ravel à Hélène et Alfredo Casella', 96.

[48] Chalupt and Gerar, *Au miroir de ses lettres*, 211.

[49] Orenstein (ed.), 'La Correspondance de Ravel à Garban (1919–1934)', 60.

[50] Colette, *Lettres à ses pairs*, 267–8.

Nothing came of this proposal: as Nichols notes, Ravel would have been most unwilling to grant Rothschild exclusive rights to the opera, intending it first for the Opéra or Opéra-Comique.[51]

The piano-vocal autograph of *L'Enfant* is dated, with rather less precision than many of Ravel's manuscripts, 'Various places, 1920–1925'. On 18 January 1925, Ravel wrote to Garban, declaring that 'the composition is finished, the transcription almost complete: I'm copying'*,[52] and on 14 February the two authors signed a contract with Durand; the opera had already been advertised in the programme for the forthcoming season of the Opéra de Monte-Carlo. With the première thus fixed for late spring, Garban and Durand – not to mention Gunsbourg – must, as Delahaye notes, have been shaking in their boots.[53] Ravel, however, would confide sanguinely to the interviewer of *Le petit monégasque*, 'And that is how and why, within six months, I finally completed *L'Enfant et les sortilèges*, confident that, despite the number of characters and the challenges of the staging, Gunsbourg, whom difficulty does not discourage but rather spurs on, would accomplish another miracle.'*[54]

L'Enfant in Monte Carlo and Paris, 1925–1926

By 12 March, Ravel had arrived in Monte Carlo, and four days later he wrote once more to Colette:

> When are you getting here? Despite the disastrous state of the parts – it's my fault... tsk... tsk... – we have managed to sort out the score, thanks to an excellent orchestra and a really extraordinary conductor [Victor de Sabata]. We rehearse tonight *à l'italienne*. The premiere is fixed for the 21st (next Saturday). The orchestra, the chorus, the soloists, the ushers[†] are enthusiastic: it's a good omen. Come quickly: your suite awaits you at the Hôtel de Paris, where the food is carefully prepared and indigestible. And if, before leaving, you have a few moments, send Durand a second verse for that celebrated aria 'Toi, le cœur de la rose...', which awaits you alone to be launched by our editors.
> See you soon. All the friendship and gratitude of your
> Maurice Ravel.*
>
> [†]I had almost forgotten Gunsbourg.[55]

---

[51] Nichols, *Ravel*, 276.
[52] Orenstein (ed.), 'La Correspondance de Ravel à Garban (1919–1934)', 62.
[53] Delahaye, '*L'Enfant et les sortilèges*', 47.   [54] Méry, 'Avant-premiere'.   [55] *OL*, letter 250.

One omission from Ravel's list of enthusiastic participants in *L'Enfant* was the dancers. This might seem surprising: after all, the resident company at the Opéra de Monte-Carlo was no less than Sergei Diaghilev's Ballets russes; the choreographer for *L'Enfant* was the 21-year-old George Balanchine, creating his first major work outside Russia;[56] and the troupe included three of the finest dancers of the twentieth century, Alicia Markova, Alexandra Danilova and Ninette de Valois. As Markova recalled: 'The very first opera ballet I was in was the world premiere of the Ravel *L'Enfant et les sortilèges*. He gave me the smoke/fire role and had me pirouetting like mad out of the fireplace; and in the second scene I was the little squirrel. I used to turn like a top, which George adored.'[57] Danilova remembered Ravel himself playing the piano for rehearsals, though she did not then know the identity of the 'little pianist' whom she directed by turn to play 'Faster' or 'Slower'. As Richard Buckle writes, only fifty years later, enquiring why Balanchine possessed an inscribed copy of the score, did she learn that her accompanist had been the composer himself.[58]

What Ravel did not tell Colette was that the rehearsals had been seriously disrupted by a stand-off between Gunsbourg, René Léon (the chief administrator of the Société des Bains de Mer, the organisation that oversaw the Opéra de Monte-Carlo) and the notoriously volatile director of the Ballets russes. Since 1922 Monte Carlo had become, in the words of Lynne Garafola, the 'winter capital and workshop' of the Ballets russes;[59] as well as presenting ballet seasons, the company was engaged to provide ballets for the operas. However, Diaghilev's relationship with Ravel had long been fraught. He seems to have had little sympathy for Ravel's music, or at least never thought it good balletic material. On his first hearing of the newly completed *Daphnis et Chloé* he had wanted to cancel the ballet altogether;[60] later he infuriated the composer by demanding cuts. Ravel continued to work with the company, orchestrating *Khovanshchina* with Stravinsky on Diaghilev's commission in 1913, but relations collapsed in 1914 when Ravel learned that Diaghilev planned to stage his Drury Lane season of *Daphnis* without the chorus.[61] He later patched things up with the Ballets

---

[56] Gottlieb, *George Balanchine*, 35.   [57] Mason (ed.), *I Remember Balanchine*, 5, 90–1.

[58] Buckle, *Diaghilev*, 451, and *George Balanchine, Ballet Master*, 33. It is unlikely that Ravel's accompanying extended beyond occasional brief demonstrations, given the tensions with Diaghilev and his undoubted desire to watch proceedings, rather than be stuck at the instrument muddling his way through his own difficult orchestral reduction.

[59] Garafola, *Diaghilev's Ballets russes*, 238.

[60] Durand, *Quelques souvenirs d'un éditeur de musique*, 16.   [61] See Nichols, *Ravel*, 168.

russes, orchestrating 'Alborada del gracioso' and Chabrier's 'Menuet pom-
peux' for their 1918 season, negotiating plans for a ballet to a scenario by
Francesco Cangiullo, and completing *La Valse*. Communications with
Diaghilev clearly remained touchy, however: 'I'm unsure whether Serge
is in Paris and, as you know, he doesn't reply to my letters', he wrote to
Misia Sert in 1920.[62]

After Diaghilev rejected *La Valse*, Ravel appears to have had nothing
more to do with him until the week before the première of *L'Enfant et les
sortilèges*, when, encountering the impresario in the foyer of the Hôtel de
Paris, Ravel apparently refused to shake his hand. Furious, Diaghilev gave
orders for his troupe to cease rehearsal, claiming that Ravel's score was 'too
difficult'. However, as Léon wrote on 14 March:

Regarding your letter in which you inform me that the piano scores for the ballets
that you must provide for the operas were given to you too late, and that M. Ravel's
music appears to you to be too complicated, it is exceedingly strange that these
difficulties should have arisen just a few hours after an incident that seems to have
taken place with M. Ravel in the lobby of the Hôtel de Paris, after which you appear
to have declared, in the presence of several witnesses, 'I will not be forced to dance
in his opera'.*[63]

Only a tense exchange of correspondence (reproduced in full in
Compendium of Sources) compelled Diaghilev to set his dancers to work
again, on pain of losing his contract with the theatre. Even after the
21 March première, however, the disturbances continued: as Gunsbourg
complained to Léon on 27 March, 'in the first act of this opera yesterday
five dancers were missing of the ten who should have danced in the little
Louis XV ballet (shepherds and shepherdesses). In response to my irate
reproaches, the stage manager M. Kremeneff told me to address my concerns to M. Diaghilev.'*[64]

Although Ravel's very public cut was the undisputed trigger for
Diaghilev's furious withdrawal of his forces, the man Ravel had described
a decade earlier as 'le plus aimable et le plus perfide d'impresarios'[65] was
also exploiting the chance to bring to a head longer-standing tensions over
rehearsal arrangements and facilities. Garafola also suggests that Diaghilev

---

[62] *Ibid.*, 208.
[63] Archives SBM; see also Druilhe, 'Les grandes créations de l'Opéra de Monte-Carlo', 7–26,
and Garafola, *Diaghilev's Ballets russes*, 240–1. I am grateful to Charlotte Lubert (Archives
SBM) for supplying copies of the original letters.
[64] Letter of 27 March 1925, Archives SBM.
[65] Letter to Edwin Evans, 20 July 1914, quoted in Nichols, *Ravel*, 169.

had been undermining Gunsbourg for some time, hoping at last to achieve his 'long-thwarted ambition for an opera house of his own':[66] after the epoch-making Ballets russes seasons of the pre-war years, it was undoubtedly galling to have his troupe earn their bread dancing for operatic warhorses like *Thaïs*, *Carmen* and *Samson et Dalila*. The incident in the foyer of the Hôtel de Paris, therefore, was less the cause of Diaghilev's intransigence than an excuse for manifesting it.

Despite these machinations, the première of *L'Enfant et les sortilèges* was a triumph. Arthur Honegger called it 'un succès éclatant';[67] Henry Prunières concluded that 'the great cosmopolitan public of Monte Carlo' had been 'conquered by the melodic charm and the spirit of this bewitching music'*;[68] and André Corneau, in a rapturous review in the *Journal de Monaco*, wrote that 'M. Ravel was the object of prolonged ovations, when, from the heights of the royal box, he appeared three times [...] to bow to the audience'.*[69]

By October 1925, the Opéra-Comique had been confirmed as the venue for the Parisian première of *L'Enfant*, and rehearsals began there on 25 November.[70] In the meantime, the opera had opened in Stockholm on 24 September and preparations were underway for a season at La Monnaie in Brussels. It made its debut there on 11 February 1926, billed with Chabrier's *Gwendoline*, a pairing that must have delighted Ravel. However, the composer attended none of these three opening nights. On 23 January, he participated in a Saturday afternoon concert of his music given by the Opéra-Comique, accompanying extracts from *L'Enfant*. The next day he left for a Scandinavian tour, travelling first to Brussels, where he oversaw a rehearsal, and then on to Hamburg, Copenhagen, Oslo and Stockholm. After a brief visit to the United Kingdom, he returned home via Brussels again, where he attended a performance of *L'Enfant* on 4 March and was warmly applauded by an enthusiastic audience.[71]

In Ravel's absence, *L'Enfant* had opened at the Opéra-Comique on 1 February, to a far more turbulent reception than it had faced in Monte Carlo. Although 'the family circle naturally applauds', wrote Roland-Manuel, 'The Institute has damned you to the seventh generation. [...] Your work is played every evening amidst the heady atmosphere of a scandal.

---

[66] Garafola, *Diaghilev's Ballets russes*, 239.   [67] Honegger, '*L'Enfant et les sortilèges*', 5.

[68] Prunières, '*L'Enfant et les sortilèges* au Théâtre de Monte Carlo', 109.

[69] Corneau, '*L'Enfant et les sortilèges*'.

[70] Letter to Roland-Manuel of 22 October, in Chalupt and Gerar, *Au miroir de ses lettres*, 215; *Registres de l'Opéra-Comique*, 1925–1926, Bm-O, micr. 3468.

[71] Cornejo, 'Maurice Ravel en Belgique', 92, 95. See also *Compendium of Sources*, letters 51 and 54.

As this never reaches the level of preventing the music from being heard, everyone is congratulating one another, especially the performers. "We're having fun", Roger Bourdin [who played the Clock and the Cat] confided to me, "we're living through historic moments".'*[72] *Comœdia*, meanwhile, dryly reported that 'The public divided itself into two camps: one of the resolute admirers, and the other of the systematic detractors. In the first scene, the saxophone phrases [*sic*], the Arithmetic ensemble, then later the duo of the cats provoked animal cries in places other than the stage – which was the only place where they had been expected.'*[73] One suspects that the Opéra-Comique audiences, in true Parisian style, were relishing the opportunity to liven up proceedings: 'The modernists applaud and boo the others', wrote Colette to her daughter, 'and during the "miaowed" duet the racket is dreadful.'*[74]

A number of reviewers took up the cudgels on Ravel's behalf, castigating the Opéra-Comique patrons for what Henry Prunières called their 'firm resolve' to 'condemn any attempt at modernity':[75] 'M.D.', in *Le Théâtre*, noted bluntly that 'the public of this theatre is too used to old-fashioned repertoire, to ancient sets, to outdated stagings. Every novelty surprises them. [. . .] This theatre needs air and we must not criticise its directors when they open the windows.'*[76] Henry Malherbe's summation – although dismissed privately by Roland-Manuel to Ravel as a 'stupid dithyramb'[77] – was equally forthright: 'May the regulars of the Place Boieldieu make no mistake: beneath the mask of humour, youth and humility, in *L'Enfant et les sortilèges* are concealed the endeavours of genius.'*[78] These responses may also owe something to opera politics: only four months earlier, Louis Masson and Georges Ricou had assumed control of the Opéra-Comique, taking over from the by-now-venerable Albert Carré (with Émile and Vincent Isola). The critics were watching closely to see what shifts in programming and direction this new team might instigate, and *L'Enfant*, Masson and Ricou's first major première, offered an ideal opportunity to position public response within the ongoing dialogues between the theatre and the musical press.

Despite the rowdy public, the balance of critical opinion was now very firmly in Ravel's favour. Although Jean Delaincourt stated blandly that 'It is difficult for us to feel any interest in a drama where the protagonists start

---

[72] *OL*, letter 264.   [73] [Anon.] '*L'Enfant et les sortilèges*'. *Comœdia*, 8 February 1926.
[74] Pichois, *Colette*, 285.
[75] Prunières, '*L'Enfant et les sortilèges* de Maurice Ravel à l'Opéra-Comique', 259.
[76] 'M.D.', 'Théâtre de l'Opéra-Comique: *L'Enfant et les sortilèges*', 7.   [77] *OL*, letter 264.
[78] Malherbe, 'Chronique musicale'.

off as different bits of the furniture'*,[79] Gaston de Pawlowski wrote that 'Ravel's music is, as one might have expected, a veritable little jewel of intelligence and originality; it abounds in treasures of the most delightful orchestral ingenuity.'*[80] Maurice Boucher concluded that the opera's ending, despite its spareness of means ('discrétion des moyens'), was so beautiful it made one weep: '*L'Enfant et les sortilèges* is a masterpiece.'*[81] Maurice Brillant, in *Le Correspondant*, remarked similarly:

Ah, but it is edifying to see this man, rich to the point of superabundance, deliberately restrain his writing [volontairement se dépouiller], to move towards an elegant simplicity, to liberate the lines, lighten the orchestra. [...] Ravel's orchestra, regardless of its richness, has always shown the most aerial lightness. 'Less *orchestrated* than *L'Heure espagnole*', Roland-Manuel wrote neatly, 'this work is more *orchestral*'.*[82]

Although most critics emphasised the richness and virtuosity of Ravel's orchestration, Brillant and Boucher were unusual in drawing attention equally to his restraint. In his use of the word *dépouiller*, in particular, alongside his quotation of Ravel's apologist and amanuensis Roland-Manuel, Brillant invoked one of the prevailing themes threaded through intellectual music criticism of the 1920s, that of the *style dépouillé* ('stripped-down style').[83] As Barbara Kelly observes, in 1921 Roland-Manuel had emphasised the notion of *un art dépouillé* in challenging Paul Landormy's assertion that Ravel's style was already outmoded by contrast with the 'very sober, very stripped-down art' of Les Six,[84] arguing, 'At a time when theories of "the stripped-down style" take hold of the avant-garde's journalistic columns, it is important to note that it is Ravel who has given us the most eloquent illustrations of this aesthetic to date.'[85] Around the time of *L'Enfant*, he would similarly declare, 'Naked simplicity and the *style dépouillé* [...] do not flourish very often in the thicket of so-called polytonality, and it is once more in Ravel's works that one finds

---

[79] Delaincourt, '*L'Enfant et les sortilèges*'.   [80] de Pawlowski, 'Répétition générale'.

[81] Boucher, 'À propos de *L'Enfant et les sortilèges*'.

[82] Brillant, '*L'Enfant et les sortilèges*'. Roland-Manuel used this description in his reviews in *La Revue Pleyel* and *Le Ménestrel*, as well as in his letter to Ravel of 23 February (*OL*, letter 264).

[83] See Kelly, *Music and Ultra-Modernism*, Chapter 5, 'In search of the musical *esprit du temps*'; see also Kelly, 'Ravel after Debussy: inheritance, influence and style', esp. 174, 180.

[84] Kelly, *Music and Ultra*-Modernism, 168; Landormy, 'Le Déclin de l'impressionnisme', *La Revue musicale* 2/4 (February 1921), 109.

[85] Kelly, *Music and Ultra*-Modernism, 59; Roland-Manuel, 'Maurice Ravel', *La Revue musicale* 2/6 (April 1921), 17.

the best examples.'[86] Georges Auric would similarly describe the opera as 'a work that is clear and liberated, where the ideas are stripped back [où la pensée se dépouille]'*.[87] Another staunch Ravelian, Jean Marnold, would also use the verb *dépouiller* to describe the conclusion of *L'Enfant*: 'hemmed with echoes of the Sonata for Violin and Cello, [the final chorus] develops and blossoms in an unadorned [*dépouillée*] limpidity'.[88]

If Paul Landormy had asserted in the immediate aftermath of the First World War that Ravel was 'already part of our past',[89] while Roland-Manuel repeatedly positioned him at the heart of the aesthetic of the 1920s, for a few older critics Ravel still appeared to represent a disturbing future. In his review of *L'Enfant*, André Messager held to the view of the composer as an aloof conjuror, full of brilliant effects with little emotional depth, and outrageously experimental for the sake of seeming modernity:

[Sensitivity and emotion] are the two sentiments that Ravel appears, with deliberate intent, to have banished from his music. He seems to have held onto nothing but the opportunity to draw out that orchestral virtuosity which is apparently the principal object of his researches. [. . .] No one is as skilled as he in the combination of timbres, the linking of unexpected sonorities, the use of the unusual facilities of the instruments, the most paradoxical harmonic combinations. But don't demand any emotion of him, still less any tenderness. He rejects everything that he considers to be a concession to bourgeois sentimentality. [. . .] What does it matter whether Ravel succeeds more or less exactly in imitating a cat or a frog? A touch of poetry would so often be better.*[90]

In his response to the Monte Carlo première, however, Prunières pre-emptively countered:

While he defends himself against it, as against a grave sin, Ravel's music is often suggestive of emotion, and in this latest work there is much of this rarest of qualities. The duet of the Child and the Princess is a moment of intense lyricism, justified by the situation, and will confound those who do not wish to admit that Ravel, under his mocking appearance, conceals a nature that trembles with the deepest sensibility.*[91]

Although Prunières emphasised the orchestral richness and lyricism of *L'Enfant*, he too noted the importance of qualities such as counterpoint

[86] Kelly, *Music and Ultra-Modernism*, 181–2; Roland-Manuel, 'Les Six devant Ravel', unpublished typescript (*c.* 1925), BnF Mus., 4 Vmo, Pièce 369, 3.

[87] Auric, '*L'Enfant et les sortilèges*'.   [88] Marnold, 'Musique' (1926), 703.

[89] Kelly, *Music and Ultra-Modernism*, 83; Landormy, 'La Musique', *La Victoire*, 18 February 1919.

[90] Messager, '*L'Enfant et les sortilèges*'.

[91] Prunières, '*L'Enfant et les sortilèges* au Théâtre de Monte Carlo', 107. Concerning Prunières's role in interwar music criticism, see Kelly, *Music and Ultra-Modernism*, esp. Chapter 3, 'Polemics and publicity'.

(like Marnold, he linked the opera with the Sonata for Violin and Cello), underlining in particular the solo flute arabesques that support the Princess's monologue as 'bear[ing] witness to his prodigious dexterity, though this is the least of its merits, for this passage, so skilfully drawn out, seems to flow from the heart, appearing utterly spontaneous and natural'. Far from restricting emotion, Prunières argued, the *style dépouillé* concentrated and focussed it.[92] Like Roland-Manuel and Brillant, Prunières thus wove his appraisal of Ravel's opera into the period's dialogues of modernity and style.

Those who saw both the 1925 and 1926 productions of *L'Enfant*, including Prunières and Charles Tenroc, were agreed that the Monte Carlo performance was the more successful, partly because of the superb Russian dancers,[93] but also thanks to a particularly lively and talented cast. 'One feels that the work was produced with love', wrote Prunières.*[94] The conducting of Albert Wolff (in Paris), however, was highlighted in almost every review, for his exceptional precision, the outstanding performance he drew from the orchestra and, not least, for conducting the work from memory 'without the least error and with an unmatchable virtuosity', as Fernand Le Borne wrote in *Le petit parisien*.*[95] Most reviewers also singled out Marie-Thérèse Gauley, who played the Child in both productions, for special praise.

L'Enfant et les sortilèges went on to make its Prague and Leipzig debuts in 1927, received a highly successful Viennese production in 1929 and a first American season in 1930, at the San Francisco Opera. But in those five years only twenty-one performances of the work were given at the Opéra-Comique. Therefore, on 20 September 1930, Ravel offered his opera once more to Jacques Rouché: 'Mon cher ami, I have withdrawn *L'Enfant et les sortilèges* from the Opéra-Comique. Would you take it in? The example of *L'Heure espagnole* persuades me that it would be much better cared for and less neglected in your hands.'*[96] Rouché agreed to take *L'Enfant*, but by May 1932 it had still not been staged at the Opéra Garnier and Ravel was writing to him once more:

---

[92] In 1928, Ravel himself would suggest something similar, saying of *Ma mère l'Oye* that 'The intention to evoke the poetry of childhood naturally led me to simplify my style and pare down [dépouiller] my writing' ('Esquisse autobiographique', *OL*, 45). See also Kilpatrick, 'The language of enchantment', 134–63.

[93] Prunières, '*L'Enfant et les sortilèges* de Maurice Ravel à l'Opéra-Comique', 259–60.

[94] Prunières, '*L'Enfant et les sortilèges* au Théâtre de Monte Carlo', 109; Tenroc, 'Les Théâtres: Opéra-Comique', 101.

[95] Le Borne, 'Courrier des théâtres'.   [96] Bm-O, LAS Ravel 10.

As you know, I withdrew the work from the Opéra-Comique, as you requested [*sic*!], and in these circumstances *L'Enfant et les sortilèges* can now only be performed on the stage of the Opéra. The difficulties that you've encountered during the last few months, and also my European tour, no doubt explain why, contrary to the promise that you gave me, *L'Enfant et les sortilèges* still has not been staged at the Opéra. But I hope that now you will be able to begin planning for it, and that the first performance of my work can be given at the Opéra in the new season, in October or November.*[97]

But Ravel was never to see another performance of his *fantaisie lyrique*, which would open at the Opéra only in May 1939. The surviving documentation offers no rationale for this delay. 'It would be good if we could finally listen to my music in silence', he said wistfully to Manuel Rosenthal in 1936.[98] Rosenthal tried to facilitate a new season but succeeded only in organising a concert performance which, with heartrending irony, took place on the day of Ravel's death, 28 December 1937. 'In the morning', recalled Rosenthal,

I had gone to see him at the clinic and, on my return, I was in tears when I had to announce the news to the musicians, the chorus, the soloists. That evening, as I was taking my bow, I saw Stravinsky's face in the dress circle, shattered, distraught. As I was leaving the stage a double bass player said to me, 'I understand that you are weeping for your *maître*, but be comforted: he, at least, didn't leave any rubbish.'[99]

---

[97] Bm-O, LAS Ravel 11.   [98] Marnat (ed.), *Ravel: Souvenirs de Manuel Rosenthal*, 191.
[99] *Ibid.*, 192.

PART II

Words and music

4 | The collaborative process

The title of this chapter might seem on first sight to be something of a red herring. Franc-Nohain's play *L'Heure espagnole* was performed and published three years before Ravel decided to make an opera out of it, while Richard Langham Smith writes, 'It would be nice to think of text and music in *L'Enfant* as one of the great collaborations of the 1920s; in fact it was rather the reverse.'[1] Ravel certainly preferred to work in isolation, or at least at a distance: the negotiations for *L'Enfant* mostly took place by letter or through the intermediary of Jacques Rouché, and it is unlikely that he had any contact with Franc-Nohain during the composition of *L'Heure*. Nor did either of his librettists hear a note of the scores before Ravel completed them. We might therefore wonder whether the collaborative process, such as it was, even merits our attention: after all, as Christopher Best puts it, 'The definitive test of a successful collaboration must be the strength of the work itself, not how sweet and amicable the working relationships between its creators prove to be.'[2]

To Ravel himself, however, the concept seems to have been real and significant: he made generous use of the terms 'collaboration' and 'collaborator' in his correspondence and in newspaper interviews, not just for *L'Enfant*, but even relative to *L'Heure*. If neither of his operas was created through close interaction with his librettists, the realisation of both nevertheless owes a very real debt to artistic exchange, both direct and oblique. Through documentary and broader aesthetic exploration, this chapter examines the language and the process of collaboration.

Ravel *au théâtre*: the ballets of 1912

Before we come to his operas, a snapshot of some of Ravel's other cross-disciplinary ventures provides useful context, highlighting both the pleasures and the pitfalls he encountered in creative collaboration. The year

[1] Langham Smith, 'Ravel's operatic spectacles', 201.
[2] Best, 'Why do choreographers and composers collaborate?', 31.

1912 saw him undertake three theatrical projects, all ballets: *Ma mère l'Oye* (developed from his eponymous duet suite), which premiered at the Théâtre des Arts on 29 January; *Adélaïde, ou, Le Langage des fleurs* (based on his piano *Valses nobles et sentimentales*), which opened on 22 April at the Théâtre du Châtelet, with Ravel conducting; and, most importantly, *Daphnis et Chloé*, first performed by Diaghilev's Ballets russes at the Châtelet on 8 June. Ravel himself wrote the scenarios for both the smaller works; for *Ma mère l'Oye* in particular he involved himself intimately in the staging as well.[3] This enterprise was a happy one; after the première Ravel wrote to Rouché, 'I didn't dare hope for the total joy, so delightful to a composer, of seeing a work for the theatre realized exactly as he had conceived it.'[4]

Ravel's collaboration with the dancer and director Natalia Trouhanova on *Adélaïde* (a project supported and partly funded by Rouché) also seems to have been straightforward:[5] he orchestrated his piano suite on Trouhanova's commission; was able to secure designer Jacques Drésa, who had worked with him on *Ma mère l'Oye*; and enjoyed his first experience of theatrical conducting. *Daphnis et Chloé*, however, was fraught from start to finish. Although its first appearance in Ravel's correspondence (a letter to Marguerite de Saint-Marceaux of 27 June 1909) evinces his excitement about the new project, it also reveals the tensions present from the very beginning of the enterprise:

I must tell you that I've just had an insane week: preparation of a ballet libretto for the next Russian season. Almost every night, I was working until 3 A.M. What complicates things is that Fokine [the choreographer] doesn't know a word of French, and all I know of Russian is how to swear. Despite the interpreters, you can imagine the flavour of these discussions.[6]

By 1910, Ravel's compositional struggles were compounded by difficulties over contracts, and he sent a long letter to the Russian-speaking Calvocoressi enlisting his help in the negotiations.[7] He was still wrestling with his score as late as April 1911,[8] and when the ballet finally went into rehearsal in the spring of 1912, tensions between Fokine, designer Léon Bakst, Nijinsky, Diaghilev and Ravel were very evident.[9] Ravel's publisher

---

[3] See Ravel's correspondence with Rouché (Bm-O, Ravel LAS); *OL*, letter 90; and Mawer, *The Ballets of Maurice Ravel*, 55.

[4] *OL*, letter 92.   [5] See Mawer, *The Ballets of Maurice Ravel*, 139.   [6] *OL*, letter 64.

[7] *OL*, letter 74.

[8] See Chailley, 'Une première version inconnue de *Daphnis et Chloé*', and Morrison, 'The origins of *Daphnis et Chloé* (1912)'.

[9] See Nichols, *Ravel*, 143–5.

Jacques Durand recalled 'loud discussions' between the Russians,[10] and Fokine would describe *Daphnis* as 'the most sorrowful work of my entire life'; the debacle even prompted him to hand in his notice.[11] Ravel, meanwhile, would write much later to Misia Sert that 'poor *Daphnis* has plenty of grounds for complaining about Diaghilev. I know it was not all on one side and that few productions have ever caused such trouble, but it wasn't always the work's fault.'[12] On 7 October 1912, he wrote to Rouché regarding a possible (unidentified) new ballet: 'I believe that the libretto of this ballet has not yet been agreed on. I would prefer to write it myself, with some guidance. The precedent of *Daphnis et Chloé*, whose libretto was a source of perpetual conflict, has made me extremely reluctant to undertake a similar experience again.'[13]

Fokine's memoirs also draw attention to the difficulties inherent in drafting the ballet's scenario, in particular noting his and Ravel's differing conceptions of the abduction scene: 'I was unable to inspire him to create musically that violent, gruesome picture which was so vivid in my imagination. I later came to reproach myself for not having insisted on this point.'[14] Deborah Mawer and Simon Morrison have both explored the composer's and choreographer's conflicting conceptual approaches, particularly concerning notions of 'Greekness'.[15] However, the key to Ravel and Fokine's collaborative difficulties may lie in Fokine's revealing later reflection: 'I tried to collaborate with Ravel to the minutest detail in conveying the various moments of action. It was essential for me to have him feel exactly as I did at each moment [. . .] It was equally important that we both should understand the meaning of each dance in the same way.'[16] In 1906, Ravel appears to have explained to Jules Renard (the poet of the *Histoires naturelles*), 'I want to think and feel the same way as you' (a point taken up in Chapter 5, and to which the Afterword returns). Being *compelled* to feel exactly the same as his obsessive Russian choreographer, however, would have been a far more problematic assignment.

All this serves briefly to illustrate several facets of Ravel as a theatrical collaborator. Firstly, the realisation of stage projects was something he clearly enjoyed, at least in principle. He liked engaging with the creative

---

[10] Durand, *Quelques souvenirs d'un éditeur de musique*, vol. II, 17.
[11] See *ibid.*, 18, and Mawer, *The Ballets of Maurice Ravel*, 82.
[12] Undated letter (*c.* 1920/21); Nichols, *Ravel*, 144.   [13] *OL*, letter 96.
[14] Nichols, *Ravel Remembered*, 43.
[15] Morrison, 'The origins of *Daphnis et Chloé* (1912)', 56–8; Mawer, *The Ballets of Maurice Ravel*, 93–103.
[16] Nichols, *Ravel Remembered*, 43.

and the technical aspects of productions: not for nothing was he the son of a brilliant engineer. However, although he had strong ideas and preferences for the realisation of his stage works, for the most part Ravel was nevertheless able to work cooperatively, respecting the *métier* of his theatrical colleagues: Rolf de Maré, the director of the Ballets suédois, who mounted *Le Tombeau de Couperin* as a ballet in 1920, wrote of 'un collaborateur enthousiaste et aimable'.[17] Although he was an eager participant in the staging of his operas and ballets, Ravel's music naturally remained his prime consideration, and he reacted swiftly and sometimes furiously to prevent it being compromised: besides his many conflicts with Diaghilev, his constant presence during the rehearsals for his operas attests to his attentiveness in this regard.

Secondly, the pathway to effective collaboration was clearly smoothed by the professionalism and goodwill of Ravel's colleagues. The bustling Opéra-Comique was accustomed to working actively with its composers and librettists; Gunsbourg and Rouché were efficient businessmen as well as adventurous impresarios. Ravel's many cordial letters to Rouché are evidence of their mutual respect, while his good working relations with stage manager Ernest Carbonne and his team at the Opéra-Comique are corroborated by a score of *L'Heure espagnole*, signed by both Ravel and Franc-Nohain, which bears a dedication in Ravel's hand to 'Ernest Carbonne, collabo sympathique'.[18] By contrast, Diaghilev's antipathy towards Ravel and his music only exacerbated the artistic, financial and personal tensions that made the Ballets russes an uneasy working environment at the best of times.

Thirdly, Ravel seems to have been a generous and courteous collaborator, provided that matters were arranged to his satisfaction. In his letter of thanks to Rouché after the première of *Ma mère l'Oye*, Ravel wrote, 'Madame [Jane] Hugard [the choreographer] also proved to be an intelligent and fine collaborator, who took it upon herself to observe my tiniest instructions, and to realize them in an elegant and sensitive manner.'[19] Even of *Daphnis*, Calvocoressi later said that 'Fokine eventually [cast] the libretto into shape to Ravel's satisfaction' (a reflection of quite a different stamp from Fokine's own).[20] Best argues that 'Making an artistic statement by committee requires either complete mutual trust or a strong hierarchy';[21]

---

[17] De Maré, *Les Ballets suédois*, 15.
[18] Sold by Alain Nicolas, *Les Neuf Muses*, spring 1989, item 27.   [19] *OL*, letter 92.
[20] Nichols, *Ravel Remembered*, 188.
[21] Best, 'Why do choreographers and composers collaborate?', 29.

Mawer assigns *Ma mère l'Oye* to the second of these categories, noting that 'Ravel seemingly enjoyed significant leadership within a collaboration that he found very satisfying'.[22] For *L'Enfant*, too, Colette seems willingly to have acceded to Ravel's suggestions for her libretto; any compromises that this partnership involved appear to have been on her side. Yet within this 'hierarchy', Ravel's correspondence also demonstrates the mutual trust, respect and artistic sympathy that existed between him and his collaborators on *Ma mère l'Oye* and *Adélaïde*; to a slighter (in documentary terms) but still evident degree between him and Franc-Nohain; and later, most pertinently, between him and Colette.

'No grand words, no grand gestures': Ravel and Franc-Nohain

A story has long circulated that when Ravel first visited Franc-Nohain to play him the score of his opera – accompanying himself at the piano and humming all the parts – the latter's only reaction was to pull out his watch and announce 'fifty-six minutes'. 'The piano transcription and the composer's inadequate speaking voice always called for the use of the audience's imagination to make up for what could not be heard... Franc-Nohain had no musical imagination', wrote Roland-Manuel (with whom this account appears to have originated).[23] Arbie Orenstein situates this meeting 'shortly before the premiere', suggests that Carré was also present, and concludes, 'Although puzzled by the adaptation, which he found cacophonous, the librettist agreed to be present at the first performance.'[24] Franc-Nohain's son Jean, who was present at that read-through, told the story a little differently, albeit long after the event: he recalled that Ravel played through the work in the presence of Franc-Nohain and his family (though not Carré), together with the conservative musicologist and critic Adolphe Boschot, the brother-in-law of Mme Franc-Nohain: 'Over the scampering, sparkling lines of my father's libretto, Maurice Ravel's music pranced delightfully, and when the admirable final quintet was complete we all waited anxiously for the official judgement. A few terrible seconds of silence

[22] Mawer, *The Ballets of Maurice Ravel*, 252.
[23] Roland-Manuel, *Maurice Ravel et son œuvre dramatique*, 52.
[24] Orenstein, *Ravel, Man and Musician*, 56.

passed. Finally, we heard a voice: "It lasts 32 minutes", said my uncle [Boschot].'*[25]

If Franc-Nohain had expected to hear *L'Heure espagnole* transformed into a typical turn-of-the-century *opéra bouffe*, he may indeed have been bemused by Ravel's score on first hearing. The opera's uninterrupted musical dialogue, its naturalistic text-setting and the rapid-fire progress of the narrative, together with the removal of the passages of text that might have lent themselves most naturally to 'bouffish' arias (see Chapter 6), would all have been startling to a writer accustomed to hearing his words in the settings of the competent but hardly daring Claude Terrasse.

Although Franc-Nohain's operatic tastes may have been conservative – no source confirms this – he was certainly musically literate: besides a good basic grasp of music theory, his poetry also reveals an accomplished familiarity with the genres, composers and artists of his era.[26] Moreover, he had been moving in progressive literary, theatrical and musical circles since the mid-1890s, counting among his closest friends Alfred Jarry (who stood godfather to Jean Nohain), André Gide and Pierre Louÿs;[27] he was an habitué of the Chat noir and was acquainted with Debussy. Nevertheless, Franc-Nohain belonged to no particular artistic alliance: as 'Nozière' wrote in 1931, 'He was never a man of factions. He had no love for agendas or dogmas.'*[28] He was a man of jovial, frank, witty and generous character, liked and respected by his colleagues and loved by his friends; indeed, a trawl of the contemporary periodicals produced not a single harsh word about the man or his art. A thorough professional, with some avant-garde sympathies, there is no evidence to suggest that Franc-Nohain would not have listened to Ravel's new score with respectful interest, even if the music may have confounded his expectations. We might in fact presume his interest to be particularly acute, given that he had first conceived the plot as a possible *opéra-comique* libretto: an outline titled *L'Heure du muletier* appears in a 1902 letter to Terrasse listing potential operatic projects.[29] Having successfully realised his original conception as a play, he must have

[25] Nohain, 'Quand j'avais onze ans'. I am grateful to Roger Nichols for sending me a copy of this article.
[26] The poem 'Musique d'ensemble', for example, from the 1900 collection *La nouvelle cuisinière bourgeoise*, invokes Czerny, *Manon*, Cécile Chaminade, the tenor Victor Capoul and the little-known composer Ange Flégier, amidst a series of puns on the notes of the scale. Franc-Nohain's innate and overt musicality were made explicit when, in 1922, his collections *Chansons des trains et des gares*, *Le Dimanche en famille* and *Flûtes* were reissued under the collective title *Le Kiosque à musique*.
[27] Rousseaux, 'Un quart d'heure avec M. Franc-Nohain'.
[28] Nozière, [Hommage à Franc-Nohain].   [29] Cathé, 'Claude Terrasse (1867–1923)', 87.

been intrigued to see it reimagined for the stage for which he had first conceived it.

Many articles about Franc-Nohain note his lively sense of humour and enjoyment of wordplay; many, too, note the perceptiveness of his writing, with its light touch often concealing acute moral and psychological insight. In 1925, Gabriel Reuillard described his depiction of contemporary *mœurs* as 'at once tender and sardonic. Willingly or not, he is a moralist in the great tradition of La Fontaine (to whom he is closest, in the cast of his mind and in his manner), La Rochefoucauld and La Bruyère. No grand words, no grand gestures.'*[30] His witty, light-footed verse, replete with colourful assonances and rhythms, and combined with a taste for fables or fairytales, has clear resonances with Ravel's own tastes and styles. In 1932, another (anonymous) critic used similar language: 'M. Franc-Nohain is a tender-hearted person, who veils his tenderness in juggling with words, rhymes [and] ideas. And he is also, after his own fashion, a philosopher.'*[31] There are echoes here of the opinions expressed of Ravel by sympathetic critics such as Henry Prunières (see, for example, his review of *L'Enfant*, quoted on p. 50), while lack of pretension and renunciation of the 'grand gesture' are as characteristic of Ravel's expressed tastes as they are of Franc-Nohain's writing. These shared aesthetic and technical preferences and concerns must have played at least an intuitive part in Ravel's attraction to *L'Heure espagnole*.

Most pertinently, as Chapter 2 observed, Franc-Nohain did not merely 'agree to be present at the first performance' of *L'Heure espagnole*: he was actively engaged with the rehearsal process, just as Ravel was. He attended the first read-through on 20 February, and the *livre de bord* records his presence at almost every rehearsal once the production had moved into the theatre; Jean Nohain recalled watching the dress rehearsal with his father and the composer from a box, as the work was 'whistled, booed, hooted'.[32] Franc-Nohain's regular attendance is perhaps the more remarkable given that he had another work in production at the same time: Terrasse's *Les Transatlantiques* premiered at the Théâtre de l'Apollo on 20 May, and the librettist was diligently attending rehearsals there, too.[33]

---

[30] Reuillard, 'Franc-Nohain'.
[31] P. L., 'L'Académie Française a décerné hier ses deux grands prix annuels'.
[32] Nohain, 'Quand j'avais onze ans'. Jean Nohain's confessor told him that the turbulent response to the première was God's punishment for his going to the theatre instead of devoting himself to religious observances: 'Maurice Ravel always smiled at that story', Nohain added.
[33] Des Essarts, 'Les Avant-premières: *Les Transatlantiques* à l'Apollo'.

Whatever (and whenever) his initial reaction, therefore, by 1911 Franc-Nohain was clearly engaged with the operatic transformation of his words. Although it would have been easy for him to hold himself aloof from the opera, he chose not to do so: Louis Laloy's emphasis on the presence of both authors 'in rehearsal after rehearsal' for the 1921 Opéra revival (see p. 26) underlines this. Even Ravel's assertion, in a 1911 interview in *L'Excelsior*, that 'I have been happy [. . .] to have as my collaborator M. Franc-Nohain, whose fantasy and wit delight me'*,[34] though primarily serving as publicity, nevertheless suggests a tangible degree of artistic engagement.

The presence of both authors at the Opéra-Comique (and later the Opéra) has further significance: Ravel and Franc-Nohain were both involved, directly or implicitly, in the development of the opera's staging, which they would almost certainly have seen as an intrinsic element of the work itself. Phillip Gossett has argued that an operatic score can never be 'entirely independent of the way in which it was first conceived and executed on stage':[35] at the Opéra-Comique (and other Parisian theatres) the staging of new operas was recorded and conserved with meticulous care so as to form a template for subsequent productions. In his various studies of nineteenth-century production books (*livrets de mise-en-scène*) of Parisian theatres, Robert Cohen has documented that 'Staging in Paris and the French provinces throughout the nineteenth century and well into the twentieth was an art of preservation rather than creation. [. . .] Staging, in a word, was not intended to be altered.'[36]

That the original staging of *L'Heure* was intended to serve as a model for subsequent productions is attested to by the multiple fair copies of the *livret de mise-en-scène*, including copies made in the 1920s and 1930s (now in the Bibliothèque historique de la ville de Paris). This material must also have been consulted for the 1921 Opéra production: among the original production material (BHVP, coll. ART, 8-TMS-02811) is a sketch labelled 'décor simplifié', which served as the basis for André Mare's 1921 set design. The original production score, meanwhile, was used for productions by the Opéra-Comique and its troupes as late as the 1960s.[37] In their

[34] [Anon.], '*L'Heure espagnole*', *L'Excelsior*, 17 May 1911.

[35] Gossett, 'Preface' to Cohen and Gigou, *Cent ans de mise en scène lyrique en France*, xii.

[36] Cohen, *The Original Staging Manuals*, xxiii. Although Jacobshagen ('Staging at the Opéra-Comique') has shown that the function of the nineteenth-century *livrets de mise-en-scène* was more mutable than Cohen allows, the importance of the original staging, both in itself and in the documented records of the *livrets de mise-en-scène*, certainly held good into the twentieth century. See also Langham Smith, 'Preface', to *Carmen: A Performance Urtext*, and 'French operatic spectacle in the twentieth century', 119–20.

[37] See Kilpatrick, 'The Carbonne copy', 99–103, 113.

presence and participation at rehearsals throughout the spring of 1911, Ravel and Franc-Nohain were thus engaging in what both would have recognised as an important process of creative collaboration. Many years later, a similarly collaborative spirit is evident in a letter in which Ravel suggested to Colette that they meet before the Opéra-Comique rehearsals of *L'Enfant* got underway – 'it's a case of taking up a [united] position before the *metteurs en scène*'*.[38] On 17 January 1926, *Le Figaro* reported that 'rehearsals are progressing busily, in the presence of the authors, M. Maurice Ravel and Mme Colette'.

Ravel and Franc-Nohain, though never close, also appear to have sustained a cordial lifelong association. In 1912, the composer allotted two of his six tickets for the première of *Adélaïde* to his erstwhile librettist;[39] sixteen years later, Franc-Nohain sent him an inscribed volume of three of his plays, including *L'Heure*: 'Pour Maurice Ravel, avec l'espoir que la *Marche Indienne* lui chantera comme *L'Heure espagnole* / son dévoué / F. Nohain' ('For Maurice Ravel, in the hope that the *Marche Indienne* will sing to him like *L'Heure espagnole* / his devoted / F. Nohain').[40] And Jean Nohain recalled that Ravel continued to visit the family, even after Franc-Nohain's death in 1934: 'On his last visit to our house, after my father's death and not long before his own, when he had almost completely lost his memory [*sic*], Ravel, smiling, indicated the old Érard that had served for the first hearing of *L'Heure espagnole*. "It lasts 32 minutes", he said.'*[41]

'It is impossible to separate the collaborators'

Many early reviews of *L'Enfant et les sortilèges* drew particular attention to the success of the work as a collaborative enterprise. 'How well [the exquisite score] is matched to the delicious fantasy of Mme Colette's

[38] Delahaye, '*L'Enfant et les sortilèges*', 63.
[39] Letter to Mlle Natalia Trouhanova, 21 April 1912; sold at auction 17 December 2013 (Salle Drouot), Catalogue ADER Nordmann, 'Archives Natalia Trouhanowa', no. 225.
[40] This volume remains in the library of Ravel's former home at Montfort l'Amaury (Musée Maurice Ravel). Franc-Nohain's name continued to surface occasionally in Ravel's correspondence: a letter to Lucien Garban of May 1925 shows him planning to 'consult with Franc-Nohain next week – tell J[acques] D[urand]' (Orenstein (ed.), 'La Correspondance de Ravel à Garban (1919–1934)', 65). In an interview in *L'Excelsior* of 24 September 1933 (*OL*, 374), Ravel mentioned a projected setting of Franc-Nohain's *Le Chapeau chinois* (another project that Franc-Nohain and Terrasse had discussed as early as 1902), but this was never more than a pipe dream.
[41] Nohain, 'Quand j'avais onze ans'.

libretto!', wrote André Corneau of the Monte Carlo production*;[42] while of the Parisian première Juliette Autran asserted, 'Two styles could not be better matched with each other than those of Mme Colette and M. Maurice Ravel. The finely detailed text of the one is completed by the witty music of the other. It all breathes and lives.'*[43] Raymond Balliman and Maurice Boucher described the collaboration in similar terms:

> To treat this original and delicate subject, M. Ravel was the best of choices – one could say the only one possible. The Ravel–Colette collaboration seems to have been ordained by the order of things, and in listening to the work it is impossible to conceive any other possible musical setting than Ravel's. [...] The union of poetry and music is such that it is impossible to separate the collaborators.*[44]

> The libretto of Mme Colette and the music of M. Ravel share the same fantasy, the same poetry, the same sort of soul. [...] Their spirit is alike, and their finer points too. [...] It is impossible to ascertain whether Mme Colette wrote for M. Ravel or M. Ravel for Mme Colette.*[45]

'Was not Ravel the musician whose heart could best understand Colette's heart?' reflected Carol-Berard, reviewing the 1939 Opéra production; 'Was it not he who could follow her most gracefully into the kingdom of dreams?'*[46]

During these early productions, nobody seems to have remarked on this artistic pairing as a surprising one, comprising a librettist famously flamboyant and a composer just as famously *pudique*. Across the decades since the première, however, this seeming disparity has come to loom large: even Colette herself, in a radio interview given shortly before her death in 1954, mused, 'Colette, Ravel, oh, but this wasn't a natural thing [une chose bien commode], Colette, Ravel, oh no!'[47]

This perception of personal incompatibility, when viewed together with the limited communication traced between Ravel and Colette, has given rise to the assumption – implicit in Richard Langham Smith's assessment, quoted at the beginning of this chapter – that there was little or no 'collaborative' process in the preparation of *L'Enfant et les sortilèges*: writer and musician remain as oddly assorted as the foxtrotting teapots and lumbering armchairs of their creation. In scholarly terms, we might trace

---

[42] Corneau, '*L'Enfant et les sortilèges*'.
[43] Autran, 'À l'Opéra-Comique: *L'Enfant et les sortilèges*'.
[44] Balliman, '*L'Enfant et les sortilèges*', 693.
[45] Boucher, 'À propos de *L'Enfant et les sortilèges*'.
[46] Carol-Berard, '*L'Enfant et les sortilèges*'.
[47] [Colette], 'Colette parle de Ravel', Radio France interview, c. 1952 (coll. Claude Moreau). The context, and Colette's self-reference in the third person, make it plain that she is referring to the *perception* of the collaboration as an unusual one.

this notion to Roland-Manuel: although in 1926 he memorably evoked 'this enchantress collaborating with this illusionist',[48] he would later write, 'One would look in vain for two more original spirits. One would be hard put to find two more incompatible [. . .] the conflict of spontaneous poetry and reflective music would inevitably have ended in catastrophe if the poet, hiding behind her colleague, had not muzzled eloquence, cut down phrases to a minimum, and the plot to one suitable for ballet'.[49] In a similar vein eight decades later, Deborah Mawer summed up the collaboration thus:

> Colette [. . .] referred to the new project by its provisional title, *Divertissement pour ma fille*, inspired by her young Bel-Gazou. Ravel countered that since he had no daughter this would not do and so, as a fundamental change, the Child became masculine. [. . .] Apart from a light-hearted, appreciative letter from Ravel of 16 March 1925, preceding the premiere, this was about it, and so Colette – who had never heard any music before the opening night – could not help feeling offended, even though she had already gained an idea of Ravel's character and composition methods. Ravel may have found working with such a high-powered, sexually extrovert and adventurous woman as Colette off-putting.[50]

(This reading entails a slight misinterpretation of the documentation, for there is no indication that the Child was ever intended to be female: Ravel's observation was directed only at the work's title and, as Colette well knew, he didn't have a son either.)[51]

The point of departure for Mawer's assessment, and most other surveys of the collaboration (though not Roland-Manuel's), is Colette's 1939 reflection on the creation of *L'Enfant et les sortilèges*, the essay 'Un salon en 1900' (partially quoted on p. 35). The salon of which Colette wrote was that of Marguerite de Saint-Marceaux where, as Gabriel Fauré and André Messager improvised outrageous Wagner spoofs and the Prince de Polignac sat and sketched, Ravel, 'perhaps secretly shy', kept his distance: 'I don't remember any particular conversation with him, no surge of friendship.'[52]

Colette's essay is the only authorial reflection on the genesis of this *féerie-ballet* that was to become a *fantaisie lyrique*. If its narrative has generally been accepted uncritically, in documentary terms it is an abbreviated and inflected history; from a great fiction writer, we should expect

---

[48] Roland-Manuel, 'La Critique: *L'Enfant et les sortilèges*'.
[49] Roland-Manuel, *Maurice Ravel et son œuvre dramatique*, 93.
[50] Mawer, *The Ballets of Maurice Ravel*, pp. 70–1; cf. note 51 below.
[51] Colette's 1919 newspaper interview, quoted on p. 39, mentions 'the heroine', which in context indicates merely 'the principal performer', as the Child is played by a woman. No source supports the contention that Colette felt 'offended' by Ravel's conduct.
[52] Colette, 'Un salon en 1900', 165–6.

no less. A re-examination of some of the documentary sources, and the introduction of others, helps to complete the collaborative picture in more detail. This leads us to Ravel's and Colette's own writings on the creative process (as well as reflections of those close to both artists), for it is here that we see the most revealing congruencies of artistic and collaborative philosophy and practice.

Chapter 3 has already documented a greater degree of interaction between composer and librettist, dealing with considerably more than the Cats' meows, than Colette admitted in 'Un salon en 1900'. We should also remember that, despite the relatively slight amount of documented correspondence, Ravel and Colette were both based in or near Paris through almost all of this period, moved in similar artistic and literary circles, and had access to telephones. We may therefore reasonably hypothesise the passage of further communications now untraceable: the opera's definitive title was not agreed upon until 1924, for example, but no record survives of the exchanges that must necessarily have preceded its adoption. Perhaps most telling in this context are the letters Ravel sent to Colette late in 1924 and just before the première (see pp. 42–4): 'Chère amie', he begins. No polite Frenchman – certainly not the punctilious Ravel – would have written 'Chère Madame' in 1919 and 'Chère amie' several years later, had he remained sealed in 'hermetic silence' in the interim.

We can quickly identify another documentary elision in Colette's 1939 account, for we know that the libretto was offered to both Dukas and Stravinsky before Ravel accepted it. Nevertheless, Colette's enthusiastic note to Rouché in the spring of 1917 – 'you have put fairies into my head' – and the warmth and admiration with which she infallibly spoke to and of Ravel leave us in no doubt that the idea of collaborating with him pleased her enormously. Ravel's response to the proffered libretto was clearly positive too, and that he seems to have suggested some possible modifications to the text is telling: given his 1912 letter to Rouché concerning the 'perpetual conflict' that beset the libretto of *Daphnis*, it suggests that he had sufficient confidence in this libretto and its author to engage with both. The degree of his involvement must remain a matter for speculation (a subject taken up in Chapter 7); although he certainly offered rather more extensive suggestions than the replacement of 'mouâu' with 'mouain', the evidence suggests that he left the actual writing and rewriting of the libretto to Colette, evincing a respect for her *métier* typical of his professional practice. In return, Colette's eagerness to accede to his suggestions (and her later rueful acknowledgement of the solitude that was necessary to him to compose) is evidence of her own respect for the *métier* of the composer.

The title 'Divertissement' appears nowhere in Ravel's correspondence, suggesting that he himself may never have used it. As Colette recalled in her 1950 memoir *En pays connu*, he certainly objected to 'pour ma fille' (and even this is evidence of more communication than 'Un salon en 1900' admits).[53] Ravel's 1919 letter to Rouché calls the work an 'opéra-dansé'; his subsequent letter to Colette refers simply to 'notre opéra'. 'The final title is not yet fixed', he wrote to Roland-Manuel on 1 August 1920;[54] two letters written that summer to Lucien Garban refer to 'X... la machine pour l'Opéra' and 'la machine lyrique sans nom'.[55] Not until the autumn of 1924 does *L'Enfant et les sortilèges* appear as such in Ravel's correspondence (and even in early 1925 it was advertised in Monte Carlo as simply *L'Enfant*). One final echo of the original title remained, however, for another undated letter from Colette to Ravel, probably written shortly before the première, suggests that Ravel intended dedicating the work to Colette's daughter: 'Cher ami, her first name is Colette, and, in full, Colette de Jouvenel. There she is, dedicatee, entering into glory through your care! She will thank you. . .'*[56]

The communications between Ravel and Colette, although relatively few, are nevertheless fascinating for what they reveal about the artistic relationship the pair had established. The informality and spontaneity of the letter Ravel sent to Colette in early 1919 (see p. 38) is all the more remarkable for being their first documented exchange of correspondence. Although he was meticulous in polite observances and formal address,[57] by 1919 Ravel and Colette had known each other for almost twenty years; if their acquaintance had never ripened into friendship, it had clearly

---

[53] Colette, *En pays connu*, 25. This story was first told by André Cœuroy, in a gossipy *avant-première* article (Cœuroy, 'Avant-première à Monte-Carlo'): 'For a long time, Colette had dreamed of writing a fairy libretto for her daughter. "How should we title it? As simply as possible: *For my daughter [Pour ma fille]*." "But I have no daughter", said Ravel, stating the obvious with his characteristic simplicity. "No daughter! That's true", said Colette. "So should we put *Pour un enfant*? Or perhaps *L'Enfant*?" We hesitated. At last, the work has just been issued from Durand with the title *L'Enfant et les sortilèges*.'*

[54] Roy (ed.), *Lettres à Roland-Manuel*, 126.

[55] Letters dated 14 June and 24 August 1920, in Orenstein (ed.), 'La Correspondance de Ravel à Garban (1919–1934)', 29, 34.

[56] Orenstein, 'Correspondance inédite', 219, but cf. Kilpatrick, 'Enchantments and illusions', 40n38. Ravel's letter of 10 February 1926 (quoted below) indicates that his intention genuinely seems to have been to dedicate the work to Colette's daughter. Why this did not eventuate is unknown; the work was published without a dedication.

[57] See Marnat (ed.), *Ravel: Souvenirs de Manuel Rosenthal*, 121.

matured into respect. The 1919 exchange reveals a mutual ease of communication and a quickness of artistic understanding: Ravel would indeed
have been delighted to learn that cinema Westerns were rolling to the
strains of *Ma mère l'Oye*. The letters are written in a spirit of comradeship
and collaborative enthusiasm, offering evidence of a thorough-going
exchange of ideas. 'Believe, *chère Madame*, in the lively artistic sympathy
of your devoted / Maurice Ravel', the composer concludes, an entreaty
whose foundation is bolstered by his letter to Roland-Manuel of 30 August
1920: 'Some inside information... I can assure you that this work, in two
parts, will be notable for its *mélange* of styles, which will be severely
criticised; this leaves Colette indifferent and me not giving a d[amn].'*[58]

These letters, together with later communications, also return continually to the word and concept of collaboration. 'To see if she still wants me as
collaborator', Ravel writes to Rouché; 'our opera' and 'an unreliable collaborator' to Colette; and to Roland-Manuel, 'I'm working at the opera in
collaboration with Colette.'[59] Almost four years later, in a May 1924 interview, Ravel said 'I am now working with Colette on a very original piece, a
kind of lyric fantasy.'[60] As with the *avant-première* interview for *L'Heure
espagnole*, Ravel was perhaps being diplomatic; certainly Colette's name
would have done nothing to harm the advance publicity for his opera. Yet,
precise as he was, Ravel might as easily have said, 'I am working on a kind
of lyric fantasy *on a libretto by* Colette.' Mawer has noted the tension
implicit in Ravel's and Fokine's respective references to 'my ballet'
(*Daphnis*);[61] in this context, Ravel's inclusive language regarding
L'Enfant is revealing. Colette's persistence in asking for progress reports,
from 1916 into the 1920s, and her enthusiastic promotion in her 1919
newspaper interview, reciprocally demonstrate that she saw herself as
actively involved in the opera's development. She had not handed over
the libretto and vanished from the scene; the progress and the destination
of *L'Enfant et les sortilèges* clearly mattered to her.

The friendly interactions, professional courtesy and collaborative spirit
between Ravel and Colette continued as their opera moved out of their
hands. On 10 February 1926, Ravel wrote to Colette from Stockholm:

Chère amie, were you at the [Paris] premiere? Our amiable dedicatee, at least, was
she able to be present for the debut of her *fantaisie lyrique*? if you love strong

---

[58]   *OL*, letter 172.   [59]   Roy (ed.), *Lettres à Roland-Manuel*, 126.

[60]   Révész, 'El gran musico Mauricio Ravel habla de su arte', *ABC de Madrid*, 1 May 1924;
Orenstein (ed.), *A Ravel Reader*, 433.

[61]   Mawer, *The Ballets of Maurice Ravel*, 82, 86.

emotions, try to get [to Brussels]. You will see the Dragonflies, the Moths, the Bats suspended by strings – something that cannot be done without danger in our own national theatre! I believe that we need to make a statement for the [Société des] Auteurs[, Compositeurs et Éditeurs de Musique] (rue Henner). Who is your agent? [...] Don't forget to declare to [your agent or mine] what percentage you calculate is owed you.*[62]

In the years that followed, the two remained in sporadic contact, mostly through their close mutual friend Hélène Jourdan-Morhange, who lived in the village of Les Mesnuls, 4 kilometres from Ravel's home in Montfort l'Amaury. Around 1929, Colette too rented a house in Les Mesnuls; her companion Maurice Goudeket then bought a house, La Gerbière, in Montfort itself (but sold it a year later).[63] Goudeket recalled, 'What a lot of people came to Les Mesnuls, almost all of whom were friends of ours too, or became so. I should never end if I were to set down the whole list of them, so I will name a few at random: the musicians Ravel, Auric, Poulenc...'[64] Their Montfort acquaintances also included Jacques de Zogheb, another of Ravel's close friends.[65] Colette and Goudeket regularly took long walks in the forest of Rambouillet – 'we knew its smallest paths', wrote Goudeket[66] – just as Ravel himself did; Jourdan-Morhange described the forest as 'his kingdom, he knew its paths and its clearings'.[67]

In the 1930s the contact waned, as the ailing composer isolated himself increasingly from the world: 'I did not have the grief of watching Ravel diminish', wrote Colette, 'At Montfort l'Amaury his solitude and his strange Belvédère kept him from public degradation.'[68] After his Parisian taxi accident in 1932,[69] though, she wrote to him with anxious affection:

Dear friend, you can imagine how much your accident has troubled and saddened us. Thanks to Moune [Jourdan-Morhange], Goudeket and I know that you are suffering, and that your temperature is still too high. We hope that your confinement will be short. Perhaps you will permit me to come and see you before I leave for Geneva? We are most affectionately your friends, and I embrace you.*[70]

'Un salon en 1900' concludes with a moving description of the composer, encountered *chez* Jourdan-Morhange, 'as grey-white as fog', though

---

[62] Delahaye, '*L'Enfant et les sortilèges*', 67.

[63] Richardson, *Colette*, 134, 136. Concerning Colette's later residency in Montfort l'Amaury-Méré, see Thurman, *Secrets of the Flesh*, 430, 449.

[64] Goudeket, *Close to Colette*, 128.   [65] Colette, *Lettres à Moune*, 33–4.

[66] Goudeket, *Close to Colette*, 88.   [67] Jourdan-Morhange, *Ravel et nous*, 29.

[68] Colette, 'Un salon en 1900', 167–8.   [69] See Nichols, *Ravel*, 332.

[70] Letter of *c*. 15 October 1932 (sold at auction, Salle Drouot, 26 June 2000), in Michel Delahaye, 'Documents dans les ventes' (2010), 28.

he still knew how to smile. On seeing me he said, in a natural voice, 'Tiens, Colette...' But he could barely force himself to speak any more, and, seated among us, he seemed as if he might dissolve into nothing between one moment and the next. [...] I believe that day Ravel spoke my name for the last time.[71]

In these passages, recounting events that were, in 1939, still in the very recent past (her essay first appeared in the *tombeau* volume *Maurice Ravel par quelques-uns de ses familiers*), we seem to find a more faithful narrative voice. But in her reflection on *L'Enfant et les sortilèges*, 'Un salon en 1900' offers an 'impression' of the collaboration that almost certainly captures more of its spirit than its substance. As any novelist will, in her essay Colette elided and reduced, drawing from disjointed and miscellaneous happenings a coherent and graceful account. She freely reshapes and disguises events, characters and emotions in the service of narrative continuity and poetic form. 'I can allow myself this small indulgence: to be veracious from time to time', she wrote in the later and franker *L'Étoile vesper*, retrospectively drawing attention to the more opaque nature of her earlier memoirs.[72]

The enchantress and the illusionist

Ravel, like Colette, was a storyteller: besides creating compelling musical narratives, he was renowned among the children of his friends as a teller of stories (see p. 234). Ravel, like Colette, was a keen observer, particularly of the animal world, which he regarded with amusement, wonder and tender affection.[73] Colette, like Ravel, could make her point with exquisite elegance combined with simplicity and straightforwardness; like him, her work blends insight and tenderness with a satirical eye and a sparkling wit.

The presence of these shared traits has been observed by numerous commentators: Langham Smith writes that 'the work may be regarded as a meeting of like minds'; Judith Thurman that the pair 'shared a private wavelength'.[74] How, then, do we reconcile these affinities with such dissimilar public personas, and in particular with the distant and mysterious Ravel portrayed in 'Un salon en 1900'? One answer lies in the words of Ravel and Colette's close mutual friend Hélène Jourdan-Morhange:

---

[71] Colette, 'Un salon en 1900', 168.   [72] Colette, *L'Étoile vesper*, *Œuvres*, vol. IV, 868–9.
[73] Jourdan-Morhange, *Ravel et nous*, 31–3.
[74] Langham Smith, 'Ravel's operatic spectacles', 204; Thurman, *Secrets of the Flesh*, 340.

this seeming disparity [of personality] has never seemed so complete to me as has often been asserted: did they not share the same artisan's care for perfecting their work? And also, in the depths of their hearts, the same small vein that welled from the same source: reticence of soul [pudeur d'âme]. [...] While the candid Ravel's *pudeur* was easily discernible, Colette, woman among women, concealed herself behind a mask of colourful spontaneity.*[75]

Jourdan-Morhange identifies two crucial points: the notion of artisanship, and that of a shared personal reticence, or *pudeur*. Ravel insistently maintained the barriers between his personal life and his *boulot*,[76] a distinction that the often autobiographical Colette may seem to have blurred. Yet, by publicly defining and declaring a personal narrative, autobiography itself can become a protective shield: as Jourdan-Morhange observes, behind Colette's mask of seeming self-revelation was a close-guarded private being. Maurice Goudeket similarly observed, 'Free as she was in speech, I shall astonish many people when I say that no one could have been more modest.'[77] Elsewhere Goudeket emphasised 'the reserve which she invariably exercised when it was a question of deep feelings';[78] Colette herself wrote to the partner of her dear friend Renée Hamon, after the latter's death: 'I expect that when you and I see each other again we shall be very calm. I have always taken immense trouble not to show emotion, and most of the time I have succeeded.'[79] There are echoes here of Ravel's well-known words to Jacques de Zogheb: 'I am Basque; the Basques feel deeply but seldom show it, and then only to a very few.'[80]

'Can I say I really knew him, my collaborator on *L'Enfant et les sortilèges*?', 'Un salon en 1900' begins.[81] In the essay's mixture of candour and evasion, we see Colette drawing these boundaries between public and private space. Implicit in her reticence is a recognition of her colleague's *pudeur*, a reluctance to intrude – even in death – upon the privacy of so intensely private a man. But in retreating from the personal in her own published reflections, Colette tacitly passed the task of writing more intimately about her collaborator to one more fitted, from closer acquaintance and being untrammelled by notoriety: Hélène Jourdan-Morhange. It was Colette who 'initiated [Jourdan-Morhange] into the *métier* of the writer', drawing her out of the depression that overtook her when 'arthritis'

---

[75] Jourdan-Morhange, *Ravel et nous*, 127–8.
[76] Steven Huebner explores this facet of Ravel's character and aesthetic in his probing chapter 'Maurice Ravel: private life, public works'.
[77] Goudeket, *Close to Colette*, 21.   [78] *Ibid.*, 38–9.   [79] *Ibid.*, 181.
[80] Orenstein (ed.), *A Ravel Reader*, 16.   [81] Colette, 'Un salon en 1900', 164.

(possibly repetitive strain injury) arrested her performing career;[82] and Colette who, providing letters and the manuscript draft page of *L'Enfant*, supported and encouraged her friend through the writing of *Ravel et nous*, one of the most insightful and eloquent studies in the Ravelian literature. It was Colette who almost certainly facilitated Jourdan-Morhange's contract with Éditions du Milieu du Monde,[83] and Colette who wrote the volume's graceful preface. And from the beginning to the end of their long correspondence, Colette addresses Jourdan-Morhange as 'Moune' – a nickname given to her by Ravel. In *Ravel et nous*, we thus may sense a second tribute, less explicit but perhaps more telling, from one *âme pudique* to another.

Most importantly, Ravel's direct and Colette's implicit separation of self and *métier* compels us to consider their collaboration in terms of what, for both of them, always came first: the practices and principles of their respective professions. 'One gives birth away from the flame, and with calculation',[84] wrote Colette, echoing Ravel's assertion that he composed with the intellectual detachment Edgar Allan Poe expounded in his essay 'The Philosophy of Composition'.[85] (We know too that Colette, like Ravel, 'read and re-read Edgar Allan Poe in Baudelaire's translation'.[86]) Another of Ravel's rare quoted reflections on the act of composition is equally revealing: 'A note at random, then a second one and, sometimes, a third. I see what results I get by contrasting, combining and separating them.'[87] How many of Colette's essays and short stories begin in similar fashion, with an idea, image or even a word, that is repeated, worked over and gradually unfolded?

An early reflection on these similar working practices came from Paul Lombard, reviewing *L'Enfant* in *Renaissance*: 'Neither of them aims for shocking effects or brutal expansiveness, rather, a luminous inspiration, a discipline that, for not being openly declared, published or proclaimed, is none the less real: we recognise it in the details, because it is there that it must be seen.'*[88] Lombard's emphasis on discipline is particularly telling here, and the word recurs in Goudeket's decisive rejection of Colette's personality and writing style as

free, uncurbed, given up to the moment – I have already had to contradict this widespread opinion several times here and to introduce the word 'severity' where it seemed to have no place. What a lot of mistakes must thus have been made, unless

---

[82] Bernard Villaret, 'Préface' to Colette, *Lettres à Moune*, 8.

[83] See Colette, *Lettres à Moune*, 214, 254. Éditions du Milieu du Monde published Colette's *Paris de ma fenêtre* (1946) and *L'Étoile Vesper* (1947).

[84] Colette, *L'Etoile vesper*, 853.   [85] Orenstein (ed.), *A Ravel Reader*, 394, 433, 454.

[86] Goudeket, 'Close to Colette', 112.   [87] Nichols, *Ravel Remembered*, 55.

[88] Lombard, '*L'Enfant et les sortilèges*'.

it is thought that discipline, strictness with oneself, and the will-power needed for composition, may be taken up and abandoned like a disguise, beside one's work-table.[89]

Both Ravel and Colette made it clear that their *métier* demanded everything that they had to give, entailing a lifelong process of learning and striving. As Roland-Manuel recalled:

[Ravel] simply could not understand that an artist might draw upon other resources than those of *métier*. When I declared one day that I was convinced I had to *start* by knowing my *métier*, he enquired with heavy irony what I intended to do the rest of the time, adding that one had to start by learning the *métier* of others and that a lifetime was not enough to perfect one's own.*[90]

'French is quite a difficult language. After forty-five years of writing one just begins to appreciate this', Colette wrote in *Journal à rebours*.[91] Ravel made the same point even more directly: 'My objective, therefore, is technical perfection. I can strive unceasingly to this end, since I am certain of never being able to attain it. The important thing is to get nearer to it all the time.'*[92] Late in life, as Colette was correcting proofs of her *Œuvres complètes*, Goudeket (who had set the project in hand) recalled that 'She would pause to say to me: "Have I really written all that? Maurice, is it possible that I've written all that?" Sometimes she would make sufficiently bold to say: "It's not so badly done, this work, you know!"'[93] Hélène Jourdan-Morhange recounted similarly that in his last years Ravel would often say, 'J'avais écrit des choses pas mal, n'est-ce pas?'[94]

In the radio interview mentioned earlier in this chapter, a very elderly Colette reflected that 'It was a pleasure to be afraid of Ravel, a mixture of fear and. . . and. . . unease and tenderness'.[95] This odd, paradoxical reflection seems to encapsulate something important about not just their relationship but the composer himself: Ravel's formidable intellect, fierce integrity and razor-sharp wit were intrinsic to his *pudeur*, often masking the warmth, kindness and spontaneity he showed to his friends. Colette's 'fear' seems to reflect at least as much on her own *pudeur* as the composer's demeanour; indeed, heard in context, her words are infused with very audible tenderness. This audio extract is profoundly moving: Colette's

---

[89] Goudeket, *Close to Colette*, 152–3.   [90] Roland-Manuel, 'Des Valses à *La Valse*', 145–6.

[91] Colette, *Journal à rebours*, *Œuvres*, vol. IV, 176.

[92] Ravel, 'Quelques réflexions sur la musique'; *OL*, 47. See also Huebner, 'Ravel's perfection'.

[93] Goudeket, *Close to Colette*, 187.   [94] Jourdan-Morhange, *Ravel et nous*, 251.

[95] [Colette], 'Colette parle de Ravel'.

voice is tired and old, her thoughts disjointed, her memory failing her – 'Maurice [Goudeket], how did I meet Ravel? . . . I don't know how I became acquainted with Ravel. . .' she begins plaintively. It is difficult in places to follow her musings, which are fragmentary and often indistinct. But throughout the two-minute extract, she returns again and again to Ravel's name, turning it over and over in her mind and mouth (with her rich rolled Burgundians *rs*) with unmistakeable warmth and affection. 'Ravel, *cher* Ravel', she calls him, and speaks of 'pleasures' and 'joys'. If she does not recount any direct interchanges or specific events, her words are vivid: 'anyone who could listen to Ravel hoped to listen to him again the next day. Ravel. . . Ah, yes, Ravel, besides, with a way of playing his own music at the piano, which was a thing that filled you with joy [une des choses que vous comblent de joie]. You know, I am not lying to you in saying this.'

Ravel and Colette were bound together by a shared sense of *métier*, a similar approach to the processes of creation and a sympathetic and rigorous conception of structural and expressive design, focussed particularly in an enjoyment of the sounds and rhythms of the French language. In the light of these aesthetic parallels, as well as the nuanced documentary history set out above, we may therefore view *L'Enfant et les sortilèges* as the result of a process of palpable artistic convergence and exchange. None of Ravel's other scores owes its very existence and form to creative interaction in the way that this one does. There is an eagerness in his letters to Colette that is rare in his correspondence: he enjoyed and was inspired by his interactions with an artist whose precepts and practices were so close to his own. In the final assessment, it is perhaps in that eagerness that true 'collaboration' lies.

5 | Songs into operas

Ravel grew up steeped in literature. As teenagers, he and Ricardo Viñes wandered the *bouquinistes* along the *quais* of the Seine, acquiring and devouring editions of Bertrand, Baudelaire and Poe. A lifelong friend of writers and poets, he was himself a poet of sorts, setting four of his own texts to music; and if his letters and reviews have little of the overt literary elegance of Debussy's, they are nonetheless notable for their incisive humour and understated flair, and for the stings that lurk in the tails of innocuously neat aphorisms. 'Almost all his œuvre', wrote René Chalupt in 1925, 'unfolds upon a literary background which, indirectly or directly, prompts the patterns of his inspiration.'*[1]

By 1907, Ravel had already produced a corpus of *mélodies* notable for their unexpected choices of text and their experimental text-setting. Writing opera was a natural development of his literary engagement, as well as his musical objectives.

As with many a composer before him, the intimate and focussed medium of song served Ravel as a compositional crucible. He used the *mélodie* to explore, test and refine his technique, in ways that relate directly to his operas – a connection he made explicit when, in 1911, he described *Histoires naturelles* as 'studies' (*études*) for *L'Heure espagnole*.[2] Direct relationships of experimentation and influence may also be traced between his 1903 *Shéhérazade* songs and the surviving fragments of *La Cloche engloutie*, and between the choral *Trois chansons* and *L'Enfant et les sortilèges*. More broadly, the qualities implicit in the texts Ravel set, and his observable techniques for transforming poetry into sung melody, provide an indispensable context for his treatment of language in *L'Heure* and *L'Enfant*.

The unconventional quality of Ravel's chosen texts is apparent from his earliest songs. The poets most beloved of late nineteenth-century

---

[1] Chalupt, 'Maurice Ravel et les prétextes littéraires de sa musique', 65. Zank similarly acknowledges 'the literary mosaic' underpinning Ravel's œuvre and aesthetic (*Irony and Sound*, 14, 16ff.), while Petersen outlines Ravel's literary tastes and influences, *Die Lieder von Maurice Ravel*, 31–8. See also Huebner, 'Ravel's poetics'.
[2] Bizet, '*L'Heure espagnole*'; *OL*, 340.

mélodistes – Banville, Leconte de Lisle, Silvestre, Hugo, Villiers de l'Isle Adam, Gautier, Verlaine – furnished Ravel with just one published song setting, Verlaine's *Sur l'herbe*.[3] Nor, in his later years, would he be drawn to bright new stars like Paul Valéry, nor the poets of the First World War generation – Louis Aragon, Paul Éluard, Guillaume Apollinaire. Instead, his texts are drawn from an eclectic mixture of Parnassians and Symbolists, poets of the Renaissance and the Enlightenment, great poets and minor ones, writers better known for prose than poetry, friends and colleagues (Klingsor, Fargue, de Régnier), plus, on two occasions, Ravel himself.

Ravel did not simply look for evocative imagery or verbal grace in the texts he chose; indeed, many are notable for their lack of it. Rather, he was interested in the myriad ways that music and words could interact with or impinge upon each other. His perception of language defined by his *métier*, he thought about words in terms of both content and form, of meaning and evocation, and of rhythms and resonances in the ear. Words, for Ravel, were to become a defining and fully integrated facet of a composition: in his operas as well as in his songs, he used distinctive patterns of textual assonance, alliteration and onomatopoeia to define his characters.

In a 1927 interview Ravel talked of Mallarmé:

We begged humbly for elucidation of the curious verses which Ravel has clothed with tone in his *Trois Poèmes* (for voice) *de Stéphane Mallarmé*. 'Useless to explain,' he answered. 'The poetry speaks to you or it does not. It is very obscure, and if once it seizes you – marvellous! I consider Mallarmé not merely the greatest French poet, but the *only* French poet, since he made the French language, not designed for poetry, poetical. It is a feat in which he stands alone.'[4]

The French language, with its plasticity, its challenging vowels and its dry expressivity, lies at the core of Ravel's operas as well as his songs. If he deemed it a language 'not designed for poetry', Ravel's 1922 article on Fauré's *mélodies* (derived from an interview with Roland-Manuel) nonetheless evokes the 'fleeting music of the French language, which is less obvious than that of Italian, for example, but how much more delicate and thus more precious!'[5]

---

[3] His setting of Verlaine's *Un grand sommeil noir* was published only in 1953, that of Leconte de Lisle's *Chanson du rouet* in 1975.

[4] Olin Downes, 'Maurice Ravel, Man and Musician', *New York Times*, 7 August 1927; Orenstein (ed.), *A Ravel Reader*, 450.

[5] Ravel, 'Les Mélodies de Gabriel Fauré', *La Revue musicale* 4/11 (October 1922); *OL*, 323.

'Sous la musique que faut-il mettre?'

Early in 1911, the journal *Musica* sent a number of composers and poets a series of questions about text and text-setting. 'What should be set to music? Good poetry or bad, free verse or prose?', they were asked (the suitability of free verse and prose for musical setting having been much debated across the preceding two decades).[6] Some of the responses were serious, some frivolous, some curt. Fauré admitted dissatisfaction with his early Victor Hugo settings and extolled the delights of Verlaine, while Debussy talked about his newest creations, *Trois ballades de François Villon*. Massenet responded with a single sentence – 'Very beautiful music has been written to terrible poems... I prefer the good ones!' – and so did Reynaldo Hahn: 'It is impossible to respond to these questions in a few words, and above all to encapsulate the entire history of vocal music.' Paul Dukas concluded that it didn't matter much anyway, because in the fashionable salons the musicians listened only to the music and the non-musicians only to the words.[7]

Ravel's reflection was one of the longest and most considered of all the responses, and the only one to set out a reasoned and practical philosophy:

> It seems to me that, in dealing with things that are truly experienced and felt, free verse is preferable to regular verse. Regular verse can, even so, produce very beautiful results, provided the composer is willing to efface himself entirely behind the poet and consents to follow his rhythms step by step, cadence by cadence, without ever displacing an accent or even an inflection. In a word, if the composer wants to work on regular poetry, his music will simply underline the poem and support it, but be unable to translate anything in it or add anything. I believe it is better, especially if you are ever dealing with emotion and fantasy, to choose free verse.*[8]

These remarks raise a number of curious points. First, most of the texts Ravel himself set adhere to rhyme schemes and metrical forms of varying degrees of regularity – including his own decidedly fantastic poems for *Noël des jouets* and the *Trois chansons*. Only *Histoires naturelles*, *Chansons madécasses* and, to a certain extent, *Shéhérazade* can be described as free verse. Second, how is one to understand phrases such as 'efface himself entirely behind the poet' and the contention that music will 'be unable to translate [. . .] or add anything [to regular verse]' ('ne pourra rien en traduire, rien y ajouter')? And can Ravel's own music ever be said to disappear

---

[6] In addition to the sources cited in the present chapter (see in particular notes 26 and 31–6), see also Macdonald, 'The prose libretto'.
[7] Ravel *et al.*, 'Sous la musique que faut-il mettre?', 40, 58–9.   [8] *Ibid.*, 59; *OL*, 293–4.

behind anything, or to content itself merely with underlining and sustaining? Some context – and perhaps a degree of contradiction – comes from Ravel's reported remarks to Jules Renard on the subject of the *Histoires naturelles*, as recorded in the latter's journal:

> I [. . .] asked him what he could add to the *Histoires naturelles*.
> 'My intention was not to add anything', he said, 'but to interpret them'
> 'In what regard?'
> 'To say with music what you say in words. [. . .] I think and I feel in music, and I would like to think and feel the same things as you.'[9]

Both passages suggest that there was, for Ravel, a clear distinction between simply 'illustrating' a poem and working in parallel with it, in the latter case expressing 'the same things' through a different medium. In this, his words oddly reflect and contradict those of Dukas, who contended, in his own *Musica* text, that 'there must be no mistake about this: *one does not set poems to music*. One provides the words with an accompaniment, and that's something else entirely. The first idea, in effect, assumes a *fusion*, the second observes a *parallel*.'[10]

The *Musica* article also emphasises the rigour of Ravel's conception of word-setting. His text goes on to apply his reflections to no less a target than the Jewel Song from Gounod's *Faust*: 'Indeed, it seems to me criminal to "damage" classical poetry', he writes, and proceeds to demonstrate how the Jewel Song 'makes a martyr' of its text, subjugating its natural metre to regular waltz-rhythms: 'The composer wanted a waltz. He counted the number of feet in these lines and found that there were twelve of them. From that point, he was not concerned about anything else, not the rhyme nor any other formal details: he wanted his waltz; the librettist wanted his twelve syllables.'* The importance Ravel placed on the integrity of poetic metre is similarly underlined in his discussion of the Jewel Song's vocalising passages: 'This is pretty and fresh and gives a sense of liveliness, a crystalline quality to the melody. But these *Ah! Ah! Ah! Ah! Ahs!*, placed in the middle of an alexandrine, make the length vary between seventeen and twenty-five [poetic] feet, and this is not useful.'*[11] Typical of Ravel is the judgement delivered in terms not of beauty but of utility.

Yet Ravel's text-setting principles, however mercilessly expressed, conceal a certain degree of flexibility, provided (as always) strict guidelines were adhered to. The composer, he is suggesting, must 'think and feel' like

---

[9] Renard, *Journal*, entry for 12 January 1907.
[10] Dukas in Ravel *et al.*, 'Sous la musique que faut-il mettre?', 58.
[11] Ravel *et al.*, 'Sous la musique que faut-il mettre?', 59; *OL*, 294.

the poet, indeed must himself *become* the poet behind whom the composer is 'effaced'. If this means the composer is unable to 'translate' or 'add' anything, he is nonetheless free to search out the music implicit in the text itself.

Assonance, alliteration and onomatopoeia

A survey of the poems – and the opera libretti – Ravel set suggests that he was drawn to texts whose effect was garnered through patterns that appeal as much to the ear as they do to the intellect. In addition to, or instead of, a formal scheme of rhyme and metre, many of his chosen poems generate a secondary layer of aural organisation through the repetition and emphasis of characteristic words and word-sounds, together with onomatopoeic patterns of rhythm and assonance. Ravel's early songs in particular often feature repeated words and word-sounds within or across lines. This characteristic is evident from his first song, *Ballade de la Reine morte d'aimer*, with its emphasis of the words *reine* and *belle/beauté*: 'En Bohême était une Reine, / Douce sœur du Roi de Thulé, / Belle entre toutes les Reines, / Reine par sa toute Beauté.' Paul Gravollet's 'Manteau de fleurs' plays on more obsessive repetitions: the word *rose* (or *roses*; also once *rosée* (dew)) ends seven of the twenty lines and appears in six more, with varying stresses and as different parts of speech (adjective and noun).[12] In Leconte de Lisle's 'Chanson du rouet', each six-line verse is constructed symmetrically around the repeated first and second (= sixth and fifth, respectively) lines. Mallarmé's 'Sainte' (see p. 236) uses the nasal [ã] vowel as either the 'A' or 'B' rhyme in each verse (which follow an ABAB pattern), and the final verse uses [ã] as not only its 'B' rhyme, but also the penultimate chime of the 'A' lines: 'Du doigt que, sans le vieux sa<u>nt</u>al / Ni le vieux livre, elle bala<u>nce</u> / Sur le plumage instrum<u>ent</u>al, / Musicienne du sil<u>ence</u>'.

Different plays of repetition and assonance are evident in Ravel's two Marot settings: 'D'Anne jouant de l'espinette' makes play with homonyms (*voy/voix*, which chime with *point* and *doits; dieux/d'yeulx* [*yeux*] and *mélo<u>dieux</u>; que/qu'eulx* [*eux*]), while 'D'Anne qui me jecta la neige' uses repeated consonant sounds for pacing and punctuation. The reflective first half of the poem is laced with sibilants, while the second part, more direct and passionate, resounds with plosive 'p's:

---

[12] The word *beauté* ends three more lines (of the five that employ *-té* as a rhyme-sound); *beauté* and *rose* are combined in the repeated 'La rose sied à sa beauté' (lines 2 and 8).

Anne par jeu me jecta de la neige
Que je cuidoys froide, certainement :
Mais c'estoit feu, l'expérience en ay je,
Car embrasé, je fuz soubdainement.
Puis que le feu loge secretement
Dedans la neige, où trouveray je place
Pour n'ardre point ? Anne, ta seule grace
Estaindre peult le feu que je sens bien
Non point par eau, par neige ne par glace
Mais par sentir ung feu pareil au mien.[13]

The taut, near-monosyllabic lines of Verlaine's 'Un grand sommeil noir' are packed with subtle repetition and alliteration – 'Je suis un berceau / Qu'une main balance / Au creux d'un caveau : / Silence, silence !' – while in the penultimate verse of Émile Verhaeren's 'Si morne!' the monotonous repetition of [i] sounds infuses that normally light vowel with bizarre heaviness, emphasised in Ravel's setting of the lines to a literal monotone (Ex. 5.1).

An equally unusual accumulation of word-sounds may be observed in the climactic line of Renard's 'Le Martin-pêcheur' (the fourth of Ravel's

Ex. 5.1 *Si morne!*, bars 32–36

13   Anne, in jest, threw snow at me / Which I certainly believed to be cold / But what I felt was fire / For I was suddenly set aflame / As fire lodges secretly / In the snow, where shall I find a place / Where I shall not burn? Anne, only your mercy / Can extinguish the fire that I truly feel, / Not by water, by snow or by ice, / But by feeling a fire that matches my own.

Histoires naturelles): 'Je ne respirais plus, tout fier d'être pris pour un arbre par un martin-pêcheur' ('I held my breath, so proud was I to be taken for a tree by a kingfisher'). The repeated *r*s hold up the flow of text, forcing the reader or singer to tread carefully and compelling a physical sense of breathlessness matching that conjured by the narrative.

These sorts of repetitions and juxtapositions of sounds and assonances are part of what led Hélène Jourdan-Morhange to declare Ravel's texts seemingly 'unsuited to being clothed with music'* ('moins aptes à être habillés de musique'):[14] they make for spiky, often ungainly vocal lines, lacking fluidity and feeling awkward in the mouth. In the same spirit as his judicious deployment of extreme registers and timbres in his instrumental music, in his songs Ravel was challenging himself, his interpreters, and the *mélodie* as a genre, by using the voice in unusual, technically demanding and more percussive ways. Similar techniques of iterated and cumulative vowel and consonant sounds may be found in both his opera libretti, becoming an element of characterisation in *L'Heure* and underpinning timbre as well as large-scale formal and narrative shapes in *L'Enfant*.

Ravel's natural inclination for alliterative or repetitive word-sounds also reveals itself plainly in his own poetry. Consider the lines depicting the vigilant angels of *Noël des jouets*: 'Et leur vol de clinquant vermeil / Qui cliquette en bruits symétriques' ('And their glittering vermillion flight / Jangling in symmetrical sounds'). Ravel combines here an evocative description with very individual onomatopoeia and complex patterns of assonance: the hard [c] and [t] consonants and light vowels of 'Qui cliquette' really do sound 'jangly', and the mirrored *clinquant*/*cliquette*, the paired fricatives *vol*/*vermeil* and the four sharp [i] vowels combine to form a secondary layer of internal wordplay. 'Ravel knew how to see and to release the essential', wrote René Dumesnil in 1938, 'and to express it he always found the right word, not only by its precise meaning, but still more by its sonority'*.[15]

In Ravel's choral *Trois chansons*, word-sounds are repeated and combined to create onomatopoeic soundscapes, in ways that literally echo in *L'Enfant et les sortilèges*. The menacing percussive effect of the sibilants in the Animals' overlapping 'Unissons-nous!' (Figs. 138–9) recalls 'Ronde', the last of the *Trois chansons*: 'Des satyresses, des ogresses, et des babaïagas, / Des centauresses et des diablesses, goules sortant du sabbat'. More threatening hisses emerge from the Numbers' chant of 'cinq et sept, cinq et sept' in the Arithmetic scene (Fig. 91; see Ex. 10.1a), an allusion

---

[14] Jourdan-Morhange, *Ravel et nous*, 134.   [15] Dumesnil, 'Maurice Ravel poète', 126.

Ex. 5.2a 'Nicolette' (*Trois chansons pour chœur mixte*), bars 22–23

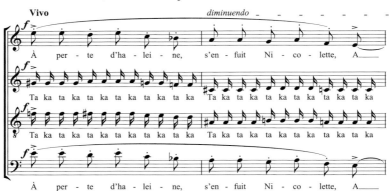

Ex. 5.2b Arithmetic scene (*L'Enfant et les sortilèges*)

highlighted by the scene's culminating indication 'Ronde folle'. An even closer affinity links the Numbers to 'Nicolette': Ravel's clog-wearing heroine flees the wolf to an amusingly onomatopoeic 'ta-ka-ta-ka-ta-ka-ta-ka' in the altos and tenors (Ex. 5.2a); the vowel and consonant sounds are those of the Numbers' repeated 'Quatre et quat'?' (Ex. 5.2b). In both works we sense the same almost tactile enjoyment of the sounds and rhythms of the language: 'Millimètre, Centimètre, Décimètre, Décamètre, Hectomètre, Kilomètre, Myriamètre, / Faut t'y mettre, / Quelle fêtre! / Des millions, Des billions, Des trillions, / Et des frac-cillions!', chants Mr Arithmetic (Figs. 83–4), echoing the dancing assonances of the 'Hamadryades, dryades, naïades, ménades, thyades, folettes, lémures' in Ravel's earlier 'Ronde'.

Ravel would also return to the quasi-naïve pastoral atmosphere of the *Trois chansons* in the scene of the Shepherds and Shepherdesses. 'Nous n'irons plus sur l'herbe mauve / Paître nos verts moutons!' they sing (Ex. 5.3c), their acerbic diminished octaves harking back to 'Nicolette'

Ex. 5.3a *Nous n'irons plus au bois*

Nous n'i-rons plus au   bois, les lau-riers sont cou - pés.

Ex. 5.3b 'Ronde' (*Trois chansons pour chœur mixte*), bars 57–60

N'i-rons plus au   bois d'Or-mon-de,   Hé-las! Plus ja - mais n'i-rons au bois:

Ex. 5.3c Shepherds and Shepherdesses (*L'Enfant et les sortilèges*)

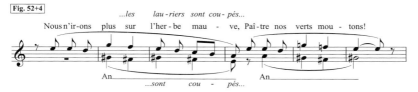

Fig. 52+4

...les   lau-riers sont cou-pés...

Nous n'ir-ons   plus   sur   l'her-be   mau - ve, Paî-tre nos   verts mou - tons!

An___   ...sont   cou - pés...   An___

(see Ex. 5.2a above, soprano and tenor), while their words echo the 'young people' of 'Ronde' ('N'irons plus au bois d'Ormonde / Hélas! plus jamais n'irons au bois'; Ex. 5.3b). In this mutual farewell to the woods, both song and scene make gentle textual and musical reference to the well-known children's song *Nous n'irons plus au bois* (Ex. 5.3a).[16] If 'Ronde' echoes the folk-tune's 3–4–5 progression (with the subdominant sharpened in Ravel's setting), *L'Enfant* suggests a rhythmic correspondence, while the soprano phrase imitates in minor mode, and the alto in the major, the tune's stepwise descent.

Both songs and opera suggest a sideways glance at the destructive ways of the world: Nicolette elopes with her repulsive lord; the enchantment of the woods has been broken. The Shepherds and Shepherdesses are succeeded by the Princess, who makes explicit the consequences of the Child's actions: by destroying the book of fairytales in which she resides, he has banished her forever into the realm of Sleep and Night. We may also see in the Shepherds and Shepherdesses, as in 'Nicolette', a nod to the stylised bucolicism of the *fête galante* via the darker re-imaginings of Verlaine. In both the songs and the opera, literary, pictorial and musical associations are thus inextricably blended, while a fleeting melodic gesture opens a window onto older traditions of folksong and fairytale.

---

[16] Debussy also quoted *Nous n'irons plus au bois* in 'Jardins sous la pluie' (*Estampes*) and the third of the 1894 *Images (oubliées)*, 'Quelques aspects de *Nous n'irons plus au bois*, parce qu'il fait un temps insupportable' (in which he also sharpens the subdominant in bars 137–45), as well as in his song 'La Belle au bois dormant' and the orchestral *Image* 'Rondes de printemps'.

Speech into song

The texts Ravel chose to set, and the qualities that he emphasised within them, reveal a composer increasingly drawn to the borderlands between poetry and music, and between speech and song. From the very beginning of his compositional career, however, Ravel was experimenting with text-setting techniques that owe more to poetic declamation and ordinary spoken language than to accepted musical practice. The first line of *Ballade de la Reine morte d'aimer* (Ex. 5.4) demonstrates the primacy to which, even as an eighteen-year-old, he accorded poetic rhythm and metre. The final syllable of *Reine* is not given a separate note (as text-setting conventions would normally demand) but apocopated in the manner of French poetry, where a 'mute' *e* that ends a line does not have to be pronounced and does not usually figure in a syllable count. The number of notes in Ravel's phrase (eight) thus tallies with Roland de Marès's octosyllabic verse. Unpublished during the composer's lifetime, this setting would have ruffled a few feathers among the arbiters of contemporary musical aesthetics.[17]

Ex. 5.4 *Ballade de la Reine morte d'aimer*, bars 4–6

After the première of *Pelléas et Mélisande*, Ravel set about exploring the practice of text-setting in a more considered and comprehensive fashion. It is no coincidence that the *Shéhérazade* songs followed hard on the heels of *Pelléas*, nor that they lie closer to Debussy's opera than anything he would ever write: Ravel himself would later say of them that 'Debussy's influence, at least spiritual, is rather evident.'[18] Reviewing *Shéhérazade*, Louis Laloy indeed noted that 'each listener immediately thinks of Debussy', but insisted that 'the disdainful epithet of imitator [should not] be flung at Monsieur Ravel: his music is not an imitative music; it has a personal accent'.[19]

Before setting his three poems, Tristan Klingsor recalled, Ravel 'took care to have me recite them out loud to him'.[20] While the textual rhythms of

---

[17] The manuscripts of several of Fauré's early songs show similar apocopations at line-ends, amended in printed editions to conventional syllabic divisions. See Howat and Kilpatrick, *Gabriel Fauré: Complete Songs*, vol. I, 137 (notes to *L'Absent*).

[18] 'Esquisse autobiographique'; *OL*, 44. See also Kaminsky, 'Vocal music and the lures of exoticism and irony', 165.

[19] *La Revue musicale* 4/11 (1 June 1904); Priest, *Louis Laloy*, 246.

[20] Dumesnil, 'Maurice Ravel poète', 125.

Ex. 5.5 'Asie' (*Shéhérazade*), bars 103–7

Klingsor's poems are meticulously translated in Ravel's setting, the melodic lines are naturalistic only in a broad gestural sense. The songs' likeness to *Pelléas* is evident in the way vocal lines, rather than tracing every inflection, tend to move in a single consistent direction across the course of a phrase, using mostly small intervals (seconds and thirds) and repeated pitches, with larger intervals generally reserved for phrase-ends. The last of the set, 'L'Indifférent', comes closest to reproducing the natural melodic inflections of its text, undoubtedly because of its more direct conversational narrative. In all three of Ravel's songs, however, and in 'Asie' in particular, naturalism bows to lyricism. As Example 5.5 (the climax of 'Asie') demonstrates, although individual phrases may echo the outlines of spoken text, in context the high tessitura, shifts of tessitura between phrases, rich accompanying textures and the occasional purely lyrical melodic gesture ensure that the listener always hears song before speech.

The surviving sketches of *La Cloche engloutie* indicate that Ravel's text-setting in this never-completed opera was based on similar principles. Example 5.6, from the first page of what remains of the score, probably dates from the summer of 1906.[21] It presents a vocal line, set over a quiet

---

[21] Reproduced in Orenstein, 'Some unpublished music and letters', plate Xa.

Ex. 5.6 *La Cloche engloutie*, sketches for Scene 1 (vocal line only)

tremolo accompaniment, that is gently evocative of the contours of the spoken voice and adheres to its rhythmic patterns, while remaining unashamedly lyrical. The melodic direction here is less regular than in *Shéhérazade*, however, and the modal inflections and moments of more tortuous chromatic motion (in the first and penultimate bars) show the composer turning away from *Pelléas* and towards *Histoires naturelles*.

Other songs of the early twentieth century – *Manteau de fleurs*, *Sur l'herbe*, *Les grands vents venus d'outremer* – employ similarly designed vocal lines, rhythmically precise relative to spoken language, but only suggestive of it in melodic terms. Of the three, the most interesting is *Sur l'herbe*, completed in June 1907 as Ravel was hard at work on *L'Heure espagnole*. One of the darkest of Verlaine's *Fêtes galantes*, 'Sur l'herbe' has little of the metric flexibility of a 'Clair de lune', 'En sourdine' or even 'Colloque sentimentale'. Rather, its short, heavily punctuated lines are weighed down with monosyllables, the first verse in particular shot through with hard consonants (*perruque, nuque*). In Ravel's setting, the alternation of conversational declamation with exaggeratedly mannered lyricism directly foreshadows the flights of Gonzalve or Inigo (the lecherous abbot and marquis are close cousins of the latter in any case), while the often dry accompaniment, the vaguely Spanish atmosphere and the shifts of metre and tempo have the flexible, text-driven pacing of *L'Heure*.

While *Shéhérazade* and *La Cloche engloutie* took their explorations of naturalistic text-setting from the starting point of lyrical singing, in *Histoires naturelles* Ravel abandoned lyricism from the outset for a drier, more conversational delivery. The rhythms are complex and irregular, the melodic contours more angular. The far more detailed and intricate notation represents a remarkable and very rapid transition, a definitive step

Ex. 5.7 'Le Cygne' (*Histoires naturelles*), bars 1–5

forward into the mature style of the composer and a new departure for the French *mélodie*, stimulated by a sophisticated conception of text-setting and the sounds of the spoken voice.

Of all the texts Ravel set, *Histoires naturelles* offer perhaps the most intriguing use of poetic assonance and onomatopoeia. 'The direct, clear language and the profound, hidden poetry of Jules Renard's words tempted me for a long time', Ravel wrote in his 'Autobiographical sketch',[22] and in the 1911 *Musica* article he called those words 'delicate, rhythmic, though rhythmic in a completely different way from classical verse'*.[23] Within the free-flowing prosody of Renard's text, we find phrases naturally falling into more regular poetic metre, often with directly expressive effect, like the restful iambs of 'Il se repose encore un peu' in 'Le Grillon', and the evocatively spacious dactyls and anapaests that end the poem: 'Dans la campagne muette les peupliers se dressent comme des doigts en l'air et désignent la lune.' The first line of 'Le Cygne' juxtaposes three different metric configurations: the onomatopoeic sibilants of 'Il glisse sur le bassin', the stronger trochaic

---

[22] 'Esquisse autobiographique'; *OL*, 45.

[23] Ravel *et al.*, 'Sous la musique que faut-il mettre?', 59; *OL*, 294.

accents of 'comme un traineau blanc' and the sleepy anapæsts of 'de nuage en nuage'.[24] The general context of flexible, unmetred verse serves to highlight such moments of metric regularity, drawing out the poems' underlying rhythmic tautness. Ravel's setting, too, seems to direct attention to these sporadic 'classical' emphases, as in the opening of 'Le Cygne' (Ex. 5.7). While he captures the natural expressive flexibility of speech, Ravel also follows the rhythms of Renard's prose-poems 'step by step, cadence by cadence, without ever displacing an accent or even an inflection' – almost, indeed, as if they were regular verse...

These local instances of expressive rhythmic emphasis find echoes in the broader design of Renard's prose-poems, where juxtaposition of shorter and longer sentences or phrases is a key dramatic tool. The brief and pragmatic opening phrases of 'Le Paon', for example, open into two long, elaborate sentences, which are dragged suddenly back to earth by the bride's prosaic failure to turn up:

> Il va sûrement se marier aujourd'hui. Ce devait être pour hier.
> En habit de gala, il était prêt. Il n'attendait que sa fiancée.
> Elle n'est pas venue. Elle ne peut tarder.
> Glorieux, il se promène avec une allure de prince indien et porte sur lui les riches
> presents d'usage.
> L'amour avive l'éclat de ses couleurs et son aigrette tremble comme une lyre.
> La fiancée n'arrive pas.[25]

These sudden shifts between stagey pronouncements and prosaic asides, and corresponding juxtapositions of rhythm and metre, would find clear echoes in *L'Heure espagnole*.

'Toute la révolution se fait autour de l'*e* muet'[26]

The première of *Histoires naturelles*, which took place at the Salle Érard on 12 January 1907 under the auspices of the Société nationale de musique,

---

[24] Bergeron also notes this natural sense of rhythm and metre, observing that the opening of 'Le Cygne' '[scans] naturally into "free" alexandrines (twelve syllables, more or less), punctuated by half-lines' (*Voice Lessons*, 280).

[25] He will surely be married today. It should have been yesterday. / In his festive garb, he was ready. He awaited only his fiancée. / She did not come. She cannot be long. / Glorious, he strolls with the allure of an Indian prince, bearing on his person the customary rich gifts. / Love brightens the splendour of his colours, and his crest trembles like a lyre. / His fiancée doesn't appear.

[26] Jean Psichari, 'Le vers français aujourd-hui et les poètes décadents', *La Revue bleue* (1891); Gribenski, '"Chanter comme des personnes naturelles"', 14.

proved to be one of the most controversial Parisian musical events of the decade. Émile Vuillermoz wrote reminiscently of the 'stupefaction' of the audience, Claude Debussy called the songs 'displaced', and even Gabriel Fauré, a staunch champion of his former pupil, reportedly said, 'I'm very fond of Ravel. But I'm not happy with people setting stuff like that to music.'[27] Auguste Sérieyx outdid himself in pomposity:

> The Société nationale is not a Music-Hall: we are certainly not opposed to a certain degree of gentle gaiety, and occasional excursions to the extreme limits of good taste can now and then provoke a discreet smile. But there is a difference between these sorts of little accidents, which can be ascribed to inexperience, and a systematic attempt at 'bluffing'; and the witty author of these *Histoires naturelles* (that is, Jules Renard) seems himself to have expressed, in his 'Martin-Pêcheur', the lesson of the unfortunate clownery introduced at the concert of 12 January: 'Not a bite, this evening'!*[28]

Ravel's choices of text, his laconic, naturalistic settings, and the conversational and sometimes sardonic interchanges between voice and piano were all calculated to surprise and provoke his audience. But what offered most fuel to his critics was his deliberate flouting of French text-setting conventions concerning the mute *e*.

The question of how to treat the mute *e* (the neutral vowel or *schwa*, [ə][29]), which is typically unvoiced in conversation but articulated in poetry, song and dramatic declamation, has vexed French writers, dramatists and composers for centuries. In the 1760s, Voltaire and Modeste Grétry were exchanging letters on the subject;[30] a similar dialogue was taken up a century and a half later in the correspondence between Romain Rolland and Richard Strauss on the subject of French prosody, *vis-à-vis* the forthcoming French version of *Salomé* (and *Pelléas et Mélisande*; see also p. 114). Rolland invested the mute *e* with a certain philosophical grandeur, equating it, in both music and poetry, with high art and culture, the

---

[27] Vuillermoz, 'L'Œuvre de Maurice Ravel', 59; Debussy, letter to Louis Laloy of 22 February 1907, *Correspondance*, 996; Nichols, *Ravel*, 89. Debussy's subsequent letter to Laloy (8 March 1907) is well known: musing on the nature of 'humoristic' music, he compared Ravel to a 'Fakircharmeur', 'who can make flowers spring up around a chair. Unfortunately, a trick is always prepared and can only astonish once!' (*Correspondance*, 998–9). See also Fillerup, 'Ravel and Robert-Houdin, magicians', esp. 130–1.

[28] Sérieyx, 'Salle Érard, Société nationale', 78.

[29] In English the *schwa* is heard on unstressed syllables (regardless of the notated vowel), such as d<u>e</u>cent, b<u>a</u>nana and s<u>u</u>pport. In French we hear the *schwa* in words such as p<u>e</u>tit and v<u>e</u>nue, but in poetry and song it is additionally articulated in syllables usually unvoiced in speech, such as ell<u>e</u>, ven<u>ue</u> and port<u>e</u>; this is the *e muet* (or *e caduc*).

[30] Gribenski, '"Chanter comme des personnes naturelles"', 5–7.

Parisian as opposed to the provincial, the classical as opposed to the decadent: 'It is less a sound than a resonance, an echo of the preceding syllable, which trembles, hangs and vanishes gently into the air.'[31]

Around and preceding the Strauss–Rolland correspondence, innumerable articles in Parisian literary, musical and theatrical journals were devoted to the mute *e*, its history, its etymology and its technical and symbolic value: in 1891, Jean Psichari even claimed that 'a veritable revolution is being created around the mute *e*'.[32] While Leconte de Lisle and Théodore de Banville argued strongly against the pronunciation of the *e* at line-ends, Jules Lemaître, in an 1893 theatrical review, deplored the tendency of actors to create additional elisions and apocopes mid-line – 'Evidently', he wrote, 'these people have no love for music'.[33]

The polemics continued into the new century. In 1903, Henry Woollett produced a *Petit traité de prosodie, à l'usage des compositeurs*, which took a few potshots at the text-setting of *Pelléas*, while 1904 saw a lively exchange of articles – which Ravel almost certainly observed with interest and perhaps amusement – that took up the contentious hypotheses of Rémy de Gourmont's 1902 treatise *Le Problème de style*.[34] Gourmont had declared that the mute *e* was in essence 'a fiction': a relic of earlier written tradition, it was no longer part of spoken language, useful only as a visual sign or 'lantern' indicating or 'illuminating' the pronunciation of the preceding consonant. In a front-page article in *Le Figaro* on 19 August 1904, Camille Saint-Saëns retaliated furiously. The elision or suppression of the mute *e*, he thundered, in the theatre, in music and even in conversation, was hastening the decline of the French language itself. Saint-Saëns invoked the 'appalling vulgarity' of the café-concert, citing by way of comparison the 'celebrated drinking song' of Victor Massé's *Galathée*, where the composer suppressed the mute *e*s at the end of his lines for illustrative effect: 'Ah! vers encor'! / Vidons l'amphor'!' But, asked Saint-Saëns, did Massé continue: 'Qu'un flot d'vin / De c' vieux vin / Calm' la soif

[31] Letter of 9 July 1905; Strauss and Rolland, *Correspondance*, 39–40.

[32] See n26 above. Helen Abbott similarly notes (*Between Baudelaire and Mallarmé*, 32) that in the many late nineteenth-century French poetic treatises, 'A particular concern [...] is the pronunciation of the *e muet* and how this affects not only the scansion of French verse, but also the rule of alternation between masculine and feminine rhymes (an issue which becomes central to the debate over the "musicality" of verse).'

[33] Gribenski, '"Chanter comme des personnes naturelles"', 14–16. In his *Petit traité de poésie française* (19–21), Théodore de Banville set out the principles of 'masculine' and 'feminine' rhymes and the treatment of the mute *e* with regard to syllable tallies and pronunciation.

[34] Gourmont, *Le Problème de style*, 'La Question de l'*e* muet', 169–90; see, in particular, 180, 189.

qui m' dévor"? Of course not: 'Instead of a bit of decent drunkenness, this would have been nothing more than a filthy orgy.'*[35]

Two months later, an extended response to Saint-Saëns's seething appeared from Ravel's friend Calvocoressi. He underlined the flexibility of the French language, noting that different *e*s have different stresses according to the words, phrases and emphases in which they find themselves, and that a commensurate flexibility was therefore demanded of writers, actors and musicians:

In contemporary language as in music, whether it concerns poetry or prose, there are some mute *e*s that are not pronounced, others that are half-pronounced and still others that are unequivocally pronounced. According to the general meaning of a phrase one mute *e*, in the same word, can be completely hidden, half-pronounced or even emphatically accentuated. Whether it's prose or poetry has nothing to do with it.*[36]

After noting that the most interesting and innovative young composers of the day were increasingly turning to prose texts for their libretti and songs,[37] Calvocoressi concluded by pointedly listing, with page and bar references, a clutch of ungainly over-accentuated *e*s in Saint-Saëns's own *Samson et Dalila*. As Gribenski concludes, 'The question of the apocope [was] not purely aesthetic, but ideological.'[38]

While the debate went on around them, by the turn of the century composers setting both prose and poetry, in opera and in song, were beginning to treat the mute *e* with a certain degree of flexibility, though generally only in isolated and unsystematic contexts. A few *e*s were left unvoiced (mostly at line-ends), the apocopations expressed variously with ties, slurs, small or parenthesised noteheads, or simply as a single note (as in Ex. 5.4 above and the end of Ex. 5.5). In *Pelléas*, Debussy treated the *e* more flexibly still, with a clearer rationale for more consistent apocopation and elision, but without approaching the nuanced treatment of *Histoires naturelles* and *L'Heure espagnole*:[39] as the critics were to protest of the latter works (if not in so many words), it was one thing to let the occasional mute *e* pass, quite another to suppress almost all of them.[40]

---

[35] Saint-Saëns, 'La Question de l'E muet'.

[36] Calvocoressi, 'Le Vers, la prose et l'*e* muet', 797. Bergeron outlines the closely related argument of the actor and singer Léon Brémont, in his 1903 treatise *L'Art de dire les vers* (*Voice Lessons*, 203–4).

[37] See also Macdonald, 'The prose libretto'.

[38] Gribenski, '"Chanter comme des personnes naturelles"', 9.   [39] *Ibid.*, 26, 28.

[40] Roger Nichols argues that 'it has strangely gone unnoticed that [Ravel] was far from consistent in this practice [the suppression of the mute *e*], and that there seems to be little or no reason as

In the context of these long-running and heated debates on the respective suitability of prose and poetry for musical setting and the treatment of the mute *e*, nothing about the timing or technique of Ravel's song cycle and opera was coincidental: the *Histoires naturelles* in particular were very clearly calculated to outrage. As Gribenski observes, Ravel's approach

> may be interpreted as a radicalisation of Debussy's innovations [. . .] In contrast to the Debussyan revolution which, from the point of view of the treatment of the mute *e* and the internal hiatus, remained nuanced and [. . .] subtle, the Ravelian revolution, as it revealed itself in *Histoires naturelles* and then in *L'Heure espagnole*, was spectacular by contrast, explicitly radical and provocative.[41]

Elden Stuart Little notes that the engraving manuscripts of *Histoires naturelles* show Ravel refining his vocal notation at a very late stage, the modifications almost entirely directed to replacing voiced *schwas* with apocopes (mostly replacing two notes of the same value and pitch with a single note, as in 'riches présents d'usage' and 'dirige vers le perron').[42] James Hurd observes that many of the discrepancies between the piano-vocal and orchestral scores of *L'Heure espagnole* (the latter postdating the former by some two years) indicate similar alterations.[43] It must remain moot, however, whether these modifications constituted a *revision* of Ravel's intentions, as Hurd suggests relative to *Histoires naturelles*,[44] or simply a clarification of them: as he rehearsed his songs with Jane Bathori, Ravel may have realised that he needed a more radical notation to express a concept that was already clear in his mind. If so, the intention that may have been at first ambiguously expressed was clarified in the final printed versions of both works. (The many minor revisions to the vocal lines in the orchestral score of *L'Heure* also reflect Ravel's careful attention to the precise interplay of voice and orchestra.) If the desire to *épater les bourgeois* was indisputably one of Ravel's motivations in setting *Histoires naturelles* as he did, at least as important was the single-minded artistic desire to test a thesis and perfect a technique.

---

to why he elided some and not others. Maybe several of the audience were simply disconcerted by not knowing when or why the next "e" would be missing' (*Ravel*, 89–90). Ravel's treatment of the *schwas* in both works, however, echoes the nuanced approach outlined by Calvocoressi in reflecting the varying poetic stresses of his texts. By the time of *L'Heure espagnole*, he had developed a more complex notational rationale for the *schwas*; see pp. 114–17 below.

[41] Gribenski, '"Chanter comme des personnes naturelles"', 38, 43.

[42] Little, 'Discrepancies and consistencies among autograph manuscripts', 36, 39–46; Hurd, 'From a peacock to apocope', 57–60.

[43] Hurd, 'From a peacock to apocope', 67–9.   [44] *Ibid.*, 62.

'Dire, plutôt que chanter'

The verb *dire* (to speak or tell) occurs frequently in the context of French song performance around the turn of the century. Concert reviews often used it interchangeably with *chanter*: 'Mlle X a *dit* quelques mélodies . . .'. (This very literal dialogue of language and performance is a central theme of Katherine Bergeron's *Voice Lessons: French Mélodie in the Belle Époque*.) The interplay of *dire* and *chanter* is equally evident in several of Debussy's reflections on opera performance: 'In the opera house they sing *too much*', he insisted; 'One should *sing* only when it is worthwhile and hold moving lyrical expression in reserve.'[45] In rehearsal for *Pelléas*, he remonstrated with Jean Périer and Hector Dufranne (Pelléas and Golaud) when they insisted on singing 'at the tops of their voices' in the usual operatic manner,[46] explaining 'the characters try to sing like ordinary people, and not in an arbitrary language made up of outdated traditions'.[47]

Half a century later, Jane Bathori explained of *Histoires naturelles*, 'If you try *speaking* the words, without singing but in time, you will understand straight away what Ravel wanted.'[48] Similar emphases emerge from Ravel's own words on *Sur l'herbe*: 'In this piece, as in the *Histoires naturelles*, the impression must be given that one is almost not singing.'[49] He made his intentions explicit in *L'Heure espagnole*, setting them out on the verso facing the first page of music: 'Apart from the final Quintet, and, for the most part, the role of Gonzalve, who sings with an affected lyricism, [the performers should] *speak* rather than *sing* [*dire*, plutôt que *chanter*]'.

This shared concern for naturalistic text-setting and quasi-*parlando* performance echoes the composer whom both Debussy and Ravel acknowledged as a crucial influence: Modest Musorgsky. In a letter of July 1868, written as he was beginning work on both *Boris Godunov* and his song cycle *The Nursery*, Musorgsky explained:

This is what I would like: for my characters to speak onstage as living people speak, but in such a way that their essential nature and force of intonation, supported by an orchestra that forms a musical canvas for their speech, shall hit the target squarely. That is, my music must be the artistic reproduction of human speech in all its subtlest twistings.[50]

---

[45] Orledge, *Debussy and the Theatre*, 49.   [46] *Ibid.*, 63.

[47] 'Pourquoi j'ai écrit *Pelléas*', in Debussy, *Monsieur Croche et autres écrits*, 63. Mary Garden similarly recalled Debussy exhorting his cast to 'oubliez [. . .] que vous êtes chanteurs' (Garden and Biancolli, *Mary Garden's Story*, 64).

[48] Laurent, 'Jane Bathori, interprète de Ravel', 64.

[49] Letter to Jean-Aubry, in Orenstein (ed.), *Maurice Ravel: Songs, 1896–1914*, xiii.

[50] Letter dated 30 July 1868; Taruskin, *Musorgsky: Eight Essays and an Epilogue*, 74.

In two interviews and a letter to *Le Figaro*, all of which appeared shortly before the première of *L'Heure espagnole*, Ravel linked his opera with Musorgsky's uncompleted one-act setting of Nicolai Gogol's *Zhenit'ba* (*The Marriage*):

I have set myself the task of transcribing a literary work, granting to the music a humoristic and pictorial role. This experiment is rather new, I think. I am only aware of one similar attempt, that of Musorgsky in Gogol's *The Marriage*; even so, the Russian composer stopped himself midway through. . . *[51]

The other roles, I believe, will give the impression of being spoken. This is what Musorgsky had wanted to achieve in Gogol's *The Marriage*, which, by the way, he never completed.*[52]

Like its direct ancestor, Musorgsky's *The Marriage*, a faithful realisation of Gogol's play. . .*[53]

The Marriage – which Musorgsky had just abandoned when he wrote the letter quoted above – was described by its composer as 'an experiment in dramatic music in prose'.[54] It received a private performance in 1868 but was not published or publicly performed during the composer's lifetime. Musorgsky clearly felt that the portion he had completed served its purpose, which was, in his own words, as 'merely' a 'preparation' for *Boris Godunov*, developing a musical vocabulary for communicating Russian text in as naturalistic and expressive a manner as possible.[55] In their respective studies of the composer (1896 and 1908 respectively, translated here from the latter), Pierre d'Alheim and Michel-Dimitri Calvocoressi both reproduced a long letter written by Musorgsky to César Cui, explaining his vision for *The Marriage*:

All this first act is, in a word, an experiment in *opéra dialogué*. I have endeavoured, as much as possible, to notate clearly these changes of tone that come to the characters in the course of the dialogue, seemingly for the most trivial of reasons and on even the most insignificant words; it's here, in my opinion, that the power of Gogol's humour is concealed.[56]

D'Alheim probably also discussed *The Marriage* in the series of lecture-recitals on Musorgsky that he presented jointly with his wife, Marie d'Olénine, in Paris in February and March 1896. These well-publicised

[51] Tenroc, '*Thérèse et L'Heure Espagnole*'.   [52] Bizet, '*L'Heure espagnole*'.
[53] *Le Figaro*, 17 May 1911; *OL*, letter 84.
[54] This description appears above the first system on Musorgsky's manuscript (Calvocoressi, *Moussorgsky*, 166).
[55] Oldani, 'Musorgsky'.   [56] Calvocoressi, *Moussorgsky*, 165.

and enthusiastically received sessions were followed, over the next five years, by numerous performances of Musorgsky's music in the city's salons and concert halls.[57] Ravel must have attended at least some of these events, for after d'Alheim's death in 1922 he wrote to Olénine, 'The name of Pierre d'Alheim marks an important era in my life as a musician. I cannot forget the day, so long ago, when, with him, you came to reveal Musorgsky's music to us.'[58] Despite Ravel's presence at the d'Alheims' events and his friendship with the Russophile Calvocoressi, however, he could not have seen a score of *The Marriage* or heard any of it performed before he composed *L'Heure espagnole*: the opera was first published only in 1908 in an edition by Rimsky-Korsakov, its text printed only in Russian. An edition with French text, translated by Raoul d'Harcourt, followed in 1911. While Ravel undoubtedly knew of Musorgsky's intentions for *The Marriage*, therefore, he could not have seen how the composer realised them before he undertook his own *opéra dialogué*.[59]

Ravel's deliberate emphasis of the links between *L'Heure* and *The Marriage* in May 1911 seems in part a tactical move, motivated by professional as well as musical reasons. Around this time he was considering orchestrating Musorgsky's opera, which he discussed in a letter to Harcourt of 21 July 1911: 'I believe that we have already spoken of the orchestration of *The Marriage*. I still feel the same way about it, that is, I would willingly undertake this interesting work. For this I am awaiting the proposals of the publisher. As soon as we are in agreement, I will set to work.'[60] Was Ravel engaging in a bit of subtle advance publicity for his new project in his newspaper 'previews'? His repeated underlining of Musorgsky's failure to complete *The Marriage* seems to be laying the groundwork in this regard. Or was the explicit connection between his own opera and Musorgsky's designed to forestall any critics who might have levelled the familiar charges of a *manque d'originalité* at this, his most ambitious work to date?

---

[57] The fascinating story of the d'Alheims' championship of Musorgsky is recounted in Tumanov, *The Life and Artistry of Maria Olenina-d'Alheim*, and Olénine, *Concerts de 1912*, 34–50.

[58] *OL*, letter 195.

[59] Calvocoressi published a brief but detailed study of *The Marriage* on its 1908 publication. He noted in particular its rhythmic freedom and suggested that the only analogous treatment of rhythm he could think of – although realised with very different intent – was in Ravel's *Miroirs*. In a footnote, he adds that 'Maurice Ravel, in his *L'Heure espagnole*, now received by the Opéra-Comique, has applied a very precise, original and free declamation, which has numerous affinities with *The Marriage*. We should note, however, that *L'Heure espagnole* was completed well before the publication of *The Marriage*' (Calvocoressi, 'Le Mariage, par Moussorgsky', 1288).

[60] BnF Mus., LAS Ravel 105.

Whatever the case, it seems plausible that the descriptions of *The Marriage* that were widely available before the opera's publication may have helped to shape Ravel's aesthetic and compositional decisions in *L'Heure espagnole*. He may even have seen or read Gogol's play: in 1896, d'Alheim wrote that it had been 'translated several times into French and performed with some success in Paris a few years ago'.[61] Ravel's chosen libretto has a similarly witty, ironic tone to Musorgsky's; like *The Marriage* it is extremely funny, fast-paced and propelled by rapid exchanges of conversation. Both operas direct their narrative through naturalistic text-setting (with the naturalism often comically exaggerated), and both support the dialogue with rapidly shifting metres, tempi and phrase-lengths. Both scores, too, employ flexible patterns of accompaniment which, although colourful, are also tightly restrained, often dry or even brusque. Although he had not seen a score of *The Marriage*, it seems that Ravel was nevertheless able to deduce some of Musorgsky's compositional processes and techniques and adapt them to his own ends.

Perhaps the most significant distinction between the two operas, however, is that while Musorgsky never abandons this pure recitative and minimalistic accompaniment – thus taking his 'experiment' to its furthest conclusion – Ravel juxtaposes this with passages of richer, more developed accompaniment, drawing on dance rhythms, Spanish idioms and expressive orchestral timbres. In granting the voices occasional brief moments of lyricism, and in particular in the extravagant effusions of Gonzalve, he sets the otherwise dry and naturalistic conversation in humorous relief. This carefully constructed opposition becomes an important structural device in a work that was no unfinished 'experiment' but complete in itself, with a strong, coherent musical as well as dramatic narrative.

Despite Ravel's explicit acknowledgements, only one reviewer noted the Musorgskian resonances in *L'Heure espagnole*: 'G.', writing in the *Revue musicale*, observed briefly that '[Ravel's] style seems to have been inspired at once by Musorgsky and by Claude Debussy, although it differs appreciably from the latter.'[62] The perceptive Louis Laloy, although he did not mention Musorgsky, did note the relationship between Ravel's opera and the 'exquisite charm' of *Histoires naturelles* (which he had previously linked with Musorgsky's *The Nursery*[63]). One of Ravel's few early champions, Laloy could recognise in both works 'the gentle soul beneath the

---

[61] d'Alheim, *Moussorgski*, 105.   [62] 'G.', '*L'Heure espagnole*', 238.
[63] *Le Mercure musical*, 15 February 1907; Priest, *Louis Laloy*, 248.

surface irony'. 'This work [*L'Heure*] is much more significant', he went on: 'never has the composer showed himself more inventive, nor more the master of the genre he has made his own'.[64] On the other hand, at least two reviewers of *L'Heure* drew parallels with *Pelléas*, though both were quick to underline the different ends to which Ravel turned his naturalistic text-setting: Paul Souday noted that 'naturally everything is turned to comedy'*,[65] while Pierre Lalo, rudely and inexplicably, wrote that *L'Heure* resembled nothing so much as *Pelléas* played on a slowed-down gramophone.*[66]

The importance of what Musorgksy attempted in *The Marriage*, Debussy realised in *Pelléas*, and Ravel underlined in *L'Heure espagnole* lies not in the degree of meticulousness with which they set their respective texts but in the fact that they sustained their 'conversations in music' for the whole course of a work. If Musorgsky had pioneered a music that reproduced 'human speech in all its subtlest twistings', it was Debussy who had brought this quality to French opera for the first time. It seems likely that it was *Pelléas*, as much as *The Marriage*, that gave Ravel the confidence to write an opera in a single long burst of accompanied, naturalistic recitative, with no chorus, and without a single big set-piece aria. What Ravel took from Debussy's text-setting in *Pelléas*, then, was the confidence to apply a principle in a very different way, trusting in his own distinct compositional voice.

After *L'Heure*, and apart from his folksong settings of 1909–10, Ravel composed nothing new for the voice until his *Trois poèmes de Stéphane Mallarmé* of 1913 – this after some eighteen song-settings plus one completed and one half-sketched opera in the years 1903–7. *Histoires naturelles* and *L'Heure* seemed to have been an effective apogee, or endpoint, for his explorations of naturalistic text-setting: in his Mallarmé *Poèmes* Ravel would construct the vocal lines after a different set of parameters. More polyphonic in conception, the voice shares the melodic material with the instruments, its lines less 'spiky' and more fluid than those of *Histoires naturelles* and *L'Heure*. Yet, unobtrusively, they again mark out inherent melodic inflections and rhythmic emphases (the latter more regularised, after the greater rhythmic formality of Mallarmé's poems). The patterns of spoken language seem, by this time, to function as a fully integrated facet of Ravel's vocal writing, working in conjunction with the symbolic and evocative demands of the text. Much of *L'Enfant et les sortilèges* is

---

[64] *La Grande Revue*, 10 June 1911; Priest, *Louis Laloy*, 259–60.   [65] Souday, 'Les Premières'.
[66] Lalo, '*L'Heure espagnole*' (1911).

characterised by a similar approach to melodic design, where fluidity of line is melded with natural patterns of accentuation (the Princess's material, for example, and the Squirrel's). More explicit naturalism nevertheless remained a resource that Ravel could call upon when necessary, as in the Child's opening monologue (and later, more fleetingly, in the *Chansons madécasses*, around Fig. 1 of 'Nahandove' and Fig. 1^{+7} of 'Il est doux', for example). In his 1925 study of Ravel's vocal music, Arthur Hoérée observed this by-now intrinsic naturalistic sense. His conclusion, that Ravel's text-setting was, in technical terms, 'a model', and his prosody 'of a perfect exactitude [...] worthy of a detailed study in itself'*, would undoubtedly have startled Lalo, Sérieyx and the denizens of the Société nationale.[67]

---

[67] Hoérée, 'La Mélodie et l'œuvre lyrique', 61.

6 | 'This archaic attempt at a modern fantasy'

In February 1924, André Berge published an extended article on Franc-Nohain's poetry. He declared that fluidity, flexibility and a skilled insouciance – art concealing artistry – were key characteristics of Franc-Nohain's style:

His rhythm is certainly not commonplace, and the rhymes that he couples together sometimes have an air of being rather astonished to find themselves in such close proximity. [...] I don't really understand the laws of prosody that he observes: those that he does not observe would be easier to determine. [...] His form is both original and independent, and no less remarkably adroit: he has a consummate artistic understanding of how to juggle with irregular lines; he has found the rhythm that matches his thoughts, which are also irregular, light and fantastic. [...] What suppleness of language! and all this with a certain little air of carelessness, which is a particularly graceful effect.*[1]

Ravel, who would censure even Verlaine for compromising 'the rules and boundaries of a most precise and formal medium',[2] would undoubtedly have recognised the *métier* that underpins Franc-Nohain's 'insouciance'. The poet did not disregard formal constraints altogether: rather, like the composer, he manipulated them from the inside, turning classical concepts of rhythm and metre to his own expressive and satiric purposes. In the Foreword ('Avis au lecteur') to *L'Heure espagnole*, as it appeared in *La Revue de Paris* in November 1904, Franc-Nohain excused, with mock-humility, his departure from the 'rules' of French verse:

In lines naively adorned with hiatuses and equipped merely with assonances – like those of our old French epics – in short lines, for the most part – like those of our old farces – in lines of varied metre – like those of Amphitryon – I amused myself by creating this fable in dialogue, its humour suitably French, its garb arbitrarily Spanish. May the reader, accustomed to the meticulous euphony, the exact rhyme

---

[1] Berge, 'Un humoriste poète: Franc-Nohain', 637–9.
[2] Downes, 'Maurice Ravel, man and musician', *New York Times*, 7 August 1927; Orenstein (ed.), *A Ravel Reader*, 450.

and the invariable metre of the classical alexandrine, grant indulgence to this archaic attempt at a modern fantasy!'*[3]

In the final scene he draws our attention to his unconventional treatment of 'the laws of prosody' when he has Gonzalve observe that the five characters 'se servent pour leurs discours / Des vers tantôt longs, tantôt courts' ('avail themselves, for their speeches / Of lines sometimes long, sometimes short').[4] This ironic exposure of his own procedures is typically Ravelian.

Poetic rhythm and metre

L'Heure presents its bawdy, farcical narrative in the guise of classical verse-drama, its dialogue couched mostly in a mixture of octosyllables and alexandrines. The octosyllable, as Clair Tisseur observed in 1893, is 'the most convenient metre to handle, as it employs the maximum number of successive syllables without a caesura' (a mid-line respiration).[5] The octosyllable is thus characterised by a 'certain rapidity', making it particularly suitable to Franc-Nohain's fleet-footed text. One of the most popular of French poetic metres since the twelfth century, the medieval octosyllable was, in Tisseur's words, 'the narrative metre *par excellence* [. . .] the rhythm of tales of adventure and of love, of edifying, historic and didactic works'.[6] Georges Pellissier observed that between the thirteenth and the sixteenth centuries the octosyllable 'was the most popular form for satiric and allegorical poems', as well as for 'mysteries, moralities, farces [. . .] moreover, it was the favourite metre of fabulists; finally, it was employed for most didactic or moral poetry'.[7] All these descriptions resonate – satirically or otherwise – with *L'Heure espagnole*: as Louis Laloy wrote in his 1921 review, 'it was not for nothing that [Émile] Faguet compared [Franc-Nohain] to La Fontaine. The praise is merited. Come and hear *L'Heure espagnole*, this modern fable.'*[8]

The twelve-syllable alexandrine is a grander and more spacious poetic metre, one that had come to prominence in the sixteenth century (notably in

---

[3] 'Avis au lecteur', Foreword to *L'Heure espagnole*, *La Revue de Paris* 11/6 (15 November 1904), 405.
[4] Because of the flexibility of rhythm and accent intrinsic to the spoken language (as discussed in Chapter 5), French verse typically prioritises syllable count over metre. Successive lines may thus employ varying patterns of stresses, as long as a consistent number of syllables is maintained.
[5] Tisseur, *Modestes observations sur l'art de versifier*, 42.   [6] *Ibid.*, 40–1.
[7] Pellissier, *Traité théorique et historique de la versification française*, 39.
[8] Laloy, 'À l'Opéra: *L'Heure espagnole*'.

the poetry of Pierre de Ronsard) and subsequently remained the great metre of heroic or tragic poetry and drama. Tisseur wrote that the alexandrine bore 'the grandest harmony [and] the most solemn tread';[9] four years after the publication of his treatise, Edmond Rostand would employ alexandrine couplets for *Cyrano de Bergerac*. Yet the alexandrine had a comedic heritage too: with irony as deliberate as Franc-Nohain's, Molière's *Tartuffe* and *L'École des femmes* are couched in rhymed alexandrines (although other of his comedies, including *Le bourgeois gentilhomme* and *Le Médecin malgré lui*, are written in prose). Franc-Nohain's choices of metre, together with his 'Avis au lecteur', thus offer a mocking nod and a wink to literary tradition.

Most of the exchanges of dialogue in *L'Heure*, together with the longer speeches, are couched in octosyllables; alexandrines are often deployed for interpolations, together with deliberately 'poetic' or dramatic remarks. When Gonzalve, in particular, drops an ornate alexandrine (in Scene IV, for example, 'L'émail de ces cadrans dont s'orne ta demeure, / C'est le jardin de mon bonheur, émaillé d'heures' ('The enamel of these clock-faces that adorn your domain / Is the garden of my happiness, spangled with hours')), the satiric use of the 'heroic form' is plain. The exchange below, from Scene III, typifies Franc-Nohain's alternation of poetic metres, in which the alexandrine Concepcion employs for her deliberately stagey instructions to Ramiro follows the rapid octosyllabic lines spoken to herself ('Tout s'arrange fort bien ainsi'). That Ramiro caps her alexandrine with a couple of his own perhaps hints at their developing relationship: later in this chapter we'll see related examples of textual and poetic mirroring functioning as commentary on the characters and their actions.

> RAMIRO
> Il fallait oser, au contraire!
> Tout muletier a dans le cœur
> Un déménageur
> Amateur!
> Et voilà qui me va distraire
> En attendant votre mari.
>
> CONCEPCION
> Je suis confuse!
>
> RAMIRO
> Cela m'amuse!

---

[9] Tisseur, *Modestes observations sur l'art de versifier*, 73.

Concepcion, *à part*

Tout s'arrange fort bien ainsi!

(Haut à Ramiro, en lui montrant la porte à droite)

L'escalier est au fond du couloir que voici . . .   [alexandrine]

Vraiment, Monsieur, vraiment, j'abuse!

Ramiro

Mais non, je vous jure, mais non!

Trop heureux de trouver une occupation! . . .   [alexandrine]

C'est moi, señora, qui m'excuse:

Je fais si piètre mine, hélas!, dans un salon! . . .   [alexandrine]

Les muletiers n'ont pas de conversation.[10]   [alexandrine]

(The lines in italics are omitted in Ravel's setting.)

Within this loosely formal metric design, conversational exchanges are often given impetus and rhythmic variation by the division of eight- or twelve-syllable lines between two characters, or by local patterns of rhyme and assonance, which are visually emphasised, in the printed play, by offset lines (as in Ramiro's 'Tout muletier . . .' above). Rhyme schemes follow similarly flexible patterns, independent of individual speeches, so that rhyme-sounds bridge and leapfrog conversational exchanges. These interlocking rhymes serve as a binding device, providing continuity and smooth narrative progression. Ravel's score reflects such textual patterns in the mirroring of gestures and phrase-shapes across passages of dialogue, as in the imitative rising figures on the chime *abuse / excuse* of Example 6.1.

If Franc-Nohain's libretto is thus carefully ordered, listeners to Ravel's opera are for the most part unlikely to notice, for the vocal lines generally

Ex 6.1 *L'Heure espagnole*, Scene III

---

[10] [Ramiro] On the contrary, it must be dared! / Every muleteer is, at heart / An amateur / Removalist! / And this will keep me occupied / While waiting for your husband / [Concepcion, aside] Everything is working out perfectly! / [aloud, to Ramiro, indicating the door at right] The stair is beyond the passage there / Truly, Monsieur, I'm exploiting you! / [Ramiro] *But no, I swear, not at all! / Too happy to find something to do!* / It's I, señora, who must beg your pardon / I cut a sorry figure in a salon, alas! / Muleteers have no conversation.

Ex. 6.2 *L'Heure espagnole*, Scene I

emphasise not the relatively regular poetic cadences, but the flexible ones of spoken French. If this practice might seem almost counter-intuitive – perhaps an ironic sort of double-bluff – in fact the formality of Franc-Nohain's text (and the informal manner in which Ravel set it) serves several important musical purposes. The poetry provides a structural reference point in an opera that consists mostly of rapid exchanges of 'naturalistic' dialogue, accompanied by orchestral fragments and inter-jections: no matter how irregular the setting, its patterns nevertheless register in the listener's ear, making it easier to follow the narrative. The design of the text also enabled Ravel to juxtapose lines that prioritise flexible spoken rhythms with others that follow the more regular tread of poetic metre, a technique he employs with deliberate dramatic effect. In Ramiro's 'Si le monstre par la montre fut arrêté, / C'est à présent la montre qui s'arrête', for example (Ex. 6.2), expressive accents and rhythms that draw out the mirrored *mon-* sounds of the alexandrine give way to prosaic and regular sextuplets, emphasised by the composer's direction *simplement*.

Shaping the libretto

'*L'Heure espagnole*, or "the hour of the muleteer", as the Spaniards say, is Franc-Nohain's comedy exactly as it was staged at the Odéon; apart from a few cuts, nothing has been changed', said Ravel in his *avant-première* letter to *Le Figaro*.[11] In fact, the cuts he made to the play were quite extensive: only three of the twenty-one scenes escaped unamended (IV, VI and XVIII); a third of the lines in the first scene are excised, and more than half of Scene XI. Ravel's cuts typically serve to compress and focus the action, as demonstrated here in the dramatic conclusion to Scene I (the cut lines shown here in italics):

[11] *OL*, letter 84.

RAMIRO

Alors que le taureau fonçait,
Et son ventre allait défoncer,
Cette montre, dans [en] son gousset,
Le préserva du coup du corne.
Vous en remarquerez la trace.

TORQUEMADA

En vérité!
Blessure de combat, ce coup de corne l'orne:
C'est une héroïque beauté.

RAMIRO

Mais *si la redoutable bête,*
Si le monstre par la montre fut arrêté,
Par un retour immérité,
C'est à présent la montre qui s'arrête.

TORQUEMADA

Nous allons donc la démonter.[12]

Even though Ravel deprived himself here of a nice play on words (*fonçait/ défoncer*) and some pleasing assonances ('coup de corne l'orne'), his cuts serve to focus musical, poetic and narrative structure, as well as to depict Ramiro's prosaic manner. The line 'Alors que le taureau fonçait' is the narrative crux of the passage: as it is overtaken by the orchestral climax, the audience must hold its breath and wait to hear just what happened 'as the bull charged'. 'Et son ventre allait défoncer' embellishes without advancing the tale: by substituting five bars of extravagant orchestral pictorialism, Ravel obviates the need for the line to be voiced. Meanwhile, the omission of intermediate rhyme-sounds emphasises the chime of those that remain, and the compression of Ramiro's anticlimactic 'Mais si le monstre' (Ex. 6.2 above) from a quatrain to a concise couplet draws the listener's ear to its assonances and mirrored meanings.

Brief consideration of several of Ravel's other cuts helps to illuminate his narrative focus. In Scene II, he omitted one of Torquemada's only long speeches, compressing the exchange that precedes it to Ramiro's simple 'Comment?':

---

[12] [Ramiro] As the bull charged / *And would have stove in his stomach* / This watch, in his fob pocket / Saved him from the horn's impact / *You will see the marks on it.* / [*Torquemada*] *Truly!* / *A combat wound, the impact of the horn adorns it* / *With heroic beauty.* / [Ramiro] But if *the redoubtable beast* / If the bull was stopped by the watch / *In an undeserved reversal,* / Now it's the watch that has stopped. / [Torquemada] / Let's open it up, then.

TORQUEMADA

Mais quelle heure est-il donc?

CONCEPCION

Trois heures!

TORQUEMADA

Sapristi!
Trois heures! comme le temps passe! . . .
Si j'avais su . . .

RAMIRO

L'excuse est farce:
Horloger, ignorer l'heure! . . .

TORQUEMADA

Vous en doutiez!
Mais c'est la conséquence inhérente au métier:
Voit-on jamais le pâtissier
Manger ses tartes et ses glaces ?
Et les gens qui vont à la chasse
Ont souvent horreur du gibier!
Si vous saviez combien, à la longue, rebute
La contemplation de l'heure et des minutes! . . .
Les horloges, Monsieur, on n'entend plus leurs coups:
Ce serait à devenir fou![13]

In a typical *opéra comique* we might imagine that this passage would naturally offer itself for an opening 'character' aria: after the initial exchange of dialogue, the music proper would get underway here. Not so in *L'Heure espagnole*. The libretto's rapid progression and Ravel's conversational text-setting underlie his decision not to set this passage: why should the clock-maker, rushing out the door, stop to sing an aria about his situation in life?

Another excision, in Scene VIII, provided the composer with an opportunity to emphasise a naughty double entendre:

---

[13] [Torquemada] But what time is it, then? / [Concepcion] Three o'clock. / [Torquemada] Heavens! / *Three o'clock? How time flies!* / *If I had known . . .* / [Ramiro] *What a comical excuse:* / *A clockmaker unaware of the time!* / [Torquemada] *You might well think so!* / *But it's an inevitable consequence of the job:* / *Do we see the baker* / *Eating his tarts and his icing?* / *And those who love to hunt* / *Often have a horror of game!* / *If you knew how much, over time, discourages* / *The contemplation of the hours and the minutes* / We no longer hear the clocks, sir, / *That way madness lies!*

Ex. 6.3 *L'Heure espagnole*, Scene VIII

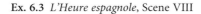

INIGO
Monsieur est homme expert à son métier!
Et faut-il que vous me quittiez ?

CONCEPCION, *à Inigo*
Non, je ne serais pas tranquille:
Le mécanisme est très fragile,
Et notamment le balancier;
J'ai besoin de tout surveiller . . .
Je demande pardon à Votre Seigneurie! . . .[14]

Ravel's tempo indications, his replacement of Concepcion's penultimate line with a suggestive ellipsis, and her hasty exit (the last few lines of the scene are also omitted) all combine to give the audience just enough time to absorb her meaning before she disappears (Ex. 6.3).

Meanwhile, in the last scene of the opera, Ravel substantially compressed the exchange which, in the play, follows Ramiro's easy extraction of Inigo from his clock: omitting Torquemada's request that Ramiro carry Gonzalve's and Inigo's clocks home for them ('Accept this ducat for your inconvenience!', declares Inigo, 'Accept this half-ducat', mutters Gonzalve), he moves straight to the clockmaker's expression of regret that Concepcion will be bereft of a clock in her bedroom. Ravel presumably considered that this entertaining exchange could diffuse the tightly focussed narrative: the dramatic action effectively ends with Ramiro's last display of strength, and all that remains to be done is comment on it. Thus, beneath the circumscribed dialogue, he sets the habanera rhythms of the

---

[14] [Inigo] *The gentleman is an expert at his job!* / And must you leave me? / [Concepcion] *No, I wouldn't be easy:* / The mechanism is most fragile / Particularly the pendulum / *I must keep an eye on everything* / I demand Your Lordship's pardon!

final quintet in motion, ensuring that there is no relinquishing of musical tension as the penultimate orchestral climax (the *fortissimo* glissandi that depict with bouffish precision the unsuccessful attempts to pull the banker from his clock) leads directly into the work's culmination.

It is easy to justify excisions such as these after the event, with the opera now better-known than the original play, and recognised as a coherent and independent entity. Nevertheless, the sorts of cuts Ravel made to Franc-Nohain's text are manifestly consistent in character and intent: allowing the most active, purposeful lines to remain, he reduced descriptive passages, omitted lines that reiterate or elaborate information already conveyed, and focussed speeches towards important rhyme-sounds and plays on words.[15] His cuts streamline the narrative of a script much wordier than most operatic libretti, making it more comprehensible when sung, and better-suited to cogent musical structuring.

Text and character

In an interview published in *Comœdia* shortly before the 1911 première, Ravel briefly delineated his procedures for dealing with Franc-Nohain's text:

> Frankly comic, with a deliciously dry wit, it has become a musical fantasy, something in the manner of the Italian *opera buffa* tradition. I have followed the conversation precisely, the emphatic or caricatured declamation of the characters; I have linked the melodic patterns to the words. I have confined myself to underlining the comic dialogue, and replaced lyricism with atmosphere, in the orchestral rejoinders and in the exaggeration of the burlesque.*[16]

As Ravel's distinction here between 'emphatic' and 'caricatured' declamation suggests, one of his primary compositional challenges was not merely to craft melodic lines that sounded natural and conversational, but to use those lines to create five individually convincing personages. While none of the characters 'sing' the orchestral motifs that typically accompany their entrances and exits (as Chapter 8 explores), their individuality is nevertheless asserted in the vocal lines themselves.

Ravel took his cue from Franc-Nohain's words: each character has different verbal tics or characteristics that inflect the melodic and rhythmic patterns of their dialogue. Torquemada's conversation is marked by the relative proliferation of dark, or 'back', vowel sounds, such as [o], [u], [ɔ]

---

[15] Concerning the omission of Gonzalve's Scene XV monologue, see p. 183 and Huebner, 'La Grivoiserie moderne', 201.

[16] Tenroc, '*Thérèse* et *L'Heure Espagnole*'; *OL*, 587n3.

and the nasal [ɑ̃]: 'Je c<u>ou</u>rs, m<u>on</u> cher M<u>on</u>sieur, je c<u>ou</u>rs'. His dark vowels are reflected in his musical portrayal: the slow tempi that accompany his entrances, for example, and the mellow string colours of his accompaniment. Although he is rather mannered in his declamation, he is also oddly unself-conscious and laconic in his delivery. His slow tempi, as well as giving time to let his dark vowels roll out, also suggest that the clockmaker enjoys the sound of his own voice; they may equally imply that his thought processes are a little laborious. (Maurice Grammont notes that the 'dark vowels' are particularly suited to expressing heaviness and languor.[17])

  Inigo's words make more caricatured play of vowel colours, and his Scene IX monologue in particular is full of amusingly overlapping word-sounds: the [ɑ̃] vowel of *t<u>an</u>t*/*inst<u>an</u>t*/*f<u>an</u>tasque*, the [a] of *f<u>oi</u>*/*conç<u>oi</u>s*, the [ɔ] of *dér<u>o</u>ge*/*pr<u>o</u>jet*/*h<u>o</u>rloge*, the [e] of *dérog<u>e</u>*/*cach<u>e</u>r*/*l<u>e</u>s*/*horlog<u>e</u>rs*, and the [ʒ] of *<u>j</u>e*/*déro<u>g</u>e*/*pro<u>j</u>et*/*horlo<u>g</u>e*/*horlo<u>g</u>ers* (the voiced equivalent of the unvoiced [ʃ] of *ca<u>ch</u>er*).

> Tant pis, ma foi, si je déroge !
> Je conçois à l'instant le fantasque projet
> De me cacher
> Dans cette horloge :
> Ces horloges sont les placards des horlogers.[18]

The interlocking assonances are reflected in Ravel's setting: the words that precede this passage are less regular in their rhythms and assonances, and are set to naturalistic recitative. 'Tant pis. . .' begins a new musical paragraph, where, against the orchestra's ungainly waltz, Ravel sets much of the text in quadruplet and quintuplet crotchets (see Ex. 8.4). The combination of cross-rhythms and tight-packed verbal assonances gives a vivid aural picture of Inigo contorting himself musically to fit the waltz-rhythms, just as he must physically squeeze himself into his clock (Louis Laloy noted this as a passage in which 'the music mocks both the subject and itself'[19]). The word *horloge* serves here as what Grammont termed *l'insistence*, and Dell H. Hymes a 'summative word':[20] it combines several of the vowel and consonant sounds emphasised in the surrounding lines, expresses the principal idea or reference point of the paragraph (and of course the opera), and, being placed at the end of the passage and effectively heard three times, has a culminating dramatic effect.

---

[17] Grammont, *Le Vers français*, 274–5.

[18] Too bad, in truth, if I'm demeaning myself! / I've just had the marvellous idea / To conceal myself / In this clock: / Clocks are the clockmaker's cupboards.

[19] *La Grande revue*, 10 June 1911; Priest, *Louis Laloy*, 259.

[20] Grammont, *Le Vers français*, 226–7; Hymes, 'Phonological aspects of style', 109–31, discussed by Bowie in *Mallarmé and the Art of Being Difficult*, 57.

Ex. 6.4 *L'Heure espagnole*, Scene XII

Inigo often ends his phrases with an upward jump of a fourth, fifth or even sixth (especially in his early scenes). This characteristic amplifies his ridiculous appearance: it is mannered and unattractively coquettish. A particularly flirtatious or fanciful sally is often punctured by a more prosaic melodic line ending with a descending inflection, as in Example 6.4 below. He tends to repeat himself, enjoys long words and involved periods – 'Mon œil anxieux interroge, / Mélancolique, l'horizon' ('My anxious eye scans, / Melancholic, the horizon') – and is fond of subjunctives: 'Car il est raisonnable, il est juste, il est bon / Que l'époux ait dehors une occupation / Régulière et périodique' ('For it is reasonable, fair and good / That the husband has an occupation / Settled and regular'). Textual contrasts in Don Inigo's speech are local: when he tries to be romantic, his poetic rhythms seem to totter beneath his weight, landing him heavily back in officious-sounding patter. Thus the cadences and alliteration evident in Example 6.4 – 'Oui, fou de toi, ô ma jolie. / Fou à faire mille folies!' ('Yes, crazy for you, oh my pretty one / Crazily ripe for a thousand follies!') – collapse into the multi-syllabic, rattling rhythms of the succeeding couplet, 'Ceci n'est qu'un commencement, / Un tout petit exercice d'entraînement!' ('This is just the beginning / A little training exercise'), a shift in character emphasised in Ravel's setting.

Ex. **6.5** *L'Heure espagnole*, Scene VIII

Ramiro's language, by contrast is generally prosaic, employing clear-cut consonants, 'masculine' rhymes and mono- or disyllables. The extract below, from Scene VIII (Ex. 6.5), shows a play of sibilants (*ça/c'est/ces*), plosive *p* and *pl-* sounds (*plus/plume/poids*) and [y] and [ɛ] vowels, in a way that suggests itself as a key 'characterising' text, in much the same manner as Inigo's Scene IX monologue ('Tant pis. . .') above:

> Mais ça n'en est pas plus ardu. . .
> C'est moins le poids, ces objets-là, que le volume;
> Car, pour le poids, c'est un fétu,
> C'est une plume ! . . .[21]

Ramiro's solidity and brusque energy are here evoked in a text that is mostly monosyllabic, with distinctive consonants falling on stressed syllables (in both text and music) that provide definition and emphasis. Such patterns of assonance are important not just in musical and textual terms, but in their implications for performance: they suggest ways of using the voice, the face and the body to communicate text and character. The comically exaggerated gestures into which Inigo's monologue lures the performer's face could serve, for example, as a basis for gestural characterisation throughout the opera. The repeated *p* sounds in Ramiro's text here likewise draw the mouth and face into very distinctive shapes and rhythms: the classic French shrug is typically accompanied by the shape of an unvoiced *p*, formed in the mouth and cheeks. This is a real Parisian *ouvrier* gesture – and Ravel tells us (in the *Comœdia* interview) that Jean Périer played Ramiro with a 'boulevard de Villette' (Parisian working-class) accent.[22]

Ramiro is the only character to develop across the course of the opera, as he is gradually seduced by the clockmaker's wife and begins to wonder what his life might be like, 'were [he] not a muleteer'. Thus, in his two

---

[21] But that won't make it more arduous. . . / It's less the weight, with these things, than the volume; / As for the weight, it's a wisp of straw, / It's a feather!

[22] Tenroc, '*Thérèse et L'Heure Espagnole*'; *OL*, 587n3.

soliloquies (Scenes X and XVI; the latter is reproduced below), Ramiro explores longer, more flexible and more expressive lines, where whole words, concepts and phrases are repeated and echoed.

Voilà ce que j'appelle une femme charmante ! . . .
[. . .]
M'avoir si gentiment ce labeur ménagé,
Tantôt emménager, tantôt déménager !
Voilà ce que j'appelle une femme charmante ! . . .
Et puis cette boutique est un plaisant séjour:
Entre chaque montée, après chaque descente,
  Nul importun, par ses discours,
N'y vient troubler ma quiétude nonchalante. . .
  Rien à dire, rien à penser :
  On n'a qu'à se laisser bercer
Au tic tac régulier de ces balanciers ! . . .
[. . .]
  Si je devais mon sort changer,
N'étais-je muletier, je serais horloger,
Dans cette horlogerie, avec cette horlogère. . .[23]

In *Le Vers français*, Maurice Grammont observed that the repetition of words and word-sounds can be used to create an effect of stasis, or of 'an infinite succession'.[24] Ramiro's lines here depict him suspended in a dream of 'what might have been', prolonging the moment as long as he can.

The muleteer's vocal lines echo the qualities of his text: the most deliberately 'natural' of the five voices, he has little in the way of extreme registers, intervals and musical mannerisms. In fact, his voice comes closest to the natural inflections of Ravel's own: the fourths and fifths that end many of his phrases corroborate Émile Vuillermoz's recollection of the composer's mordantly humorous sallies that typically ended with the 'abrupt' inflection of a falling fourth.[25] These descending intervals, evident in Example 6.5 above, give Ramiro's speech a resolute and matter-of-fact character. In his two monologues, however, the muleteer has more rising

---

[23] That's what I call a charming woman! . . . / [. . .] / To have so kindly provided me with this household task / Sometimes to move things in, sometimes to move them out! / That's what I call a charming woman! . . . / Moreover, this shop is a pleasant destination: / Between each ascent, after each descent, / Nobody bothering me with speeches / Intrudes on my relaxed silence. . . / Nothing to say, nothing to think; / One can just allow oneself to be rocked / By the regular tick-tock of these pendulums! . . . / [. . .] / If I had to change my fate, / Were I not a muleteer, I would be a clockmaker, / In this clock shop, with this clockmaker's wife. . .

[24] Grammont, *Le Vers français*, 211–12. [25] Vuillermoz, 'L'Œuvre de Maurice Ravel', 59–60.

inflections, both mid-phrase and at phrase-ends, and his tessitura expands, covering a twelfth ($b\flat$ to f'). These qualities emphasise the more fanciful, exploratory character of his words and, set against his normal commonplace manner, deepen our understanding of his character.

Gonzalve's language is more colourful and more consciously (and conventionally) poetic than anybody else's. He too juggles with repeated words and word-sounds, in much more obvious, exaggerated ways than his colleagues: 'Ton cœur ballant, ton cœur battant' (Scene IV), 'Au rythme qui se casse, à la rime cocasse' (Scene XXI) and 'De sapin, de chêne ou de cèdre?' (Scene VI), whose sibilants are immediately echoed in Concepcion's 'Oui, c'est fou, je te le concède, mais cède!' (Ravel emphasises the near-homonyms *cèdre* and *cède* with *portamenti*.) Flamboyantly disregarding the famous Mallarméen dictum not to name the thing but evoke it, Gonzalve almost always names his subject first, before embroidering it with metaphors and similes: 'L'émail de ces cadrans dont s'orne ta demeure, / C'est le jardin de mon bonheur, émaillé d'heures' ('The enamel of these clock-faces that ornament your domain / Is the garden of my happiness, spangled with hours'). His analogies, although picturesque, are often less inspired than comically obvious (ticking clock as heartbeat, enclosing clock as coffin). While this might be read, as Steven Huebner argues, as deliberate exposure of Symbolist metaphor,[26] it equally seems to lampoon poetic extravagance and mediocrity of a more generic type (and Gonzalve's lament on entering his clock in Scene VI – 'Il me plaît de franchir ton seuil, / Entre ces planches clos, comme dans un cercueil' ('It pleases me to cross your threshold / Between these closed boards, as if in a coffin') – is perhaps closer to the Baudelaire of 'La Mort des amants' than it is to Mallarmé). As Chapter 9 explores, the empty derivativeness of Gonzalve's poetry is mirrored in his music, the most conventionally 'operatic' of the five characters, with its extravagantly wide intervals (many of his effusions begin with ostentatious octave leaps) and mannered 'Spanish' turns.

Concepcion, alone of all the characters, generally speaks rapidly, her phrases, in Ravel's setting, mostly based on small intervals (seconds, thirds, repeated pitches), with occasional 'spikes' – sudden upward or downward jumps of a fifth or sixth – that suggest irritability. On her first appearance, Concepcion's words, edgy and irascible, emphasise plosives and fricatives, percussive consonant sounds that can effectively be spat out. Her spiteful aside about Torquemada's physical capacities, for example, juggles the

---

[26] Huebner, 'La Grivoiserie moderne de Ravel', 205. All quotations from this article are taken from Huebner's original English text (personal communication, 6 June 2013).

consonants [v] and [m] and the incisive vowels [ã] (*en*), [a] (*avare*), [e] (*avez*) and [u] (*vous*), again adding an additional layer of aural characterisation through evocative patterns of alliteration and assonance (see Ex. 9.4a):

De force musculaire, oui, vous avez sujet
De vous montrer avare, ou, du moins, ménager :
        Vous n'en avez pas à revendre !²⁷

Concepcion is quick-witted and quick-spoken and manifests more varied and passionate emotional responses than anyone else. Perhaps as a result, the character, assonances and rhythms of her text are mutable, adapting themselves to her mood and sparring partner. With Ramiro, she tends to speak in short and generally straightforward phrases, less metred than when she is with Gonzalve. In Scenes IV, V and VI, she matches her language to the latter's extravagant poeticising, capping alexandrine with alexandrine, echoing assonances and employing poetic similes and more ornate grammatical constructions. In vivid contrast to her earlier rapid-fire consonants, in the passage below the [l] and [n] consonants suggest a lengthening of their accompanying vowel-sounds:

        Oui, mon ami. . . Dépêchons-nous !
Ne perdons pas, à de vaines paroles
        L'heure qui s'envole,
        Et qu'il faut cueillir.²⁸

There is also a neat contradiction implicit between the languorous sounds of her words and their imperative meanings, a quality echoed and ironically subverted in Ravel's score. As Jessie Fillerup observes, the dialogue in Scene IV juxtaposes conflicting tempi (Concepcion repeatedly attempting to hurry Gonzalve along, the poet continually slipping back to a languid *Lent*) that underline 'the characters' [. . .] inability to communicate with each other'.²⁹

For Inigo, Concepcion has few words to offer: most of her lines to him are brief admonitions. Her responses to Gonzalve also become increasingly brusque, her language separating itself from his as she physically rejects him. The contrast between words that mould themselves around those of

---

²⁷ For muscular strength, you have grounds indeed / To show yourself miserly, or, at least, to be economical: / You don't have any of it to spare!
²⁸ Yes, my friend. . . Let us hurry! / Let us not waste in useless words / The hour that is flying / And must be plucked.
²⁹ Fillerup, 'Purloined poetics', 204; see also p. 180 below.

her companions, and those that set in rude relief their linguistic mannerisms (Inigo's wordiness, Gonzalve's extravagance), is a subtle structural
effect woven into Franc-Nohain's language. Concepcion's textual flexibility
accords with her dramatic importance, for she is the lynchpin of her opera,
the central dramatic force who determines (or tries to) the course of the
narrative. As Chapter 9 explores, this textual quality found equivalence in
her musical portrayal, leading Christine Souillard to describe the operatic
Concepcion as 'an image, a phantasm present in the [musical] language of
each [of her suitors]'.[30]

Naturalism, comedy and rigour – and the mute *e* again

That the plasticity of French poetic rhythm and metre can provoke confusion elsewhere on the continent is typified by Richard Strauss's bewildered response to *Pelléas et Mélisande*: as he wrote to Romain Rolland,
'Yesterday I read through Debussy's *Pelléas et Mélisande* again, and I am
once more very uncertain about the principles of French declamation
when sung. Thus, on page 113, I found "CheVEUX, CHEveux, DE
cheveux". For heaven's sake, I ask you, of these three ways there can
really only be *one* which is right.'[31] But, as Rolland explained, 'the great
difficulty with our language is that for a very large number of words,
accentuation is variable – never arbitrary, but in accordance with logical
or psychological reasons. When you say to me: ". . . Of these 3 (cheveux)
only one can be right", what you say is doubtless true of German, but not
of French.'[32]

If Strauss ever studied the score of *L'Heure espagnole*, he would have
observed Ravel variously accentuating *hor-LOGE* and *HOR-loge*, *MU-le-
tier* and *mu-le-TIER*, according to character, mood and tempo. He might
also have noticed that, in just the first scene of the opera, the word *montre*
appears variously set to a single note, two separate notes and two tied notes.
As he had done in *Histoires naturelles*, in *L'Heure espagnole* Ravel allowed
most of the mute *e*s to be apocopated, or barely voiced. He gave careful
thought to varying shades of pronunciation and emphasis, employing five
different ways of setting the syllables linked to a *schwa* (the neutral vowel;
see p. 89). These are set out below (Ex. 6.6), using that flexible word *montre*

---

[30] Souillard, 'Commentaire littéraire et musical', 88.
[31] Letter dated 2 August 1905; Strauss and Rolland, *Correspondance*, 53.
[32] Letter dated 9 August 1905; Strauss and Rolland, *Correspondance*, 55–6.

Ex. 6.6 Variant notations for mute *es*

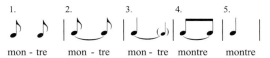

as an example: (1) two individual notes; (2) notes tied but not beamed together; (3) a note tied to a small note-head, which may be parenthesised (this notation is used only a handful of times); (4) notes tied and beamed together; (5) a single note.[33]

In *Histoires naturelles*, Ravel had relied for the most part on just two notations, those of categories (2) and (5) above; notation type (4), which is by far the most frequently employed for the *schwas* of *L'Heure espagnole*, appears on just six occasions in the song cycle. His distinction between two main notational forms in *Histoires naturelles* is principally designed to allow for the aural and vocal qualities of different word-sounds. Hard final consonants like *-ique*, *-ale*, *-ade*, *-ite* and *-ose* are more likely to be set to a single note, particularly at the end of a line, while softer word-sounds such as *-re*, *-lle*, *-ne*, *-me* and *-ge*, which need more time for enunciation, generally receive tied notes: as Jane Bathori explained, 'he wanted singers to suppress the pronunciation of the mute *es* almost completely, while at the same time retaining their rhythmic value'.[34]

The more flexible notation of *L'Heure espagnole* expands this delineation of unvoiced and partly voiced *schwas* to a more complex hierarchy of spoken articulation: the *schwa* is clearly voiced when notated as in category (1) above, unvoiced when notated as in category (5), and part-voiced for categories (2), (3) and (4). The published orchestral score suggests a further subtle distinction between categories (2) and (4). The vocal score shows syllables in both categories separated by hyphens wherever space allows. The orchestral score maintains this underlay for syllables in category (2), but frequently prints syllables in category (4) conjointly beneath the first note of the pair, even where hyphenated syllables would fit easily. Although inconsistently realised, it could be hypothesised that this distinction in the underlay between beamed and separate notes was intended as a deliberate

---

[33] Hurd explores some of these notational issues ('From a peacock to apocope', 38–49, 57–66), but does not delineate a clear rationale for Ravel's usage, instead concluding (49) that 'the supposedly scrupulous Ravel was surprisingly unspecific in detailing the execution of his notation in these two works [*Histoires* and *L'Heure*]'. See also note 40 to Chapter 5 above.

[34] Laurent, 'Jane Bathori, interprète de Ravel', 64.

clarification, indicating that the *e* as notated in category (2) is fractionally more articulated than that of category (4).[35]

In *Histoires naturelles* Ravel was setting prose-poems, ungoverned by the conventions of poetic rhythm and metre. In *L'Heure espagnole*, however, he was dealing with a text of a more formal design, of regularised line-lengths and meticulous arrangements of rhythm and rhyme. How did the composer who took Gounod to task for 'damaging' classical verse (see p. 78) reconcile Franc-Nohain's textual rigour (and his occasional deliberate abandonment of it) and his own strictures on text-setting with his goal of conversational, naturalistic declamation, and the intrinsic flexibility of the language? The answer seems to lie in that diverse array of notational resources. In Ravel's score, where mute *es* count towards syllable tallies they tend to be articulated (even if only lightly), and when they do not (at line-ends and caesurae) they are usually elided, apocopated or barely voiced. Thus, in Torquemada's Scene II alexandrine 'Les horloges, monsieur, on n'entend plus leurs coups:', the word *horloges* is articulated as three syllables (and three notes), while a few bars later, in the octosyllables 'Si vous croyez que c'est léger, / Une horloge, et facile à prendre!', *horloge* receives two syllables and two notes. Inigo's waltz in Scene IX (see Ex. 8.4) similarly varies the notation of *horloge* according to its poetic emphasis: when it ends a line ('De me cacher dans cette horloge') the second syllable is set to a single minim, but where it falls mid-line ('Ces horloges sont les placards des horlogers.') it receives two tied crotchets.

While syllable tallies were thus clearly an important consideration, Ravel's notational variety suggests that other musical and poetic concerns also shaped this differentiated treatment of the mute *e*. Purely musical and practical issues of rhythmic definition, legibility and clarity of articulation are naturally of the first importance, but his notation also varies according to the expressive and dramatic context. Within a passage of dialogue, rhyme-sounds and patterns of assonance are likely to be notated in the same way (as in the chime *abuse/excuse* of Ex. 6.1 above); again this relates to the varying length and emphasis of final consonant sounds. Vocal tessitura and the direction of a melodic line also play a part: ascending or questioning phrases are more likely to articulate or half-articulate the *schwa* than are decisive descending phrases. Example 6.2 above

---

[35] There are very few hyphens in Ravel's orchestral manuscript because there was no space to fit them in. Those that do appear are most commonly found between bars or under longer notes; they always fall between articulated syllables and never precede a mute *e*. Ravel occasionally pencilled lines from syllables to notes to clarify the underlay; otherwise he trusted the engraver to work out which syllable belonged under which note.

demonstrates this, with the varied setting of the word *montre* (set first as a pair of tied notes and then as two separate notes) principally determined by Ramiro's transition from dramatic storytelling (in alexandrines) to prosaic explanation. In Scene XIX, Inigo laments 'Et personne pour me haler!... Personne!...': the first instance of *personne*, where it forms part of an octosyllable, notates *-sonne* as a pair of tied and beamed quavers, while the repetition gives just a single plaintive quaver. Gonzalve fully articulates the *schwas* in his opening serenade, but when he slips back into a more conversational manner the final syllables of *poétique, musique* and *sérénade*, all falling at line-ends, receive only a single syllable. Concepcion articulates more *schwas* when she is conversing with the declamatory Gonzalve than she does with the matter-of-fact Ramiro. Complex and nuanced, Ravel's notational rationale was thus carefully considered and meticulously applied.

'A most precise and formal medium'

In 1911, Émile Vuillermoz remarked that the characteristic inflections of Ravel's own voice could be heard in the utterances of the five characters of *L'Heure espagnole*.[36] Nearly three decades later, he would make the same claim, in the 1939 collection *Maurice Ravel par quelques-uns de ses familiers*. Linking *Histoires naturelles* with *L'Heure*, in the latter essay he wrote of Ravel 'seeking to liberate French lyric prosody', and 'daring to challenge' 'arbitrary vocal conventions'.[37] Despite the outrage his prosodic 'audacities' provoked, Vuillermoz wrote, Ravel 'would not deviate an inch from the path that he had chosen, for when something appeared to him to be logical and correct, he was prepared to fight to the death for it'.[38]

Despite their shared content, the tone of Vuillermoz's 1911 appraisal was quite different: far from being whole-heartedly admiring of the composer's meticulous skill in realising his characters, Vuillermoz was highly dubious about the value and implications of this naturalistic text-setting:

The music is wedded to the melodic contours of the words with a fatiguing servility, reproducing the verbal inflections with excessive humility. [...] If this fashion for tracing the words in music catches on, logically we will find ourselves with as many different sorts of prosody as there are French provinces, the melodic curve of a *marseillaise* invective being essentially different from that of a Norman

[36] Vuillermoz, 'Les Théâtres: *L'Heure espagnole*', 68.
[37] Vuillermoz, 'L'Œuvre de Maurice Ravel', 59–60; see p. 111 above.   [38] *Ibid.*, 58–61.

epithet. [...] In listening to a 'quasi parlando' recitative we will know at once whether the composer is from Toulouse, or if he first saw the light of day at Lons-le-Saunier!*[39]

Vuillermoz's reshaping of his observations in the 1939 *tombeau* volume echoes the changing perceptions of Ravel's technique and style already observed in the pre- and post-war responses to *L'Heure*, and in Arthur Hoérée's 1925 emphasis of the 'perfect exactitude' of Ravel's text-setting (quoted on p. 00). In his 1939 essay, an extended study of Ravel's work and style, we see Vuillermoz seeking to define the composer's legacy of modernity and innovation.

Rather surprisingly, Alfred Bruneau's otherwise negative review of the 1911 *L'Heure espagnole* offered a more nuanced reflection on Ravel's text-setting, recognising that, while the dialogue of four of the five characters was essentially naturalistic, Ravel's recitative nevertheless moulds itself slightly differently around each of them: 'The freedom of [Ravel's] writing here becomes an anarchy that often crosses the limits. But we must note the clear and differentiated portrayals of each of the characters, the exactitude with which they, abandoning [conventional operatic] syllabic or melodic procedures, reproduce the multiple inflections of ordinary language.'*[40] The interviews Ravel gave before the première, together with his explanatory letter to *Le Figaro*, again underline the importance he placed on getting text right, in musical terms:

The French language has its accents and musical inflections, just as much as any other, and I do not see why one should not take advantage of these qualities *so as to try and observe the correct prosody* [emphasis mine]. The comedy must be derived not, as in operetta, by the arbitrary and comical accentuation of words, but by the unusual nature of the harmonies, the rhythm, the melodic design and the orchestration.[41]

Ravel's words spring from the same clearly defined rationale as had his strictures on *Faust*. Distorting the rhythms and inflections of a text for comic effect is, he suggests, a rather cheap trick, not particularly amusing in itself – at least, not for a whole opera. Rather, the impact and wit of a libretto will be heightened if the musical treatment of the text is rigorous, just as the humour carefully built into the orchestral accompaniment will interact more audibly with the words.

---

[39] Vuillermoz, 'Les Théâtres: *L'Heure espagnole*', 68.   [40] Bruneau, 'Théâtres de concerts'.
[41] *OL*, letter 84.

With Ravel's increasing confidence and boldness in naturalistic text-setting came not just flexibility but a commensurate exactitude: the formality that underpins Franc-Nohain's words is thus reflected, albeit most subtly, in Ravel's music. In freeing himself from the conventions of musical text-setting, the composer imposed different constraints, of poetic rhythm, rhyme and metre, and of musical notation. But alongside these technical concerns is a more creative extension of the practices Ravel had developed in his songs: in *L'Heure espagnole* he made the assonances and rhythms of the language work for him as an essential tool of characterisation.

Several commentators have observed that the close relationship between *Histoires naturelles* and *L'Heure* extends beyond text-setting procedures to melodic material; Jankélévitch noted particular connections through the characteristic interval of the falling fourth (discussed in more detail in Chapter 8).[42] Chapter 5 also noted that songs and opera are linked in their interplay of shorter and longer lines, elaborate descriptions and prosaic asides. Underlying this characteristic is a more fundamental structural and conceptual quality: the establishment and subversion of the listener's expectations. Ravel undermines our expectations from the very opening of the first of the *Histoires*, 'Le Paon'. He offers us eight bars, *sans hâte et noblement*, with a characteristic rhythmic gesture and an unremarkable harmonic progression through the subdominant, supertonic and dominant before a tonic arrival in bar 9. But just as the listener is primed for the first vocal entry, the voice anticipates it, entering a bar before it 'should' (Ex. 6.7), not with a grand opening statement to match the piano's, but with a colloquial aside, picking up in the middle of a thought and ending in the perfect cadence: 'He will surely be married today.' Where does one go from there? To an almost parenthetical observation – 'It should have been yesterday.' With those laconic remarks, the expected narrative rhythm of the song and the cycle is disrupted before it has even been established.

Subversion of expectations is an indispensable tool in the comic arsenal, and one that is intrinsic to *L'Heure espagnole* as both play and opera, in textual, musical and dramatic terms. We see it in Franc-Nohain's text, in the constant puncturing of grand statements with matter-of-fact remarks. Such patterns are hinted at even in the deliberately ungainly sequence of explanatory, parenthetical comparisons that characterises his prefatory 'Avis au lecteur'. We see a similar quality in the tensions between the sounds and the meanings of words, evident in Concepcion's exhortations to Gonzalve in Scene IV (their meaning imperative, their word-sounds

---

[42] Jankélévitch, *Ravel*, 31–2; see also Clifton, 'Maurice Ravel's *L'Heure espagnole*', 20–6.

Ex. 6.7 'Le Paon' (*Histoires naturelles*), bars 6–10

languorous), as well as in Ravel's musical amplification of these tensions (the slower tempi that seem almost to be clutching at Concepcion's impatient heels). The undercutting of expectations can also become a structural tool: Ravel's excision of possible 'arias' (Torquemada's Scene II and Gonzalve's Scene XV monologues, for example) at once streamlines the action and subverts the audience's conceptions of *opéra bouffe*, just as Franc-Nohain's use of poetic metre (and his justification of it in the 'Avis au lecteur') plays on and undermines the usages long associated with his chosen formats. In later chapters, we'll see how Ravel used 'Spanish' gestures, leitmotivic techniques and certain important harmonies in precisely similar fashion, positioning them within and against conventional forms. Composer and playwright thus make maximum use of their audience's repositories of musical, literary and theatrical convention, while simultaneously subverting their expectations of genre and style.

7 | A portrait of an opera-ballet

It is perhaps surprising that, over the course of a long career, to which theatre and music were both central, Colette did not write more for the stage.[1] As Mari Ward McCarty writes, 'Theatrical references surface at every stage of the text, from the basic level of the word itself to the overall ambiance of an entire book. [. . .] Colette sees her characters as performers in the limelight [. . .] no other novelist has ever infused an entire life's work with the depth and breadth of theatrical metaphor we see in Colette'.[2] Yet, as we will see, Colette's one work written explicitly for the theatre, *L'Enfant et les sortilèges*, is in many respects oddly untheatrical. Its stage directions are poetic and highly detailed, including extensive descriptions of characters' appearances, movements, gestures, vocal qualities and feelings, as well as of their physical surroundings. In *L'Heure espagnole* whole pages pass without stage directions. In the first episode of *L'Enfant*, by contrast, there are more than three times as many words of direction as sung text, and throughout the libretto the dialogue is regularly punctuated by long descriptive paragraphs. But despite this wealth of explanatory detail, there is little in the way of technical directives. 'La scène' ('the stage') is occasionally mentioned, but nowhere do we find a character 'exiting stage left'; rather, they 's'éloignent', 'disparaissent' or 's'en vont'; the Princess disappears not through the trap but 'sous la terre'. The directions are full of adverbs and adjectives, evocations and analogies: the page of the book on which the Child is lying rises 'like a slab of marble'; the Child uses the poker 'like a sword' to attack the wallpaper; the armchair (Fauteuil) hobbles 'like an enormous toad'. They even include some spoken words: in the opening scene, we read 'Cette main se lève, interroge de l'index, et la voix de Maman

---

[1] A capable pianist, Colette was for some years a professional music as well as theatre critic; music and musicians wind their way through all her published writings (particularly the autobiographical works). Maurice Goudeket wrote that 'Her ear and her memory for music were faultless and she was never mistaken as to either the key or the tone of what she was hearing, being particularly sensitive to the perfect relation of movements and able to read a score' (Goudeket, *Close to Colette*, 68). See also Crosland, 'Colette and Ravel', 116–19; and Langham Smith, 'Colette as critic'.

[2] McCarty, 'The theatre as literary model', 125–6, 133.

demande: "Bébé a été sage? Il a fini sa page?"' ('The hand rises, with a questioning index finger, and Maman's voice asks: "Has Baby been good? Has he finished his lesson?"').[3] At the very end of the opera, as we will see, directions and spoken text merge again, in a way that seems more novelistic than theatrical.

The narrative of *L'Enfant* is episodic but uncomplicated. There are relatively few passages of dialogue, so the text is primarily descriptive; the purpose of individual scenes and arias is for the most part characterisation and reflection. In his 'Autobiographical Sketch', Ravel called *L'Heure espagnole* 'a sort of conversation in music' ('une sorte de conversation en musique'), but of *L'Enfant* he reiterated 'the predominant concern with melody' ('le souci mélodique qui y domine'), relating it directly to the form of the libretto.[4] His vocal writing is more lyrical and melodic and less meticulously realistic, a technique suited to the magical happenings of the story: as Marie-Pierre Lassus points out, song (*chant*, from the Latin *cantare*) is literally at the core of 'enchantment'.[5]

The Child begins the opera more anti-hero than hero, and although his character develops as the work progresses, he is never exactly heroic. He fights no dragons, breaks no spells – in fact, he never leaves the confines of a house and garden described as 'Norman', no faraway land but a setting of comfortable familiarity. But this very ordinary, very human protagonist nevertheless traces a path of transgression, reparation and transcendence, illuminated by magical events, that is located firmly within the genre of the fairytale. Max Lüthi writes that fairytales deal with the basic motifs of human existence: 'life and death; good and evil; temptation and intrigue; weakness and innocence; despair, guidance and assistance'.[6] Almost all these motifs are present in *L'Enfant et les sortilèges*. We may even see Colette's peaceful Norman house as a true fairytale location, the years of the First World War having banished such settings to the realm of nostalgic imagination.

L'Enfant is set in motion by one of the commonest of all fairytale premises: an instruction (to work) is disobeyed and the consequences of this violation are severe. The Child's destructive rage is countered by the uprising of the creatures; in between these episodes he passes through a series of magical or fantastic encounters, which gradually equip him with the self-knowledge to make reparation. His initial disobedience is annulled

---

[3] References to the libretto are drawn from its publication in Colette, *Œuvres*, vol. III, 151–69.
[4] 'Esquisse autobiographique'; *OL*, 45–6.   [5] Lassus, 'Ravel, l'enchanteur', 40.
[6] Lüthi, *Once Upon a Time*, 73.

by his final act of repentance; that this should take the form of binding a squirrel's paw when he had previously injured the caged squirrel is both a structurally apt mirroring of events and a perfect fairytale response.

Although the Child does not go journeying in a physical sense, his story nevertheless traces the path of the fairytale's traditional wandering hero, who meets all sorts of magical characters in his quest. The journey itself is internalised, symbolised in the Child's path to repentance. His binding of the squirrel's paw is a moment of symbolic transformation, a revelation of the hero's true nature that has the same dramatic function as the breaking of an enchantment. The story's apotheosis and the Child's reward are expressed not through the outward, jubilant trappings of immense wealth, astonishing beauty and an adoring spouse, but in inner reactions and behaviours. At the end of the opera, the Child is still a child, but through his repentance and newfound maturity the world has changed for the better.

The libretto and the score

It seems likely that the manuscript Colette originally presented to Jacques Rouché differed fairly considerably – in detail, if not in substance – from the final libretto, as published by Durand in 1925 (separately from the piano-vocal and orchestral scores). Ravel seems never to have received a 'definitive' fair copy of the revised libretto before he completed the opera; we know Colette was still sending him piecemeal revisions until as late as the autumn of 1924 (see p. 42). Although Christine Milner notes Ravel's 'exemplary fidelity' to Colette's text,[7] the final version of the libretto seems to have been reciprocally informed by Ravel's compositional process.

A few discrepancies between the published libretto and score offer us glimpses of Ravel's approach to his text. In the scenes of the Cup and Teapot, the Shepherds and Shepherdesses, the Arithmetic scene and the Animals' uprising, the composer introduced repetitions of lines and whole swathes of text; as we will see below, these amplify Colette's local patterns of repetition and emphasis. He also made a few minor amendments to the ordering, allocation and division of lines, notably in the dialogue of the Fauteuil and Bergère and the scene of the Shepherds and Shepherdesses. These sorts of adjustments reflect a flexibility commensurate with the descriptive nature of much of the sung text.

---

[7] Milner, 'Note sur le texte' to *L'Enfant et les sortilèges*, in Colette, *Œuvres*, vol. III, 1342.

Ex. 7.1 The Child cries for his sword

A more striking divergence between libretto and score emerges in the Child's desperate cry for his sword at the end of the Princess's scene ('Mon épée! Mon épée!'): in the libretto alone, this is preceded by the words 'Je vaincrai!' ('I will triumph!'). By omitting this positive assertion, Ravel curtails the narrative, leaving the Princess's own final cry ('À l'aide!') effectively unanswered: the Child's 'Mon épée!' is transformed from a call to arms to an empty lament. His musical setting confirms this, as the rising figure of the first two iterations of 'Mon épée!' is inverted and compressed on the third occurrence, underlining the Child's helplessness (Ex. 7.1).

In a musico-psychoanalytical reading, Peter Kaminsky convincingly argues that Ravel's realisation of the scene depended on the dramatic necessity of 'simultaneously empower[ing] and disabl[ing] the Child: on the one hand, to give him the strength and magical power of the Knight with the *potential* to rescue the Princess; on the other to nullify this potential as a painful consequence of his having torn the book'.[8] Ravel's elimination of the words 'Je vaincrai!' not only underlines his 'disabling' of the Child: by focussing his final lines on the repeated 'Mon épée!', he recalls the threefold iteration of the same word at the scene's climactic passage ('Ah! qu'il vienne avec son épée! Si j'avais une épée! Une épée!').[9]

The one scene that we know to have been entirely rewritten during the opera's long gestation is that of the Cup and Teapot. The sole surviving page of the libretto in Colette's hand (Fig. 7.1) is an early draft of this scene, in which the Cup is not Chinese, but of Limoges porcelain. As the Teapot explains, this is why she can say nothing but 'Fouchtra!' – 'It means "shame!"' Nor is this Teapot the black American boxer-figure that would eventually emerge, but the 'english théière [. . .] de votre gram'ma!', his comically accented French scattered not with pugilistic *franglais* but with

---

[8] Kaminsky, 'The Child on the couch', 322.

[9] Kaminsky posits that the sword is represented by the 'long-awaited' dominant harmony that arrives at this climax (as the Child concludes 'Je saurai te défendre' – *ibid.*, 324–8), although he slightly mistranslates the Child's words: the Child longs for but does not actually take ownership of the sword at this point (singing rather, '*If* I had a sword . . .'). He claims the sword as his own only as the Princess disappears.

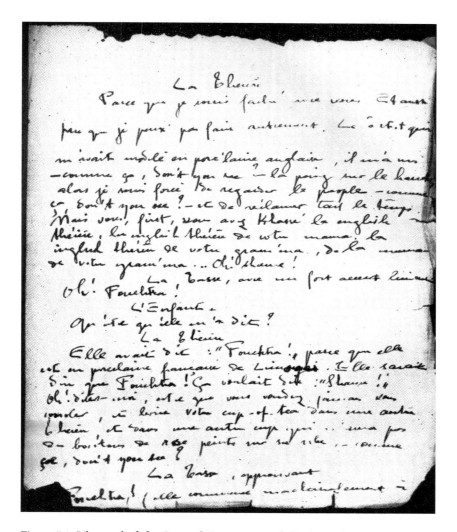

Figure 7.1 Libretto draft for Cup and Teapot scene of *L'Enfant et les sortilèges*

phrases like 'cup-of-tea' (the phrases shown in italics below are in English in the original):

LA THÉIÈRE

Because I am [souis] angry with you. And also because I can't do anything else. The artist who modelled me from English porcelain, he made me – like that! *Don't you see?* My fist on my hip, so I am [souis] forced to look at everyone – like that, *don't you see?* – and to complain all the time. But you, *first*, you have broken [*khassé*] the *english* teapot, the *english* teapot of your Mama, the *english* teapot of your *gram'ma*, of your Mama's *gram'ma*. . . *Oh! Shame!*

LA TASSE, with a strong *limousin* accent:

Oh! Fouchtra!

L'ENFANT

What did she say to me?

LA THÉIÈRE

She said 'Fouchtra!', because she is made of Limoges porcelain. She can't say anything but Fouchtra! It means '*Shame!*' oh! Tell me, would you ever want to console yourself and drink your *cup-of-tea* from another teapot, and in another cup, without pink buttons painted on her dress, like that, *don't you see*?

LA TASSE, approvingly :

Fouchtra! (she begins involuntarily to [. . .]*

It is not hard to see why this scene was rewritten: the Teapot's speeches are too long, his sentences too complicated, and the text, in this early version, lacks the patterns of repetition and assonance that lend the libretto its natural rhythmic emphases.

Ravel's correspondence with Colette shows that this version had been superseded even by February 1919 (see p. 38): 'a single couplet, with refrain', he writes, a description that matches neither the initial nor the ultimate versions of the scene. As the final version clearly incorporates the most important of Ravel's general suggestions ('the cup and the teapot, in old Wedgwood – black – singing a ragtime'), we might also wonder if some of the words themselves could also have been the composer's own. If their Sitwellian nonsense is vintage Colette, the sentiments hidden within are characteristically and ironically Ravelian: 'since we don't understand, it will always sound Chinese!' ('Puis' kong-kong-pran-pa, / Ça-oh-râ toujours l'air chinoâ' [Puisqu'on [ne] comprend pas / Ça aura toujours l'air chinois]). Manuel Rosenthal also notes the touches of soldier's slang in the Cup's lines – 'Kek t'as [qu'est ce que tu as] foutu d'mon kaoua?' ('What the hell have you done with my kava?') – as typical of Ravel, who delighted in the expressive possibilities of argot.[10] A few other moments also prompt speculation as to how much the composer's ideas and interventions informed the finished libretto. The scatological punning of the croaking Frog – 'Je ne connais pas la ca-ca-cage' – is typical of Colette's wordplay,

---

[10] Marnat (ed.), *Ravel: Souvenirs de Manuel Rosenthal*, 135. Colette would also have been familiar with soldier's argot: her then husband Henry de Jouvenel was a soldier, and she spent some time during the early part of the war caring for wounded soldiers.

but his first words, 'Kékékékécékéça?' ('Qu'est ce que c'est que ça [What's that]?'), echo a 1908 letter from Ravel to Ida Godebska ('Monday I received a card from... Bourbonne-les-Bains! Then, nothing. Kécèkécèkécélà?'[11]). As previously noted, the Arithmetic scene in particular is redolent of Ravel's choral *Trois chansons* of 1914–15: the plays of assonance are so close that the scene's subtitle 'Ronde' (the title of the third of Ravel's songs) seems to make the allusion explicit.

Passages such as these have given rise to conjecture about the provenance of particular words, phrases and even scenes.[12] Colette certainly appears to have given permission for minor reworkings of her text: 'we'll take out the words wherever they get in the way'*, she wrote to Stravinsky in 1916 (see p. 36). Given that the Cup and Teapot scene was certainly passed back and forth, we may wonder whether other scenes, too, were developed to a certain extent in collaboration (through now-untraced correspondence, telephone conversations or meetings, as suggested in Chapter 4). However, the number of clear echoes of Colette's other writings serves to put the general question of the libretto's authorship well beyond doubt. In its expressive setting of animal voices, with their characteristic tics and figures of speech, we recognise immediately the Colette of *Dialogues de bêtes*, together with the many other depictions of animals and animal voices threaded through her novels and memoirs. In her 1921 piece 'Celle qui en revient' (*Dialogues de bêtes*), for example, the words of the Bergère (a sheepdog, in this case) echo the Dragonfly and Bat of *L'Enfant*: 'Seuls... seuls... seuls. [. . .] Quoi? Que cries-tu? Ils t'emportent? Ah! pas sans moi, pas sans moi!...'[13] More striking correspondences emerge from a wartime Christmas tale, 'Conte pour les petits enfants des poilus', which first appeared in *Le Matin* on Christmas Day 1915 and was later incorporated in *La Paix chez les bêtes*. The appearance of the marten here seems to prefigure both the Cat and the Frog of *L'Enfant*:

---

[11] *OL*, letter 53. Orenstein traces this onomatopoeic touch to *La Cloche engloutie*; in his 1925 review of *L'Enfant*, Henry Prunières also noted that a much earlier equivalent can be found in Aristophanes' *The Frogs*.

[12] See, for example, Orenstein, *Ravel, Man and Musician*, 193 ('Although all the modifications in Colette's libretto cannot be fully determined, it is clear that Ravel was responsible for the ragtime [. . .] the squirrel's aria, and many of the dances'). Marcel Marnat, in conversation with the author (July 2007), hypothesised that much of the final libretto was Ravel's work. Rosenthal's memoirs, as cited above, also implicitly assume that the touches of soldiers' slang were the composer's. Larner, on the other hand, suggests that 'Ravel probably made fewer changes than is generally assumed' (*Maurice Ravel*, 184).

[13] Colette, *Douze dialogues de bêtes*, *Œuvres*, vol. II, 63–4.

Something, suddenly, leaped and stopped: a fine yellow marten, newly garbed by the harsh months, hunting. She sat down like a squirrel, groomed her tail, scratched, looked at the moon.

'Psss, psss', called the soldier.

The marten made a comical leap, as if her whole body had burst out laughing, and disappeared.[14]

Like *L'Enfant*, the story depicts a council of animals surrounding a fallen human, in this case debating which of them should donate their hide to the soldier, who is freezing to death in his sleep: '"Do you want a hide? Take my hide, my fine hide. It's thick, a bit ugly, hard-wearing, it's a hide. . . " "Not so fine as mine. . ."' Like the Child, the soldier wakes amid the beasts bringing succour: protected by a coverlet of falling snow and the animals themselves, 'his young blood still throbbed, magically warmed, as throbbed the generous blood of the well-clad beasts'.[15] As Margaret Crosland notes, 'Was [*La Paix chez les bêtes*] so far from *L'Enfant et les sortilèges*? I think not, for no one part of her writing was entirely isolated from any other.'[16]

Rhythm and rhyme, affect and timbre

If Ravel did retouch parts of Colette's libretto (we can now only guess), it thus seems likely that his amendments were fairly minimal. Any revisions he made must have been undertaken with extraordinary alertness to established continuities of poetic and linguistic design, for there are no 'seams', no sense of piecemeal assemblage or reworking. Rather, a remarkable textual coherence runs beneath the contrasting episodes.

Unlike *L'Heure espagnole*, the libretto of *L'Enfant* has no consistent basis in metre, rhyme or poetic rhythm. In the printed libretto, some passages of text – notably the Fire's aria and the dialogues of the Bat, Frog and Squirrel – are set out in unbroken prose paragraphs; others are laid out as poetry. The only instances of perceivable rhyme schemes occur in Arithmetic's 'Millimètre, / Centimètre, / Décimètre, / Décamètre. . .', as well as in the Clock's scene; the latter opens (after his 'dinging') with a six-line AAABBA stanza, while the second part of his monologue employs a more flexible design based around several key 'chimes', notably the [e] of *passer, veiller, mutilée, changé* and *sonner*, and the [œ] of *heure, douleur* and *demeure*. It is not coincidental that these scenes, featuring the work's

---

[14] Colette, *La Paix chez les bêtes*, Œuvres, vol. II, 153–4.   [15] *Ibid.*, 155–6.
[16] Crosland, 'Colette and Ravel', 123.

two most 'regulated' characters, also include two of the only passages that maintain a consistent number of syllables across more than two or three lines. The Dragonfly's 'Où es-tu? / Je te cherche. . .' and the first few lines of the Animals' uprising (quoted below) also follow more regularised metric patterns, but otherwise the lines fall mostly as unmetred free verse.

Despite this poetic flexibility, however, Colette's text presents several key unifying elements. The first of these is the repetition and emphasis of words and phrases within and across episodes. We observe this particularly at the beginnings of lines: the Child's fivefold 'J'ai envie de. . .' in the opening scene; the repeated 'Plus de. . .' of the Fauteuil and Bergère; the Shepherds' and Shepherdesses' 'Las, notre chèvre. . . / Las, nos agneaux. . . / Las, nos cerises zinzolin!', whose emphatic rhythm foreshadows the thrice repeated 'Toi, . . .' of the Child's little aria; and the Clock's literal chiming of the hours in his reiteration of the word *heure* all typify this sort of iterative syntax. Repetitive word-sounds and gestures are exploited *par excellence* in the Arithmetic scene and the Animals' uprising, the latter set out here as it appears in the libretto:

C'est l'Enfant au couteau !
C'est l'Enfant au baton !
Le méchant à la cage !
Le méchant au filet !
Celui qui n'aime personne
Et que personne n'aime !
Faut-il fuir ?
Non! Il faut châtier.
J'ai mes griffes !
J'ai mes dents !
J'ai mes ailes onglées !
Unissons-nous, unissons-nous ![17]

These gestures impart a natural rhythm and metre to lines that are otherwise mostly unmeasured and fluid in their patterns of accentuation.

Besides promoting unity on a local level, and establishing a general sense of rhythmic cohesion and emphasis, textual repetitions are a key aspect of the opera's narrative pace and perspective. In his study 'Colette et la

---

[17] It's the Child with the knife! / It's the Child with the stick! / The wicked one with the cage! / The wicked one with the net! / The one who loves nobody, / And whom nobody loves! / Must we flee? / No! He must be punished. / I have my claws! / I have my teeth! / I have my taloned wings! / Let us unite, let us unite!

poésie', Henry Bouillier tellingly observes that, in contrast with Mallarmé's dictum to evoke rather than name, for Colette 'to name is to give meaning and life to reality, to concentrate the subject, to restore its savour, form, colour'.[18] In *L'Enfant* she names and names again: messages, narrative, ideas and images are built up and reinforced precisely through patterns of repetition and accumulation. Thus the four desires ('J'ai envie de. . .') preceding the Child's 'J'ai envie de mettre Maman en pénitence!' have a cumulative effect: to 'put Maman in the corner' becomes the sum of all desires. The Clock's fourfold repetition of the word *heure* illustrates his story; and the Child's image of the Princess is conjured phrase by phrase through the iterative syntax of 'Toi, le cœur de la rose'.

Michel Mercier recognises a further dramatic function of such repetitions, observing that the consequences of the Child's destructive actions are made immediately apparent in the very language of the Fauteuil and Bergère: 'the Child believes himself free, [but] he does not know that by his refusal and his violence, he has begun a sequence of "fair's fair"; to his two "plus de" ["Plus de leçons! Plus de devoirs!"], the Fauteuil responds with five "plus de"'.[19] While a twofold statement followed by a fivefold one may not seem entirely 'fair', the Child's opening monologue, with its five-times repeated 'J'ai envie de. . .' provides a more precise gestural mirroring. We thus see localised patterns and emphases becoming structural building blocks, as early as the opera's second episode. Ravel clearly recognised and built upon this aspect of textual design, underlining and echoing iterative phrases with shared melodic and rhythmic gestures. In the Arithmetic episode and the final scenes, he further exploited and built upon these patterns through the additional repetition, overlay and fragmentation of textual and melodic material.

Further examination of the libretto, at the level not of words but of word-*sounds*, reveals textual patterns that are less obvious but perhaps more potent. Much of the underlying textual coherence derives from subtle onomatopoeia: as Marie-Pierre Lassus has explored, the characters of the individual creatures are all shaped as much by the sounds of their words as by their meanings.[20] Thus, the scenes featuring inanimate creatures (Fauteuil and Bergère, Cup and Teapot, Clock, Fire, Arithmetic) and negative emotions (the rebellious and angry Child) are distinguished by hard, incisive word-sounds, such as the consonants p/t/k and clenched-teeth

---

[18] Bouillier, 'Colette et la poésie', 170.　　[19] Mercier, '*L'Enfant et les sortilèges*: Analyse', 58.

[20] Lassus, 'Ravel, l'enchanteur', 43–4; see also Kilpatrick, '"Jangling in symmetrical sounds"', 10–12.

fricatives [ʒ] (of *je*), and [s], together with the [a] (of *chat*) and nasal [ɔ̃] (of *bon*) vowels. Lassus terms this linguistic affect 'la parole agressive'.[21] The living creatures – the fairytale Princess and the Animals in the Garden – emphasise softer, slower and lighter sounds (which Lassus labels 'la parole tendre'): the consonants b/d/g, the fricative [z] (*rose*), the light [i] (*libre*) and [ɛ] (*aime*), and the drawn-out [ø] (*jeu*), [œ] (*cœur*) and [o] (*rose*) vowels.[22] The contrast between these two linguistic affects can be seen clearly if we compare the Fire's words (quoted here as they appear in the score) with the Dragonfly's:

LE FEU

Je réchauffe les bons, mais je brûle les méchants.
Petit barbare, barbare imprudent, tu as insulté à tous les Dieux bienveil-
   lants qui tendent entre le malheur et toi le fragile barrière !
[. . .]
Gare au feu dansant ! Gare, gare, gare, gare à toi ![23]

＊ ＊ ＊

LA LIBELLULE

Où es-tu ?
Je te cherche
Le filet,
Il t'a prise. . .
Ô toi chère,
Longue et frèle
Tes turquoises,
Tes topazes
L'air qui t'aime
Les regrette
Moins que moi. . .[24]

In addition to the 'hard' [a] and [ɔ̃] vowels and [ʒ], [s] and [f] fricatives in the Fire's aria, the proliferating rolled *r* sounds give a threatening percussive edge to her words. Lassus also observes that Ravel's choice of the [a] vowel for the coloratura passages – 'the most intense sound in the language' – has an immediate effect in '[overpowering] the will of the

[21] Lassus, 'Ravel, L'enchanteur', 43–4.   [22] *Ibid.*, 45.
[23] I warm the good, I burn the bad / Little savage, unwise savage, you have insulted all the friendly gods / Who keep the fragile barrier between you and unhappiness! [. . .] / Beware of the dancing fire! Beware, beware, look to yourself!'
[24] Where are you? / I search for you / The net / He has caught you. . . / O you, dear one, / Long and fragile, / Your turquoises, / Your topazes, / The air that loves you / Mourns them still less / Than I do. . .

Child'.[25] (Maurice Grammont lists [a] among the *voyelles éclatantes* and notes the importance of such vowels in the expression of anger.[26]) The Dragonfly's aria, by contrast, is filled with [i], [ε] and [z] sounds that lengthen and soften the consonants around them (the Dragonfly's *chère* against the Fire's *méchant*; the Fire's *réchauffe* against the Dragonfly's *filet*). Ravel's alertness to these contrasted linguistic affects is evident in the rhythmic and timbral colourations of the two passages: in the Fire's aria (Ex. 7.2a) the 'hard' vowel sounds fall on the downbeats, with the attack of consonants reinforced by the staccato string accompaniment and the woodwind doublings. By contrast, in the Dragonfly's aria (Ex. 7.2b) sustained string chords draw out 'soft' vowel sounds and gentle sibilants are emphasized by rhythmic placement, articulation and orchestral colouring.

While these passages each exploit a single linguistic affect, other scenes contrast 'hard' and 'soft' word-sounds directly. In the waltz of the Bat, for example, the 'hard' phrases ('Rends-la moi!') are accompanied by pizzicato strings (decorated with woodwind arabesques), but at the soft [ε] of the Child's murmured 'sans mère!' the strings play *arco* for a single bar. Maman's first words to the Child stress the hard [e] and [a] vowels ('Bébé a été sage? Il a fini sa page?'), and are accompanied by incisive woodwind chords. When she exhorts the Child to repentance ('Regrettes-tu ta paresse?'), the softer *schwas* and languid double consonants are emphasised by the opera's first string chords (Ex. 7.3). The Child sticks out his tongue, Maman's words become sharp again and the winds accompany her sharp sibilants and echoing [ɔ] vowels: 'Voici le goûter d'un méchant enfant: du thé sans sucre, du pain sec. Restez tout seul jusqu'au dîner' ('Here is a snack for a naughty child: sugarless tea and dry bread. Stay here by yourself until dinner'). Ravel's changing timbres draw attention equally to Maman's change of mood (from caressing to admonishing) and to the contrasted sounds of her words: because word-sounds are so intricately woven into the structure of the libretto, emotional, linguistic and timbral affect thus work in inextricable conjunction.

Word-sounds, text-setting, orchestral colour, characterisation and narrative progression are similarly bound together in the Child's two extended solos. Despite the emphasis Ravel placed upon the innate lyricism of *L'Enfant*, the Child's opening monologue (Ex. 7.4) is as naturalistic as anything in *L'Heure espagnole* (though it perhaps looks more directly to the child of Musorgksy's *Nursery* songs). Ravel's setting meticulously

---

[25] Lassus, 'Ravel, l'enchanteur', 42.   [26] Grammont, *Le Vers français*, 263, 266–7.

Ex. 7.2 Contrasted textual and timbral affect

a. The Fire

b. The Dragonfly

Ex 7.3 Contrasted textual and timbral affect in Maman's dialogue

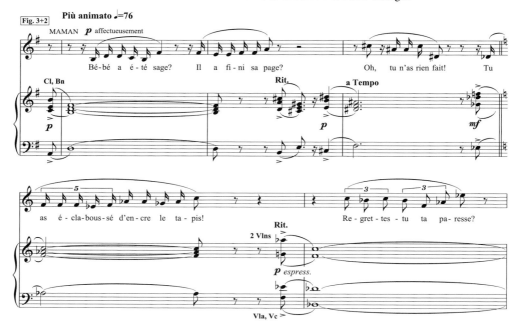

Ex. 7.4 Child's monologue

captures the accents of a petulant and tired small child, and the incisive timbre of the accompanying oboes heightens the aural impact of the words. His increasingly ambitious and excited demands are mirrored in phrases that rise across progressively broader intervals, while his concluding line encapsulates his protestations by inverting the melodic motion, decisively delineating the descending octave *e″–e′* within which the preceding phrases are centred. The final 'en pénitence' could not more plainly express bad-tempered rebellion, with determined accents on even the final weak *-ce*.

The Child's other extended solo, his little aria 'Toi, le cœur de la rose', is a pivotal structural moment: at the exact midpoint of the opera (pp. 50–1 of the 101-page vocal score; it occurs around the 22-minute mark of the 45-minute work), the Child, lamenting the loss of his fairytale Princess, finds himself able to express love, tenderness and sorrow. Here too, words and word-sounds are an intrinsic element of musical portraiture. No longer hard and emphatic, the Child's words stress sweeter, more drawn-out assonances:

Toi, le cœur de la rose,
Toi, le parfum du lys blanc,
Toi, tes mains et ta couronne,
Tes yeux bleus et tes joyaux...
Tu ne m'as laissé, comme un rayon de lune,
Qu'un cheveu d'or sur mon épaule,
Un cheveu d'or... et le débris d'un rêve...[27]

The round, repeated [l] sounds in lines 1, 2, 5 and 6 and the soft *schwas*, slow [o] and [œ] vowels and gentle sibilants (ro<u>s</u>e, ly<u>s</u>, te<u>s</u> <u>j</u>oyaux, te<u>s</u> <u>y</u>eux, <u>ch</u>eveu, lai<u>ss</u>é) all reveal the Child's changing state of mind, at least as much as the actual meanings of the words. In Ravel's setting, the bad-tempered naturalism of the opening monologue is replaced by tender lyricism, where brief flights of melody alternate with reiterated B♭s (the dominant, in the E♭ tonality; see Ex. 11.1b), unresolved, lingering and hesitant. The longer vowel sounds are underlined by pulsing strings, blended with sustained horn, clarinet and bassoon chords and countermelodies – warmer and more rounded woodwind timbres than the oboe, which Ravel reserves for the shift to the minor key and the Child's direct expression of loss. Articulation, rhythmic placement and instrumental timbres thus consistently shape the

---

[27] You, the heart of the rose, / You, the perfume of the white lily, / You, your hands and your crown, / Your blue eyes and your jewels... / Like a ray of moonlight, you have left me nothing / But a golden hair on my shoulder, / A golden hair... and the ruins of a dream...

libretto's linguistic affects into an integral part of the opera's characterisation and drama. In particular, the opposition of wind/percussion/pizzicato string textures and the lusher sounds of *arco* strings is a defining quality of its colouristic structure.

Magic words

If the words of Colette's libretto impinge directly upon the timbral design of *L'Enfant et les sortilèges*, they also help to define its broader architectural gestures. We may trace this in particular through the repetition and emphasis of certain key words – 'magic words' in a sense, for they instigate and delineate crucial events. In the opening scene, the Child, rampaging around his room, cries 'Je suis très méchant! Méchant, méchant, méchant!', then 'Je suis libre, libre, méchant et libre!' Both lines feature direct repetitions of words – *méchant* and *libre* – that encapsulate the narrative. In this scene, they act as invocations, the 'magic words' that set the wondrous events in motion. As the Child sings his final 'méchant et libre!' he goes to sit in an armchair, which moves away: the 'enchantments' have begun. In the scenes that follow, Fauteuil and Bergère, Clock, Fire and Shepherds and Shepherdesses all use the word *méchant* before the Trees, in the Garden scene, turn the word directly on the Child – 'Oh, méchant!' (Fig. 104^{+4}). In the Animals' uprising the word is propelled to the forefront of the texture in a crescendo of menace (quoted here from Ravel's score, specifically the alto line): 'C'est le méchant, c'est le méchant à la cage! C'est le méchant, c'est le méchant au filet!'[28]

While the Princess's scene evokes the idea of freedom (if she could only escape from her 'wicked enchanter'), and the flight of the Dragonfly seems intended to depict it, after the opening scene the word *libre* is not heard again until the reappearance of the creature who first appeared physically caged, the Squirrel: 'Le ciel libre, le vent libre, mes libres frères au bond sûr d'un vol' ('The free sky, the free wind, my free brothers leaping as if winged'). Again, the word *libre* sounds three times, and here too it works magic: it prompts the Child to acknowledge his loneliness, before the explosive single-word invocation 'Maman!' unleashes the Animals' rage.

The word *sage* also figures as a *mot clé* for both librettist and composer, imparting a large-scale reciprocity to the first and last scenes. Maman's first

---

[28] Huebner also notes the reiteration of the words *libre* and *méchant*, 'Ravel's Child', 86.

words are 'Bébé a été sage?', and in the closing bars Ravel has the Animals sing in overlapping chorus 'Il est bon, l'Enfant, il est sage, bien sage, si sage...' The reiteration alerts us to the word's double meaning: when applied to children (and animals) *sage* means 'well-behaved' – Maman initially uses it thus – but in a broader sense it also means 'wise'. We have come full circle, closing with the words of the opening, yet we are not quite back where we started: the very sense of the word has grown, like the Child himself.

In his 1977 study of the fairytale, F. André Favat described the importance of the repetition of words, phrases and actions, which not only fill out the narrative but also heighten tension and postpone its release.[29] Such patterns often centre around threefold gestures: a genie will give three wishes; we must watch the two stepsisters try on the glass slipper before Cinderella slips it onto her foot; and although the woodcutter and his wife twice fail to lose Petit Poucet and his brothers in the woods, we know very well that their third attempt will be successful. In a fairytale, the third time is always the moment of transfiguration. Already noted above in the Child's despairing cry for his sword, we may also recognise these patterns in Maman's 'Et songez à votre faute! / Et songez à vos devoirs! Songez, songez surtout au chagrin de Maman!' The third line (with its double repetition of *songez*) is at once summative and transformative: the exhortation to 'consider Maman's sorrow' is the last straw for the Child, sparking his violent rebellion. Similarly, it seems no coincidence that the Child later calls for his mother with two three-part reflections ('Ils s'aiment. Ils sont heureux. Ils m'oublient... / Ils s'aiment... Ils m'oublient... Je suis seul...'); Chapter 10 details the summative musical (as well as textual) function of this line. In this context, the threefold iterations of *méchant* and *libre* emerge as 'magic words' indeed, inextricably part of a fairytale heritage.

But the opera is also defined by another 'magic word', one so obvious that when *L'Enfant* was performed in Leipzig in 1927 and Vienna in 1929 it was even given the title *Das Zauberwort* [*The Magic Word*]: *Maman*. The word *Maman* is sung by both the Child and Maman in the opening scene; by the Child, unaccompanied, after the Squirrel's aria; by the summoning Animals; and by the Child once more, in the final bar. The Child himself uses the word three times and each has a distinct and significant dramatic effect. On its first appearance, 'J'ai envie de mettre Maman en pénitence', the word is a summation of all his rebellious desires. His second

[29] Favat, *Child and Tale*, 52.

articulation of 'Maman!' is drawn from him, 'in spite of himself', after the Squirrel's aria and the appearance of the two Cats, lovingly entwined on the Garden wall, eventually bring him to a full realisation of his loneliness and misery: here the word encapsulates his desolation and desperate need for aid. His third and final voicing of 'Maman', in the opera's final bars, is an affirmation of love and tenderness.

Musically, the word 'Maman' is associated with the interval of the descending fourth, undoubtedly chosen to mirror its natural spoken inflection. In its first invocation, however, the word is set not to a descending but an *ascending* fourth, the only ascending interval in that decisive downward phrase (Ex. 7.4 above). Ravel thus alerts us to the Child's mutinous state of mind by inverting Maman's interval, even before we hear it in its 'proper' guise. The three iterations of the word *méchant* that conclude the first part of the Child's tantrum are each set to a falling fourth – a gesture that, by recalling Maman's interval, directly conveys his rebellion.

Similarly subtle gestures of suggestion and inference occur throughout the opera, ensuring that while all we ever see of Maman (according to Colette's directions) is a very large skirt, her image and idea are never far from the stage. Mr Arithmetic chants 'zanne, zanne, zanne' and 'toffe, toffe, toffe' to repeated fourths, and most of the Clock's phrases end with the falling fourth. The female Cat's miaous make frequent use of the same interval, and even the accompaniment to the Fire's aria swings relentlessly across perfect fourths (dominant-tonic). The falling fourth also becomes a consequent to the characteristic rising semitone + fifth antecedent gesture that characterises much of the musical material in the Garden scene (see pp. 207–8). Even when not stated openly, the fourth is often used to shape key phrases: many of the Princess's lines span descending fourths, while both the Bat ('Le nid plein, les petits') and the Squirrel ('la prison') employ descending third + second motifs. The creatures' first *tutti* murmur of 'Maman!' (Fig. 145^{-1}) is a falling fourth, and in their final unaccompanied fugal chorus they use the same interval for the repeated word 'l'Enfant', suggesting perhaps that the Child has himself attained the tenderness and wisdom of Maman.[30]

Ravel chose to represent 'Maman' not only with an interval but also a cadence, a modally inflected imperfect (ii–V) progression (Ex. 7.5a). We first hear this cadence upon Maman's entry, where repeated statements of it (moving from the tonic of G by whole-tones to E♭) illustrate her

---

[30] See also Prost, 'Maurice Ravel: *L'Enfant et les sortilèges*', 79, and p. 229 below.

Ex 7.5 'Maman' cadence

a. First presentation (effective ii–V)

b. Final appearance (effective V–I)

conversation with the Child. The cadence makes a gestural return after Maman's punishment, its falling fourths stretched to tritones that under-line the 'wrongness' of the situation, before being restated in its original form and pitch as she departs. In the closing moments of the opera, the Animals' cries for 'Maman!' are surmounted by a threefold statement of her cadence, now played by the full orchestra.[31]

Earlier in this chapter, we noted Henry Bouillier's observation that for Colette the very act of naming imparts meaning and life. By contrast, Ravel's musical image of Maman is built up on the edge of our perception: in Mallarméen fashion, we might argue, she is implied, suggested, but not named (that is, musically defined) outright. In the last bars of the opera, however, the patterns suddenly coalesce. The wandering oboe melody of the opening returns, doubled by two violins, and the Child sings 'Maman!' to a falling fourth above a reprise of the 'Maman cadence', which functions now as a modal perfect cadence (the same harmony and falling fourth above a V–I bass; Ex. 7.5b). With word and gesture at last united, the

---

[31] For further discussion of the 'Maman cadence', see Kaminsky, 'Of children, princesses, dreams and isomorphisms', 39–42.

naturalistic falling fourth, we realise, echoes the classical sigh gesture: as the Child breathes 'Maman!' in loving relief, the audience too may exhale at last.

In this context, the published libretto of *L'Enfant* offers us another intriguing glimpse of Ravel's conception of the narrative and its structure. Colette sets out the final moments thus:

> LES BÊTES, toujours plus haut
>
> « Maman! »
>
>> *Une lumière paraît aux vitres, dans la maison. [. . . Les Bêtes] laissent l'Enfant seul, droit, lumineux et blond, dans un halo de lune et d'aube, et tendant ses bras vers celle que les Bêtes ont appelée:*
>
> Maman!
>
> Il est sage. . . si sage. . . il est bon, il est sage. . . si sage. . . si sage. . .[32]

In his score, Ravel reversed the last two lines, repeating Colette's last words *ad infinitum* and inserting the explicit reference to the Child himself ('Il est bon, l'Enfant, il est sage. . .'), an addition that reflects directly on his choice of the falling fourth for the word 'l'Enfant' in that passage. More strikingly, however, Colette's libretto suggests that the final 'Maman!' is allocated not to the Child but to the Animals. After the Squirrel's aria prompts his plaintive call for his mother, according to the libretto the Child does not speak again for the rest of the opera.

Christine Milner observes a telling likeness between the summoning of 'Maman!' and a passage from Colette's 1909 novel *L'Ingénue libertine*: 'Her mouth trembled, holding back her tears, and holding back too that word which could heal all her terrors, summoning embraces, light, shelter: "Maman. . . "'[33] The correspondence here is not only evident in imagery but also in syntax. In the libretto, only the typeface and alignment of 'Maman' make it clear that the word is voiced at all: were it refashioned as a novel, the sentence would conclude more ambiguously, 'celle que les Bêtes ont appelée: Maman!' The word 'Maman' would appear unvoiced, *retenu* as it is in *L'Ingénue libertine*. Milner observes that 'It was undoubtedly through inadvertence that Colette did not indicate the change of

---

[32] [The Beasts, getting continually louder] Maman! / *A light appears at the window, in the house. [. . . The Beasts] leave the Child alone, upright, luminous and fair, in a halo of moon and dawn, stretching his arms towards she whom the Creatures have summoned:* / Maman! / He is wise. . . so wise. . . he is good, he is wise. . . so wise. . . so wise. . .

[33] Milner, 'Note sur le texte' to *L'Enfant et les sortilèges*, 1345, citing p. 728 of *L'Ingénue libertine* (*Œuvres*, vol. I).

character, clearly showing that it is the Child who utters ["Maman!"]'.[34] Yet comparison of libretto with score suggests rather a deliberate modification on Ravel's part; moreover, a writer of Colette's craft and theatrical experience is unlikely to have been unaware of the lack of clarity in her attribution.

We must therefore wonder whether the libretto's closing ambiguity is deliberate. Did Colette deliberately step back and allow Ravel to decide the final turn of their plot? Without further documentation, it is impossible to say. Nevertheless, Michel Mercier suggests that 'Ravel could not be satisfied, like Colette, with a voiceless hero'.[35] By turning the Animals' last words into a gentle fugal chorus, where overlay and repetition gently echo and invert the galloping polyphony of their fury; by their repeated naming of the Child; and most of all by reassigning the final 'Maman!' to the Child alone, Ravel reveals the strength and coherence of his structural concept: meaning, gesture, harmony, text and orchestral timbres are compellingly united in this culminating bar.

A *féerie-ballet*, a fantasy-libretto

In her 1936 memoir *Mes apprentissages* Colette wrote, 'Musical contours and the [written] phrase are born of the same elusive and immortal pair – sound and rhythm.'[36] Her lifelong musical engagement undoubtedly helped to shape a writing style notable for something akin to a composer's feel for resonance, metre and cadence: as Margaret Crosland put it, 'it is her feeling for rhythm, harmony, and the general musicality of words that creates those beautifully balanced phrases and sentences, long and short, which make her prose into poetry without ever becoming that unsatisfactory thing, poetic prose'.[37] Maurice Goudeket wrote that 'It was the turn of her sentences which Colette worked over most, as if she wanted to make them always more faithful to her own internal rhythm, in harmony with her exacting ear.'[38]

The libretto Colette delivered was thus defined in large part by vocal affect and aural effect. Its evocative play of rhythm and assonance and its overall textual coherence, coupled with its striking affinities with Ravel's own poetry, suggest that composer and librettist shared an intriguingly interdisciplinary sense of what an operatic libretto might be, were words to

---

[34] *Ibid.*, 1346.   [35] Mercier, '*L'Enfant et les sortilèges*: Analyse', 66.
[36] Colette, *Mes apprentissages*, *Œuvres*, vol. III, 1069.   [37] Crosland, 'Colette and Ravel', 116.
[38] Goudeket, *Close to Colette*, 45.

be shaped by musical sense and music by textual sonorities. Nevertheless, the libretto is also remarkably prescriptive, in its very detailed description of the appearance and movements of the different creatures, in the characteristic rhythms and assonances of their words, and in the many musical and aural evocations woven through the text. In accepting this specificity of description and direction, we may recognise a delineation of a compositional *cadre* that is particularly characteristic of Ravel.

In 1920, Diaghilev described Ravel's *La Valse* as 'the portrait of a ballet. . . the painting of a ballet'.[39] The libretto of *L'Enfant et les sortilèges* might be best described as 'the portrait of an opera-ballet'. A published libretto serves quite a different purpose from that of a published playscript: the latter is often intended for performance, but the former can only be followed or read independently. In the absence of a complete manuscript (or even any more than that single early page of draft), we may therefore wonder how much the printed libretto of *L'Enfant* represents a deliberate re-imagining and re-presentation of Colette's text. Its lengthy and poetic stage directions seem as much a description of an imagined scene as instructions for its theatrical realisation, while the ambiguity of the closing lines is redolent of Colette the novelist. If Colette's writings are threaded with the language and projections of the theatre, it is thus doubly ironic that this, her one published theatrical work, seems designed to be read, and savoured, on its own, quasi-novelised terms.

[39] Poulenc, *Moi et mes amis*, 179.

PART III

The compositional web

8 | The 'calling cards' of *L'Heure espagnole*

For all the Manons, the Carmens and the Fausts appearing every week on Parisian stages during the first decade of the twentieth century, there was no compelling need for an ambitious young French opera composer to define himself relative to Massenet, Bizet or Gounod. Rather, as Tony Aubin put it in 1945:

> To be a great musician, but to be neither Wagner, nor Fauré, nor Debussy: there was the first difficult problem for someone reaching maturity, in age and in technique, at the beginning of the century. To write for the theatre without sacrificing oneself either to the historic forms of opera or to the *verismo* of the Italian school; above all to avoid expressing oneself through any sentiment that suggested a lyric overflow from Tristan, and no less to set one's face against anything that hinted at Mélisande's inimitable reserve: there was yet another redoubtable problem.[1]

Wagner's music was being performed constantly in Paris from the 1880s until the First World War, in concert halls as well as opera houses. His aesthetic had fundamentally influenced a generation of French opera and the whole climate of French music and musical opinion.[2] Even Ravel had succumbed a little to the lure of Bayreuth in his Prix de Rome cantatas, admittedly written for a jury steeped in high Romantic opera tradition. As Barbara Kelly observes, he 'would never again write anything so Wagnerian, or so suggestive of the nineteenth-century operatic tradition he would later wish to supplant'.[3] And that he did indeed wish to supplant it was clear: 'Today, now that we are free and the terrible influence of Wagner does not disturb us anymore', he said in a 1924 interview;[4] elsewhere, he called that influence 'pernicious' and potentially 'disastrous'.[5]

---

[1] Aubin, 'L'Œuvre lyrique', 22.

[2] See *inter alia* Huebner, *French Opera at the Fin de Siècle*; Schwarz, *Wagner-Rezeption*; and Suschitzky, 'Fervaal, Parsifal, and French national identity'.

[3] Kelly, 'History and homage', 8.

[4] André Révész, 'El gran musico Mauricio Ravel habla de su arte', *ABC de Madrid*, 1 May 1924; Orenstein (ed.), *A Ravel Reader*, 432.

[5] Ravel, 'Contemporary music' (Rice Institute Lecture, 7 April 1928), in Orenstein (ed.), *A Ravel Reader*, 45; Orenstein, *Ravel, Man and Musician*, 123.

While Wagner held sway at the Opéra Garnier (in the first decade of the century few months passed without at least two different Wagner operas on the bill, and many months saw three or four), at the Opéra-Comique *Pelléas et Mélisande*, 'originally a *succès de scandale*', as David Grayson puts it, had 'rapidly bec[o]me a *succès d'estime*'.[6] Recognised as an epoch-making work from the day of its 1902 première, *Pelléas* was staged in every season but two (1905–6 and 1909–10) in its first decade and would receive its hundredth performance on 25 January 1913. Even more than Wagner, *Pelléas* was a potent and inescapable presence for a young composer seeking to enter the opera theatre in 1907, especially one labouring under the tag of *debussysme*.

In the course of a decisively negative review of the première of *L'Heure*, August Sérieyx would observe, 'Special rhythms are attached to certain characters like the muleteer and the banker, just as they are to a Walther or a Beckmesser; it's enough to say that we are in the presence of a work conceived and ordered according to the traditional means magisterially enshrined by the master of Bayreuth.'[*7] In equipping Ramiro with a light, uneven march figure, and Inigo with pompous Baroque dotted rhythms, Ravel was indeed nodding to 'the master of Bayreuth'. But if Sérieyx had noted the technique, he failed spectacularly to recognise its purpose. 'My music is unequivocally French. Anything except Wagnerian', Ravel said in a 1932 interview.[8] If he adopted an unabashedly Wagnerian procedure in *L'Heure espagnole*, it was to a purely satirical end. Moreover, the deliberation – even ponderousness – with which Ravel ushers his characters on and off stage is, as we'll see, an unambiguously ironic riposte not just to Wagner but to *Pelléas et Mélisande* as well.

Motivic organisation

When he made the decision to turn Franc-Nohain's *L'Heure espagnole* into an opera, Ravel was ascribing himself a set of challenges and parameters that were not only peculiar in themselves, but also essentially unique in operatic terms. He had an odd and unbalanced cast, with four male players who have no relationship beyond their shared interest in the sole woman, Concepcion. He had a backdrop that was Spanish, but self-consciously

---

[6] Grayson, 'Debussy on stage', 80.   [7] Sérieyx, 'Chronique musicale'.
[8] C. B. L., 'Ein Nachmittag bei Maurice Ravel', *Neue freie Presse*, 3 February 1932; Orenstein (ed.), *A Ravel Reader*, 488.

rather than authentically so. 'A big Catalan – that is to say Norman – clock', writes Franc-Nohain, setting the scene, while in the closing passages we hear that there is only 'un peu d'Espagne' about the whole affair.

Most importantly, Ravel had not a purpose-written libretto but a play. His text was an independent entity, which did not need music to cohere, communicate and entertain. He had a busy and fast-moving plot, responding to immediate issues and concrete, local events, rather than broad or abstract concerns. Within its single narrative focus – Concepcion's attempts to bring one of her lovers up to the mark – the story changes direction scene by scene. Its patterns of appearance and disappearance are meticulously arranged but irregular; they do not naturally lend themselves to clear-cut musical forms. Layered as it is with puns and double meanings, Franc-Nohain's tight-packed verse is also conceived to amuse and entertain in its own right. With this in mind, one of Ravel's chief concerns in setting this script must have been the simple obligation not to get in the way of the words: as he put it, 'the theatrical action itself demanded that the music be only the commentary on each word and gesture'.[9] A certain degree of self-effacement was necessary to avoid imposing structures that could obfuscate the narrative, although they might be clear and logical on their own terms.

Ravel thus needed a music that was principally organised on the same local level as the libretto. It had to illuminate, underline and comment, but without drawing too much attention to itself. The common focus of the four male characters, and the rapidity with which they appear and disappear, meant that they needed, musically, to be instantly identifiable and distinct. The use of characteristic motifs would thus naturally have suggested itself. The motifs had to be concise: there was no point in creating an eight- or even a four-bar musical signature for a character who might be on stage for only five or six bars. And they had to be flexible, to encapsulate the characters themselves, the ever-changing configurations in which they appear, and the continually reshaped motivations on which they act.

What Ravel created was a set of motifs that lend themselves easily to extension, combination and dissection. They can appear in different modes, with altered intervals and with different orchestration or rhythmic emphases. Most importantly, they are recognisable even when reduced to a melodic outline, a single harmonic entity, a rhythmic cell or sometimes even a timbral suggestion. These motifs naturally form a structural basis for

---

[9] [Anon.], 'Avant-première: *L'Enfant et les sortilèges*', *Le Gaulois*, 20 March 1925; *OL*, 349.

the opera: as the drama is propelled by rapid exchanges of dialogue, so the music would be driven by the interweaving of these characteristic gestures.

In Ravel's completed score, there are few bars that are devoid of motivic material – that is, material linked with a character or action, possessing distinctive melodic, harmonic or rhythmic characteristics, that recurs or relates to other recurring material.[10] The three most characteristic motifs are those attached to Ramiro, Inigo and (jointly) Torquemada and his clocks. Gonzalve is represented not by a single motivic signature but by an affect of highly stylised Spanishness (discussed further in Chapter 9). Concepcion uses a few distinctive melodic gestures, harmonic concoctions and timbral combinations (one gesture in particular characterises her dialogues with Ramiro), but she seemed to require no single defining leitmotif. As the only woman and the central axis of the plot, onstage for most of the opera, she is unmistakeable.

The first bar of Ravel's Introduction presents the motif that characterises both Torquemada's workshop and the clockmaker himself (Ex. 8.1a). Freed from the regular rhythm of its first appearance, it is equally recognisable in the jota that carries Torquemada off the stage at the end of Scene II (Ex. 8.1b),

Ex. 8.1 'Clock' motif

a. Introduction, bar 1

b. As jota, Scene II

---

[10] For a related discussion of Ravel's treatment of his motifs, with particular reference to Bergson's theory of comedy, see Huebner, 'Laughter: In Ravel's time', especially p. 236. See also Souillard, 'Commentaire littéraire et musical', and Clifton, 'Maurice Ravel's *L'Heure espagnole*', 164–230.

Ex. 8.1 (cont.)

c. As habanera, Scene IV

Ex. 8.2 Ramiro's motif

a. Scene I

b. Scene III

while Gonzalve transforms it into his first extravagant habanera in Scene IV (Ex. 8.1c). The motif's most important feature is its melodic shape, a descending figure ending in an upward turn.

Ramiro too has a characteristic melodic gesture, but the most important quality of his motif is the rhythm ♩ ♪♪ ♩ (or its equivalent). Appearing first in Scene I, as Ramiro describes his duties (Ex. 8.2a), the re-presentation of the motif at the beginning of Scene III (Ex. 8.2b) completes it with a falling fourth. Although his theme manifests itself in various modal guises and with

Ex. 8.2 (cont.)

c. Scene XXI (as habanera)

Ex. 8.3 Inigo's motif

a. First appearance, Scene VII

b. Motif inverted, Scene VII

some intervallic flexibility, that instantly identifiable rhythmic cell is always present. The motif is thus just as recognisable when it appears translated into a habanera – as at the end of Scene XVIII and in the final quintet (Ex. 8.2c) – as in the irregular 7/8 and 9/4 metres of its first appearances.

Inigo appears to the stately dotted rhythms of the French overture (Ex. 8.3a), which evoke his formality, self-satisfaction and taste for the grandiose gesture. Ravel underlines these qualities with a little mock-academicism, inverting the motif (marked *très expressif* in Ex. 8.3b) as Inigo tries to introduce a note of pathos to his wooing.

Inigo's motif also lends itself to fragmentation and combination. In Scene IX its three descending steps, transferred to the minor mode, set off a gently repetitive waltz, before the original motif returns as a trombone countermelody (Ex. 8.4). While Ramiro's motif, like his speech, is short and to the point, Inigo's verbal prolixity is thus musically matched by his repetitiveness: his second slow waltz, in Scene XIX, similarly combines a vapidly repetitive melodic cell with a restatement of his original motif.

A fourth motivic element is less obvious but more pervasive, present in some form in almost every scene. This is a line that descends through three or more semitones, appearing most commonly as an isolated melodic fragment (often as a countermelody), but equally amenable to incorporation within a harmonic motion. In the latter guise, it is an important element of the Introduction, in the two series of chromatically descending chords beneath the cacophony of the clocks (bars 16–21 and 33–4), as well as in the descending bass of Inigo's Scene IX waltz (system 3 of Ex. 8.4). As a more recognisable melodic motif, its first appearance comes in Scene II, as Torquemada peevishly concedes that he is unable to carry the clocks himself (Ex. 8.5).

While this motif is most commonly heard, as here, descending against a sustained chord, other recognisable appearances include its transformation into habanera rhythm at the beginning of Scene VI (see Ex. 9.1 below) and as a countermelody to Inigo's baroque dotted rhythms in Scene VII (Ex. 8.3 above). Often hidden within the texture, this gesture is linked not with a character but with a concept: maintaining the association initially granted it in Scene II, throughout the opera it implies or lampoons physical (sexual) incapacity.[11] The dialogue between Concepcion and Inigo in Scene XII makes this comically explicit: Ex. 8.6 shows the motif variously as a *tremolando*, a melodic line in the violas, a *portamento* descending bass, appoggiatura figures and sliding strings.

Besides its obvious *buffo* application, the descending motif also has direct harmonic implications: it naturally associates itself with the characteristic chromatic appoggiaturas of the Spanish-tinged Phrygian mode.

---

[11] Huebner notes this motif, with particular regard to its sexual connotations ('La Grivoiserie moderne', 201), but does not explore its pervasiveness across the opera.

Ex. 8.4 Inigo's motif as waltz, Scene IX

Ex. 8.5 Descending chromatic figure, Scene II

Ex. 8.6 Descending chromatic figures in Scene XII

a. *Tremolando* and viola countermelody (indicated with arrows)

In Scene XV, for example, the motif does not appear in melodic form, but over the E pedal of Gonzalve's soliloquy the harmony emphasises F♯ and F♮ stresses (Ex. 8.7).

In more compressed form, three adjacent semitones are heard simultaneously in a chord that Ravel characteristically uses as a marker of

Ex. 8.6 (cont.)

b. Sliding trombones

'Spanishness': the Phrygian-coloured harmony of a seventh chord super-imposed on a pitch a tritone distant from the chord's implied resolution (in Ex. 8.8 an A^7 chord – the dominant seventh of D – perched on G#).[12] This is one of Gonzalve's signature gestures, heralding his arrival at the end of Scene III (Fig. 15^{-3}) and emphasised during his little aria in Scene XIX ('Adieu, cellule...'; see also p. 181). Throughout the opera the triple-semitone combination thus serves alternately as melody and harmony, *couleur locale*, satiric comment and core binding element.

---

[12] As a cadential appoggiatura this chord can also be traced back through Schumann and Chopin – it underpins the culminating cadence of the latter's *Barcarolle* – to Beethoven and Bach; see Howat, *The Art of French Piano Music*, 67, 352n9. Ravel also uses it at the start of 'Scarbo', and cadentially at the end of 'Les Entretiens de la Belle et de la Bête', but in 'Spanish' guise the harmony characterises the 'Habanera' of his *Rapsodie espagnole* (originally the first movement of the two-piano *Sites auriculaires*) and the central passage of 'Alborada del gracioso', and makes an appearance in the *Vocalise-Étude en forme de Habanera*.

Ex. 8.6 (cont.)

c. 'Sighing' figures

d. Sliding strings

One further harmonic device serves an instantly recognisable motivic and satirical purpose: the chord which, at strategic moments, ceases to function as a standard half-diminished and assumes the unmistakeable aura of a Tristan chord. As Huebner observes, this harmony is deployed at moments of dramatic or sexual tension: it occurs – at Wagner's pitch – as Concepcion interrupts Inigo's increasingly pressing advances (Ex. 8.9a),

Ex. 8.7 Chromatic movement as 'Spanish' harmony, Scene XV

Ex. 8.8 Triple-semitone clash (harmony of Fig. 15^{-3})

and launches her unaccompanied 'Sans horloge!'[13] Concepcion makes her first entrance over a series of half-diminished chords (Fig. 7^{+2}); the same chord marks her impatient 'Oui, mon ami...' between Gonzalve's effusions in Scene IV (Example 8.9b); another one punctuates her offer to accompany Ramiro upstairs with Gonzalve in his clock (Scene VIII, Fig. 39^{+6}), another her decision to send Inigo upstairs in a clock (Scene XIII, Fig. 66^{+5}) and yet another Inigo's extraction from that clock by Ramiro in the final scene (Fig. 117). Usually offset by rests and often accented, the chord is aurally distinguished from the harmonies on either side of it: flourished under the noses (or ears) of the audience, it gleefully proclaims 'Thwarted Desire!', rather in the manner of a silent movie placard. But Ravel's use of the Tristan chord has a dual function: while mocking its very obviousness, he also uses it as a deft compositional shorthand, compressing a clutch of extra-musical associations into a gesture of the utmost concision and immediacy.

The reiteration of these principal motifs and motivic elements determines the organisation of the music that encompasses them: the opera's architectural coherence derives from their development, fragmentation, juxtaposition and superimposition. As we've already seen in part, the motifs, being few, distinct and self-contained, can each be reduced to a single basic gesture. Any instance of ♩ ♫ ♩ rhythm or an emphasised falling fourth is enough to identify Ramiro, while Inigo can be recognised by the

[13] Huebner, 'La Grivoiserie moderne', 199–201.

Ex. 8.9 Strategic 'Tristan' chords

a. Scene VII

b. Scene IV

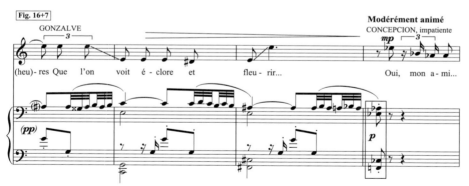

first four notes of his motif, and a slow-moving descending chordal figure will always evoke the clocks. Examination of the third scene of the opera illustrates the way in which a relatively straightforward exchange of dialogue is underpinned by subtle thematic complexity. The scene opens as Torquemada leaves and Concepcion is alone with Ramiro: it is here that

Ex. 8.10 Concepcion's motif, Scene III

the real action begins. The opening material evokes Concepcion's frustrated confusion, with the parallel major sevenths of cor anglais and bass clarinet hinting at her petulance. This material will reappear in Concepcion's dialogue with Ramiro in Scene V, and the final descending triad also echoes in Scene XXI (bar 4 of Example 8.14 below); though not consistent enough to function as a 'leitmotif', it has a clear local identifying function.

Concepcion's lament for her lost 'jour de vacances' is immediately followed by Ramiro's theme (Ex. 8.2b above), which appears for the first time with its culminating falling fourth. This interval, as Chapter 11 explores, is a Ravelian signature; in *L'Heure* it becomes Ramiro's signature as well, strongly evident, as Chapter 6 noted, in his vocal lines as well as in his orchestral accompaniment. In this first appearance, however, the falling fourth also echoes the opening gesture of Concepcion's material. This connection is emphasised in the chords that accompany her next line (Ex. 8.11), which both extend the first bar of Example 8.10 and reinforce Ramiro's falling fourth. Concepcion's allusion to the clocks ('Cette horloge, monsieur. . .') is accompanied by an echo of the clock motif, as developed early in the Introduction. The reference is heightened by a strong whiff of the opening tonality, the E minor chord an obvious tonal reminiscence.

Ex. 8.11 Integration of Concepcion's motif with clock motif

Ramiro responds to Concepcion's 'hesitating' question about the weight of the clocks with a reprise of his motif ('Ça, Madame? C'est une paille . . .'; Fig. 13). Their subsequent exchange at Fig. 13[+3] (Ex. 8.12) is captured in three bars that juxtapose his and Concepcion's motifs directly, the falling fourth serving to link them (the same combination recurs in Scene V, at Fig. 25). Also present (in the tenor, indicated by arrows in Ex. 8.12) is the characteristic three-note descending chromatic gesture, which returns, unadorned, to accompany Concepcion's words 'Tout s'arrange fort bien ainsi!' (Fig. 14[+6]). This direct musical echo of Torquemada's Scene II plaint (Ex. 8.5 above) is a sly warning that things may not 'arrange themselves' quite as easily as she imagines. The scene closes with a final echo of Concepcion's motif, with its falling fourth and dissonant sevenths ('Vraiment, Monsieur, vraiment, j'abuse!'), before Ramiro's motif leads directly into the jota rhythms that herald the appearance of Gonzalve.

In this very early scene, Ravel is already beginning to explore the juxtaposition and combination of his motifs in ways that function as both musical argument and extra-musical commentary: the overlapping of Ramiro's and Concepcion's themes in these passages seems to hint at their eventual union.

Detached from its surroundings, Ramiro's falling fourth functions as a motivic cell in its own right. In the conversation between Concepcion, Ramiro and Inigo in Scene XIII, for example (Ex. 8.13a), the fourth becomes an accompanying gesture beneath a brief reprise of the waltz-figure from Inigo's Scene IX soliloquy (Ex. 8.4 above). It also recurs in a series of quickfire motivic juxtapositions as Gonzalve exits his clock in Scene XIX (Ex. 8.13b). Here the cell recalls not only Ramiro but the cuckoo that called – with an uncharacteristic fourth, rather than a third – at the

Ex. 8.12 Juxtaposition and combination of Ramiro's and Concepcion's motifs

beginning of the scene: in both cases the flute carries the top line, making a very recognisable timbral connection. This is immediately followed by two bars of a habanera fragment that echoes Scene XIV (Fig. 70), then two bars of the descending chromatic figure.

Another neat example of motivic melding comes from the beginning of Scene XXI (Ex. 8.14). Here, Ramiro's motif (signalling his return to the stage with Concepcion) alternates with a melodic fragment that combines a spiralling 'Spanish' gesture – heard in Gonzalve's effusions in Scene IV and Inigo's sardonic evocation of 'les poètes' in Scene XII (Fig. 62; see p. 185) – with the descending triad that ended Concepcion's motif in Scene III (Ex. 8.10 above). The same phrase, with the descending triad slightly modified, reappears in the first passage of the final quintet (Fig. 121^{+2}). In these examples we see the characteristic falling fourth acting rather like a

Ex. 8.13 Motivic juxtapositions

a. Scene XIII

b. Scene XIX

Ex. 8.14 Motivic melding, Scene XXI

chemically unstable element, bonding enthusiastically with other motifs and fulfilling both harmonic and melodic functions with equal facility. More fancifully, in *L'Heure* we may recognise most literally the composer as the 'Swiss [or Spanish] watchmaker' that Stravinsky famously called him. If, like Torquemada, we lift the lid of the watch – or if we look beneath the vocal line of the opera – we see functioning within it these interlocking motivic cogwheels, advancing and controlling the narrative as they regulate time itself.

The inescapable clocks

This brings us to the clocks of *L'Heure espagnole*, who are characters in their own right. They have a motif, which they share with their maker Torquemada (Ex. 8.1 above), and they play a crucial role in determining the course of the action. The clocks intervene at key moments, prompting thoughts, responses and actions from the other characters: as Ramiro muses in Scene XVI (Fig. 78[+3]), a clock strikes twelve, representing (or impelling) his hour of decision: 'If I had to change my fate, / Were I not a muleteer, I would be a clockmaker, / In this clock shop, with this clockmaker's wife. . .', he concludes. Elsewhere, cuckoo clocks offer cheekily apt interpolations: one effectively introduces Torquemada by sounding just before his first words, another punctures Inigo's impassioned wooing of Concepcion at the end of Scene VII (Ex. 8.9a above), and a third carols just after Concepcion takes Ramiro off, at the beginning of Scene XIX. In the last instance, as noted above, the traditional falling third is extended to a falling fourth – an unmistakeable indication that it is Ramiro who has successfully cuckolded Torquemada at last. Concepcion herself is entirely

Ex. 8.15 'Clock' motif and 'Marche funèbre'

aware of the significance of the cuckoo clocks: in Scene XII, mistaking Inigo's coy imitations for one of the clocks in the shop, she exclaims 'And this is a fine moment / To talk of cuckoos here!' Sardonic comment also comes from the mechanical trumpet player and 'little rooster': both end their performances (Fig. 2^{+3}, Fig. 3, Fig. 50^{+3}) with downward chromatic slides. With this allusion to the characteristic descending chromatic figure, Ravel suggests a direct relationship between the automatons and 'real' characters: in exaggerated miniature, the clocks echo and mock the failures of human stratagems and mechanisms.

Because the clocks are so well endowed with personality, the characters themselves seem to regard them as fellow-actors. They all relate to the clocks, talk about and to them, and interact with them physically and intellectually. For Gonzalve, as noted in Chapter 6, the clocks serve as poetic inspiration, as he turns them into a series of entirely predictable metaphors. In Scene VI he invokes the music of the Introduction to accompany his enclosure in the clock, with the opening motif comically transferred to the tuba (Ex. 8.15). Above this, an unmistakeable horn allusion to the 'Marche funèbre' from Chopin's B♭ minor Sonata (op. 35) offers a cartoonish illustration of the coffin he is imagining.

Don Inigo has little respect for the clocks: he climbs into one thinking it will be good for a laugh. The clock, however, has its revenge, as he gets hopelessly stuck. The lack of poetry in Inigo's disposition is matched by the inescapably physical way he relates to the clocks: he lumbers in (with difficulty) and cannot get out again. As Huebner suggests, for Inigo in particular the clocks also serve as sexual metaphors, as in the

Ex. 8.16 Development of Ramiro's motif, Scene X

less-than-subtle 'Qu'à l'intérieur j'ai voulu pénétrer' (Scene XX) and the mournful 'Lorsque j'eus tant de peine à entrer, faut-il déjà sortir?' (Scene XII).[14] Ramiro, meanwhile, initially maintains a firmly practical approach to the clocks. Yet from the beginning there is a sense that they appeal to the thread of lurking lyricism and fantasy in his character. The drama with which Ramiro recounts the history of his uncle in the Barcelona bullring – saved by his pocket-watch – hints at this feeling for romance, and in his two later soliloquies the chimes and mechanical noises send him into a more reflective mood. For him the clocks are magical in themselves – he marvels at them – and a form of escapism, for they prompt him to fantasise about what his life might be like, were it not for his mules. He too begins to associate the clocks with women, but in more philosophical terms than his rivals: 'When I see these subtle machines assembled here / All these tiny springs, so easily confused, / I think of the mechanism that is / woman, a mechanism just as complicated! It is difficult to understand it!'

[14] Huebner, 'La Grivoiserie moderne', 198–9.

As Ramiro, in his Scene X and XVI soliloquies, begins to contemplate his life and character, his motif and that of the clocks begin to intertwine. Scene X (Ex. 8.16) opens with an *expressif* statement of his motif, legato over a pedal note, with its falling fourth stretched to a sixth and a modified final turn. This evolves into a new melodic fragment, which reinstates the falling fourth and retains the distinctive ♩ ♫ ♩ rhythm, while recalling the outline of the original clock motif – for it is the clockmaker's shop and its mechanical inhabitants, as least as much as the clockmaker's wife, who have prompted these new thoughts. The scene concludes with Ramiro returning, *avec mélancolie*, to reality (Fig. 52): 'All the skill Fate has granted me / Is limited to carrying clocks', he muses, his new lyrical theme descending from the violins to a solo cello and heard beneath a restatement of his original motif, staccato once more.

The clocks are recalled even more directly in Ramiro's second soliloquy, in Scene XVI (Ex. 8.17).[15] The scene opens in the same manner as Scene X, with an *expressif* statement of Ramiro's motif. This gives way, as Ramiro looks around the shop, to a modified restatement of the original clock motif, which echoes not just bar 1 of the Introduction but the upward motion and reprise of the same figure a fourth higher in bars 4–6 (bars 3–4 of Ex. 8.17). The third and fourth chords of the clock motif are, in this passage, moved respectively up and down a tone, creating Ramiro's falling fourth between them. As well as being a neat evocation of his engagement with the clocks, the resultant motif would also become a Ravelian signature: near-identical gestures may be found in *Ma mère l'Oye* ('Le Jardin féerique'), *Daphnis et Chloé* ('Danse religieuse'), *Le Tombeau de Couperin* ('Menuet') and the first movement second subject of the G major Concerto.

The exigencies of Torquemada's profession give Concepcion the chance to entertain her suitors, so she has a certain affection for the clocks; moreover, they provide the solution for getting those suitors up to her bedroom. But because of her complicated machinations, Concepcion, more than any of the other characters, is disturbed by the clocks. She thinks and speaks of time as the other do not: 'time weighs on me!', she repeats in Scene XVII. In Scene IV, she repeatedly emphasises time's passing, as she tries to get Gonzalve to pay attention to her – 'this fleeting hour', 'this only hour', 'the time has come', 'time is measured pitilessly'. As she encourages him 'Let us not lose ourselves in fruitless words / The hour is flying / And must be caught' (Fig 16^{-3}), a reprise of the opening clock motif suggests

[15] In an intriguing discussion of what he terms the 'primal scene', Puri notes the structural importance of Ramiro's two soliloquies (which serve to divide the opera into three roughly equal parts), relative to the opera's Introduction (*Ravel the Decadent*, 78).

Ex. 8.17 'Clock' motif with Ramiro's falling fourth, Scene XVI

that she is right to be anxious. At the end of her aria in Scene XVII, she beats with her fists on the front of the clock concealing Gonzalve, her rage seemingly directed equally at the poet and at time itself.

Jessie Fillerup cogently argues for the opera's (unconscious) engagement with the contemporary debates of Einstein and Bergson concerning the perception and measurement of time: '*L'Heure* is a work that not only functions "in time", like any other, but is explicitly *about* time [. . .] As Ravel challenges perceptions of musical time through tempo, rhythm, meter, and performance duration, he questions the mechanisms – clocks, space, experience, and memory – that "measure" time, sounding a theme central to the Einstein–Bergson debate.'[16] Indeed, as she argues, 'Franc-Nohain employs several references to time and mortality in the play, but Ravel seems to take the playwright's conceit one step further, making Time the opera's primary subject and star.'[17] The point of all this, however, is not to instigate a metaphysical discussion (Fillerup covers this ground admirably[18]) but to

[16] Fillerup, 'Purloined poetics', 191.   [17] *Ibid.*, 189.

[18] See *ibid.*, 168–221. Puri argues that 'the opera is founded in a decadent experience of time as an existential prison' (*Ravel the Decadent*, 14). See also Souillard, 'Commentaire littéraire et musical', 89; Langham Smith, 'Ravel's operatic spectacles', 192–3; and Huebner, 'Laughter: In Ravel's time', 239.

Ex. **8.18** Echo of clock motif, Scene I

recognise the importance of the clocks as a dramatic and thus musical force throughout *L'Heure espagnole*. As well as the Introduction's symphony of mechanical noises, echoed in the interjections of chimes and carillons at intervals throughout the opera, the motivic material associated with the clocks has a core unifying function. The two key musical ideas set out in the Introduction – the opening 'clock' motif and the series of chromatically descending chords – are inescapable presences throughout the whole opera, in subtle emphasis of the narrative-defining power of the clocks.

Although the opening motif (Ex. 8.1 above) recurs directly, in the same intervallic and rhythmic form, in only five scenes (I, II, IV, VI and XX), its characteristic outline – a descending figure, generally spanning the interval of a fifth and curling upwards at the end – returns in many other guises. As we've seen, it merges with Ramiro's motif to accompany his soliloquies (Exx. 8.16–8.17); the muleteer also introduces himself, in Scene I, with a 7/8 figure that descends in first-inversion chords through the interval of a fifth (in the oboe and clarinets) and concludes with the strings playing a rising third (Ex. 8.18). This fragment will return in the final scene as Concepcion remarks, 'Regulier comme un chronomètre'; it is a nice touch of irony that this 'regular chronometer', like the original clock motif, is in a decidedly irregular metre.

Scenes IV–V present a series of variants on the clock motif (Ex. 8.19), beginning with Gonzalve's direct quotation at Fig. 16 (see Ex. 8.1c above). Each of these fragments moves in a predominantly downward direction, offset with an upward turn; each of them descends through a fifth (sometimes diminished) and each of them includes an interval of a third within their otherwise stepwise motion. The same gestural outline is recalled in the sinuous oboe line that accompanies Concepcion in Scene XVII when she laments the imminent return of Torquemada (Ex. 8.20); here again, the

Ex. 8.19 Variants on 'clock' motif, Scenes IV–V

Ex. 8.20 'Clock' motif variant, Scene XVII

melody moves through a descending fifth, countered with a final upturned third. The last three chimes of a clock striking six reinforce a sense of thematic affinity.

Codes, cards and *Pelléas* again

In a 1902 interview in *Le Figaro*, Debussy deplored Wagner's use of leitmotifs as 'calling-cards' – 'I must confess that I find this procedure somewhat gross', he said.[19] Yet, as has often been noted and discussed, Debussy too aligned certain motifs, harmonies and gestures in *Pelléas* with characters, symbols, ideas and psychological states.[20] Robin Holloway describes his motivic procedures thus: 'Every motif shares the same intervals with every other; they can be fragmented into accompaniment or ostinato; every ostinato or accompaniment can emerge as a motif; and

---

[19] Langham Smith (trans. and ed.), *Debussy on Music*, 80–1.

[20] Debussy's use of characteristic motifs in *Pelléas* has been explored by many commentators, from Louis Laloy's 1905 article 'Le Drame musical moderne: Claude Debussy' (Priest, *Louis Laloy*, 165–87) onwards. In *French Opera at the Fin de siècle*, Huebner argues that 'the ubiquity of leitmotifs in progressive *drame lyrique* [...] rendered [Debussy's] decision to use them quite unremarkable' (73). See also Orledge, *Debussy and the Theatre*, 91–7; Langham Smith, 'French operatic spectacle in the twentieth century', 125; and, more generally, Holloway, *Debussy and Wagner*, Abbate, '*Tristan* in the composition of *Pelléas*', and Nichols and Langham Smith, *Pelléas et Mélisande*, 140–83.

the harmony everywhere consists of these same intervals superimposed into chords.'[21]

As it happens, Holloway's words are also a fair summation of Ravel's musical procedures in *L'Heure espagnole*. Other descriptions of Debussy's motivic treatment in *Pelléas* also resonate strongly with *L'Heure*: Robert Orledge's description of 'a direct musical response to a given scenario or dramatic text, almost in what might be termed cinematographic "moment" form';[22] and Elliott Antokoletz's identification of 'a kind of "leit-sound" capacity' that 'contributes to the symbolic association of different musical events'.[23] We've seen Ravel doing something akin to the latter in the flute that links the 'cuckoo' falling fourths at the beginning and middle of Scene XIX of *L'Heure* (Figs 94[+1], 97[+4] and 98[+2]; see Ex. 8.14 above): the first instance is 'just' a cuckoo, but the last is definitely Ramiro, and thus we retrospectively identify him with the earlier cuckoos too. More subtly, but just as decisively, Ramiro's increasing fascination with Concepcion is evoked when his motif appears in its *expressif* form at the beginnings of Scenes X and XVI, clothed in the instrumental timbres of Concepcion's material in Scene III (cor anglais, clarinet and bassoon, plus bass clarinet in Scene XVI).

Yet alongside these intricate motivic relationships we find a joyous abandonment of Debussyan subtlety. Ravel's characters are introduced by their themes as circus turns by a ringmaster. Their motifs are 'calling-cards' indeed, ceremoniously presented on every visit and flourished under the noses of the audience. The characters even take their cues from each other's musical signatures: at the beginning of Scene XIII, Concepcion is alerted to Ramiro's approach not by his voice, it seems, but by his motif. The first production made this explicit, relocating Franc-Nohain's direction that she 'quickly closes the clock where Inigo is hidden' (which in the printed score is shown above Ramiro's opening words, at Fig. 64[+3]), back to the first bar of the scene (Fig. 64), as the first notes of his motif are heard.[24]

In *Pelléas*, it is not just Mélisande who is lost in the forest: most of the characters are following misty paths, with no knowledge of their

---

[21] Holloway, *Debussy and Wagner*, 137. Holloway adds (136–7) that 'It is precisely in his employment of Wagnerian leitmotifs in *Pelléas* that Debussy stands furthest from his original [. . .] The music in *Pelléas* actually *reacts* to the words rather than, as in Wagner, being the expression and embodiment of them.'

[22] Orledge, *Debussy and the Theatre*, 88.

[23] Antokoletz, *Musical Symbolism in the Operas of Debussy and Bartók*, 121; see also 86–8. Wenk also explores Debussy's motivic use of timbre, *Debussy and Twentieth-Century Music*, 43–6.

[24] Original production score, coll. Roy Howat.

destinations. In *L'Heure espagnole*, by contrast, the audience knows, just as the characters themselves seem to, that they are witnessing or taking part in a farce, a dance in which each step is foreseen and measured – orchestrated, most literally – from the outset. The orchestra shares the role of storyteller with the singers, ushering the characters on and off and prompting their decisions and reflections. It also serves as commentary (and in this it is perhaps more novelistic than cinematographic): the orchestra communicates with the audience behind the backs of the characters, as it were, with interpolations like the cuckoos, the sardonic and ubiquitous descending chromatic gesture, and the spotlighted Tristan chords. Where Debussy's orchestra illuminates the emotional depths and conflicts of his *dramatis personæ*, Ravel's often undermines his characters, delighting in their littleness and exposing the cogwheels and pulleys of their narrative (most obviously in the final quintet, where the sarrusophone blurts the bass note that Inigo cannot reach, Fig. 126^{-3}).

Like *Pelléas*, *L'Heure* is a music of association, a coded music, for characters who themselves speak in code. The inhabitants of Allemonde speak a language of symbols, and so do the characters in Torquemada's shop. But if words and motifs, in *Pelléas*, are symbols for things and ideas, in *L'Heure* words often stand for other words: theirs is a language of wicked double meanings, cheeky euphemisms and punning wordplay. Concepcion puts Inigo off by exclaiming 'J'ai les déménageurs!' as an Englishwoman might say that she 'has the painters in' (both are euphemisms for menstruation); she emphasises the fragility of the clock's mechanism – 'especially the pendulum!'; and Inigo explains how he had 'wanted to penetrate the interior' – of the clocks, of course. Their music, like their conversation, forms a complex and endlessly referential web of ideas, gestures and phrases; their 'calling cards' become playing cards, endlessly shuffled and re-dealt.

In 1896 Ricardo Viñes, in his journal, had described Ravel 'trembling convulsively and weeping like a child' at a performance of the *Tristan* Prelude, saying 'It's always like this, every time I hear it.'[25] While Ravel was also a devoted *pelléastre*, attending every performance of the 1902 opening season, by March 1904 Viñes would record, of an evening spent with 'toute la bande', 'we laughed a lot at a parody done by Ravel and Delage of *Pelléas et Mélisande*'.[26] If *L'Heure espagnole* makes game of *Pelléas* and Wagnerian

---

[25] Gubisch, 'La Vie musicale à Paris', 190 (entry for 1 November 1896).
[26] *Ibid.*, 201 (entry for 24 March 1904).

grand opera, it does so from the inside, turning technical procedures back on themselves and using them to generate humour.

It can have been little more than coincidence that the same baritone, Jean Périer, created the roles of both Pelléas and Ramiro at the Opéra-Comique. Nevertheless, this coincidence was an extraordinarily happy one, whose significance cannot have been lost on Ravel. The relationship of *L'Heure espagnole* to *Pelléas et Mélisande* may perhaps be best viewed as parody in a serious, classical sense. Ravel measured up his canvas after the principles Debussy had explored and allocated himself a similar set of materials or techniques with which to work, then used these techniques to produce an outcome signifying something utterly different. Roy Howat has explored the relationship between Ravel's 'Ondine' and Chopin's A♭ Étude, op. 25 no. 1, in related terms;[27] we may similarly view Ravel's *Valses nobles et sentimentales* relative to Schubert's *Valses nobles* and *Valses sentimentales*, and recognise the same principle again in his joking comment on the final scene of *Daphnis et Chloé*: that he had put the score of Rimsky-Korsakov's *Shéhérazade* on the piano and tried to copy it.[28] Despite the debt it owes to *Pelléas*, *L'Heure* is unequivocally Ravelian. As Barbara Kelly notes, 'At the heart of his teaching methods, Ravel emphasised mastery of technique through the imitation of models; originality would emerge from "unwitting infidelity to the model".'[29] The extent of Ravel's innovation, in *L'Heure espagnole*, perhaps shows itself most clearly in the way he made these frameworks and techniques utterly his own.

---

[27] Howat, *The Art of French Piano Music*, 79
[28] Reported by Manuel Rosenthal, in Nichols, *Ravel Remembered*, 44.
[29] Kelly, 'History and homage', 10, quoting Roland-Manuel, 'Des Valses à *La Valse*', 145.

9 | From Carmen to Concepcion

On 17 May 1911, *Comœdia* published a gossipy interview with Geneviève Vix, who was about to create the role of Concepcion in *L'Heure espagnole*:

'What, you have come to ask for my impressions of my new role of Concepcion! You know how I avoid all interviews! It's a betrayal! No, no, I will tell you nothing... Anyway, I have nothing to tell; I am not the right person to speak to you about *L'Heure espagnole*...' And the penetrating, disconcerting eyes of Mlle Geneviève Vix are quick to express all the resentment of which the singer is capable.

'Permit me... It is several years now since Franc-Nohain and Maurice Ravel chose you to create the role of their heroine... It's a position...' 'Which does not justify indiscretion.'

All at once, I resort to stronger persuasion. 'In the name of our old friendship, tell me how you play Concepcion!' And I take on a profoundly sorrowful air and exclaim, 'Camarade, mon amie, ne ferez-vous rien pour moi?' This quotation from Carmen and my woebegone expression dispel the wrath of my patient – Mlle Geneviève Vix has a tender heart.*[1]

The 'exclusive' interview with Vix (who goes on to say nothing very much about how she plays Concepcion or anybody else) was titled 'Mlle Geneviève Vix and *L'Heure espagnole* – from Carmen to Concepcion'.

This juxtaposition of characters and operas was hardly unexpected: any Spanish-themed opera given in Paris in the early twentieth century was inevitably going to be viewed relative to *Carmen*, especially one staged at the Opéra-Comique. Although the opera's 1875 opening season had been a notorious failure (remembered thus not least because of the untimely death of its composer three months after the première), *Carmen* had made a triumphant return to the Opéra-Comique in 1883 and was never out of the repertoire thereafter. We can safely assume that almost every audience member during the 1911 run of *L'Heure espagnole* would have been familiar with Bizet's masterpiece; most of them would have seen it numerous times. As both *the* 'Spanish' opera and the theatre's flagship work, *Carmen* cast a long shadow.

[1] Prudhomme, 'Mlle Geneviève Vix et *L'Heure espagnole*'.

Of the original production sources for *Carmen*, Richard Langham Smith observes that 'some details in the *mises en scènes* are to be found nowhere else, explaining elements of the opera that neither the scores nor the libretto revealed'.[2] The 1911 staging material for *L'Heure espagnole* – including the original production score, fair copies of the *mise-en-scène* and the costume and set designs – likewise reveals technical procedures and narrative glosses not communicated in the libretto or score.[3] These records help to show us how the five characters were first realised: how they looked, how they moved, how they related to each other, and how they acted out their Spanishness. Considered alongside the history, perceptions and caricatures of *espagnolade*, they play a vital role in tracing how Franc-Nohain's libretto and Ravel's score incorporate and lampoon contemporary perceptions of Spain and Spanishness.

Carmen and *espagnolade*

For audiences and critics in 1875, *Carmen* provided ample material for outrage. The protagonist's moral laxity, the rowdy female chorus and the onstage murder were all new and shocking, and were targeted in indignant reviews.[4] Nevertheless, the opera's transformation into stunning success owes much to the paradoxical familiarity of its foreignness. Geographically close, recognisably European, but demonstrably 'other', Spain offered nineteenth-century Parisians, in Hervé Lacombe's words, 'a "near" or "backyard" exoticism [. . .] the exoticism of the middle class'.[5]

In the Preface to his Performance Urtext of *Carmen* (Peters Edition), Langham Smith cogently summarises the

passion for Spanish themes (not to mention the exotic in general) in French artistic ventures in the middle of the nineteenth century [. . .] Spanish music of one sort or another permeated every genre, and was seen in every Parisian musical venue from the private salon, through the Theatre, to Opera, Ballet and, of course, Zarzuela.

---

[2] Langham Smith, 'Taming two Spanish women', 97.

[3] For a full discussion of the original production material, see Kilpatrick, 'The Carbonne copy'.

[4] Macdonald, '*Carmen*'. See also Wright (ed.), *Dossier de presse: Carmen (1875)*.

[5] Lacombe, 'The writing of exoticism', 157. Concerning broader questions of musical exoticism, see the many writings of Ralph Locke, notably including *Musical Exoticism* and 'A broader view of musical exoticism'; Born and Hesmondhaigh (eds.), *Western Music and its Others*; Bellman (ed.), *The Exotic in Western Music*. Studies with a specifically French perspective include Fauser and Everist (eds.), *Music, Theater, and Cultural Transfer*, and Fauser, *Musical Encounters at the 1889 Paris World's Fair*.

Paris was full of Spanish customs and the community even held bullfights in Montmartre.[6]

By 1889, Julien Tiersot could complain, as Michael Christoforidis puts it, that 'Spain was everywhere': in his reflection on Spanish music at the Exposition Universelle, Tiersot described 'bullfights to right and left; Spanish choral societies here, Spanish soirées there; at the Cirque d'hiver Spanish fiestas, orchestra, dance, *estudiantina*; at the Exposition the gypsies from Granada'.[7]

This thriving culture of *espagnolade* furnished Bizet and his librettists with a rich repository of images and idioms, many of them long familiar to Opéra-Comique audiences: Lacombe has documented how some of *Carmen*'s tropes, and its use of popular idioms, were already well established even within this more limited frame.[8] As early as 1857, as Kerry Murphy notes, the critic Léon Lespès could 'despairingly [ask] *opéra comique* composers, "Why don't you go to China or India, Lapland or Patagonia, leave off that country where *the eye of a young girl gleams under the mantilla*?"'[9] Carmen herself may have been shocking, but her setting – although depicted with a greater degree of authenticity than the audiences of the Opéra-Comique were accustomed to – was not.

By the last decade of the nineteenth century, a changing operatic climate, as Samuel Llano explains, 'further helped to mitigate perceptions of difference in *Carmen*. Thanks to *verismo* and naturalism, Parisian operatic audiences grew accustomed to onstage death and violence.'[10] Langham Smith details the beginnings of a different but related cultural shift: by around 1910, although flamboyant *espagnolade* still flourished, nineteenth-century conceptions of Spain were starting to be 'subjected to critical review'.[11] On the operatic stage, we may observe these perceptual changes intertwining in the two operas of Raoul Laparra, *La Habanera* (1908) and *La Jota*, which premiered in spring 1911, just a few weeks before *L'Heure espagnole*. Laparra, a year younger than

---

[6]   Langham Smith, 'Preface', to *Carmen: A Performance Urtext*. In addition to the sources cited in the notes that follow, see also Lesure (ed.), *Echanges musicaux franco-espagnols*, and Jambou (ed.), *La Musique entre France et Espagne*.

[7]   Tiersot, *Promenades musicales à l'Exposition*, 276, quoted in Christoforidis, 'Foreword' to Llano, *Whose Spain?*, xi.

[8]   Lacombe, 'L'Espagne à l'Opéra-Comique avant *Carmen*'. See also Hoffmann, *Romantique Espagne*, who documents (Appendix III) what Murphy describes as a 'staggering' number of French theatrical works on Spanish themes across the period 1780–1850 (Murphy, 'Couleur locale or the real thing', 295).

[9]   Murphy, 'Couleur locale or the real thing', 305, quoting Léon Lespès, *La France musicale*, 4 October 1857.

[10] Llano, *Whose Spain?*, 165.

[11] Langham Smith, 'Ravel's operatic spectacles', 190; he cites articles in the Parisian *Revue hispanique* and Julián Juderias's *La Leyenda negra*, which includes a chapter summarising 'the view of Spain from surrounding Europe' (nn8–9).

Ravel, was a fervent admirer and scholar of Spanish music and culture (he was also a fluent Basque speaker, for which Ravel respected him greatly). In 1914 he would contribute an extended article on Spanish music ('La Musique et la danse populaires en Espagne') to the *Dictionnaire du Conservatoire*, tracing musical characteristics and forms from every region of Spain: among the many musical examples (on p. 2369) is the melody Ravel adopted for his 1910 'Chanson espagnole'. As Llano demonstrates, Laparra's approach to *espagnolade* was consciously 'authentic', a quality he sought to set against the 'imagined' Spain of *Carmen*: in his 1935 monograph *Bizet et l'Espagne*, Laparra labelled *Carmen* 'une œuvre d'intuition, mais non une œuvre vécue' ('an *imagined*, but not an *experienced* work').[12]

Laparra's passion for Spanish authenticity was shared by Albert Carré, who went so far as to transport the cast and crew of *La Habanera* to Burgos to gather *couleur locale* in preparation for the production.[13] However, neither of Laparra's operas held their place in the repertoire: their violence, gruesome realism, the reluctance or inability of the critics to recognise what Laparra was trying to achieve, and the failure of the music itself to live up to all that Laparra claimed for it, contributed to their lack of success.[14] Laparra's former composition teacher Gabriel Fauré noted 'an overuse of typical rhythms that entails a fatal monotony':[15] overwhelmed by self-conscious authenticity, Laparra's writing often lacks a consistent musical narrative and a clear, independent compositional voice.

Ravel's Spain

Ravel's Spain, by contrast, is more sinuous, more assimilated within his own musical language. Christine Le Bordays described his hispanicism as in 'perpetual flux. Fluid and ductile, it slips easily into different moulds, and its sincerity of tone depends on his adhesion to his chosen atmosphere.'[16] As Spain was France's 'familiar exotic', for Ravel it was more directly a 'famili*al* exotic',[17] a heritage consciously adopted as his own. 'From your (or from my) homeland, a thousand wholehearted

---

[12] Laparra, *Bizet et l'Espagne*, 42, cited in Llano, 'Spanish traditions', 100.

[13] Llano, 'Spanish traditions', 125, 134.

[14] See *ibid.*, 113–17, and Llano, *Whose Spain?*, ch. 3 ('Citizens or savages? The Spaniards in Raoul Laparra's *La Jota* (1911))'.

[15] Fauré, '[*La Habanera*]', *Le Figaro*, 27 February 1908.

[16] Le Bordays, 'L'Espagne ravélienne', 44.

[17] Parakilas, 'How Spain got a soul', 184 (emphasis mine).

greetings', he wrote to Joaquín Turina in 1911,[18] and he later recalled that his Basque mother had sung him to sleep with Spanish lullabies.[19] Ravel's parents had met in Madrid in 1872, and Marie Ravel spoke Spanish better than French: Manuel de Falla described her as 'a lady of exquisite conversation, in always impeccable Spanish'.[20]

Arriving in Paris in June 1875, three months after both the première of *Carmen* and Maurice Ravel's birth, the Ravel family settled in the 9th arrondissement, the district that reaches from the Opéra to the foot of Montmartre. Apart from a brief venture into the 5th arrondissement between 1896 and 1899, they were to remain in the 9th (in various apartments) until 1901.[21] The Ravels were thus close to the émigré Spanish community which, as Elaine Brody notes, had settled mainly in the eastern part of the 9th arrondissement and in the neighbouring 18th – a circumstance that reflects interestingly on the later description of *L'Heure espagnole* as 'a Spain seen from the heights of Montmartre'.[22] The Ravel family must have maintained some acquaintances within the expatriate community, as it was through their mothers that Ravel and the Catalan pianist Ricardo Viñes became acquainted ('the long-haired boy called Mauricio' first appears in Viñes's diary in November 1888).[23] Brody writes that the adolescent Viñes regularly attended events mounted by the Société Nationale d'Acclimatation (organised by some of the early Spanish émigrés), adding that he would 'also drop in at odd times [...] sometimes with friends like "Mauricio"'.[24]

Ravel's compositional output began and ended in Spanish mode (*Sérénade grotesque* of 1893, and *Don Quichotte à Dulcinée* of 1933), including three major works explicitly Spanish in inspiration (*Rapsodie espagnole*, *L'Heure espagnole* and *Boléro*), as well as a clutch of movements and minor works: the two-piano 'Habanera' of 1895 (*Sites auriculaires*), later transferred to *Rapsodie espagnole*; *Pavane pour une Infante défunte*, 'Alborada del gracioso', the 1907 *Vocalise-Étude en forme de Habanera*, and the 1910 'Chanson espagnole'. The Concerto for the Left Hand also exudes strong whiffs of Spanishness, and even the Concerto in G hints at a

---

[18] Delahaye, 'Documents dans les ventes' (2009), 48.

[19] See Roland-Manuel, *Maurice Ravel*, 19–20, and Narbaitz, *Maurice Ravel: un orfèvre basque*, 85.

[20] Falla, *On Music and Musicians*, 94; first published in Falla, 'Notas sobre Ravel', *Isla* 17 (Cadiz, 1939): 'señora cuya exquisita conversación, siempre en claro español'.

[21] Nichols, *Ravel*, 7, 10.

[22] Brody, *The Musical Kaleidoscope*, 171, and Tenroc, 'Thérèse et *L'Heure espagnole*'; OL 587n3. The 18th arrondissement includes Montmartre.

[23] Gubisch, 'Les Années de jeunesse d'un pianiste espagnol en France', 12.

[24] Brody, *The Musical Kaleidoscope*, 172.

slowed *bolero* rhythm in its last movement.[25] To this catalogue we might add the Basque rhythms of the Trio, and Ravel's planned (but never completed) concerto on Basque themes, entitled *Zazpiak Bat* (*The Seven are One*) in honour of the Basque region, whose seven provinces straddle the Spanish border.

By 1907 Ravel felt himself very literally at home in Spanish mode: Manuel de Falla, who became acquainted with him that summer, wrote of the 'subtly genuine Spanishness' he recognised immediately in *Rapsodie espagnole*.[26] Like Debussy's hispanicism – and the majority of musical *espagnolade* – Ravel's has a distinctly Andalusian flavour: his melodies take on an emphatically Phrygian tint, echoed and reinforced harmonically; dance rhythms, never far away in any of his music, come to the fore (especially the jota, malagueña and habanera); and his orchestra is spiced with castanets and tambourines. All these elements are foregrounded in *L'Heure espagnole*, and all, for Opéra-Comique audiences in 1911, were unmistakeable markers of Spanishness.

However, none of the opera's characteristic motifs, as presented in Chapter 8, are themselves intrinsically 'Spanish', although their flexibility means that they can appear in Spanish guise (the moulding of the initial 'clock' figure into jota and habanera rhythms, for example, and the transformation of Ramiro's motif into a habanera in the final quintet – see Exx. 8.1 and 8.2). Identifiably 'Spanish' material – that is, displaying characteristic melodic turns, dance rhythms and harmonies – occupies something less than half of Ravel's score, forming, as James Parakilas notes, 'a barely audible substratum to the singing'.[27] As Gonzalve contemplates his clock in Scene VI, for example, the melancholy chromatic descents gesture at habanera rhythms (Ex. 9.1), but it is only after his chain of flamboyant habaneras in the preceding two scenes that we recognise them as such, so fleeting is the resemblance.

Parakilas further contends that 'though there are "Spanish" rhythms and vocal embellishments galore in this work, they are rather indiscriminately applied'.[28] To charge this composer with a lack of discernment is to tread perilously; nothing in this fleet-footed score is 'applied' without precise intent. But if we read Parakilas's 'discrimination' as 'taste', we come a little closer to the mark. Spanish (or 'Spanish') music is not integral to the opera's meticulous motivic structure. Rather, most of it is heard within a recognisably parodic context: the more flamboyant its Spanishness, the

---

[25] See Howat, *The Art of French Piano Music*, 144. Concerning Ravel's Spanish music more generally, see also Llano, 'España en la vitrina'.

[26] Falla, *On Music and Musicians*, 94.   [27] Parakilas, 'How Spain got a soul', 186–7.

[28] *Ibid.*, 186.

Ex. 9.1 *L'Heure espagnole*, Scene VI

more ironic its purpose. Thus Ramiro's account of 'mon oncle, le toréador' – saved by the watch in his breast pocket, that most obvious of clichés – is comically overdone, with its flamenco rhythms and Andalusian harmonies; Gonzalve's serenades are overloaded with Spanish-tinted arabesques and languid habanera rhythms; and the final quintet, as Langham Smith remarks,

> is a brilliant double-parody, firstly of flamenco vocal techniques and Spanish inflections, and secondly of eighteenth and nineteenth-century operatic traditions. [. . .] Trills and swoops; cascading semiquavers punctuated by overdone harp arpeggios; staccato chordal singing; and *notes Eiffel* for everyone – all these dirty tricks constantly refer to the triplet-duplet rhythm of the habanera.[29]

Ravel's 'indiscriminate' application of Spanishness emerges here – and in the passages considered below – as a calculated ploy, echoing and parodying the equally indiscriminate nature of much contemporary *espagnolade*.

More subtle Spanish references emerge from the opera's first scene, which opens with the bass descending through the Phrygian-coloured tetrachord E-D-C-B, a pattern that Langham Smith labels 'the hallmark of Spanish folk music'.[30] In fact, this descending bass is a compressed echo of the Introduction, which takes twenty-two bars to move through the same tetrachord. The arrival of the B, in the Introduction (Fig. 2^{-1}), marks a very audible transition, interrupting a series of whole-tone steps down through an octave (the arrival back at the tonic E marks the beginning of Scene I), and heralding a new orchestral texture (low brass replace the contrabass, and tremolo strings yield to wind scales beneath the call of the 'trumpet- [actually horn-] playing automaton'). As it happens, one of the most obvious predecessors for this four-step progression – at Ravel's pitch, too – is the 'Chanson Bohème' that opens Act 2 of *Carmen*.

---

[29] Langham Smith, 'Ravel's operatic spectacles', 199.   [30] *Ibid.*, 196.

Ex. 9.2a Bizet, *Carmen*, Entracte to Act IV, bars 1–9

Ex. 9.2b *L'Heure espagnole*, 'Aux arènes de Barcelone'

If this subtle correspondence is unlikely to have triggered memories for the first audiences of *L'Heure espagnole*, they may have pricked up their ears at a far more obvious one: Ramiro's dramatic description of the 'arènes de Barcelone'. This, the opera's first instance of very obvious Spanishness, cannot but have reminded the more alert listeners of the *arènes* of Seville (Ex. 9.2).

From this point, however, although certain melodic turns and dance rhythms may have brought *Carmen* briefly to mind (Christine Souillard, for example, calls Gonzalve's Scene IV serenade 'à la manière de *Carmen*', without citing any precise resemblance[31]), there is no recognisable moment of direct pastiche or quotation. Musically at least, this target was too cheap a shot.

With the musical shadows of *Carmen* only fleeting in *L'Heure espagnole*, a more pungent vein of parody lies within Ravel's own œuvre. In Scene XV Gonzalve, abandoned by a furious Concepcion, muses on his 'enveloppe de chêne' to the accompaniment of a languidly Andalusian melody, instantly recognisable as the principal theme from the middle section of 'Alborada del gracioso'. The passage is also redolent of the 'Feria' from *Rapsodie espagnole* (composed in tandem with *L'Heure*), which, like 'Alborada', positions a slower, Phrygian-coloured passage between flamboyant outer sections. Gonzalve's 'Adieu, cellule...' in Scene XIX echoes the

---

[31] Souillard, 'Commentaire littéraire et musical', 96. Marcel Marnat similarly notes 'wicked allusions to [...] *Carmen*, which had become the fetish work of the Opéra-Comique', though he gives no specific examples ('Ravel en représentation', 14).

Rapsodie's 'Malagueña', with its jaunty triple-time bass melody, chains of descending chords, oscillating semitones and repeated-chord patterns. These latter correspondences are perhaps more generic, testimony to the repository of harmonic, melodic, rhythmic and timbral gestures that characterises Ravel's 'Spanish style'. Concepcion's 'O, la pitoyable aventure', by contrast, seems almost to pastiche the 'Feria'. It shares the same spiralling melodic figures, the jota rhythms, the glissando gestures, and the descending chromatic lines in the bass (compare bars 10–12 of the 'Feria' with the *Pressez* bars in Concepcion's aria); it too includes a slower central section ('Maintenant, le jour va finir', Fig. 87). But, despite Concepcion's best attempts, 'O, la pitoyable aventure' never really gets off the ground. Without the rhythmic momentum of the 'Feria', these disparate elements cannot be bound together; the first section constantly lapses into slower tempi (the 'Alborada' theme makes a reappearance), in bitter echo of Gonzalve's failure, in Scene IV, to match Concepcion's lively pace. Ravel not only up-ends our operatic expectations here – this is his leading lady's one aria, and it ends just as we think it is finally getting going – but, in doing so, he turns his ironic eye inwards. 'Et ces gens-là se disent Espagnols!' laments Concepcion; 'you call *this* Spanish?', we can almost hear Ravel asking.

A Spanish lover

Gonzalve's Scene IV entrance and serenade offer another example of the way in which Ravel's score – and Franc-Nohain's libretto – lampoons several targets at once. The inherently parodic nature of the opera's 'Spanish' music is obvious from the moment Gonzalve's voice is heard. Vocalising *dans les coulisses*, he is a caricature before he even appears onstage: the Opéra-Comique audiences of 1911 would have instantly recognised the advent of the over-romantic serenading tenor. There is also a more specifically parodic context to Gonzalve's entrance. Lacombe observes of mid-nineteenth-century Opéra-Comique libretti that 'Spanish romance is exteriorised and extroverted, a declaration of love that could be considered showy, nearly in bad taste'.[32] Gonzalve offers ample evidence that this archetype was still a ripe target by the early twentieth century. 'A serenade under a balcony, accompanied by guitar if at all possible, is nearly mandatory in any "Spanish" drama', Lacombe writes.[33] Little wonder,

---

[32] Lacombe, 'The writing of exoticism', 153.   [33] *Ibid.*, 152.

then, that the 1911 production had Gonzalve entering, 'by the door on the right with great liveliness – his hat on his head. Gonzalve advances onto the stage, swaying as if he is playing the guitar – very conceited.'[34] His air guitar makes a reappearance when the 'Caprice de femme' inspires him to a 'Chanson' in Scene V (Fig. 26[+5]). There may be no balcony, but Gonzalve makes do.

Against these theatrical backdrops, already priming us for parody, at Gonzalve's entrance we hear Ravel's orchestra evoking the timbre of the guitar in strings and harp; melismatic vocalising conjuring flamenco idioms (Langham Smith notes that the passage emphasises the 'upper and lower leading-note effect frequently found in the improvisatory passages of flamenco song (*salida*), and in guitar playing (*falsetas*)'[35]); and Ravel's special harmonic marker of Spanishness in the sustained opening chord, a dominant seventh on A, superimposed on a G# pedal (see Ex. 8.8). While Langham Smith accurately terms the serenade 'a studied piece of Spanish pastiche', Ravel is also pastiching himself yet again: the pointed reiteration of this harmony and the accompanying textures are both almost identical to the central passage of 'Alborada del gracioso', his own earlier Spanish serenade (itself something of a parody, at least in its title). These ironic references perhaps give weight to the humorously self-deprecating parallel Manuel Rosenthal reported Ravel as drawing, late in life, between Gonzalve's mannered extravagance and his own youthful adoption of a consciously dandified persona, apparently declaring that the poet was 'himself, as a young man'.[36]

As the scene and the opera progress, we find Gonzalve displaying all the 'exteriorised and extroverted' gestures of the showy Spanish lover. The original *mise-en-scène* paints him as incurably flamboyant in his gestures: moving downstage 'en faisant des grâces', indulging in an exaggerated double-take upon discovering Inigo concealed in the second clock (Scene XIX), and exiting his clock in Scene XIV with wild spins, vividly depicted in

---

[34] Original production score, coll. Roy Howat. See Kilpatrick, 'The Carbonne copy', 120–2.

[35] Langham Smith, 'Ravel's operatic spectacles', 197; on p. 198, he cites two examples of similar flamenco passages, drawn from Raoul Laparra's above-mentioned article in the *Dictionnaire du Conservatoire*.

[36] Marnat (ed.), *Ravel: Souvenirs de Manuel Rosenthal*, 26. Rosenthal's reflections on *L'Heure*, however, are dubious in several respects, as discussed on pp. 192–3 below; this may cast doubt on his coupling of Ravel with Gonzalve. Huebner nevertheless echoes Rosenthal in linking Ravel, as composer/narrator, with the tenor as the 'poet/singer' of the work, arguing that 'the material facts of a creative artist of Iberian descent [*sic*] who expressed himself in updated Spanish idioms, yet who also loved Mallarmé, create an obvious parallel' (Huebner, 'La Grivoiserie moderne', 209). Ravel's engagement with the concept and figure of the dandy is central to Puri's *Ravel the Decadent* (though Puri has oddly little to say about *L'Heure*, and does not mention Gonzalve at all in this context).

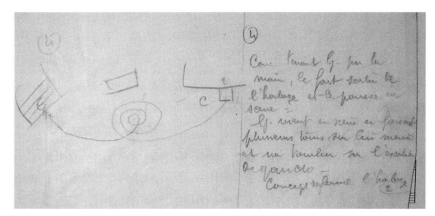

Figure 9.1 Gonzalve's extravagant exit from his clock (Fig. 68^{+10}), as depicted in the 1911 production score

the original production score (Fig. 9.1). Gonzalve's melodrama and affectation, his exaggerated movement to the music and his enormous gestures indicate that his theatrical persona mirrored the satiric extravagance of Ravel's musical portrayal.

Gonzalve's opening serenade has him displaying a showy quintilla (a Spanish/Catalan verse form consisting of five-line verses in rhymed iambic tetrameter) and a fine Andalusian-tinted tune, both presumably 'composed' specially for the occasion:

Enfin revient le jour si doux.
– Harpes, chantez, éclatez, salves ! . . . –
Enfin revient le jour si doux,
Le jour où, d'un époux jaloux,
Ma maîtresse n'est plus l'esclave.[37]

But the inadequacy and self-conscious artifice inherent in his character are also evident from his opening phrases, for poem and music do not match. Textual rhythms, which Ravel observes so meticulously for the other characters, are here uneasily compressed and distorted by the melody: the unimportant article *le* twice falls on a downbeat and the strong first vowel of *éclatez* is squashed in offbeat semiquavers. Most strikingly, the climax of the passage – the sustained top $g''\#$ – falls on the insignificant and awkward word *d'un*, the important words that follow (*jaloux*, *maîtresse*) swallowed in the subsequent chain of cascading semiquavers (Ex. 9.3).

---

[37] At last the sweetest day returns. / – Sing, harps, break out, applause! . . . – / At last the sweetest day returns, / The day when my mistress / Is no longer the slave of a jealous husband.

Ex. 9.3 Gonzalve's opening serenade

Gonzalve's shortcomings are also reflected in the original *mise-en-scène*, which hints, in several moments of embarrassed self-consciousness, at his failure to believe entirely in his own poeticising. At Ramiro's first return to the stage, in Scene V, Gonzalve 'ignores him and examines the marionettes, pretending not to have noticed him'. Similarly, after Torquemada's reappearance, Gonzalve 'returns behind the counter looking all about him, pendulums, watches etc.' – that is, anywhere but at Torquemada.[38] Were he in truth the flamboyant Spanish serenader portrayed in the score nothing would shatter his impervious self-absorption, but both unexpected entries plainly disconcert him.

Steven Huebner also notes the uncomfortable cut of the tenor's Spanish costume, terming his music 'misplaced'.[39] Of the Scene XV soliloquy Franc-Nohain wrote for Gonzalve (mostly omitted from Ravel's setting), Huebner notes that 'Gonzalve explicitly rejects Hispanicism in favour of classical culture':[40] 'Ah ! How greatly do we need / To return to you, pure classical sources / And may our eloquence be devoted / To the imitation of the Greeks and Romans'. Given this forthright dismissal, Ravel's musical portrayal of Gonzalve in exaggeratedly Spanish popular idioms is, as Huebner observes, rather paradoxical: 'it was [Ravel] who took the initiative to lend Spanish colour to Gonzalve's language, an initiative that actually went against the grain of Franc-Nohain's character [...] Thus the comic paradox: one would hardly expect a symbolist with rarefied taste to express himself in popular idioms.'[41] No matter how Gonzalve might like to perceive himself, however, the caricature of the extroverted Spanish lover was very clearly in Franc-Nohain's sights as well as Ravel's. In bringing him on with what is clearly a serenade – and a Spanish verse form, at that – Franc-Nohain is directly responding to the comic-theatrical tradition of the Spanish serenade and extroverted Spanish romance. Moreover, Ravel's clear awareness of Huebner's 'comic paradox' is evident in Gonzalve's failure to meld his popular idioms with his 'rarefied' poetry.

---

[38] Fair copies of the original *mise-en-scène*; BHVP, coll. ART, 4-TMS-03775.
[39] Huebner, 'La Grivoiserie moderne', 201.   [40] *Ibid.*, 206.   [41] *Ibid.*

Nevertheless, Gonzalve, too caught up in his own poeticising to attend to the matter in hand, indisputably lampoons targets well beyond the culture of *espagnolade*: foolish lovers and wilting aesthetes, like duped husbands, unfaithful wives and sexual incapacity, have provided comedic fodder across many centuries, languages and cultures. Besides the Symbolists, we might link him to late nineteenth-century aestheticism, so memorably mocked in Gilbert and Sullivan's *Patience* (it is no coincidence that both *Patience* and *L'Heure* are frequently restaged in 1960s 'hippie' settings); or equally to the empty romantic extravagance Shakespeare parodied when, in *Two Gentlemen of Verona*, he had Proteus counsel Thurio:

You must lay lime to tangle her desires
By wailful sonnets [. . .]
Say that upon the altar of her beauty
You sacrifice your tears, your sighs, your heart.
Write till your ink be dry, and with your tears
Moist it again [. . .]
After your dire-lamenting elegies,
Visit by night your lady's chamber-window
With some sweet consort. To their instruments
Tune a deploring dump. The night's dead silence
Will well become such sweet-complaining grievance.[42]

Jessie Fillerup also recognises a broader frame of pastiche and parody for Gonzalve, looking beyond Spanish idioms to consider his opening scene relative to broader stylistic norms of the serenade. In this context at least, she writes,

Gonzalve did everything 'right': he used a compound meter (6/8), a moderate to slow tempo, [. . .] a soft dynamic (*pianissimo*), and plucked, arpeggiated accompaniment on a string instrument (the harp). His text [opened] with an exclamation of longing ('At last, the day so sweet returns. . . '). When Gonzalve diverged into abstract territory, he adopted a tried-and-true tactic [. . .] in which the lover woos the beloved through flowery metaphor.[43]

Perhaps more pertinently, all this best serves to illustrate the multifarious nature of Franc-Nohain's satire, as well as Ravel's. The Spanish garb of *L'Heure espagnole* provides an instantly recognisable focus and colouring, a subset of clichés and stereotypes that are all the funnier for tapping into

---

[42] Shakespeare, *Two Gentlemen of Verona*, Act 3 scene ii; *The Norton Shakespeare*, ed. Greenblatt, Cohen, Howard *et al.*, 114–15.
[43] Fillerup, 'Purloined poetics', 207.

much broader targets. In the same manner, the play's echoes of the *commedia dell'arte*, perhaps most evident in the characters of Torquemada (something of a Pantalone) and Inigo (an unmistakeable Dottore), are sharpened when viewed through the prism of contemporary French stereotypes of Spanish masculinity ('ces gens-là se disent Espagnols!').[44] Gonzalve may be a Symbolist, therefore, but he is 'Spanish' first.

Concepcion and the habanera

Gonzalve's abstraction is mocked by Don Inigo in Scene XII: the latter's 'Les poètes, affairés. . . ' (Fig. 62) returns to the music of the Scene IV serenade (Fig. 17). This is the only point in the opera at which one character directly parodies another, reprising a very recognisable chunk of material. But the passage is also remarkable in another respect: with the exception of the final quintet, it is the only moment at which Inigo adopts the characteristic rhythms of the habanera. This deliberately stylised evocation is a ploy to ingratiate himself with Concepcion, for the habanera is very much her dance. Although he is actually describing and imitating Gonzalve, his adoption of habanera rhythms – however little they suit him – seems intended to convey to Concepcion that he is moving, as it were, to her beat.

Concepcion's musical association with the rhythm and gestures of the habanera is apparent from her first scene, in her mocking dismissal of her husband's physical prowess (see Ex. 9.4a below). In Scene XIV she vocalises a habanera, 'évasive et rageuse', over Gonzalve's raptures; in Scene XVIII her decision to take Ramiro upstairs *sans horloge* is accompanied by habanera rhythms; and the flamboyant habanera idiom of the final quintet seems partly intended to reflect her control of the narrative. Huebner suggests that, throughout *L'Heure espagnole*, 'Spanish musical idioms, especially Habanera rhythms, are attached to sexual competence.' He argues that this pattern is established in Concepion's first habanera, sardonically evoking the 'force musculaire' in which Torquemada is lacking, and is made plain in the final quintet, which celebrates the triumph of the

---

[44] Clifton traces some of these *commedia dell'arte* connections ('Maurice Ravel's *L'Heure espagnole*', 154–8). Pantalone is often portrayed as 'a lecherous old merchant who dotes on an only daughter Columbina', or a miser with a young wife. The Dottore (or Graziano) is 'learned but gullible [. . .] speaking pompous absurdities' (*ibid.*, 154–5). Langham Smith discusses the perception of the degenerate male Spaniard, evident in many writings of the time, in 'Ravel's operatic spectacles', 191.

'amant efficace'.[45] I would argue for a more specific association, as well as a more general one. Most immediately, the habanera is intrinsic to the characterisation of Concepcion, both as she presents herself and as she is imagined by the other characters: Gonzalve, for example, indulges in habaneras only when spinning fantasies around Concepcion and her domain. But the dance is also emblematic of broader French stereotypes of feisty Spanish femininity, which in the opera are personified and satirised in the character of Concepcion, and which previously had been most explicitly realised – and in large part defined by – the figure of Carmen.

As Parakilas puts it, 'For almost two hundred years now, the "soul of Spain" has been lodged above all in the body of the Spanish dancer, evoked by music that plays on the rhythm of one or another of the famous Spanish dance types.'[46] Lacombe and Murphy have similarly documented the centrality of dance in French constructions of Spanishness.[47] In late nineteenth- and early twentieth-century France, no dance was more famous, and more associated with the 'soul of Spain' (and Spanish women), than the habanera. Even in Spain the habanera was a naturalised 'exotic' dance: evolving from the French *contredanse* in early nineteenth-century Cuba (thus *havanaise/habanera*), it had arrived in Spain only mid-century. (As J. Peter Burkholder notes, even the *contredanse* derives from the English 'country dance'.[48]) Thus, as Manuel de Falla explained, the habanera was 'the song [*sic*] most in vogue when [Ravel's] mother lived in Madrid':[49] it was the latest arrival from the New World. Falla continues, 'This was the same time as Pauline Viardot-García, famous and well acquainted with the best composers in Paris, spread the *habanera* among them. That is why that rhythm, much to the surprise of Spaniards, went on living in French music although Spain had forgotten it half a century ago.'[50] As it happens, Ravel's piano teacher in his teenage years – and later the dedicatee of his *Rapsodie espagnole* – was Charles de Bériot, the nephew of Pauline Viardot (and son of the equally renowned La Malibran). Nevertheless, the prolongation into

---

[45] Huebner, 'La Grivoiserie moderne', 201–3. He does not mention that the passage extolling the 'amant efficace' in fact reprises Ramiro's motif (see Ex. 8.2c), a correspondence that neatly backs up his thesis.

[46] Parakilas, 'How Spain got a soul', 142.

[47] Lacombe, 'L'Espagne à Paris au milieu de XIXe siècle', 406–11; Murphy, '*Couleur locale* or the real thing', 296–9.

[48] Burkholder, 'Music of the Americas and Historical Narratives', 414.

[49] Falla, *On Music and Musicians*, 95.

[50] *Ibid.*, 95; Burkholder notes, however, that the habanera had established itself within the *zarzuela* tradition ('Music of the Americas and Historical Narratives', 414).

the twentieth century of the French obsession with the habanera arguably owes less to the celebrated García family than to one habanera in particular: Carmen's most famous aria, 'L'amour est un oiseau rebelle'.

The first instance of habanera rhythms in *L'Heure espagnole* (Concepcion's 'De force musculaire') and the last, in the final quintet, are linked melodically, rhythmically and tonally (Exx. 9.4a–b). We might also sense a gestural affinity with 'L'amour est un oiseau rebelle' here (particularly around the latter's 'L'amour est enfant de Bohème'), which is underlined by the echoing of the last cadential flourish of Carmen's aria in the final vocal turn of the quintet (Ex. 9.4c–d).

Ex. 9.4 Habanera figures

a. *L'Heure espagnole*, Scene II

b. *L'Heure espagnole*, final quintet

Ex. 9.4 (cont.)

c. *L'Heure espagnole*, final vocal flourish

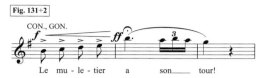

Le mu - le - tier   a   son___ tour!

d. Bizet, *Carmen*: 'L'amour est un oiseau rebelle' (Habanera), final vocal flourish

Si   je   t'ai - me, prends garde à___ toi!

We should be wary of making much of this relationship: similar gestures
are traceable in many other late nineteenth- and early twentieth-century
pieces of musical *espagnolade*, including Ravel's own 'Habanera' (*Sites auriculaires / Rapsodie espagnole*), never mind the earlier collections of folksongs
and dances that often served as part-source or inspiration.[51] What is significant here is not literal musical correspondence, nor indeed whether or
not Ravel was deliberately alluding to *Carmen*, but rather gestural likeness
and dramatic effect, viewed within the framework of the opera as a whole.
This returns us to the question of how cultural context shaped the perceptions of the first audiences of *L'Heure espagnole*, how the first production
reciprocally responded to those perceptions, and how both performance and
reception now inform our understanding of the opera itself.

'The Spanish woman, [. . .] being close to France, possesses the advan-
tages of the European woman as well as the "je ne sais quoi" of the exotic
woman', writes Hervé Lacombe. She is, therefore, 'the most troubling of
them all'.[52] Richard Langham Smith outlined the tenacity of the French
idea of 'the mythical over-sexed Spanish female' (although he notes that, as
a married woman receiving suitors, Concepcion 'is undoubtedly closer to a
French stereotype than a Spanish one').[53] Like Carmen, Concepcion is the
lynchpin of her opera, about whom the other characters orbit; like Carmen,
she is rapacious, fiery and peremptory, in control of her story and her life.
As partly noted in Chapter 6, Concepcion also shares something of the
textual and musical mutability of her predecessor, who, as Ralph Locke

---

[51] Not least of these is the 1872 collection *Echos d'Espagne*, which includes Sebastien Yradier's 'El
arraglito', the tune upon which Bizet's celebrated habanera was based. Ravel's personal library
also contained a mid-nineteenth-century collection of habaneras.

[52] Lacombe, 'The writing of exoticism', 157.

[53] Langham Smith, 'Ravel's operatic spectacles', 190–1.

notes, 'shifts her musical style depending on the individual or group being addressed'.[54] Thus, as Carmen 'has mastered the art of echoing the Gounod-like lyrical-passionate manner of Don José',[55] so Concepcion, whose natural manner of speech is abrupt and angular, can nevertheless match Gonzalve's lyricism with her own (around Figs. 18–19 in Scene IV, for example).

In the 1911 staging records, Concepcion emerges as much the most vividly portrayed character of the five: no one else is granted half so many adverbs. Every movement she makes is lively and aggressive: the *mise-en-scène* describes her variously as *furieuse* and *vive*; she descends the stairs 'at a run' and 'throws herself' into the arms of Gonzalve. She is the only character to run or laugh and, despite Gonzalve's posturing, the only one to dance: in this last trait in particular, she makes her Spanishness most explicit. She pushes and pulls her various lovers around the stage, forcibly restraining them or bundling them unceremoniously in and out of clocks. During 'O! La pitoyable aventure', the production score specifies that she 'moves to the right of the stage to break objects and bibelots, then moves upstage and searches for something else to break'. A few pages earlier she had thrown Ramiro's watch to the ground, *furieuse*, in her frustration with Gonzalve – indeed, the fair copy of the *mise-en-scène* records that she throws the watch *at* Gonzalve.[56] Like Carmen, Concepcion is also a consummate actor, deliberately assuming moods and gestures for dramatic effect: her weary subsiding into a chair as she protests that the clock in her bedroom will have terrible effects on her nerves (Fig. 53^{+7}) is masterly. The original production score (alone) also records that Concepcion follows close on Ramiro's heels as they leave, *sans horloge*, in Scene XVIII ('Elle le talonne'), and as they mount the stairs she 'pushes him'.

Not only does Concepcion's fiery portrayal evoke the figure of Carmen, the sketches for her costume (contained within the staging material at the Bibliothèque historique de la ville de Paris) also bear a striking resemblance to the first Carmen, Célestine Galli-Marié, as she was depicted in a famous 1884 portrait by Henri-Lucien Doucet. Even the pose – half-turned away, hand on hip, provocative chin – is similar, the classic 'Spanish' stance also evident in postcards and pictures of other Opéra-Comique Carmens (notably Emma Calvé and Marguerite Merentié), and traceable at least to Goya, whose 1797 *Portrait of the Duchess of Alba* shows a near-identical stance (Fig. 9.2). In fact, Geneviève Vix as Concepcion resembled not so much Galli-Marié as the Carmen she played herself (Fig. 9.3): she appears

[54] Locke, 'A broader view of musical exoticism', 506.   [55] *Ibid.*
[56] BHVP, coll. ART, 4-TMS-03775.

Figure 9.2 From left: Francisco Goya, *Portrait of the Duchess of Alba* (1797); Célestine Galli-Marié as Carmen (1884); Costume design for Concepcion (1911); Geneviève Vix as Concepcion (1911)

Figure 9.3 1912 photo-montage showing the Opéra-Comique's Carmens. Left to right: Emma Calvé, Lucienne Bréval, Marie Delna, Germaine Bailac, Marthe Chenal, de Nuovina, Maria Goy, Georgette Leblanc, Marié de l'Isle, Blanche Deschamps-Jehin, Célestine Galli-Marié, Marguerite Mérentié and Geneviève Vix. *Musica* 117 (June 1912).

in a photomontage of the theatre's Carmens in the June 1912 edition of *Musica*, assuming the same stance.

The audience at the première of *L'Heure espagnole* would therefore have seen in Concepcion a singer whom most already knew as an interpreter of

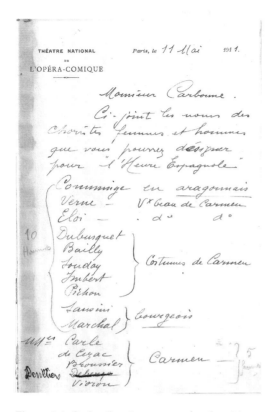

Figure 9.4 Opéra-Comique memo dated 11 May 1911, detailing stage-walkers'
costumes for *L'Heure espagnole*

Carmen, moving around the stage with something of Carmen's fire, and
wearing an outfit that reinforced her connection with that character.
Moreover, she was set against a background of choristers dressed in
costumes that would have seemed strangely familiar. In the 1911
L'Heure, we learn from the production material, stage-walkers were called
upon, passing back and forth now and again in the street beyond
Torquemada's shop window. Although they served primarily as *couleur
locale*, they may also have stimulated subtle recollections of the busy out-
door scenes of *Carmen*, for a memo bound into the 1911 production score
specifies that the chorus members involved (ten men and five women)
would be dressed in costumes from that opera (Fig. 9.4).[57] Although this

---

[57] An Opéra-Comique dossier of casting and costumes for 1908–11 shows the *Carmen* chorus (for
September 1909) in costumes described variously as 'Élégant', 'Peuple', 'Officier', 'Soldat', 'Un
Maraîcher', 'Andalou', 'Moine', 'Marchand de Chevaux', 'Un dormeur', 'Porte bagage', 'Gendarme',
'Marchand de Mules', 'Major Blanc', 'Marchand d'Eau', 'Marchand de Coqs', 'Marchand d'Olives'
and 'V^x Beau' (Bm-O, Rés. Pièce 81; the dossier unfortunately ends shortly before *L'Heure* appears
in the repertoire).

costuming was an obvious and natural economy on the theatre's part, alert audience members could have recognised the familiar garments: inside the shop it may have been eighteenth-century Toledo, but the street beyond looked suspiciously like 1830s Seville.

All this provides vital context for the musical echoes of *Carmen* in *L'Heure espagnole*. Ravel, well aware of Opéra-Comique traditions and the preferences of its patrons, must, when composing the opera, have given thought to its visual realisation. Heard in isolation, the fleeting reminiscences of *Carmen* might have passed with barely a raised eyebrow. In the context of the première's costumes, gestures and performers, as well as the traditions of the theatre itself, they are unmistakeable.

'Gallic humour in Spanish costume'

Against the larger-than-life characters of Gonzalve and Concepcion, and the entirely ridiculous Don Inigo, we might consider Ramiro – unsentimental, matter-of-fact and restrained in movement and gesture – as less remarkable. There is little in Ravel's score or Franc-Nohain's libretto to prompt us; his taciturnity and matter-of-fact delivery leave less opportunity for colourful characterisation. Ramiro sets the other caricatured personages in relief, placed as he is almost outside the piece, trotting on and off as the others expound extravagantly, centre-stage.

Manuel Rosenthal, in his memoirs, reflected in some detail on the characters of *L'Heure espagnole*. Explaining that Ravel 'had spoken to him at length' about the work, Rosenthal described Ramiro alone as an essentially Spanish and parodic creation:

Ramiro [. . .] 'has no conversation'. Here, Ravel is mocking the 'Spaniard of opera'. The others could be drawn from any society at all, but not Ramiro: he is the tough Spaniard, the bullfighter. He is an avatar of Escamillo in *Carmen*, who is equally bereft of conversation: he is a bullfighter, he knows how to kill the bull, he swaggers about, that's it.[58]

Beyond the additional connections Rosenthal draws between *L'Heure* and *Carmen*, however, there is more to Ramiro than he allows. First, Franc-Nohain is unlikely to have had Escamillo primarily in mind when creating the character of Ramiro, though the resemblance was presumably clear to Ravel. (Huebner has traced Franc-Nohain's 'morale de Boccace' to its literary foundations, demonstrating the connections between Franc-Nohain's tale and Boccaccio's *Decameron*, as retold by La Fontaine in *Le*

---

[58] Marnat (ed.), *Ravel: Souvenirs de Manuel Rosenthal*, 26–7.

Muletier – nouvelle tirée de Boccace.[59]) Moreover, of all the five characters, Ramiro is the only one to reveal a hint of self-awareness, developing over the course of the opera; he alone moves between a prosaic public face and more fanciful private reflection. Indeed, a 1932 letter from Ravel to Jane Bathori specifically notes that the role of Ramiro demands 'much subtlety', and draws attention to his poetic flights.[60]

Against the creation of Ramiro as *Carmen*-parody, Rosenthal sets the other characters, particularly Concepcion and Gonzalve, outside the frame of *espagnolade*: he claimed that Ravel saw his ensemble as 'A handful of very different characters, who, he said [...] represented all of society. Concepcion is not *a* woman, but *woman*. Woman, who, like a puppet play, manipulates every sort of masculine humanity.'[61] Besides the uncharacteristically (indeed, implausibly) misogynistic tone of this portrayal, Rosenthal's summation overlooks the vital musico-dramatic point: however Franc-Nohain conceived her, Ravel cannot have been unaware of the parallels between Concepcion and one very particular woman.

Rosenthal's identification of Ramiro alone as Spanish parody, and his rejection of Spanish stereotypes for the others, brings us to a key contradiction. The opera's Spanish music is almost exclusively the province of Concepcion and Gonzalve: after his lively recounting of the Barcelona bullfight, Ramiro reverts to a conversational manner, Inigo assumes Spanish rhythms only to mock them ('Les poètes...'), and while Torquemada's rapid departure at the end of Scene II sees his characteristic clock motif transformed into jota rhythms (Ex. 8.1b above), were the setting not Spanish we might hear the passage merely as a fast waltz.

In his 1904 foreword to *L'Heure espagnole* (quoted in full on pp. 99–100), Franc-Nohain terms his play a fable 'd'humeur honnêtement gauloise et de costume arbitrairement espagnol'. There are echoes here of Théophile Gautier who, as Parakilas eloquently puts it, 'In his travels, in his writings [...] tries on the "Spain of my dreams" as a costume, to see how disconcerting it looks on him, to see what it shows him about France'.[62] A French play in Spanish costume... as Huebner remarks, 'In light of Concepcion's stereotypical remarks about her Spanish brethren, this seems a bit odd.'[63] But Huebner's extrapolation, that 'As far as [Franc-Nohain] was concerned the action could have been situated anywhere else', ascribes to the playwright an intention that is not clear from his text. Beyond mere caprice, Franc-Nohain's word *arbitrairement* suggests the

[59] Huebner, 'La Grivoiserie moderne', 193–9.   [60] *OL*, letter 325.
[61] Marnat (ed.), *Ravel: Souvenirs de Manuel Rosenthal*, 26.
[62] Parakilas, 'How Spain got a soul', 148.   [63] Huebner, 'La Grivoiserie moderne', 206.

assertion of choice: the 'arbitrariness' of the Spanish locale does not necessarily make it less carefully chosen and presented. While tapping into archetypes well beyond the culture of *espagnolade*, in the context of their time and place the characters are decisively Spanish creations, dramatically and musically: the rapacious Concepcion, who assumes the sexy, amoral persona of Carmen; Ramiro, the sturdy, apparently stolid muleteer/*torero*; the serenading Gonzalve; and the collective lack of virility among Concepcion's rejected lovers all caricaturing French perceptions of a decadent Spain.

Yet 'Spanishness', in *L'Heure espagnole*, is indeed little more than a costume; beneath its mantilla, the work is in truth 'honnêtement gauloise'. The play's only use of conversational Spanish is Concepcion's infuriated exclamation 'Cortijo!' at the end of Scene XIV – which Ravel omitted, along with Gonzalve's rejection of *la langue espagnole*, as noted above; the only linguistic concessions to *couleur locale* are the occasional 'señora', Concepcion's 'doña sol', and a few place references. It would in fact be no difficult matter to remove any hint of Spanishness from the play and perform it as an Edwardian drawing-room comedy, or in Louis XIV costume *à la manière de* Molière, or in 1960s California. But in the context in which it was written, Spanishness is integral. It may be merely the 'costume', but it matters nonetheless. It matters because, had Franc-Nohain chosen a different garb for his 'fable', Ravel would very probably never have set it in the first place. It matters, too, because without *Carmen* and the culture of *espagnolade*, the resultant opera might never have made it to the stage of the Opéra-Comique. Just as the elements of *Carmen* that were initially deemed most shocking and most 'foreign' – the violence, Carmen's overt sexuality – came to be acceptable within (and because of) its Spanish setting, Concepcion's dominance, vitality and rapaciousness were admissible in turn through her positioning as a daughter of Carmen – and a daughter raiding her mother's wardrobe, too.

The Spanishness of *L'Heure espagnole* matters equally because the first production – an understanding of which critically shapes our perspective of the opera itself – located the opera firmly in the tradition of *Carmen*. The juxtaposition is explicit in Geneviève Vix's interview, already cited in part at the head of this chapter. 'I am very happy to be playing Concepcion in a Spain quite different from that of *Carmen* or [Laparra's] *La Jota*', Vix declared,[64] just as Ravel's *avant-première* interview described 'a comical Spain, a Spain seen from the heights of Montmartre, with neither mysticism nor earthiness [*truculence*]'.[65] Performer and composer between

---

[64] Prudhomme, 'Mlle Geneviève Vix et *L'Heure espagnole*'.
[65] Tenroc, '*Thérèse* et *L'Heure espagnole*'; *OL*, 587n3.

them thus establish *L'Heure espagnole* within the context of other Spanish operas, while emphasising its difference. A poem by 'Trial', which appeared in *Paris-Midi* on the eve of the première, subtitled 'À la manière de Franc-Nohain', echoed them both:

Ah, ah, ah, Carmen ! Carmencita !
Habanera, Jota,
Fini tout ça !
C'est l'Espagne pour vieux gaga . . .
Les véritables Espagnoles
Sont natives des Batignolles ![66]

Ravel identified a different Parisian arrondissement but the same principle: Jean Périer, he noted, 'is an actor of astonishing flexibility; his Boulevard de la Villette accent couldn't be funnier'*.[67]

The January 1921 season of *L'Heure espagnole* in Brussels saw Ravel's opera staged as the curtain-raiser to Laparra's *La Habanera*. It must have been an intriguing, perhaps unsettling evening. In *La Habanera* and *La Jota*, Laparra was writing self-consciously 'authentic' Spanish music set to an inherently Spanish narrative in a vividly depicted Spanish locale. Ravel was attempting something quite different: the image of a Spain viewed 'from the heights of Montmartre' is the key to the 1911 conception of *L'Heure espagnole*. Hence a Gonzalve who would not have been out of place on a music-hall stage, Périer's working-class Parisian accent, and a Concepcion whose costume and characterisation echoed the Opéra-Comique's figurehead, Carmen herself. As well as the bullrings of the émigré Spaniards, the heights of Montmartre were the home of the Parisian cabarets, where clichés were lampooned and passions lasted only as long as the song or the bottle. In his 1921 review, Gaston Lebel called the libretto 'chatnoiresque, essentiellement parisien':[68] had Concepcion in her bolero jacket and ruffled skirt appeared at Franc-Nohain's old haunt, the Chat noir, she might well have sung an exaggerated 'L'amour est un oiseau rebelle' to the accompaniment of a café piano.

These parallels between *Carmen* and *L'Heure* were embedded in the latter from the outset, as Ravel cannot but have been acutely aware: the first audiences were always going to make some sort of connection between the two Spanish women. So, in production, the choice may well have been

---

[66] 'Ah, ah, ah, Carmen! Carmencita! / Habanera, Jota, / All that's done with! / That's Spain for old dodderers. . . / The true Spanish women / Are natives of the Batignolles!' ['Trial'], 'La Salle'.

[67] Tenroc, '*Thérèse et L'Heure espagnole*'; *OL*, 587n3.   [68] Lebel, '*L'Heure espagnole* à l'Opéra'.

made not to diminish the parallels, but to emphasise – indeed caricature – them. If Carmen is little more than a shadow in Ravel's score, she is subtly foregrounded in the opera's original *mise-en-scène*. We may see this as a bold dramatic ploy, a staging concept that was innovative in its referential, reflexive nature and, by the same token, ironically nostalgic. The failure of the first audiences (those Opéra-Comique subscribers and die-hard *Carmen* aficionados) to recognise and appreciate this inherent parody undoubtedly contributed to the limited success of *L'Heure espagnole* in the 1911 season. In a way, this production foreshadowed the Wedgwood Teapot of *L'Enfant*, who sings 'since we don't understand it will always sound Chinese!' Did anyone in that first audience wonder whether they themselves, with their passion for *Carmen*, for *espagnolade*, and for exoticism of occasionally dubious authenticity, were having their legs gently but firmly pulled?

10 | The 'big, small world' of *L'Enfant et les sortilèges*

In the latter years of the nineteenth century, children became an increasingly vital part of the French consciousness. The passing of a series of laws concerning education and child labour formalised philosophical conceptions of childhood, necessarily defining it (in Caroline Steedman's words) 'not just as a category of experience, but also as a time-span'.[1] A massive upsurge in the publication of children's literature reflected the ever-increasing proportion of children attending school,[2] while Parisian toyshops proliferated astonishingly from the 1860s.[3] Symbolic acknowledgement of a new social order came from Hippolyte Durand, who published a book in 1889 (a good year for symbols) titled *Le Règne de l'enfant*. By 1924, the culture of *messieurs les enfants*[4] had become so entrenched that the journal *Les Annales politiques et littéraires* could devote an entire issue to 'L'Enfance', reacting in part against a perceived excess of child-centredness. Articles contrasting the degeneracy and precocity of the 'modern child' with the good old days 'when children never questioned the orders they received'[5] alternate with others depicting, in Baudelairean prose, the peace and focussed intimacy of childhood as a haven from the hectic and decadent Zeitgeist.[6]

Colette – who herself contributed an article to this issue – depicted in the Child of *L'Enfant* a character and a childhood typical of those imagined in *Les Annales*. Firmly locating him within a time, place and even social class, she stipulates, 'A Norman house, old, or, better, old-fashioned', with the elegantly furnished nursery suggesting a comfortably situated family and a Child – loved, if spoiled – who has never known want. In 1925, Xavier Léon would describe him as 'the "standard" type of modern child: badly raised, lazy and bad-tempered, already leaning towards all the harmful instincts of the human race, in love with destruction and cruelty'.[7] Jean Boutiller,

---

[1] Steedman, *Strange Dislocations*, 7. See also Heywood, *Childhood in Nineteenth-Century France*.
[2] Crubellier, *L'Enfance et la jeunesse*, 358.   [3] Clark, 'France', 290.
[4] *Ibid.*, 283 ('Children had become *messieurs les enfants*, around whom the household centred').
[5] Bidou, 'Enfants et parents', 51.
[6] The articles in this issue are summarised in Schillmöller, *Maurice Ravels Schlüsselwerk*, 75–6.
[7] Léon, 'L'Enfant et les sortilèges', 166.

reviewing the Paris première in the journal *L'Enfant*, praised the opera for its realistic presentation of a child familiar to parents everywhere: 'All parents understand the battles – open or covert – that they must wage against the instinctive untruthfulness, laziness, brutality, even ferocity, of their charming little fallen angels.'[8]

In thus echoing something of the contemporary reflections on children and childhood, *L'Enfant et les sortilèges* was also the apex of a musical and artistic trend. As French literature moved from Hugo towards Gérard Nerval (*Sylvie*) and thence to Alain-Fournier (*Le grand Meaulnes*) and Proust, and artists like Berthe Morisot and Mary Cassatt began to paint children vigorously engaged with their surroundings, the composers of the Third Republic turned from the idealised Romantic childhood of Schumann's *Kinderszenen* towards the overflowing nurseries and exuberant family life of their busy, vital Parisian society. From Bizet's *Jeux d'enfants*, composed in the year following the Republic's proclamation, to Fauré's *Dolly*, Debussy's *Children's Corner* and *La Boîte à joujoux*, Caplet's *Un tas de petites choses*, Inghelbrecht's *La Nursery*, and a host of individual piano pieces and songs, children and childhood came to life, in musical terms, as never before.[9] In Ravel's own œuvre, besides *L'Enfant et les sortilèges*, we find the little song *Noël des jouets* and the 1922 *Berceuse sur le nom de Fauré* (dedicated to the newborn son of his friend Roland-Manuel), as well as *Ma mère l'Oye*, a duet suite composed for children to perform, in which childhood and fairytale both find expression.

But despite this wealth of music about childhood, very few works attempted to depict actual children: even *Dolly* and *Children's Corner*, written for and about two particular little girls (half-sisters, at that), are not so much portraits as landscapes with figures. Amidst all these well-stocked nurseries (and in the light of the culture depicted in *Les Annales*), we can perhaps understand why W. Wright Roberts, in the first of a pair of 1928 articles entitled 'Child studies in music', lamented: 'More and more [music about children] has concerned itself with a cargo of externals – toys, machines, mechanical things, and less with inward vision [. . .] There is a limbo of modern music, stocked with marches of tin soldiers and laments for broken dolls and the other mechanical properties of the child's world as

---

[8] Boutiller, '*L'Enfant et les sortilèges*', 186.

[9] Among the many other composers of musical *enfantines* were Déodat de Séverac, Louis Aubert, Alfred Bruneau, Gabriel Grovlez, Xavier Leroux, Albéric Magnard, Massenet, Pierné, Poulenc, Roussel and Satie. Musorgsky's *Nursery* songs, published, like *Jeux d'enfants*, in 1872, played a key role in this tradition. The history of musical *enfantines*, relative to philosophical and cultural perceptions of childhood, is explored in Kilpatrick, 'The language of enchantment', Chapters 1–2.

seen by the trivially minded adult.'[10] Roberts's second article mused, 'Since [Musorgsky's] day, it is to be feared, those who have written music about children have often treated them as "so many amusing dolls"':[11] children and the trappings of childhood, he suggests, had become conflated, the living beings reduced to the level of their inanimate companions.

In her 1999 essay 'Outside Ravel's tomb', Carolyn Abbate looked through the words of Vladimir Jankélévitch to Baudelaire's 1853 essay *The Philosophy of Toys*. Ravel's œuvre as a whole, Jankélévitch writes, is 'a profusion of patent toys, puppets and animated automata that are created and set in motion everywhere in his music by a mind occupied with a mimed version of life'.[12] His words, as Abbate points out, echo Baudelaire's depiction of Madame Panckouke's toy room, 'a chamber where [...] the walls were invisible, so deeply were they lined with toys; the ceiling had vanished behind a great flowering bouquet of toys, which hung down like wonderful stalactites'.[13] Ravel's depiction of the Garden in *L'Enfant*, Jankélévitch suggests, is less a vibrant natural environment than a 'great humming aviary', while, as Abbate notes, 'even [Ravel's] domestic animals are artificial. In *L'Enfant*, lambs come in shades of rose, and goats in amaranthine violet.'[14]

In *L'Enfant*, the 'cargo of externals' – toys, pets, lavish surroundings – unquestionably appear to dominate the story as they dominate the stage and even the published score: in André Hellé's cover painting, Clock, Chairs, Teapot *et al.* loom over the Child, who crouches fearfully at the lower right-hand corner. But if he spends much of the opera literally or metaphorically sidelined, the Child nevertheless holds centre-stage as the curtain rises, cataloguing in the plainest of language his desires and frustrations. And from the side of the stage, as this chapter explores, the Child shapes the musical as well as the dramatic narrative, through evolving musical forms, melodic and harmonic gestures and timbral colourations. Reviewing the 1929 Viennese production for the *Musical Times*, Paul Bechert wrote astutely that the opera depicted 'a big, small world, seen through the eyes of a child; a French child to be sure, and decidedly one of the twentieth century'.[15] In this 'big, small world', we trace the interplay between vivid sensory experience and entrancing imagination, between the trappings of childhood and the focussed vision of an inner world.

---

[10] Roberts, 'Child studies in music' (I), 16.
[11] Roberts, 'Child studies in music' (II), 157, quoting a letter from Musorgsky to Stasov.
[12] Jankélévitch, *Ravel*, trans. Margaret Crosland, 78.   [13] Abbate, 'Outside Ravel's tomb', 495.
[14] *Ibid.*, 496.   [15] Bechert, 'Musical notes from abroad: Vienna', 558.

Structural exchange and expansion

A minuet, *bel canto* coloratura, musette, 'Valse américaine', foxtrot, jazz, a Massenet pastiche, a hint of Puccini. . . as Matthias Schillmöller observes, the kaleidoscopic musical idioms of *L'Enfant* can, in performance, seem as bewildering to the listener as they do to the Child on stage.[16] But the opera's surface disjunction conceals a coherent underlying structural narrative, which amplifies patterns and reciprocities inherent in Colette's libretto. On the broadest scale, the nursery and Garden scenes are linked through shared patterns of dramatic and musical architecture. The latter part of each follows the same essential progression: in a pivotal encounter (respectively with the Princess and the Squirrel), a greater degree of interaction and exchange prompts a transformative moment of realisation, followed by a pause for reflection; this is succeeded by a whirlwind 'ronde' that ends in chaotic disintegration. From the wreckage, threads of musical material emerge (the Child's abortive dialogue with the Cat; the contrabassoon fragments tiptoeing beneath the Animals' dialogue), which are gradually rewoven into the final part of the scene. The two mad 'rondes' also relate musically, with chromatic and step-wise movement around the pivot note C (overlaying different bass lines; Ex. 10.1); both use the rhythm and driving energy of repeated words with cutting consonants ('quatre et quat'' and 'cinq et sept' for the Numbers; 'C'est le méchant' and 'Unissons-nous!' for the Animals); and both end with *fff* climaxes that plummet into obscurity as the Child collapses. Annotations in two Opéra-Comique vocal scores, almost certainly made during rehearsals for the 1926 Paris première, underline the correspondence, labelling the rising of the Animals 'Ronde méchante' (against the printed 'Ronde folle' of the Arithmetic scene), and indicating that in each scene the Child is surrounded to the point of invisibility ('les chiffres l'entourent', in the Arithmetic scene; 'l'enfant [*sic*] disparaît d'un cercle de bêtes' in the Garden scene).[17]

In the Animals' uprising, however, we see not just a musical echo of the Arithmetic scene but a larger dramatic mirroring. As the Child's rage had formed the third and last section of the opera's first episode, so the response of the creatures reciprocally occupies the first section of the

---

[16] Schillmöller, *Maurice Ravels Schlüsselwerk*, 108. The stylistic aspects of the different episodes, and their use of pastiche and satirical elements, are explored in, *inter alia*, Prost, 'L'Enfant et les sortilèges: l'infidélité aux modèles', 59–63; Harwood, 'Musical and literary satire in Maurice Ravel's *L'Enfant et les sortilèges*'; and Saint-André, 'Commentaire musical et littéraire'.

[17] Bm-O, A830c and F1775.

Ex. 10.1 Musical correspondence across the two 'rondes'

a. Arithmetic scene

b. Animals' rising

similarly tripartite final episode (whose divisions fall after the Child's collapse, Fig. 140, and after the summoning of Maman, Fig. 150). In structural and dramatic terms the second mad 'ronde' is a delayed but direct inversion of the Child's own destructive fury.

Within individual episodes, Ravel also uses structure as a narrative tool. Divisions across and within scenes often mark patterns of mathematical precision: in the scene of the Shepherds and Shepherdesses, for example, the opening passage in the Æolian mode, 46 bars in length, divides into two 23-bar segments (the midpoint falling at 'Las, notre chèvre amarante', Fig. 53). The central A major passage is divided just as precisely, the 'ballet des petits personnages' (Fig. 56) and the soloists' 'L'Enfant méchant...' (Fig. 58) each occupying 21.5 bars. In these exact bisections, we see the Child's actions – tearing Shepherds from Shepherdesses on his wallpaper – reflected most literally.[18]

The Child's opening monologue has an equivalent formality of design: belying the seemingly aimless oboe figurations, it falls neatly into

---

[18] Similarly precise bisections, on a larger scale, are evident in the 'Passacaille' of the Piano Trio and the finales of the G major Concerto (see Howat, *The Art of French Piano Music*, 49) and 1927 Violin Sonata; in the last of these the reprise of the opening material, at Fig. 8, falls halfway between the start of the movement and the beginning of the coda at Fig. 16.

Table 10.1 Organisation of first episode

Fig.	Bars	Action	Musical material
–	11	Prelude	Oboe figurations
1	11	Curtain rises	Oboe figurations, contrabass melody
2	11	Child sings	Oboe figurations, contrabass melody
3^{+2}	10	Maman enters (conversation)	'Maman cadence', with fragments of Child's oboe melody
5	5	Maman's punishment	*Allegro*; dissonant chordal appoggiaturas
5^{+4}	10	Maman urges repentance	'Maman cadence' (falling fourth becomes tritone)
7	17	Child sings ('Ça m'est égal!')	Melodic lines based around falling fourth, punctuating chords
9	41	Child wreaks havoc	Orchestral; bitonality
14^{+4}	17	Child sings ('Je suis libre...')	Melodic lines based around falling fourth, punctuating chords

three 11-bar segments of near-strophic repetition. On the second iteration (Fig. 1), the contrabass is woven into the texture; on the third (Fig. 2), the Child begins to sing. Maman's scene comprises two 10-bar sections, based around sequential presentations of the 'Maman cadence' (see p. 139), which frame the 5-bar *Allegro* of her punishment. The Child's rage falls again into a meticulously balanced ternary form: the passages setting his two defiant outbursts ('Ça m'est égal!' and 'Hourrah! Plus de leçons!') are both 17 bars long (the latter counted to the bar of silence preceding the *Lento, maestoso* of the Fauteuil and Bergère); between them fall the 41 bitonal bars of his destructive rage.

The first episode as a whole thus forms three sections, each comprising a tightly knit three-part structure (see Table 10.1). With the Child holding the stage alone for the first and third sections, this large-scale tripartite sequence also takes on a ternary element, at least in dramatic terms. This serves both to bind the episode and to set it apart from what follows: the enclosed, self-referential structures suggest that the Child's understanding of the world is inward-looking and intensely concentrated, and that he is the axis about which the narrative revolves.

Taking a cue from the Child's behaviour, the scenes that follow are complete in themselves, inward-looking and non-referential. The

Fauteuil (Armchair) and Bergère echo the tightly measured ternary forms of the opening scene in their elegantly clumsy Minuet and Trio; the Clock attempts something similar, though his mechanism runs down when he embarks on the reprise of his 'A' section; and the Teapot's foxtrot and Cup's *chinoiserie* are simultaneously (and bitonally) reprised as they dance. As Christine Prost observes, these three episodes, linked by their shared 'afternoon' setting and featuring the opera's most frankly comic creations, may be viewed collectively as a triptych of duet – solo – duet,[19] reciprocating the solo – duet – solo arrangement of the opening episode.

If the Cup and Teapot's duet makes no reference to the Child, it nevertheless prompts him to a moment of reflection: 'O ma belle Tasse chinoise. . .' he murmurs, 'stricken', as they disappear (see Ex. 10.5 below). The direction *atterré* bears a twofold meaning: the Child is not only stricken with fear and wonder, but for the first time begins to realise the damage he has wrought. From this point we see a concomitant relaxation of structure, the ternary forms starting to open outwards. The Fire traces an expanded quasi-rondo (ABA'B'CA), while the scene of the Shepherds and Shepherdesses concludes by hinting at an embryonic arch form, reprising earlier material much compressed and in reverse order: first the conclusion of the A major dance, now back in the Æolian mode of the opening ('L'Enfant ingrat. . .'), then the lament for the fantastically coloured pastoral world ('Las, notre chèvre amarante!') and finally the opening 'Adieu, pastourelles. . .'

Each of these five early episodes (Chairs, Clock, Cup and Teapot, Fire, Shepherds and Shepherdesses) presents a different response to the Child. The Chairs challenge his security and self-importance by ignoring him, even as they pronounce his downfall; the Cup and Teapot do not even acknowledge him; and the Shepherds and Shepherdesses again refer to him only in the third person. The Clock, by contrast, addresses the Child, albeit dismissively ('laissez-moi au moins passer!') as he staggers helplessly about the room. The central passage of his aria introduces for the first time the idea of 'what might have been': had the Child not torn out his pendulum, he could have continued to sound the hours, each like the other forever more. The formally indecisive conclusion of the scene, as it depicts the running down of his mechanism, also seems to take subtle account of these hints of repercussions, and of a past (and future) lost.

The Fire confronts the Child with his wrongdoing more directly: 'You have brandished the poker, upset the kettle, scattered the matches [. . .] you

---

[19] Prost, 'Maurice Ravel: *L'Enfant et les sortilèges*', 77.

have insulted all the friendly gods who keep the fragile barrier between you and unhappiness'. Above the uncompromising rhythms of her accompaniment, her use of the familiar *tu* makes her message blunter still. She threatens the Child not with deprivation, as did the Chairs ('No more cushions for his sleep'), but with personal injury ('Beware [...] you will melt like a snowflake on her scarlet tongue!'), the vertiginous vocal writing reinforcing the threat of imminent danger. Again, direct interaction with the Child seems to prompt a degree of formal flexibility: the Fire's opening material returns for the last time not in the tonic C major but in F. This unexpected shift to the subdominant opens into the extended coda, as the Fire's dance with the 'grey, rippling and mute' Cinders leads the narrative towards the more fluid evening scenes.

Like the Clock, the Shepherds and Shepherdesses recall the Child's happy infancy: to them he gave his first smile. Now they look more directly to a barren future: 'never again will we pasture our green sheep upon the purple grass'. In their ability to look both forwards and backwards they foreshadow the Princess, who will turn their experience back on the Child himself. She is the only character to reflect on the immediate past ('She whom you called in your dream, last night. / She whose story, begun yesterday...'): if the Child can dismiss the nostalgic reminiscences of his first smile, the Princess's appeal to the emotions of 'yesterday' is far more potent. This greater temporal and emotional awareness seems reflected in the episode's structure, as the embryonic arch form of the Shepherds and Shepherdesses is transformed into a fully realised arch (Table 10.2).

Appearing over harp arpeggios (A), the Princess's fragile existence is conjured not only in the sparse textures of her monologue (B) but also in her use of the imperfect tense ('tu appelais [...] tu te chantais [...] tu me cherchais'): her shift to the decisive *passé composé* ('Mais tu as déchiré le livre') heralds the more richly orchestrated central (C) passage, which itself presages an ominous future ('Que va-t-il arriver de moi?'). The emotional core of the Princess's scene, this central part too divides into a smaller ternary arch. At its heart is the dialogue between Child and Princess who, over *portato* flute arpeggios, lament the loss of the magical talismans of bluebird and necklace; but its climax is the Child's impassioned 'Ton Chevalier? Le Prince au Cimier d'aurore?' At the midpoint of the episode (starting at bar 41 of 81 bars), this reprises the legato woodwind arpeggios of Fig. 65, now reinforced with harp and strings. Melodically, it looks back farther again: as Example 10.2 demonstrates, the Child's lines map onto the Princess's opening ones, a reminiscence emphasised by the modulation back to the E♭ of her monologue. In this discovery, through

Table 10.2 Organisation of Princess's episode

Fig.	62	63	64	65	66	67	68	69	70	71	72
Section	A	B		C(a)	C(b)		C(a)		B	A	
Characters	Princess appears	Princess		Princess	Princess and Child		Child		Princess	Princess disappears	– Child left alone
Musical/ timbral material	Harp arpeggios (with str.)	Solo flute		Legato ww. arpeg.	*Portato* flute arpeg. (joined by cl.)		Legato ww. arpeg., harp, str.		Solo flute	Harp arpeggios (with str.)	Hn, Cl. B.
Bars		9 [26 bars]		27	34 [25 bars]		41		52	62 [24 bars]	76 [6 bars]

Ex. 10.2 Child's lines 'map' over Princess's

imitation, of his own lyrical voice, we see the lessons of the Princess reflected most plainly.

But if the Child's newfound ability to love and a burgeoning desire to protect and cherish, rather than harm, are reflected in the scene's expansive lyricism, he is still confined by mirrored structures. Accompanied once more by a solo flute, the Princess laments the Child's inability to defend her against the wicked enchanter, before the harp arpeggios of the scene's opening return as Sleep and Night reclaim her.

With the Princess disappears the gift of song: too weak, perhaps, to continue in this vein alone, the Child reverts to a near-monotone in 'Toi, le cœur de la rose', essaying only the most tentative of lyrical gestures. In this brief moment of repose, the opera's temporal midpoint, the reiterated pitches B♭ and D – the questioning dominants of the E♭ and G minor tonalities – begin to draw us away from the reflexive patterns of the early scenes. In the hectic *ronde* that follows, Arithmetic and his number chorus set up two contrasting ideas, the four-bar phrases of 'Deux robinets coulent...' (Fig. 75) and the 2x2-bar settings of outrageous sums ('Quatre et quat'? Dix-huit!'; Fig. 80). But when the A section returns (Fig. 84), after the 'Millimètre, centimètre...' transition, all order is lost;

the *ronde* becomes *folle* and is driven to the point where it can only shatter and disintegrate. The Cats' duet also pulls us away from ternary forms, but in a different direction: its solitary motif is continuously developed until it too reaches an unsustainable intensity, and we suddenly find ourselves in the Garden.

If these indoor episodes suggest something of a patchwork quilt, the ensuing Garden scene is a single tapestry into which the Child is inextricably woven. That he sees himself no longer as a separate entity but part of a broader environment is immediately clear: he opens his arms and sings, 'Ah, what joy to find you again, Garden!', finally welcoming the world and drawing it to himself. As he thus places himself within the scene, the Child's growing awareness and tenderness are matched by the greater integration of characters and musical material. At the reprise of the Dragonfly's waltz, for example (Fig. 110), the animal noises of the scene's opening return, together with the song of the nightingale (anticipated at Fig. 100 by flute and slide whistle and now sung in reality), reflecting the Child's growing awareness of the unity of the natural world. In addition to this literal reprise, the first half of the Garden scene (until the moment of the Animals' uprising) is bound together through commonalities of rhythm, metre and melodic material. Two principal musical ideas alternate and overlap: the 'nocturne' material, with parallel open-fifth string chords and 'natural' sounds (including the knocking, croaking dyads of the Frogs); and the chain of waltzes, mostly based on the melodic gesture of a rising semitone and fifth. This figure first appears in the duet of the two Cats (bracketed in Ex. 10.3a), before returning, enharmonically re-spelt, in the waltz of the Dragonfly, where it is paired with a consequent figure that momentarily traces Maman's falling fourth (Ex. 10.3b). The Bat's waltz in turn makes subtle reference to this consequent (the falling fourth inverted to an ascending fifth; Ex. 10.3c), before the flute takes up the Dragonfly's theme in a seamless introduction to the dance of the Frogs (Exx. 10.3d–e), itself based on constant reiterations of the semitone + fifth motif.

The same waltz motif then introduces the Squirrel's aria (Fig. 132; see Ex. 10.4 below). As the aria ends, the reappearance of the two Cats prompts another reprise of the motif, in direct echo of their duet, which is succeeded in turn by a fragment of the nocturne material.

The recapitulation of material in the Squirrel's aria underlines its summative dramatic function: opening with the unifying semitone + fifth motif over the sustained chords and piano arpeggios of the Dragonfly's

Ex. 10.3 Garden scene, waltz motif

a. First appearance, Cats' duet

b. Becomes antecedent to a falling-fourth consequent, Dragonfly's waltz

c. Consequent sketched in Bat's waltz

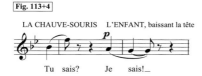

d. Prelude to 'Danse des rainettes'

e. Antecedent as principal melodic gesture, 'Danse des rainettes'

waltz, it loosely echoes the soaring rise and final descent of the 'Danse des rainettes' (the Squirrel's last words, 'tout miroitant de larmes', are a transposed reprise of the corresponding final notes of the 'Danse des rainettes'), with a direct echo of the Dragonfly's final repeated 'Rends-la moi!' heard in the orchestra beneath the Squirrel's second 'ce qu'ils reflétaient' (Fig. 133^{+1}). The aria is thus literally and conceptually a summation of the creatures' plaints. In its mapping of its vocal line over earlier material, we also find an echo of the Princess's scene, an episode of parallel structural and dramatic importance.

The Child released

If the Princess's scene had brought to a climax the interwoven motifs of love and loss, the Squirrel's aria represents the culmination of another core theme, that of enclosure and liberation. The Child initially declares himself free, but as events unfold he comes to realise that he is constrained both emotionally and physically by the consequences of his naughtiness. The Squirrel, conversely, regains his own lost freedom. The dialogue between Squirrel and Frog sees their black-key pentatonic melody struggling, as Peter Kaminsky puts it, 'against the Child's prevailing key of D major, just as they struggle in vain to escape from the cage'.[20] But while the Child's explanatory plea holds to his D major ('La cage, c'était pour mieux voir ta prestesse', Ex. 10.4), the Squirrel's bitter 'Oui, c'était pour mes beaux yeux' pulls the tonality suddenly into flat keys. To an echo of the opening of the Garden scene (alternating fifths on F and E♭), the Animals begin to gather, and the reiterated D♯ of the Frog/Squirrel dialogue (via its enharmonic equivalent E♭) becomes the dominant to the A♭ of the aria. The emphatic repetition of the key word *libre* here proves that the Child cannot escape the Animals' wrath – though he can at last make reparation. In this slowly dawning recognition of his confinement, we see the Child's emotional horizons paradoxically expanding.

The Squirrel's aria also sees the resolution and transformation of another musical thread woven through the fabric of the opera. Rejected by the Chairs, rebuffed by the Clock and ignored by the Cup and Teapot, the Child is initially little more than a bewildered onlooker to a fantastic parade. But, as noted above, the Cup and Teapot prompt his first sung words (apart from a couple of frightened interjections) since his destructive fit: 'Ô, ma belle tasse chinoise!' ('Oh, my beautiful Chinese cup!'). Stopping for the first time to reflect, the Child at this moment begins to understand and acknowledge the damage he has done. His line appropriates the Cup's pentatonic scale, while the accompanying celeste blends the wandering oboe melody of the opera's opening with the figurations of the Cup's solo (Ex. 10.5).

French-Swiss child psychologist Jean Piaget used the term 'egocentric' to describe the thinking of 'Preoperational' children (in the age range 2–7 years): such children can only view the world 'in terms of their own perspective'.[21] This Child, aged 'six or seven' (in Colette's description), stands on the cusp of Piaget's Preoperational and Operational Periods. A key factor in the shift from the Preoperational to the Operational stage is

[20] Kaminsky, 'Ravel's late music', 250.   [21] Siegler and Alibali, *Children's Thinking*, 40.

Ex. 10.4 Prelude to Squirrel's aria

the development of the ability to take on different perspectives and under-stand processes of transformation.[22] At this key moment, we see a cogni-tive/emotional development mirrored in music: the Child, melding the

[22] Huebner also considers Piagetian theories in his chapter 'Ravel's Child'.

Ex. 10.5 Child appropriates Cup's pentatonic scale

Cup's material with his own, is learning to take on different perspectives; he is beginning to grow up.

In structural terms, this line has a further significance, for it employs a pattern that the Cup did not: a pentatonic scale descending across a full octave. This gesture recalls the final statement of the Child's opening monologue (see Ex. 7.4), which similarly descends through an octave in a pentatonic context (the vocal line itself uses just four of the five pitches; the missing F# is in the oboe part).[23] A near-identical figure is heard at the Child's effective declaration of love for the Princess, the climactic 'Ton Chevalier?...' (Fig. 68; see Ex. 10.2 above). We find another echo in the early bars of the Garden scene, as the Child opens his arms and sings, 'Ah, what joy to find you again, Garden!' (Ex. 10.6a). Here, another key moment in his development – the recognition of joy, love and newfound tranquillity – is conveyed in a descending phrase within whose diatonic F major tonality we find the same pentatonic collection as 'Ton Chevalier?...' Later, in the Dragonfly's aria, the Child's agonised acknowledgement of his wrongdoing is similarly set to a descending pentatonic scale (Ex. 10.6b).

Underlining the profound dramatic and emotional impact of their scenes, both the Squirrel and the Princess (Ex. 10.2 above) employ these descending pentatonic gestures, the only two characters other than the Child to do so. The Squirrel's line, however, spans not an octave, as did the other statements, but a minor seventh, descending from e″♭ to f′ (Ex. 10.7). As she concludes, the harmony traces descending fifths towards the tonic A♭. The Child's response is a remarkable indicator of his growth. The resolution is suspended as he sings 'Ils s'aiment. Ils sont heureux. Ils m'oublient . . .' ('They love each other. They're happy. They forget me . . .'). This almost parenthetical passage – the Child is singing only to himself – is not itself pentatonic. As he ends the line, however, the harmony finally arrives at A♭, and he sings 'Ils

---

[23] Kaminsky also notes this blending, or 'contextualisation', of the 'stereotypical Chinese element' with the '"purer" non-tonal pentatonicism of the prelude' ('Ravel's late music', 254n26).

Ex. 10.6 Child's reflections

a. Garden 'Nocturne'

b. Dragonfly's waltz

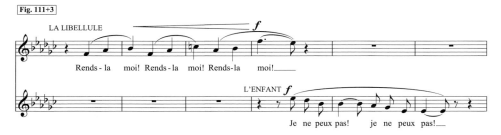

s'aiment... Ils m'oublient... Je suis seul... ' ('They love each other... They forget me... I'm alone...'), on that missing E♮, which sounds as a resolution of the Squirrel's line. The Child's words show that he has reached a nadir of loneliness and remorse, impelling him to call for his mother 'in spite of himself'. Yet by completing and resolving both the Squirrel's scale and the underlying cadence, the Child has also reached another important milestone: he has entirely repented of his earlier behaviour. Although he has yet to bind the little Squirrel's paw, it is at this moment, musically, that he is freed.

Orchestration and the grotesque

Alongside this structural unfolding and these key melodic gestures, orchestral colourations function as indicators of the Child's state of mind and the world around him. As we saw in Chapter 7, certain timbral effects are paired with important words and linguistic affects; more generally, throughout the opera, the wind and brass are used principally for the 'inanimate' objects and for the expression of negative emotions (boredom, rage), while bowed strings convey remorse and tenderness, and portray the natural world. The winds thus dominate the first half of the work: they create bitonal havoc with the percussion to depict the Child's 'frenzy of

Ex. 10.7 Child completes Squirrel's pentatonic scale

perversity'; a bassoon and contrabassoon herald the Fauteuil and Bergère; plaintive clarinets, oboes, bassoons and flutes accompany the *pastorale*; the Princess is introduced by that fragile flute; winds and brass rudely punctuate the phrases of Mr Arithmetic. In the Garden scene, by contrast, the strings come to the fore: pedal chords in the opening nocturne; *portamento* accompaniment for the trees; soaring violins in the 'Danse des rainettes'; the tender progression that leads to the Squirrel's aria; the rich chords of the reiterated 'Maman' cadence.

In addition to this large-scale orchestral painting, there are brief moments of string-tinted illumination. Amidst the winds, percussion and pizzicato strings that depict the Chairs and the Clock, Ravel twice briefly adds a solo bowed instrument. Sliding down through the interval of a second as the Fauteuil sings, 'No more cushions for his sleep' (Ex. 10.8a), the solo cello suggests the vanishing (deflating?) cushions that are the first visible consequences of the Child's destructive actions. In the Clock's aria, a single contrabass shadows the line 'Moi, moi qui sonnais de douces heures' (Ex. 10.8b). This, the opera's first instance of expressed regret, opens the episode's more nostalgic central section; the change of timbre is reinforced by the shift from plucked strings to harp for the accompanying chords.

In the central section of the Princess's scene the strings gradually take hold, swelling around the woodwind arpeggios; at the climactic phrase ('Ton Chevalier?'), the first violins double the Child's line. In the Garden scene, when the Bat makes plain to the Child that the death of his mate has left the children motherless and the Child murmurs 'Sans mère!', the strings, hitherto pizzicato, stop plucking to bow for a single bar. The final reprise of the perambulating oboe theme in the opera's closing bars, doubled by two violins, thus becomes a timbral reconciliation that evokes the Child's newfound compassion.

Subtle manipulation of orchestral timbres serves different purposes. In the Child's interaction with the Trees, *portamenti* in the lower strings are heard against lurching chords in the lower winds, punctuated by the aeoliphone

Ex. 10.8 Solo strings reinforce the consequences of the Child's actions

a. Chairs

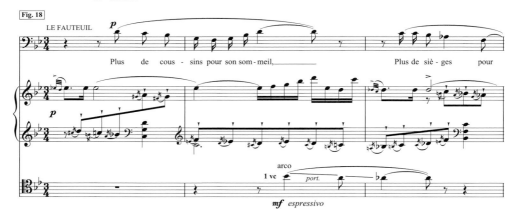

b. Clock

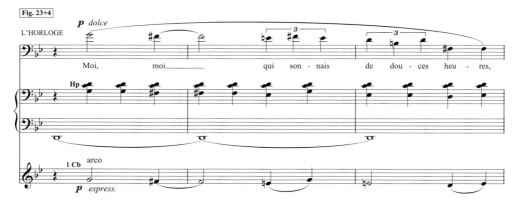

(wind machine). These strangely distorted combinations are calculated to emphasise the sliding tritones in the vocal line, a blend that gives the episode the trappings of the grotesque. A similarly exaggerated *parlando* style, with slides, exaggerated intervals and zig-zagging melodic lines, characterises the episode of the Fauteuil and Bergère; Ravel's score reinforces the affinity by indicating that Fauteuil and Tree 'may' be sung by the same person. Here too we find instrumental as well as vocal distortion, with the accompanying luthéal[24] bending the piano sound towards the timbre of a harpsichord, while ungainly appoggiaturas destabilise the formal gait of the minuet. In

---

[24] An attachment to the piano mechanism, with several different 'stops' that alter the timbre.

this scene, the word *grotesque* comes from Colette herself, in her description of the dance – 'compassée [measured] et grotesque'.

Of all the strange characters that inhabit *L'Enfant et les sortilèges*, the Chairs, with their blend of comic and sinister elements, and human and animal characteristics, are the most literal grotesques (the Fauteuil moves away from the Child 'like an enormous toad', accompanied in Ravel's setting by a croaking contrabassoon that underlines its comic earthiness). Jessie Fillerup writes of the opera as a whole that 'It might be argued that Ravel employs the grotesque as a tactic of alienation: by juxtaposing archaic and modern musical styles, he creates the disorienting *vertige* that distances the child from reality.'[25] With Chairs and Tree representing the Child's first encounter in each half of the opera, their shared grotesque characters serve to tumble him headlong into the world of the *sortilèges* (he might have imagined, in the opening bars of the Garden scene, that in reclaiming the Garden the enchantments were at an end). The *Oxford English Dictionary* suggests that one role of the grotesque is to promote empathy (Victor Hugo's Quasimodo is such a character). If the Child does not interact with the Fauteuil and Bergère, and if they neither lament their plight nor ask for pity, they are nevertheless the first to point out the repercussions of his wrongdoing, laying the foundation for his subsequent moral development. In his interaction with the Trees, we reciprocally find the Child's first attempt to make amends: as they lament their wounds, the Child, 'moved to pity', presses his cheek against a trunk. This, his first physical gesture of repentance and love, sees him literally and metaphorically united with the Trees.

The Child alone

The seeming abstraction of children and childhood in musical *enfantines*, noted at the beginning of this chapter, generally holds true on the opera stage as well: child characters tend to appear less as living beings than as symbols (innocence, purity, sacrifice, nostalgia, truth, helplessness). Often mute, they are unable to express emotions, thoughts or desires of their own: in Bellini's *Norma* and Verdi's *I due foscari*, for example, they are hostages and bargaining tools, while Puccini's Dolore (*Madama Butterfly*) is a symbol by his very name.[26] In 1919, as Ravel was beginning work on

---

[25] Fillerup, 'Purloined poetics', 327. See also Zank, *Irony and Sound*, 170–1.
[26] The young princes of *Boris Godunov* (Feodor) and *Pelléas et Mélisande* (Yniold) made a more decisive presence upon the operatic stage. Both characters capture an authentically childlike voice in their directness and focus on the moment at hand, and in their readiness and simplicity

L'Enfant et les sortilèges, Richard Strauss was writing for an offstage 'chorus of unborn children' in *Die Frau ohne Schatten*. These unreal, unseen children are projections of the fears and desires of the opera's adult protagonists – but, as Elizabeth Giuliani observes, Strauss merely makes explicit what his predecessors had already intimated.[27] Dolore, Norma's children and Lucrezia's (in *I due foscari*) have little more concrete existence than the disembodied voices of the unborn.

By his very existence, therefore, the Child of *L'Enfant et les sortilèges* is an unusual figure. He is distinctive, individual, energetic and noisy, with a voice, a mind and a will of his own. With his body he destroys and then repairs: his actions impact upon his world. He listens and speaks to things, rends and tears, embraces, binds them, hides behind them. He has the capacity to communicate, first his boredom and rage, then his bewilderment and fear, and finally his remorse and compassion. No other operatic child (in a mainstream repertoire work) exists as the central and exclusive focus of his opera, to be given such depth of characterisation and – perhaps most importantly – to grow and develop as the work progresses.

Because the Child does spend much of his opera as an onlooker, it is easy to overlook the importance, in musical and structural terms, of his developing character. The Child's musical purpose is at times obvious: his reflections between scenes in the first half serve to punctuate as well as link the narrative from each episode to the next, providing continuity through their shared pentatonic content. In broader terms, the Child's growth is reflected in the expansion and integration of musical forms; it emerges equally from Ravel's orchestration, as the wind-dominated opening gives way to the warm string sounds of the Garden scene.

In endowing its protagonist with no name beyond 'L'Enfant', the opera seems at first to nod to the typical operatic abstraction of children and childhood. Yet his namelessness renders him not an abstract but an utterly individual creation: he needs no other name because his world is created around him, and grows with him. As his development shapes the musical narrative, so this Child has the potential – and, by the work's conclusion, the wisdom – to shape his own destiny.

---

of response. Nevertheless, both exist more as prisms to refract the events going on about them than as active participants in the drama.

[27] Giuliani, 'La Musique et l'enfance', 61.

11 | A Child of his time

The years of the long gestation of *L'Enfant et les sortilèges* fall within those of Proust's *À la recherche du temps perdu*, which was published serially between 1913 and 1927. In September 1916, meanwhile, convalescing after a bout of dysentery, Ravel was reading Alain-Fournier's 1914 novel *Le grand Meaulnes*, a strange tale of the irreconcilable gulf between reality and a childhood ideal.[1] The protagonists of both novels attempt to recapture a past concentrated in idealised childhood experience, though Meaulnes (in the words of Catherine Savage) is 'less concerned with the experience of the past, which Proust's narrator will find meaningful and satisfying, than with his attempt to live it again'.[2] Alongside the novelised explorations of Proust and Alain-Fournier, the process of retrieving – or at least retracing – the childhood self, with its attendant memories, repressions and traumas, was brought literally to the public and intellectual consciousness in the early twentieth century by Sigmund Freud and his disciples, for whom childhood experience represented a pathway to adult wholeness and healing.

In its dialogues of modernity and nostalgia, destruction and reparation, focussed through the figure of the Child, the narrative of *L'Enfant* unites several of the primary cultural absorptions of its era. One of the opera's great strengths is that its far-reaching themes, held within a straightforward narrative and realised by a fantastic cast, can support myriad interpretations. However, in theatrical terms, *L'Enfant* presents an unusually complicated and potentially prescriptive prospect for designers and directors, since Colette's descriptions of setting and scale are far more complex and specific than those provided by most opera librettists. As Émile Vuillermoz noted in his review of the 1939 Opéra Garnier production:

The task imposed on the designer and the costume designer is outside human capabilities. To realise a lyric drama in which the characters are armchairs, tables, a kettle, a tea service, the cinders in the hearth, cats, squirrels, frogs, dragonflies and a naughty little boy *en travesti*; to make the furniture, the animals and the people

---

[1] Orenstein, *Ravel, Man and Musician*, 75n10. In the post-war years Ravel would seriously contemplate a fantasy for cello and orchestra based on *Le grand Meaulnes*.

[2] Savage, 'Nostalgia in Alain-Fournier and Proust', 170.

painted on the walls sing, walk and dance, to give a body and a face to imponderables – this is obviously an unachievable 'order'.[3]

Yet since literal realisation is impossible, the opera is also a liberating work to stage. Its performance history is rich and colourful, and the scholarly literature hardly less so. This chapter juxtaposes a few representative productions with some of the prevailing strands of musical and contextual scholarship, as it seeks to reconcile the opera's conceptual sophistication with its practical challenges.

Wartime, modernism and nostalgia

In February 1981 *L'Enfant et les sortilèges* was staged at the Metropolitan Opera in New York, in a production created by John Dexter and David Hockney and conducted by Ravel's friend and former student Manuel Rosenthal. It was the last work in a triple bill: Satie's *Parade* was the curtain-raiser, followed by Poulenc's *Les Mamelles de Tirésias*. The three works were bound together by their links to the First World War,[4] with Matisse-inspired décor and emphasis of shared music-hall elements; the sets for *Tirésias* and *Parade* were dominated by barbed wire and spectre-like figures in gas masks (elements that reappeared less obtrusively in *L'Enfant*). Dexter focussed his underlying narrative through imagery of children as the observers, victims, perpetrators and healers of violence. The reshaped narrative of *Parade* thus centred on a 'wonderstruck' child watching circus performers playing to troops in the trenches; at the conclusion, the protagonist Harlequin led the 'archetypal innocent child' into a happier world.[5] The Harlequin reappeared at the end of *L'Enfant*, this time leading the Child into what critic Donal Henahan described as 'a new world of kindness and sensitivity'.[6]

Children are an eternal symbol of renewal, and the France of Ravel's lifetime was consciously renewing itself. In celebrating the promise and pleasures of children and childhood, works such as *Jeux d'enfants*, *Dolly*, *Children's Corner* and *Ma mère l'Oye* also epitomise the confident and forward-looking Belle Époque. In the years of the First World War,

---

[3] Vuillermoz, '*L'Enfant et les sortilèges*'.

[4] Russell, 'David Hockney's designs for Met Opera's *Parade*'. Composed between 1940 and 1944 and first performed in 1947, *Les Mamelles de Tirésias* is based on Apollinaire's 1917 play.

[5] Kisselgoff, 'Ballet: *Parade*'s dances made into curtain-raiser'.

[6] Henahan, 'Met Opera's *Parade*, captivating triple bill'.

however, the image of the child took on powerful and poignant new significance. The suffering of the children of Belgium became a powerful symbol of devastation and lost innocence: hungry children, homeless children, fatherless children and, most potently of all, murdered and mutilated children, all loomed large in the public imagination.[7] Debussy's song *Noël des enfants qui n'ont plus de maison* was written for a concert given by one of the Belgian relief organisations; Ravel's choral *Trois chansons* of 1914–15 (which turn fairytale narratives to distorted ends) arguably also gesture to the images of violated childhood then dominating the popular press and public imagination.[8] After the war, therefore, the image of the child as the bringer of renewal and hope was doubly potent.

Studies of *L'Enfant* by Marcel Marnat, Pascale Saint-André and Michel Faure each draw out themes of conflict and reparation, focussed through an explicitly socio-political lens: all three, for example, see in the revolt of the Animals against the Child/tyrant the power and influence of the Marxist Left in interwar France.[9] If Marnat writes, in inverted commas, of the 'Cartel des gauches' (referring to the Socialist-Radical alliance that followed the 1924 elections) and the 'classes soumises', Faure unhesitatingly applies the labels of *bourgeoisie* and *prolétariat*, while Saint-André invokes the emotive ideal of 'une ère libre et fraternelle', arguing that the hints of *La Valse* in the 'Danse des rainettes' act as a symbol of revolution.[10]

These parallels, although they may usefully inform our understanding of the opera within a cultural and political milieu (and related imagery may be powerfully apt in performance), are more reflective of the opera's intuitive connection with the Zeitgeist than they are intrinsic to the work itself. (Indeed, given that the libretto predates the unrest of the 1920s, we might as easily read it back to the French Revolution, or 1830, or 1848, or 1871...) That said, wartime and post-war themes of conflict and renewal

---

[7] See Horne and Kramer, *German Atrocities, 1914*, 185, 204. Manuel Rosenthal recalled Ravel saying that after the war ended, 'everyone remembered what had been said of the Germans, who cut off the hands of little children, killed pregnant women and did so many other terrible things' (Marnat (ed.), *Ravel: Souvenirs de Manuel Rosenthal*, 134). See also Kilpatrick, 'The language of enchantment', 220–3.

[8] See Kilpatrick, '"Into the woods"'.

[9] Marnat, *Maurice Ravel*, 561, 565; Faure, *Musique et société du Second Empire aux années vingt*, 85; Saint-André, 'Commentaire musical et littéraire', 27, 30.

[10] While the 'Danse des rainettes' undoubtedly recalls *La Valse*, it is gesturally much closer to the seventh of the *Valses nobles et sentimentales*, a work notably lacking in revolutionary overtones. In 1922 Ravel specifically asserted that *La Valse* 'has nothing to do with the current situation in Vienna, nor any symbolic significance in that respect' ('C.v.W.', 'Het Fransche Muziekfeest', *Die Telegraaf*, 30 September 1922; Orenstein (ed.), *A Ravel Reader*, 423.)

are indisputably woven through *L'Enfant et les sortilèges*. Although it was completed amidst the troubled and chaotic relief of the 1920s, in conception it is a wartime opera, whose concluding gestures of reparation and forgiveness resonate with particular potency in the time and place of its creation. 'Nobody can explain why [the war] went on so long', said Dexter in 1981; 'Nobody said "Stop". Nobody ever says "Stop".'[11] As the last work on the Met programme, *L'Enfant* encapsulated and resolved the themes of *Parade* and *Tirésias*, and the Child's binding of the Squirrel's paw took on a significance that reached back to the earlier works: it was he who was finally able 'to say "Stop"'. The implication was plain: as Dexter said, 'children can redeem the world'.[12]

But if it is firmly located in its post-war setting, *L'Enfant* also very obviously looks back, in its 'smooth blending of all styles from all eras, from Bach up to... Ravel!'[13] Time, and the passage of time, are key underlying themes, evoked most plainly in the scenic transition from afternoon to twilight to moonlight to the glimmerings of dawn. However, audiences may recognise in the Child's experiences a more fundamental progression, from childhood towards maturity. Jorge Lavelli's 1975 Milan production (reprised at the Opéra Garnier in 1979) explicitly played on this concept, conceiving the work as a rite of initiation into an understanding of time and loss, and expanding the significance of the Princess's scene to the work as a whole: 'the projection of a memory of childhood, with all the nostalgia of a moment lost forever'.[14]

Maturity comes with memory, and knowledge of the irretrievability of *temps perdu*. The Clock's lament for the 'sweet hours' and the Shepherds' and Shepherdesses' 'Nous n'irons plus. . .' are brought home to the Child in his lament for the lost Princess, the little aria 'Toi, le cœur de la rose'. Gazing across the barrier of the Great War as the Child himself looks back in regret, Ravel here invokes the most popular of *fin-de-siècle* opera composers, Jules Massenet. His acknowledged model was *Manon's* aria 'Adieu, notre petite table':[15] the two passages share a tempo marking, the direction *sostenuto*, a simple triadic accompaniment, and certain melodic and harmonic gestures (Ex. 11.1). The arrival of Arithmetic, however, with the harshly dissonant chord and 'tremolo dental' in the trumpet and winds, makes it plain that the time of Massenet has passed: as Steven Huebner

---

[11] Russell, 'David Hockney's designs for Met Opera's *Parade*'.   [12] *Ibid.*

[13] [Anon.], 'Avant-première: À l'Opéra de Monte-Carlo'; *OL*, 349.

[14] Jorge Lavelli, 'Le Cauchemar de l'initiation'.

[15] Marnat (ed.), *Ravel: Souvenirs de Manuel Rosenthal*, 31.

Ex. 11.1a Massenet, 'Adieu, notre petite table' (*Manon*)

Exx. 11.1b-c Ravel, 'Toi, le cœur de la rose' (*L'Enfant et les sortilèges*)

notes, the juxtaposition 'produces as wide a stylistic rupture as any enacted on the opera stage at this time'.[16]

A more subtly nostalgic thread is woven through the Garden scene, with its many references to Ravel's own music: *La Valse* and the *Valses nobles et sentimentales* in the waltz sequence, and, perhaps more potently, the fairytale evocations of *Ma mère l'Oye*. The opening of the scene, with its sustained string chords and haunting birdcalls, directly recalls the 'Prélude' that Ravel added to his 1912 ballet score (Exx. 11.2a–b show a literal harmonic correspondence, at the entry of the frog and insect chorus), while the characteristic consequent figure of the Garden scene (Ex. 10.3b above) is strongly reminiscent of 'Les Entretiens de la Belle et de la Bête' (Ex. 11.2c), the latter's falling fifth replaced here by a falling fourth. The 'knocking' dyads of the 'Danse des rainettes' hark back to the grumblings of the Beast, and the Beast's own

---

[16] Huebner, 'Ravel's Child', 81.

Ex. 11.2 Correspondences between *Ma mère l'Oye* and *L'Enfant*

a. 'Prélude' (*Ma mère l'Oye*), bar 43

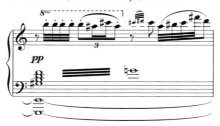

b. Garden scene (*L'Enfant*)

c. 'Les Entretiens de la Belle et de la Bête' (*Ma mère l'Oye*), bars 17–23 (cf. Ex. 10.3)

ancestor Belzébuth, the 'chien sombre' of *Noël des jouets* (Exx. 11.2d–f), while the Squirrel's 'Sais-tu ce qu'ils reflétaient' shares the sighing figures and tonal centre of bars 68–71 of 'Petit Poucet' (Exx. 11.2g–h). These last two passages, moreover, both evoke a child lost and lonely in an outside world that has become threatening and unfamiliar.

Finally, the threefold reiteration of the cadence that signals the return of Maman recalls the conclusion of 'Le Jardin féerique', with its soaring strings and harp glissandi as well as its tolling fourths. The Garden thus becomes another 'Jardin féerique', magical, joyous and transcendent. The *OED* suggests that nostalgia may entail 'longing for familiar surroundings': we might thus read, in these correspondences with Ravel's earlier compendium of fairytales, the Child's longing not just for the 'lost domain' of his fairytale Princess but also for the familiar environment depicted through his creator's characteristic musical language.

Ex. 11.2 (cont.)

d. *Noël des jouets*, bars 25–6

e. 'Les Entretiens de la Belle et de la Bête' (*Ma mère l'Oye*), bars 49–58

f. 'Danse des rainettes' (*L'Enfant*)

g. 'Petit Poucet' (*Ma mère l'Oye*), bars 68–71

h. Prelude to Squirrel's waltz (*L'Enfant*)

Most works of theatre expect us to identify with a protagonist, but also to see more, and to see differently. In *L'Enfant* this duality is foregrounded. The vision of the Child is the vision of the audience, as Colette's stage directions make explicit: 'Enter Maman (or rather as much as can be seen of her, with the very low ceiling and the entire scale of all the furnishings and all the objects in exaggerated dimensions in order to make more striking the smallness of the Child).' But while Ravel and Colette want us to experience the world through the Child's eyes, in his parade of pastiches the composer engages in an independent dialogue with his audience: the Child does not know he is paraphrasing Massenet, but we do. Nostalgia is an adult emotion, most often bound up with longing for childhood (as Chapter 10 observed, it is the Princess's appeal to the emotions of 'yesterday' that moves the Child most); and although *L'Enfant* is one of the few works in the mainstream repertoire that children can immediately enjoy, opera is nevertheless a primarily adult medium. Thus, as Fillerup observes, the audience's own memories 'transform their past into a place that never was. The unreality of their nostalgia mapped onto the theatrical experience could be said to create a shared aesthetic and experiential space that accepts both memory and magic as "real."'[17]

Because this passage from childhood to maturity, set within its archetypal fairytale idiom, is so recognisable and so readily abstracted, it is easy to forget that for the Child at least, what happens on stage is real. Ravel and Colette interweave fairytale and reality, imagination and sensation, to depict the small protagonist's physical environment in precise and colourful detail while granting him the enclosed, fantastic vision of a child in a world that is entirely his own, of which he is the centre and which no adult can truly penetrate. The intensity of a child's imagination and experience, married with the enchantments of the fairytale, were explicitly evoked in Hockney's designs for the

---

[17] Fillerup, 'Purloined poetics', 327.

1981 Met production, which emphasised childlike primary colours in unexpected and fantastical combinations (the Garden became a forest of red-trunked, blue-leafed trees), and in Michel Terrasse's designs for the 1950 Opéra-Comique season, with their kaleidoscopic palate of purples, greens and oranges and a Child whose pink and black jacket, blue trousers and golden hair suggest something of Saint-Exupéry's Little Prince. The designer of the 1929 Viennese production, Eugène Steinhof, described his Garden scene as 'a few very simple lines to capture the trembling waves of colour, much atmosphere and little reality, a translucent landscape, as if it were engraved upon iridescent glass, a mirage captured by a child's imagination!'[18] Childish fantasy also seems to have inspired Maurice Sendak's designs for the 1987 Glyndebourne production, which set the first scene within small, enclosed nursery surroundings – more realistic in themselves than Hockney's looming walls – but surrounded them with the luxuriant, magical garden of *Where the Wild Things Are* (the framing narrative of Sendak's much-loved picture book being akin to that of *L'Enfant*).

When the opera returned to Glyndebourne in 2012, its sets, by Barbara Limburg, abandoned the nursery altogether. With the edges of the stage often lost in darkness ('I have never witnessed such eloquent use of black space', wrote reviewer Rodney Milnes[19]), the production oddly reflected the words of Alain-Fournier, who wrote in 1906 that his future book (*Le grand Meaulnes*) would be 'a continuous coming and going between dreams and reality – "dream" meaning the immense, indefinite life of childhood, hovering above the other and endlessly reverberating with echoes of the other'.[20]

Dreams in a more literal sense shape the reflections of scholars including Carolyn Abbate, Mattias Schillmöller and Christine Prost, whose analyses are predicated on the basis that the fantastic events take place within the Child's imagination, or even his sleep. Abbate concludes her powerful reading of the opera by writing that the Animals' tentative vocalising of 'Maman' reveals 'a critical point about the "enchanted" nature of all we have heard up to the instant the Child becomes unconscious. The Animals, the trees, the teapot, the wallpaper, the book: none of these things could speak, dance or sing. They had *seemed* to, but their animation and voices are now understood as an illusion'.[21] Like Prost, who describes 'the

---

[18] Steinhof, '*L'Enfant et les sortilèges* à l'Opéra de Vienne'.

[19] Rodney Milnes, '*L'Heure espagnole* and *L'Enfant et les sortilèges*'.

[20] Palmer, 'Debussy, Ravel and Alain-Fournier', 270.

[21] Abbate, 'Outside Ravel's tomb', 512, 515; see also Schillmöller, *Maurice Ravels Schlüsselwerk*, 108. Fillerup engages with Abbate's thesis in her study 'Ravel and Robert-Houdin, magicians'; see in particular 154–8.

imaginary world of the child' (not quite the same as 'a child's imagination'),[22] and like Huebner, who writes that listeners 'never seem invited to relinquish a position of superiority towards [the Child]',[23] Abbate prioritises here the perspective of the adult, watching knowingly from beyond the proscenium arch. But if Ravel and Colette were attempting to evoke the vivid colours of childhood fantasy, they were also depicting not just an 'imaginary world', but a story that 'accepts both memory and magic as "real"'. The chairs, clocks and cups don't *seem* to come to life – in the opera, they really do. They do for the Child, who is still of an age to believe such things possible, and they do for us, because we watch the story through his eyes. The Child is grounded in the potent and magical reality of childhood, where the most peculiar situations can be accepted as the status quo, and he is the fulcrum of his tale; for him, the 'illusion' is utterly real.

Childhood is at once the period in which we live most in the realm of the creative imagination, and in which our physical experience of the outer world is perhaps most intense. This Child reacts to the 'enchantments' with shock: he never expected his armchair to sing or his clock to walk. He never questions their existence, however, nor does he challenge the magical atmosphere by denying the right of inanimate objects to move and dance and sing. Like a fairytale protagonist, he accepts the magical events as real and powerful: although he may have found himself in a fairytale by accident, once there he does not fight the story but unquestioningly becomes part of it – as Ravel himself observed, 'the "marvellous" is completely natural inside the head of a little boy'.[24] What happens to the Child is no dream-sequence but a fantastic reality: he touches and speaks to the creatures and they respond to him. If his powerlessness through much of the opera might seem dreamlike, his final act of reparation is not.

'My mother's house'

If an audience's perceptions of *L'Enfant* are necessarily infused by their own memories of childhood then, even more surely, we might argue, are the shape and atmosphere of the work itself informed by the childhoods – imagined and recalled – of the opera's creators. As Peter Ackroyd argued in his 2005 biography of Shakespeare: 'If there is one aspect of a writer's life

---

[22] Prost, 'Maurice Ravel: *L'Enfant et les sortilèges*', 78.   [23] Huebner, 'Ravel's Child', 72.
[24] Méry, 'Avant-première'.

that cannot be concealed, it is childhood. It arises unbidden and unannounced in a hundred different contexts. It cannot be denied or misrepresented without severe psychic disturbance on the surface of the writing. It is the very source of the writing itself and must necessarily remain undefiled.'[25]

Although they grew up in very different environments, both Ravel and Colette enjoyed close family lives and largely happy childhoods. Most importantly, both were devoted to their mothers, acknowledged their profound influence on their creative lives and were devastated by their deaths. As Colette wrote in 1953, 'I always remained in touch with the personage who, little by little, has dominated all the rest of my work: the personage of my mother.'[26]

While the character of Maman is absent from the stage for most of the opera – and her face, according to Colette's libretto, never appears at all – her character focusses the narrative and her presence is subtly but pervasively recalled as the story unfolds. Chapter 7 demonstrated the significance of the falling fourth and cadence associated with Maman; to this one might add the dramatic symbolism of characters such as the Princess, in whom Jacques Dupont persuasively identifies a mother-figure: the mother is the Child's first *bien-aimée*, and the Princess's disappearance, which implies the finality of death, is dramatically mirrored when the Child realises that his killing of the Bat has left the baby bats without their own mother.[27] Ravel makes the impact of the Child's wrongdoing absolutely plain here, with his 'Sans mère!' directly echoed by the Bat's 'C'est ta faute!' (Ex. 11.3).

Besides its parallels with various of Colette's earlier stories, the libretto of *L'Enfant* has much in common with her autobiographical works of the 1920s, which semi-mythologise her Burgundian childhood and her mother Sido (her depictions of the family garden, in the 1922 memoir

Ex. 11.3 Melodic mirroring between Child and Bat

---

[25] Ackroyd, *Shakespeare*, 43.

[26] Colette, 'Preface' to *My Mother's House* and *Sido*, trans. Una Vincenza Troubridge and Enid McLeod, 19.

[27] Dupont, 'Visages de l'enfance, sortilèges de Colette', 24.

La Maison de Claudine, resonate particularly strongly with the words that set the Garden scene of *L'Enfant*). Equally telling is the way in which the opening of *La Maison de Claudine* inverts the opera's implicit and explicit yearning for 'Maman' with its repeated cry, 'Où sont les enfants?' As Sylvia Berkman wrote in the *New York Times* (reviewing the 1953 reissue of Colette's memoirs):

'Where Are the Children?' the opening sketch of *My Mother's House* is named, and the haunting question underlies the substance of the entire book. 'Where are the children?' Colette's mother would cry, and, leaving her ample, busy house, would stand, head lifted, in the garden she had shaped, to seek, inquire and protect. The children have disappeared, secret and intent, into preoccupations of their own; in the garden, yes, but for this moment invisible. Sido, the vigorous, the abundant, could neither find nor guard them there.[28]

We have already noted the correspondence between the summoning of 'Maman!' and the tearful longing of Minne for her mother in *L'Ingénue libertine* (p. 140); there are hints, too, of Colette's 1921 depiction of wounded soldiers on the battlefields calling for their mothers: 'le cri, le soupir, qui errait, sorti des bouches fraîches et des barbes grises: "Maman"' ('the cry, the sigh, that hovered, drawn from fresh mouths and grey beards: "Mama"').[29]

Colette's own daughter was born in July 1913, less than a year after Sido's death in September 1912. The libretto of *L'Enfant* thus arguably reflects something of not just Colette's grief for her mother, but also her own, still-unfamiliar motherhood (a role that did not come easily to her). We may wonder whether, as she wrote the libretto of what she originally intended to be a *Divertissement pour ma fille*, Colette was attempting to recreate the figure of her wise, present and devoted mother in herself.

If its characters and storyline were not of his making, Ravel must have recognised the emotional potency Colette's narrative held for him. Given the strength of his attachment to his own mother, it is also tempting to superimpose the figure of a desolate Ravel upon the character of the Child: as Marie Ravel's death, in January 1917, forced Ravel to abandon the fantasies of childhood, so the Child, rejected by his phalanx of creatures, is left calling desperately for 'Maman!' The Child's initial furious rejection of his mother might equally be likened to Ravel's occasionally complex relationship with his own: Maurice and Édouard Ravel both lived with their parents well into adulthood and Marie, devoted to her sons, was

[28] Berkman, 'The images of childhood'.   [29] Colette, *La Chambre éclairée*, *Œuvres*, vol. II, 915.

probably over-protective and occasionally stifling (Ravel once jokingly described her as a 'monster'[30]).

Although attempts to draw parallels between the composer and his subject can be no more than speculative, a more revealing connection may be perceived at a level deeper than the opera's narrative. From a musical perspective, that crucial interval of the falling fourth opens a window from *L'Enfant* onto Ravel's work more generally. The innumerable reiterations of the interval in *Histoires naturelles* and in the vocal line as well as the accompaniment of *L'Heure* – the works in which Ravel most consciously sought to reproduce the rhythms and inflections of the spoken language – uphold Émile Vuillermoz's assertion that the inflection was natural to his voice and thus his compositional ear (see p. 111). Motifs using or based around falling fourths characterise much of *Ma mère l'Oye* as well as the opening of the *Sonatine*, 'La Vallée des cloches' and the central section of 'Noctuelles' (*Miroirs*), key moments in *Daphnis et Chloé*, and the G major Concerto. In the words of Deborah Mawer, the fourth is Ravel's 'signature interval, objectified across his repertory'; Jean-Claude Téboul called it 'the driving force of his melodic stream'.[31] Perhaps, then, in *L'Enfant* Ravel deliberately linked the word *Maman* with this most characteristic of his melodic gestures, acknowledging the significance of his mother to his life and work as a whole.

Whatever its psychological bearing, however, the purpose of the falling fourth is above all else musical, matching the natural spoken inflection of the word *Maman* and serving as a binding motivic gesture: Ravel would never have woven in such a tribute had it not first satisfied his compositional requirements. We may, therefore, view *L'Enfant* simply as a homage or *tombeau*. Sido, who gave her daughter her love and sympathetic understanding of nature, and Marie, without whom Ravel, as he said himself, 'could never have composed *Ma mère l'Oye*',[32] are undoubtedly memorialised in an opera that celebrates fantasy and fairytale, a childlike ability to perceive the magic inherent in the natural world, and maternal, filial and pantheistic tenderness and love.

For his 1975 Milan production, Jorge Lavelli paired *L'Enfant* with Stravinsky's *Œdipus Rex*: the former he described as a *nuit blanche*, but the latter was a *soleil noir*, and his colour palate was correspondingly

[30] *OL*, letter 119.

[31] Deborah Mawer, 'Musical objects and machines', 48; and Téboul, 'Le Langage musical dans la musique de piano de Ravel' (Ph.D. diss., Paris: Sorbonne, 1978), quoted in Prost, 'Maurice Ravel: *L'Enfant et les sortilèges*', 79.

[32] Jean Françaix, *De la musique et des musiciens*, 164.

monochrome. In this juxtaposition Lavelli made near-explicit a particularly pervasive strand of interpretation and analysis of *L'Enfant et les sortilèges*. A post-war opera centred on one individual Child, and the conflict and resolution between child and mother, offers obvious scope for interpretative speculation; when combined with the singular private lives of its two creators, the temptation of psychological and, in particular, psychoanalytical representation seems irresistible.

The first commentator to seize upon the opera's psychoanalytical implications was Melanie Klein, who presented an analysis of the work to the British Psycho-Analytical Society just four years after its première. Knowing little or nothing of Ravel or Colette, Klein made no attempt to project the symbolism of the opera onto its creators, but dealt with it as an independent entity. Her reflections on sadism as a response to a situation of distress or danger, and the image of the 'good' or 'bad' parent, were regarded as particularly innovative and important, as Nicola Glover writes:

> This paper is very significant, from both a clinical perspective, as well as laying the foundation for a Kleinian aesthetic. For the first time Klein connects creativity with deep early anxieties, and she regards the urge to create arising from the impulse to restore and repair the injured object after a destructive attack.[33]

However, as Klein's paper makes clear, her analysis was based not on *L'Enfant et les sortilèges* itself but on a review of the 1929 Viennese production by Eduard Jakob in the *Berliner Tageblatt*. Klein did not attend a performance; she had not read Colette's libretto; she had not heard a note of Ravel's score. As a result of this transit across three languages and four countries (from French into an Austrian production sung in German, to a Berlin review and thence to a paper written in English and given in London), her account unsurprisingly omits key features of the libretto and distorts numerous others: for example, the line 'J'ai envie de manger tous les gâteaux' ('I want to eat all the cakes') becomes, in her paper, 'I'd like *best of all* to eat up all the cake *in the world*'.[34] In a major emphatic shift, a desire that is both achievable and just one of several expressed wants becomes both an impossible fantasy and the (oral) culmination of all desires. Similar loose translations and contingent misconstructions abound, not least through her emphasis of the opera's entirely different

---

[33] Glover, *Psychoanalytic Aesthetics: The British School*, Chapter 2 ('Essentials of Kleinian theory').
[34] Klein, 'Infantile anxiety-situations', 440.

German title *Das Zauberwort* (*The Magic Word*).[35] Most seriously, Klein's focus is almost entirely on the Child's rage and the perambulations of the inanimate *sortilèges*, while the Garden scene is only fleetingly acknowledged, and the episode of the Princess – the narrative heart of the opera – goes unmentioned. Her analysis thus crucially de-emphasises the Child's process of transformation and reparation: in the words of Carol Mavor, 'one questions her thorough emphasis on the Child's destructive acts and her lack of attention in regard to the boy's feminine (maternal) acts'.[36] Joseph Schwartz, meanwhile, observes that Klein's extreme language and darkly tormented view of the Child are troublingly characteristic of her work as a whole: 'Klein's account of infancy is a maelstrom of threats and deprivation, of destruction, of fears of retaliation, of an ever-present malevolence, of terrible anxiety, of terror [. . .] a tale of gothic horror.'[37]

The most interesting and significant aspect of Klein's paper thus lies not so much in its conclusions (at least for opera scholars) as in its very existence: it is a pertinent indicator of the increasingly reciprocal relationship that developed during the 1920s between psychoanalysis and the creative arts. The libretto of *L'Enfant et les sortilèges* predates the first widespread publications of Freud and Jung in French translation (Freud's works were appearing in French in the years immediately following the First World War, Jung's by the mid-1920s[38]), but in its conception and treatment of its subject the opera again proves its strong connections with the spirit of the age. The debate on the merits of psychoanalysis was a touchstone of Parisian intellectual life in the post-war period, when the early championship of André Gide and the Surrealists established an immediate connection with literature and philosophy:[39] in an extended 1921 article Albert Thibaudet decried the failure of the publishing house Alcan to include Freud alongside their editions of Schopenhauer, Nietzsche and Bergson.[40] Thibaudet also observed, as did Louis Cazamian three years later, the impact of psychoanalysis on contemporary creative arts: the latter argued that 'The novel and the theatre of today [. . .] are full of the latent or manifest presence of Freudianism'.[41] It can thus be argued that *L'Enfant* typifies a crucial shift in twentieth-century theatre, prompted or stimulated in part

---

[35] Kilpatrick, 'The language of enchantment', 247–51, explores these issues in detail. Among the studies to have drawn on Klein's reading of the opera are Milner, 'Le Corps de Sido'; Langham Smith, 'Ravel's operatic spectacles'; Kristeva, *Le Génie féminin: Colette*; and Huebner, 'Ravel's Child'.

[36] Mavor, 'The unmaking of childhood', 35.   [37] Schwartz, *Cassandra's Daughter*, 197.

[38] Mordier, *Les Débuts de la psychanalyse en France*, 141.

[39] Turkle, *Psychoanalytic Politics*, 99.   [40] Thibaudet, 'Réflexions sur la littérature', 467.

[41] Cazamian, 'La Psychanalyse et la critique littéraire', 450.

by psychoanalytic theory and its associated literary and artistic impact. On the operatic stage, this was demonstrated by the increasing focus on the self and the accompanying interiorisation of motive and impulse: as George Martin put it, 'In the nineteenth century the hero battled forces outside himself; in the twentieth he battles those within.'[42]

Central to psychoanalytic theory is what Caroline Steedman describes as 'the idea that the core of an individual's psychic identity was his or her own lost past, or childhood'.[43] The importance of the role played by childhood in the formation of the adult self is a key underlying motive of *L'Enfant*. Similarly, that the protagonist is a child; that he is given no other name *but* 'the Child'; that he is endowed with such depths of feeling and the capacity to understand, respond and develop – all these characteristics can be seen partly as a reflection of the impact of psychoanalysis on the creative arts.

If one remains within the Austro-German school, the opera's fairytale setting would seem to lend itself more easily to a Jungian than to a Freudian (or Kleinian) approach. According to Jung, the cross-cultural commonalities in fairytales prove that they are a vital conduit for the expression of the collective unconscious – that which is 'shared in a mystical way by all humankind, [containing] the deeper, universal and primal aspects of the personality'.[44] The characters and narrative idioms of fairytales mirror archetypes Jung identified within the human psyche; *L'Enfant et les sortilèges*, which is deliberately placed in the fairytale tradition, can also be seen as expressive of some of these archetypes. The powerful, nurturing Maman thus has something of Jung's Great Mother, while the Child's reconciliation with his world links him to Jung's archetypal Child, who functions as a symbol of renewal and rebirth.

Jung offers two more key functions of the child-motif or archetype: '"Child"', he wrote, 'means something evolving towards independence. This it cannot do without detaching itself from its origins: abandonment is therefore a necessary condition, not just a concomitant symptom.'[45] Here, perhaps, is the Child of the first half of the opera, violently detaching himself from his familiar surroundings, then – through the Princess – moving more consciously towards independence through an understanding of loss. Secondly, Jung's archetypal Child is also the 'one who makes whole', a 'uniting symbol' and a 'bringer of healing'.[46] If Ravel and Colette's Child is at first more destroyer than healer, another Jungian archetype

---

[42] Martin, *A Companion to Twentieth-Century Opera*, 10.
[43] Steedman, *Strange Dislocations*, 4.
[44] Moore and Fine, *Psychoanalytic Terms and Concepts*, 17.
[45] Jung and Kerényi. *Introduction to a Science of Mythology*, 121.   [46] *Ibid.*, 115.

offers further explanation. The Child's rage can be seen as a manifestation of his Shadow, the 'dark side' of the human personality, in Jungian terms: 'all those uncivilised desires and motions that are incompatible with social standards and our ideal personality'.[47] The Animals in the Garden, communicating more directly and more passionately than the inanimate creatures, are, like Jung's archetypal Animal, closely in touch with their true natures. By guiding the Child to recognition of his Shadow, they also help him to discover his own true self, thereby reconciling the conflicting parts of his personality.

A further intriguing Jungian connection is suggested by the characters of the Princess and the Fire, who seem to express different elements of the Anima (the feminine elements of the male psyche). The Princess appears as a young woman, but with an aura of experience; she is wise, but mysteriously so; she appears from and disappears into the earth: all these qualities are typical of the Anima.[48] The dangerously flickering Fire typifies a darker, more perilous and threatening projection of the Anima, intensified by the scene's progress from light into shadow. Ravel's stipulation that Fire and Princess should be played by the same singer seems to heighten this dichotomous representation of the Anima. Late in life Jung admitted that his theories had mostly been arrived at intuitively before he argued out their logic in detail, often only to show their viability in professional terms. In his casting specifications, Ravel – who had almost certainly not heard of Jung's concept of the Anima/Animus – appears similarly to have intuited an archetype that Jung explored independently.

Ravel's Child

Carefully placed inside a yellow box in the library of Ravel's house, Le Belvédère in Montfort l'Amaury, is a 'Lilliput [Post-]Card' inscribed in the hand of a very young child: 'Monsieur Ravel' on one side, and 'Merci mon grand ami – Giselle' on the other. The card is a simple and touching testimony to Ravel's natural affinity with children, and his love of the accoutrements, occupations and fantasies of childhood.

Ravel's ease of communication with children was remarked upon by many of his friends. There are still a few Montfortois who number among their earliest memories Monsieur Ravel stopping to speak to them in the

---

[47] Fordham, *An Introduction to Jung's Psychology*, 50.
[48] Walrond-Skinner, *A Dictionary of Psychotherapy*, 54.

street;[49] several of his friends recalled that he was wont to disappear during formal dinners, to be found later playing with the children of the house.[50] All these anecdotes stress Ravel's lack of condescension: he was direct and straightforward and addressed children with a gentle seriousness, entering easily into their activities and conversation (his birdlike stature may have helped too). He was also a fine storyteller: as Mimie Godebska wrote, 'There are few of my childhood memories in which Ravel does not find a place [. . .] I had a predilection for Ravel because he used to tell me stories that I loved. I used to climb on his knee and indefatigably he would begin, "Once upon a time. . ."'[51]

Beyond his natural affinity with children, the 'childlike' aspects of Ravel's own personality were highlighted by many of his friends. As an adult, they wrote, Ravel retained 'the candid soul', 'the purity', 'the spontaneity', 'the ingenuity' and 'the joyous astonishment' of childhood.[52] 'I think that he never forgot anything that was young and joyful', wrote Guy de Pourtalès; 'To him, the little world of childhood was always a fairyland, woven with enchantments and with music.'[53]

Children, Adam Gopnik writes, 'compel us to see the world as an unusual place again'.[54] The concept of childhood seems to have held a natural resonance for a composer who delighted in seeing things from unexpected perspectives, or from several perspectives at once. In the memory, the idea and the experience of childhood, Ravel found a perennial freshness of inspiration and vision. His image of childhood was not that of a Rousseau, Jean Paul or Schumann, a Hugo, Baudelaire or Proust. It was no metaphor for an essential goodness or purity of spirit, nor was it a 'lost domain' or abandoned Eden. More simply, Ravel retained a sense of active engagement with childhood, as real and present experience. The changing, developing protagonist of *L'Enfant et les sortilèges* thus reflects not only a twentieth-century understanding of childhood but also the perspective of its creator, who understood the state as at once present and transient. This Child is not stuck in shimmering Romantic stasis: real time passes and he grows up.

---

[49] Recounted by Claude Moreau and Marie-Huguette Hadrot, in conversation with the author, Montfort l'Amaury, July 2004.

[50] Nichols, *Ravel Remembered*, 19.

[51] Mimie Godebska Blacque-Belair, 'Quelques souvenirs intimes de Ravel', 189.

[52] Vuillermoz, 'L'Œuvre de Maurice Ravel', 2; Chalupt, 'La Féerie et Maurice Ravel', 130; Jourdan-Morhange, 'Ravel à Montfort l'Amaury', 164; Klingsor, 'L'Époque Ravel', 133; Jourdan-Morhange, quoted in Sanson, *Maurice Ravel*, 106.

[53] de Pourtalès, 'Petit hommage à Ravel', 35.   [54] Gopnik, *Through the Children's Gate*, 14.

The effectiveness of the 1981 Met production of *L'Enfant* – to fix on one representative example – lay in its eloquent unification of fairytale imagery (bright colours, mystery and magic) with tangible connections to the wartime and post-war culture of the opera's creation (barbed wire and gas masks; Matisse and music hall). This carefully judged interplay of fantasy and reality powerfully amplified themes inherent in the opera itself. More abstract production concepts, in over-emphasising symbolic or psychological aspects of the opera, may run the risk of missing or obscuring not just this essential dialogue, but with it much of the musical, dramatic and conceptual sophistication that underlies the opera. 'Complexe, mais pas compliqué' was one of Ravel's teaching mottos; the underlying complexity might speak for itself all the better for not being cluttered with 'complications'. It was originally conceived as a 'Divertissement', after all.

Afterword

À la fenêtre recelant
Le santal vieux qui se dédore
De sa viole étincelant
Jadis avec flûte ou mandore,

Est la Sainte pâle, étalant
Le livre vieux qui se déplie
Du Magnificat ruisselant
Jadis selon vêpre et complie :

À ce vitrage d'ostensoir
Que frôle une harpe par l'Ange
Formée avec son vol du soir
Pour la délicate phalange

Du doigt, que, sans le vieux santal
Ni le vieux livre, elle balance
Sur le plumage instrumental,
Musicienne du silence.[1]

Stéphane Mallarmé, 'Sainte'

In December 1896, the 21-year-old Ravel set to music Stéphane Mallarmé's poem 'Sainte'. It was a bold and unusual undertaking on several counts. His previous attempts at song-setting had been limited to Roland de Marès's *Ballade de la Reine morte d'aimer* (1893) along with a couple of Verlaine poems, *Le ciel est, par-dessus le toit* (left incomplete) and *Un grand sommeil noir* (1895).[2] Moreover, no established composer had yet published a

---

[1] In the old window holding / The old sandalwood losing its gilding / Of her viol that sparkled / Once with flute and lute, / Is the pale Saint, showing / The old book that unfolds / Streaming with the Magnificat / Once at vespers and at compline: / At this monstrance window / Brushed by a harp the Angel / Formed with her evening flight / For the delicate phalanx / Of the finger, that, without the old sandalwood / Without the old book, she balances / On the instrumental plumage / Musician of the silence. (trans. Rosemary Lloyd; Lees, *Mallarmé and Wagner*, 137.)

[2] Orenstein, 'Some unpublished music and letters', 291–6; see also Chalupt and Gerar, *Ravel au miroir de ses lettres*, 59. Ravel's setting of Marot's 'D'Anne jouant l'espinette' also dates from December 1896.

Mallarmé *mélodie*, the poet's famed complexity and the intense and see-mingly self-sufficient musicality of his words appearing to negate their translation into song.[3]

What, then, drew Ravel to this poem? He is unlikely to have known that Mallarmé had described 'Sainte', in a letter to Théodore Aubanel, as 'un petit poème mélodique, et fait surtout en vue de la musique' ('A small melodic poem, made above all with music in mind').[4] He was probably attracted initially by its musical imagery, a quality common to many of his song texts. But Ravel must also have recognised, as have most subsequent commentators, that 'Sainte' is one of the poems in which Mallarmé's quest for a new, musicalised poetry is best embodied, in imagery and technique.

The form of 'Sainte' is outwardly straightforward – almost literally foursquare, with its iambic tread, its octosyllables and its four four-line stanzas. With minimal punctuation, it unfolds in one long sentence, complete, poised and impassive. The first two stanzas each present a self-contained image (the old sandalwood of the viol, the old book of the Magnificat), sharing rhyme sounds and mirroring syntax. But from the midpoint of the poem a transformation takes place. The third and fourth stanzas are bound together with a single supple phrase in which, as Heath Lees writes, 'the line-by-line clarity of the first two stanzas gives way to a sinuous and complex musical "prose" which [. . .] builds longer, more plastic, iridescent phrases that activate their own musical movement'.[5] The poem's central image, that of the Saint's 'delicate fingertip', is pre-sented as an *enjambement* across the third and fourth stanzas ('la délicate phalange / Du doigt'). In Lees's reading, Mallarmé's first stanzas depict the loss of purpose and meaning in old, ritualised art forms, but the latter ones evoke the creation of a new art, poetry and music 'symbolically fused into one through the suspended axis of the saint's fingertip, the human point of creativity where the act of musical sound production fuses with the shaping idea and creates the conditions for a magical instant of *extase*'.[6]

The calm regularity of Mallarmé's first stanzas is echoed in Ravel's quiet chords and regular 4/4 metre, the even quavers of his vocal line, the

---

[3] Debussy, Eugène Lacroix and Edmond Bailly had all made settings of 'Apparition'. Debussy's (dating from 1884) remained unpublished until after his death. Lacroix's and Bailly's were both published in 1894; the latter, an 'adaptation musicale', is closer to accompanied recitative than to *mélodie*.

[4] Lees, *Mallarmé and Wagner*, 136. Ravel may, however, have known that the poem had first been published (in 1865) with the title 'Sainte Cécile jouant sur l'aile d'un chérubin'.

[5] *Ibid.*, 138.

[6] *Ibid.*, 141. Gayle Zachmann offers a similar interpretation: *Frameworks for Mallarmé*, 154–6.

Ex. 12.1 Sainte, bars 20–4

indication (for piano) *sans aucune nuance jusqu'à la fin*, and the near-strophic echoing of harmonic and melodic content (the second stanza re-presents the harmonic material of the first a fifth lower and reprises melodic gestures). But from that midpoint (bar 16 in Ravel's song), a transformation occurs: above the crotchet pulse, a piano countermelody floats above the voice, offsetting the metric regularity with 2- and 4-beat phrases that cut across the barlines. Against these accent shifts and differentiated phrases, Mallarmé's rhythmic plasticity also emerges in the vocal line's play of triplet and duplet rhythms. The voice carries the key *enjambement* in a single phrase, the change of stanza falling in a bar of 1/4 above the piano's bare bass crotchet (Ex. 12.1).

Why did Ravel set 'Sainte'? At twenty-one, he was soaked in literature as well as music. He haunted the *bouquinistes*, spent afternoons discussing poetry with Ricardo Viñes, and had already recognised the importance of Poe (whom Baudelaire and Mallarmé also acknowledged as a key influence) in his own creative thought. His voracious reading, his engagement with experimental artistic circles (in the early 1890s he was introduced – by his father – to the Auberge du Clou, a haunt of poets, musicians, *chansonniers* and artists), and his very choice of 'Sainte' all suggest he was well aware of the currents in contemporary literary and artistic discourse. As writers and *philosophes* acknowledged and debated what Helen Abbott describes as the 'profound influence of musical criteria on poetic composition during the nineteenth century',[7] the young Ravel perhaps wondered how that influence might be turned back on itself. He could hardly have been unaware of the Wagnerian resonances in 'Sainte' – indeed, he set it just weeks after Viñes described him weeping helplessly at the *Tristan* Prelude.[8] But there is nothing of Wagner in his setting; harmonically, it is closer to Satie. Rather, Ravel, like Mallarmé, looks beyond *wagnérisme* to the core of his creative practice. His choice of 'Sainte' and his setting of it exemplify not just his keen intellectual and literary awareness but also his conscious fascination, from the beginning of his professional life, with the transposition and synthesis of artistic idioms across boundaries of genre and style.[9]

Ravel would become a composer drawn to exploring borderlines and borderlands. He probed the spaces between genres and mediums: play and opera, opera and ballet, poetry and prose, song and speech. He translated imagery and technique across art forms, seeking to discover in their fusion something original, coherent and complete. 'I have set myself the task of transcribing a literary work [. . .] This experiment is rather new', he said of *L'Heure*, and in interviews around the première of *L'Enfant*, as well as in his 'Autobiographical Sketch', he emphasised both its stylistic independence and the importance of the libretto in determining musical parameters ('The predominant concern with melody derives naturally from the story').[10] While opera is by definition a form founded in the unification of the musical, literary and dramatic arts, Ravel's also play more explicitly than most on notions and syntheses of genre. This quality is evident in the

---

[7]   Abbott, *Between Baudelaire and Mallarmé*, 9.

[8]   Gubisch, 'La Vie musicale à Paris', 190 (diary entry for 1 November 1896). In its second version, Mallarmé's 'Sainte' was published in 1883, at the height of the 'second wave' of *wagnérisme*; Lees traces its relationship with Wagnerian thought (particularly as expressed in Wagner's *Lettre sur la musique*): *Mallarmé and Wagner*, 136–42.

[9]   In 1925 René Chalupt observed, 'Ravel was not afraid to tackle *Sainte* as early as 1896; if he allowed this youthful work to appear in the collection of songs published by Durand [in 1907], it was obviously because he was satisfied with this early realisation. It is surprising that a composer of twenty-one years of age had not only developed such technical assurance, but also sufficient intellectual maturity to penetrate the spirit of the poem and situate it musically in the atmosphere of aloof serenity that it demanded [. . .] Ravel's art is in essence akin to that of Mallarmé; spontaneity plays no part, and even the sensuality encountered therein stems from an intellectual origin. The craft of neither the musician nor the poet will permit the slightest weakness, and inspiration is linked with the perfection of form'* (Chalupt, 'Maurice Ravel et les prétextes littéraires de sa musique', 68–9).

[10]   Tenroc, '*Thérèse* et *L'Heure espagnole*'; *OL*, 351, 46.

many appellations – *comédie lyrique, opéra bouffe, opérette, comédie musicale; opéra dansé, opéra fantastique, opérette américaine, fantaisie lyrique* – he attached over the years to *L'Heure* and *L'Enfant* respectively; we may recognise the same principle in his subtitle *symphonie choréographique* to *Daphnis et Chloé*.

Ravel's 'borderlands' were also those of perspective and style. Both his operas meld seemingly incongruous techniques and forms: leitmotifs, dry recitative and flamboyant Spanishness in *L'Heure*, and the panoply of models united in *L'Enfant*. In so doing, however, both works traverse the space in which parody and pastiche are transfigured into the authentic and original voice: 'Each time that he appears to imitate [pasticher]', wrote Jean Roy of *L'Enfant* in 1939, 'Ravel enters still more profoundly into the secret of his own music'.[11] In both operas, too, as in most of Ravel's œuvre, we find the play between cool irony and sensuous *tendresse*, confounding the critics (and sometimes audiences and scholars as well), as he sought the liminal space where *insensibilité* is transfigured into intense *sensibilité*. 'Since we cannot express ourselves without exploiting and thus transforming our emotions', he said in 1931, 'would it not be better at least to be fully aware [conscient], and to acknowledge that art is the supreme imposture? What is sometimes called my lack of sensibility is simply a scruple not to write just anything.'[12]

In his 1928 Autobiographical Sketch, Ravel described his image of Greece in *Daphnis* as 'that imagined and depicted by French artists at the end of the eighteenth century', and defined his intention in *Ma mère l'Oye* 'to evoke the poetry of childhood'; the passing ascription of another art form, poetry, adds a further perceptual twist to a work where music and storytelling are already intertwined.[13] He separately acknowledged the importance of such processes of refraction – passing one subject through the *cadre* (frame) of another – when, speaking of the *Miroirs*, he quoted Shakespeare: 'The eye sees not itself, but by reflection, by some other things.'[14] Thus, in *L'Enfant*, imagery of childhood, of memory and nostalgia, of modernity and destruction, is viewed through the prism of the fairytale narrative. And does *L'Heure* consider human foibles through the lens of *espagnolade*, or does the genre of the farce frame French notions of Spanishness?

---

[11] Roy, 'Ravel et les sortilèges'. See also Ravel's well-known comments on imitation and innovation, partly quoted on p. 171 above; Roland-Manuel, 'Des Valses à *La Valse*', 145.

[12] Ravel, 'Mes souvenirs d'enfant paresseux'; Orenstein (ed.), *A Ravel Reader*, 395.

[13] 'Esquisse autobiographique'; *OL*, 45–6.

[14] Addendum to the 'Esquisse autobiographique'; *OL*, 489n17.

'I like to tell adventures in music!', Ravel told a Danish interviewer in 1926.[15] Much of his œuvre dwells in a space where music and narrative are conceptually and structurally intertwined, a quality evident not just in the many pieces with explicitly literary or extra-musical agenda, but also in the amenability of works such as *Valses nobles et sentimentales* and even *Le Tombeau de Couperin* to ballet staging. The epigraphs heading many of Ravel's piano pieces imply melding of musical and poetic content, while *Ma mère l'Oye* and *Gaspard de la nuit* are directly informed by literary structure: the former, prefiguring *L'Enfant*, translates the techniques and idioms of the fairytale, while the latter twines the near line-by-line evocation of its three wildly Romantic poems with the rational tread of the Classical sonata form.[16] The 'Pantoum' of the 1914 Piano Trio, meanwhile, not only takes a verse form (one used by Baudelaire) as its title, but meticulously translates its formal design as well.[17] We can sense the fusing fingertip of Mallarmé's 'Sainte' equally in the stunning structural, gestural and textual synthesis of the final bars of *L'Enfant*, and in the years of focussed compositional exploration that underpin the directive '*dire, plutôt que chanter*' in *L'Heure*. And while Colette consciously sought rhythm and harmony in her prose, and Franc-Nohain's poetry resounds with musical puns and plays of assonance, Ravel, in André Mirambel's 1939 summation, had 'the qualities of a prosodist, not only in his choice of subjects [...] but also in his handling of musical language, which he constructs in the manner of a [written or spoken] phrase; one could say that Ravel elevated musical language to the heights of musical prose'*.[18]

Ravel, then, sought to refract both perspective and technique. It is little wonder that he was drawn to Franc-Nohain's playful undermining of the forms of 'classical' poetry, and later to Colette's quasi-novelised libretto, both intrinsically prismatic not just in perspective but also in form. While he was a composer drawn to the 'spaces between' in idea and imagery, what took him into, through and beyond those spaces was compositional craft. We may recognise this quest for the liminal in all aspects of his technique, from the unexpected fusions and diffusions of orchestral timbre (the contrabass harmonics that open *L'Enfant*, for example) to the integration of literary idioms with musical forms; in the harnessing of pastiche in the service of his original musical language, and in his assimilation of the

---

[15] X. M., 'Maurice Ravels Ankomst', *Berlingske Tidende*, 30 January 1926; Orenstein (ed.), *A Ravel Reader*, 440.

[16] See Kilpatrick, 'Therein lies a tale', and Howat, 'Ravel and the piano', 81–7.

[17] See Newbould, 'Ravel's *Pantoum*'.

[18] Mirambel, 'L'Inspiration grecque dans l'œuvre de Ravel', 116.

rhythms and cadences of spoken language into sung melody. We see this quality, too, in his setting of the transformative moment of *Sainte*. The harmonic shift in bar 23 is a beautiful piece of word-painting, illuminating the image of the saint's fingertip like a stream of sunlight. Still more potent is Ravel's musical emulation of Mallarmé's formal tension: while each stanza is offset with a bar of 1/4, only at this point do we recognise those bars as structural preparation for the crucial transition, the single beat now capturing the paradoxical melding and disjunction of the poem's pivotal phrase.

In the 1931 article 'Memories of a lazy child', Ravel suggested that Manet's painting *Olympia* exuded the same spirit as Chabrier's piano piece 'Mélancolie', simply 'transferred [transposée] to another medium'.[19] The same verb appears in his Autobiographical Sketch, relative to the 1914 *Trois poèmes de Stéphane Mallarmé*: 'I wished to transpose Mallarmé's poetry into music'.[20] In this context, Ravel's reported words to Jules Renard – that he wanted 'to say with music what you say in words'[21] – emerge as part of a considered and consciously realised compositional philosophy: 'For me there are not several arts but one alone. Music, painting and literature differ only in their means of expression.'[22] Although we might feel the shadow of Wagner hovering again here, *Gesamtkunstwerk* was never a Ravelian dream. Rather, he wanted to work from the inside out, to *become* the poet, the artist, the craftsman. 'It is the musician who allows one to hear clearly what is not said', wrote Wagner in the conclusion of his *Lettre sur la musique* (a thesis that resonates in Mallarmé's 'Sainte'), 'and the infallible form of his echoing silence is the *infinite melody*'.[23] Yet in the end, it is the performer who bridges the space between composer and audience, and the proscenium arch that becomes the refracting prism. Little wonder, perhaps, that although the 1921 audiences at the Opéra Garnier 'clamoured' for the composer, and Ramiro (M. Couzinou) peered hopefully inside one of Torquemada's clocks in search of him, as reviewer Georges Le Fèvre wrote, 'the author of *L'Heure espagnole* was not to be found in there'*.[24]

---

[19] Ravel, 'Mes souvenirs d'enfant paresseux'; Orenstein (ed.), *A Ravel Reader*, 394.

[20] 'Esquisse autobiographique'; *OL*, 46.

[21] Renard, *Journal*, entry for 12 January 1907; see p. 78 above.

[22] Ravel, 'Mes souvenirs d'enfant paresseux'; Orenstein (ed.), *A Ravel Reader*, 393.

[23] Wagner, *Quatre poèmes d'opéras précédes d'une lettre sur la musique à M. Frédéric Villot (15 septembre 1860)*; quoted in Lees, *Mallarmé and Wagner*, 139.

[24] Le Fèvre, 'À l'Opéra: *L'Heure espagnole*'.

Bibliography

Manuscripts, libretti and printed scores

L'Heure espagnole

Autograph vocal score: coll. Robert Owen Lehman, on deposit at Pierpont Morgan Library, NY. Signed and dated 'Maurice Ravel – terminé à la Grangette 10/ 1907'. 64pp.

Autograph orchestral score: Harry Ransom Center, University of Texas at Austin; Carlton Lake Collection, Box Folder 301. Signed, undated. 212pp.

Published scores: Paris: Durand, 1908 (vocal) / 1911 (orchestral and miniature); D.&F. 7073 and 7314.

Text: *La Revue de Paris* 11/6 (15 November 1904), 405–30; Paris: Charpentier, 1905 (play); Paris: Durand, 1909 (libretto).

L'Enfant et les sortilèges

Autograph vocal score: coll. Robert Owen Lehman, on deposit at Pierpont Morgan Library, NY. Signed and dated 'divers lieux, 1920–25'. 75pp.

Autograph orchestral score: formerly in the archives of Éditions Durand, new reportedly in the Bibliothèque du Palais Princier, Monaco (with thanks to Manuel Cornejo).[1]

Published scores: Paris: Durand, 1925; D.&F. 10699 (vocal) and D.&F. 13019 (orchestral and miniature).

Text: Paris: Durand, 1925; Colette, *Œuvres*, vol. III, 151–69 (see below).

Archival sources

Archives de la Société des bains de mer de Monte-Carlo (SBM)
   Correspondance Diaghilev–Léon–Gunsbourg, 1925.
   Original set designs by Alphonse Visconti, 1925.

---

[1] Although Zank (*Maurice Ravel: A Guide to Research*, 326) lists the orchestral autograph as being held at the Harry Ransom Center, University of Texas at Austin, in fact the score was not included in the collection of autograph mss. acquired by Carlton Lake in 1983 (from the Durand archives) for the HRC.

Bibliothèque historique de la ville de Paris (BHVP), Fonds de l'Association de la Régie théâtrale (ART)

Staging material for *L'Heure espagnole*:

4-TMS-03773 Complete fair copy of *mise-en-scène*, recorded against 1909 edition of the libretto.

4-TMS-03774 Watercolour sketches for two costume and set designs.

4-TMS-03775 Complete fair copy of *mise-en-scène*, recorded against 1905 edition of the play.

4-TMS-03776 Complete fair copy of *mise-en-scène*.

4-TMS-03777 Gouache sketches for costume and set designs.

8-TMS-02811 Set designs, directions for *bibelots mécaniques* and *mise-en-scène* for Scene I only, recorded against 1909 edition of the libretto.

8-TMS-02812 Unmarked 1923 edition of the play.

Bibliothèque nationale de France

Bibliothèque-musée de l'Opéra (Bm-O)

Dossiers d'œuvres: *L'Heure espagnole*, *L'Enfant et les sortilèges*.

Dossiers d'artistes: Colette; Franc-Nohain; Ravel.

Fonds Rouché: pièce 406, LAS Colette de Jouvenel.

Lettres autographes signées (LAS): Colette; Dukas; Rouché; Ravel.

Ravel, Maurice. *L'Heure espagnole*. Piano-vocal score, A735d. Paris: Durand, 1908. Ex. coll. Pierre Ladrière, containing reviews and programme of the 1911 production; signed by the cast, conductor and *régisseur*.

L'Enfant et les sortilèges. Piano-vocal scores, A830c and F1775 (Fonds Opéra-Comique). Paris: Durand, 1925. Used in rehearsal for both the 1926 and 1950 Opéra-Comique productions, they show numerous non-autograph performing annotations. On the inside front cover of F1775 the date '30 novembre 1925' appears in pencil (rehearsals for *L'Enfant* began on 25 November 1925).

Registres de l'Opéra-Comique, 1910–11 (micr. 3453); 1925–6 (micr. 3468).

Département des Arts de spectacle (BnF AdS)

Dossier Maurice Ravel, 8-RO-4167.

L'Enfant et les sortilèges: Recueil factice, 8-RF-55196.

Franc-Nohain: Recueil factice des articles biographiques, 8-RF-59492.

Franc-Nohain: Recueil factice des articles critiques, 8-RF-59496.

L'Heure espagnole: Recueil factice, 8-RF-59459.

Département de la Musique (BnF Mus.)

Bathori, Jane. 'Quelques mots sur Maurice Ravel'. 4° Vm Pièce 896.

Fonds Montpensier: Maurice Ravel.

LAS Ravel (Maurice): VM-BOB 23243

Programmes de spectacles donnés au Théâtre du Vieux-Colombier de 1917 à 1928. Rés VM DOS-117 (05).

Roland-Manuel. 'Les Six devant Ravel'. Unpublished typescript (*c*. 1925). 4 Vmo, Pièce 369.

Coll. Roy Howat

Original production (*régie*) score for *L'Heure espagnole*. Paris: Durand, 1908. Annotated mostly in the hand of *régisseur* Ernest Carbonne, and including detailed plans of the set and props, descriptions of and cues for *bibelots mécaniques*, and various additional documentation.

Contemporary criticism

L'Heure espagnole

[Anon.] '*L'Heure espagnole*'. *L'Excelsior*, 17 May 1911.

'Premières représentations: Gaité-Lyrique [*sic*] – *L'Heure espagnole*'. *Le petit journal*, 20 May 1911.

Bellaigue, Camille. 'Revue musicale'. *Revue des deux mondes* 6/4 (1 July 1911), 217–28.

Bertelin, Albert. '*Thérèse* [. . .] *L'Heure espagnole*'. *Comœdia illustré* 3/18 (15 June 1911), 581–4.

Bidou, Henry. '*L'Heure espagnole*'. *Opinion*, 7 January 1922.

Bizet, René. '*L'Heure espagnole*'. *L'Intransigeant*, 17 May 1911.

Boschot, Adolphe. 'La Musique: À l'Opéra – *L'Heure espagnole*'. *L'Écho de Paris*, 7 December 1921.

Brillant, Maurice. '*L'Heure espagnole*'. *Le Correspondant*, 25 December 1921.

Bruneau, Alfred. 'Théâtres de concerts'. *Le Matin*, 18 May 1911.

Chalupt, René, 'Le Mois du musicien'. *La Phalange* 5/49 (20 July 1910).

Chantavoine, Jean. 'Chronique musicale: *L'Heure espagnole*'. *Revue hebdomadaire* 20/6 (24 June 1911), 579–80.

Cornet, Charles. 'Société musicale indépendante'. *Le Guide musical* 56/25–6 (19/26 June 1910), 492–3.

de Curzon, Henri. '*L'Heure espagnole* de Maurice Ravel'. *Le Guide musical* 55/4 (24 January 1909), 70–1.

Daubresse. 'La Semaine à Paris'. *Le Guide musical* 57/20–1 (14/21 May 1911), 392.

Duvernois, Henri. 'Franc-Nohain'. *Comœdia*, 4 December 1921.

Faguet, Émile. 'La Semaine dramatique'. *Journal des débats*, 20 March 1905.

Fauré, Gabriel. '*L'Heure espagnole*'. *Le Figaro*, 20 May 1911.

le Fèvre, George. 'À l'Opéra: *L'Heure espagnole*'. *Bonsoir*, 8 December 1921.

'G.'. '*L'Heure espagnole*: comédie musicale en un acte'. *La Revue musicale (Revue d'histoire et de critique)* 11/11 (1 June 1911), 238–9.

Hahn, Reynaldo. '*L'Heure espagnole*'. *Le Journal*, 21 May 1911.

Lalo, Pierre. 'La Musique [. . .] *L'Heure espagnole*'. *Le Temps*, 28 May 1911.

   'La Musique [. . .] *L'Heure espagnole*'. *Le Temps*, 3 February 1922.

Laloy, Louis. 'La Musique [. . .] *L'Heure espagnole*'. *La grande revue* 67 (10 June 1911), 627–8.

   'À l'Opéra: *L'Heure espagnole*'. *Comœdia*, 7 December 1921.

Lebel, Gaston. '*L'Heure espagnole* à l'Opéra'. Unidentified periodical [Bm-O, Dossier d'œuvre: *L'Heure espagnole*].

Marnold, Jean. 'Musique'. *Mercure de France* 91 (16 June 1911), 866–70.

Prudhomme, Jean. 'Mlle Geneviève Vix et *L'Heure espagnole*: de Carmen à Concepcion'. *Comoedia*, 17 May 1911.

'S., L.'. 'Opéra – *L'Heure espagnole*'. *Le Gaulois*, 7 December 1921.

Sérieyx, Auguste. 'Chronique musicale – Opéra-Comique – *L'Heure espagnole*'. Unidentified periodical [BnF AdS, Recueil factice: *L'Heure espagnole*].

Souday, Paul. 'Les Premières – Opéra-Comique – *L'Heure espagnole*'. Unidentified periodical, 20 May 1911 [BnF AdS, Recueil factice: *L'Heure espagnole*].

Tenroc, Charles. 'Les Avant-premières: *Thérèse* et *L'Heure espagnole* à l'Opéra-Comique'. *Comœdia*, 11 May 1911.

Trial. 'La Salle – À la manière de Franc-Nohain'. *Paris-Midi*, 18 May 1911.

Vuillemin, Louis. 'Théâtre National de l'Opéra-Comique: *L'Heure espagnole*'. *Comœdia*, 20 May 1911.

Vuillermoz, Émile. 'Les Théâtres: *L'Heure espagnole* – *Thérèse* – *Le Martyre de Saint Sébastien*'. *S.I.M. Revue musicale* 7/6 (15 June 1911), 65–70.

See also Zank, *Maurice Ravel: A Guide to Research*, items R162–89, and Kilpatrick, *The Operas of Maurice Ravel: A Compendium of Sources* (www.cambridge. org/9781107118126).

L'Enfant et les sortilèges

[Anon.] 'Mme Colette, librettiste d'un ballet de Maurice Ravel'. Unidentified periodical, 13 December 1919 [BnF AdS, Recueil factice: *L'Enfant et les sortilèges*].

   '*L'Enfant et les sortilèges*', *Comœdia*, 4 and 8 February 1926.

Arnoux, André. 'Avant-première: *L'Enfant et les sortilèges*'. Unidentified periodical [BnF Mus., Fonds Montpensier (Ravel)].

Auric, Georges. '*L'Enfant et les sortilèges*'. *Les Nouvelles littéraires*, 11 April 1925.

Autran, Juliette. 'À l'Opéra-Comique: *L'Enfant et les sortilèges*'. *Le Soir*, 3 February 1926.

Balliman, Raymond. '*L'Enfant et les sortilèges*'. *Lyrica* 5/48 (February 1926), 693.

Bechert, Paul. 'Musical notes from abroad: Vienna'. *The Musical Times* 70/1036 (June 1929).

le Borne, Fernand. 'Courrier des théâtres'. *Le petit parisien*, 2 February 1926.

Boucher, Maurice. 'À propos de *L'Enfant et les sortilèges*'. *L'Avenir*, 2 February 1926.

Boutiller, Jean. '*L'Enfant et les sortilèges*: Fantaisie lyrique de Madame Colette et de M. Maurice Ravel'. *L'Enfant* (1926), 183–6.

Brillant, Maurice. '*L'Enfant et les sortilèges*'. *Le Correspondant*, 25 February 1926, 619–24.

Carol-Berard. '*L'Enfant et les sortilèges*'. *L'Époque*, 19 May 1939.

Charpentier, Raymond. '*L'Enfant et les sortilèges*'. *Comœdia*, 2 February 1926.

Cœuroy, André. 'Avant-première à Monte-Carlo: *L'Enfant et les sortilèges* de Colette et de Ravel'. *Paris-Midi*, 20 March 1925.

Corneau, André. '*L'Enfant et les sortilèges*'. *Journal de Monaco*, 24 March 1925.

'D., M.'. 'Théâtre de l'Opéra-Comique: *L'Enfant et les sortilèges*'. *Le Théâtre*, April 1926, 7.

Delaincourt, Jean. '*L'Enfant et les sortilèges*'. *Nouveau siècle*, 6 February 1926.

Honegger, Arthur. 'Théâtres de musique: *L'Enfant et les sortilèges*'. *Musique et théâtre* 3 (15 April 1925), 5.

Léon, Xavier. '*L'Enfant et les sortilèges*'. *Le Ménestrel* 87/14 (3 April 1925), 166–7.

Lombard, Paul. '*L'Enfant et les sortilèges*'. *La Renaissance*, 27 February 1926.

Malherbe, Henry. 'Chroniques musicale: *L'Enfant et les sortilèges*'. *Le Temps*, 3 February 1926.

Marnold, Jean. 'Musique'. *Le Mercure de France* 186/666 (15 March 1926), 701–6.

Méry, Jules. 'Avant-première: *L'Enfant et les sortilèges*'. *Le petit monégasque*, 21 March 1925.

Messager, André. 'Chronique – Les Premières – *L'Enfant et les sortilèges*'. *Le Figaro*, 4 February 1926.

de Pawlowski, Gaston. 'Répétition générale à l'Opéra-Comique: *L'Enfant et les sortilèges*'. *Le Journal*, 2 February 1926.

Prunières, Henry. '*L'Enfant et les sortilèges* au Théâtre de Monte-Carlo'. *La Revue musicale* 6/6 ('Maurice Ravel', April 1925), 105–9.

'*L'Enfant et les sortilèges* de Maurice Ravel à l'Opéra-Comique'. *La Revue musicale* 7/5 (March 1926), 258–60.

Roland-Manuel. 'La Semaine musicale: Théâtre de l'Opéra-Comique – *L'Enfant et les sortilèges*'. *Le Ménestrel* 88/6 (5 February 1926), 60–1.

'La Critique: *L'Enfant et les sortilèges*'. *La Revue Pleyel* 29 (15 February 1926), 60–1.

Rouché, Jacques. '*L'Enfant et les sortilèges*'. *Le Jour*, 16 May 1939.

Roy, Jean. 'Ravel et les sortilèges'. Unidentified journal (1939) [Bm-O, Dossier d'œuvre: *L'Enfant et les sortilèges*].

Steinhof, Eugène. '*L'Enfant et les sortilèges* à l'Opéra de Vienne'. *L'Art vivant* 105 (1 May 1929).

Tenroc, Ch[arles]. 'Les Théâtres: Opéra-Comique: *L'Enfant et les sortilèges*'. *Le Courrier musical* 28/4 (15 February 1926), 101.

Vuillermoz, Émile. '*L'Enfant et les sortilèges*'. *L'Excelsior*, 19 May 1939.

See also Zank, *Maurice Ravel: A Guide to Research*, items R278 & R281–98, and Kilpatrick, *The Operas of Maurice Ravel: A Compendium of Sources* (www. cambridge.org/9781107118126).

Secondary sources

Abbate, Carolyn. *In Search of Opera*. Princeton University Press, 2002.

'Outside Ravel's tomb'. *JAMS* 52/3 (Fall 1999), 465–530.

'*Tristan* in the composition of *Pelléas*'. *19th-Century Music* 5/2 (Fall 1981), 117–41.

Abbott, Helen. *Between Baudelaire and Mallarmé: Voice, Conversation and Music*. Farnham: Ashgate, 2009.

Ackroyd, Peter. *Shakespeare: The Biography*. London: Chatto and Windus, 2005.

ADER Nordmann. *Lettres et manuscrits autographes*. Catalogue of sale, 17 December 2013 (Salle Drouot). Paris: ADER Nordmann.

d'Alheim, Pierre. *Moussorgski*. Paris: Société du *Mercure de France*, 1896.

Antokoletz, Elliott. *Musical Symbolism in the Operas of Debussy and Bartók*. New York: Oxford University Press, 2004.

Araiz, Oscar. '*L'Enfant et les sortilèges*: un adulte avec une tête d'enfant'. Theatre programme: *L'Enfant et les sortilèges*. Grand Théâtre de Genève, 1989.

Aubin, Tony. 'L'Œuvre lyrique'. In Marguerite Long, Tony Aubin, Léon-Paul Fargue, Arthur Hoérée, Georges Pioch and Hélène Jourdan-Morhange, *Maurice Ravel*. Paris: Les Publications Techniques et Artistiques, 1945, 21–4.

de Banville, Théodore. *Petit traité de poésie française*. Paris: Charpentier, 1883.

Bartlet, Elizabeth C. 'Archival sources for the Opéra-Comique and its "Registres" at the Bibliothèque de l'Opéra'. *19th-Century Music* 7/2 (Autumn 1983), 119–29.

Bellaigue, Camille. 'Un grand musicien réaliste: Moussorgski'. *Revue des deux mondes* 5/2 (15 April 1901), 859–60.

Bellman, Jonathan (ed.). *The Exotic in Western Music*. Boston: Northeastern University Press, 1998.

Berge, André. 'Un humoriste poète: Franc-Nohain'. *Le Correspondant* 96/1474 (25 February 1924), 636–56.

Bergeron, Katherine. *Voice Lessons: French Mélodie in the Belle Époque*. New York: Oxford University Press, 2010.

Berkman, Sylvia. 'The images of childhood' [review of Colette, *My Mother's House* and *Sido* (trans. Troubridge and McLeod)]. *New York Times*, 29 November 1953.

Best, Christopher. 'Why do choreographers and composers collaborate?' *Dance Theatre Journal* 15/1 (1999), 28–31.

Bidou, Henry. 'Enfants et parents'. *Les Annales politiques et littéraires* 42/2163 ('L'Enfance'), 51.

Le Bordays, Christine. 'L'Espagne ravélienne'. *CMR* 2 (1986), 44–61.

Born, Georgina, and David Hesmondhaigh (eds.). *Western Music and its Others: Difference, Representation and Appropriation in Music*. Berkeley: University of California Press, 2000.

Bouillier, Henry. 'Colette et la poésie'. *Cahiers Colette* 15 (1992), 165–71.

Bowie, Malcolm. *Mallarmé and the Art of Being Difficult*. Cambridge: Cambridge University Press, 1978.

Brody, Elaine. *Paris, The Musical Kaleidoscope: 1870–1925*. London: Robson, 1988.

Buckle, Richard. *Diaghilev*. London: Weidenfeld and Nicolson, 1979.

   George Balanchine, Ballet Master. New York: Random House, 1988.

Burkholder, J. Peter. 'Music of the Americas and historical narratives'. *American Music* 27/4 (Winter 2009), 399–423.

Calvocoressi, Michel-Dimitri. '*Le Mariage*, par Moussorgsky'. *S.I.M. Revue musicale* 4/12 (15 December 1908), 1284–90.

   'Le Vers, la prose et l'*e* muet'. *Le Guide musical* 50/44 (30 October 1904), 795–800.

   Moussorgsky. Paris: Alcan, 1908.

Carré, Albert. *Souvenirs du théâtre*. Paris: Plon, 1950.

Cathé, Philippe. 'Claude Terrasse (1867–1923)'. Ph.D. diss., Université de Paris Sorbonne, 2001.

Cazamian, Louis. 'La Psychanalyse et la critique littéraire'. *Revue de littérature comparée* 4 (1924), 449–75.

Chailley, Jacques. 'Une première version inconnue de *Daphnis et Chloé* de Maurice Ravel'. In *Mélanges d'histoire littéraire (XVIe–XVIIe siècle): offerts à Raymond Lebègue*. Paris: Nizet, 1969, 371–5.

Chalupt, René. 'La Féerie et Maurice Ravel'. *La Revue musicale* 19/187 ('Hommage à Maurice Ravel', December 1938), 128–34.

   'Maurice Ravel et les prétextes littéraires de sa musique'. *La Revue musicale* 6/6 ('Maurice Ravel', April 1925), 65–74.

Chalupt, René, and Marcelle Gerar. *Ravel au miroir de ses lettres*. Paris: Lafont, 1956.

Chopin, Frédéric. *Selected Correspondence of Fryderyk Chopin*. Coll. and ann. Bronislaw Edward Sydow, trans. and ed. Arthur Hedley. London: Heinemann, 1962.

Clark, Linda. 'France'. In Joseph M. Hawes and N. Ray Hiner (eds.), *Children in Historical and Comparative Perspective*. Westport, Ct.: Greenwood, 1991, 277–304.

Clifton, Keith. 'Maurice Ravel's *L'Heure espagnole*: genesis, sources, analysis'. Ph. D. diss., Northwestern University, 1998.

Cohen, H. Robert. *The Original Staging Manuals for Twelve Parisian Operatic Premières*. New York: Stuyvesant, 1991.

Cohen, H. Robert, and Marie-Odile Gigou. *Cent ans de mise en scène lyrique en France*. Preface by Phillip Gossett. New York: Pendragon, 1986.

'La Conservation de la tradition scénique sur la scène lyrique en France au XIXe siècle: les livrets de mise en scène et la Bibliothèque de l'Association de la Régie Théâtrale'. *Revue de musicologie* 64/2 (1978), 253–67.

[Colette]. 'Colette parle de Ravel'. Radio France interview, date unknown (coll. Claude Moreau).

Colette. *En pays connu*. Paris: Ferenczi, 1950.

 Lettres à Moune et au Toutounet, 1929–1954, ed. Bernard Villaret. Paris: Des femmes, 1985.

 Lettres à ses pairs, ed. Claude Pichois and Roberte Forbin. Paris: Flammarion, 1973.

 My Mother's House and *Sido*, trans. Una Vincenza Troubridge and Enid McLeod. London: Secker & Warburg, 1969.

 Œuvres. 4 vols., ed. Claude Pichois. Paris: Gallimard [Bibliothèque de la Pléiade], 1984–2001.

Cornejo, Manuel. 'Maurice Ravel en Belgique', *CMR* 13 (2010), 74–125.

 See also under Ravel.

Cornejo, Manuel, and Dimitra Diamantopoulou. 'Maurice Ravel et Pierre Lalo: une lettre oubliée de Maurice Ravel au directeur du *Temps* (Avril–Mai 1907)'. *CMR* 12 (2009), 22–43.

Crosland, Margaret. 'Colette and Ravel: The Enchantress and the Illusionist'. In Eisinger and McCarty (eds.), *Colette: The Woman, the Writer*, 116–24.

Crubellier, Maurice. *L'Enfance et la jeunesse dans la société française, 1800–1950*. Paris: Colin, 1979.

Debussy, Claude. *Correspondance (1872–1918)*, ed. François Lesure and Denis Herlin. Paris: Gallimard, 2005.

 Monsieur Croche et autres écrits, ed. François Lesure. Paris: Gallimard, 1971. English edition: *Debussy on Music*, trans. and ed. Richard Langham Smith. New York: Knopf, 1977.

Delahaye, Michel. 'Documents Ravel dans les ventes et collections publiques et privées'. *CMR* 8 (2004), 93–110; *CMR* 12 (2009), 44–55; *CMR* 13 (2010), 10–28.

 'L'Enfant et les sortilèges: Colette-Ravel-Diaghilev'. *CMR* 13 (2010), 31–73.

 (ed.) 'Lettres de Ravel à la famille Gaudin de Saint-Jean-de-Luz'. Part 1: 'Du Prix de Rome à la guerre, 2/8/1901–20/9/1916'; Part 2: '1919–1927'. *CMR* 9–10 (2005–6 & 2007), 13–58 & 14–56.

Duchesneau, Michel. *L'Avant-garde musicale et ses sociétés à Paris de 1871 à 1939*. Spirmont: Mardaga, 1997.

Dumesnil, René. 'Maurice Ravel poète'. *La Revue musicale* 19/187 ('Hommage à Maurice Ravel', December 1938), 124–7.

Dupont, Jacques. 'Visages de l'enfance, sortilèges de Colette'. *L'Avant-scène opéra* 127 (January 1990), 23–6.

Durand, Jacques. *Quelques souvenirs d'un éditeur de musique*, vol. II. Paris: Durand, 1925.

Druilhe, Paul. 'Les grandes créations de l'Opéra de Monte-Carlo: *L'Enfant et les sortilèges* de Maurice Ravel'. *Annales monégasques* 9 (1985), 7–26.

Eisinger, Erica Mendelson, and Mari Ward McCarty (eds.). *Colette: The Woman, the Writer*. University Park: Pennsylvania State University Press, 1981.

des Essarts, F.-D. 'Les Avant-premières: *Les Transatlantiques* à l'Apollo'. *Comœdia*, 17 May 1911.

de Falla, Manuel. *On Music and Musicians*, ed. Federico Sopeña, trans. D. Urman and J. M. Thomson. London and Boston: Marion Boyars, 1979.

Faure, Michel. *Musique et société du Second Empire aux années vingt*. Paris: Flammarion, 1985.

Fauser, Annegret. *Musical Encounters at the 1889 Paris World's Fair*. University of Rochester Press, 2005.

Fauser, Annegret, and Mark Everist (eds.). *Music, Theater, and Cultural Transfer: Paris, 1830–1914*. Chicago and London: University of Chicago Press, 2009.

Favat, F. André. *Child and Tale: The Origins of Interest*. Urbana, Ill.: National Council of Teachers of English, 1977.

Fillerup, Jessie. 'Purloined poetics: The grotesque in the music of Maurice Ravel'. Ph.D. diss., University of Kansas, 2009.

'Ravel and Robert-Houdin, magicians'. *19th-Century Music* 37/2 (Fall 2013), 130–58.

'Ravel's lost time'. *Journal of the Royal Musical Association* 139/1 (2014), 205–20.

Fordham, Frieda. *An Introduction to Jung's Psychology*. London: Penguin, 1953.

Françaix, Jean. *De la musique et des musiciens*. Paris: Fondation Polignac, 1999.

Garafola, Lynn. *Diaghilev's Ballets russes*. New York and Oxford: Oxford University Press, 1989.

Garban, Dominique. *Jacques Rouché: l'homme qui sauva l'Opéra de Paris*. Paris: Somogy Éditions d'Art, 2007.

Garden, Mary, and Louis Biancolli. *Mary Garden's Story*. London: Michael Joseph, 1952.

Giuliani, Elizabeth. 'La Musique et l'enfance'. *L'Avant-scène opéra* 127 (January 1990), 58–62.

Glover, Nicola. *Psychoanalytic Æsthetics: The British School*. Chapter 2: 'Essentials of Kleinian theory'. *Psychoanalysis and Psychotherapy*, accessed 30 October 2013, www.psychoanalysis-and-therapy.com/human_nature/glover/chap2.html.

Godebska Blacque-Belair, Mimie. 'Quelques souvenirs intimes de Ravel'. *La Revue musicale* 19/187 ('Hommage à Maurice Ravel', December 1938), 189–91.

Gopnik, Adam. *Through the Children's Gate: A Home in New York*. London: Quercus, 2007.

Gottlieb, Robert. *George Balanchine: The Ballet Maker*. New York: HarperCollins, 2004.

Goudeket, Maurice. *Close to Colette*, trans. Enid McLeod. London: Secker & Warburg, 1957.

de Gourmont, Rémy. *Le Problème de style: questions d'art, de littérature et de grammaire*. Paris: Mercure de France, 1902.

Grammont, Maurice. *Le Vers français: ses moyens d'expression, son harmonie*, 2nd edn. Paris: Champion, 1913.

Grayson, David. 'Debussy on stage'. In Simon Trezise (ed.), *The Cambridge Companion to Debussy*. Cambridge: Cambridge University Press, 2003, 61–83.

Gribenski, Michel. '"Chanter comme des personnes naturelles": apocope de l'*e* caduc et synérèse chez Debussy et quelques-uns de ses contemporains'. *Cahiers Debussy* 31 (2007), 5–57.

Gubisch, Nina. 'La Vie musicale à Paris entre 1887 et 1914 à travers le journal de R. Viñes'. *Revue internationale de musique française* 1/2 (1980), 154–248.

'Les Années de jeunesse d'un pianiste espagnol en France (1887–1900): journal et correspondence de Ricardo Viñes'. Unpub. thesis, Paris: Conservatoire de musique, 1971.

Gunsbourg, Raoul. *Cent ans de souvenirs... ou presque*. Monaco: Éditions du Rocher, 1959.

Haine, Malou. 'Cipa Godebski et les Apaches'. *Revue belge de musicologie* 60 (2006), 221–66.

Harwood, Gregory. 'Musical and literary satire in Maurice Ravel's *L'Enfant et les sortilèges*'. *Opera Journal* 29/1 (1996), 2–16.

Henahan, Donal. 'Met Opera's *Parade*, captivating triple bill'. *New York Times*, 22 February 1981.

Heywood, Colin. *Childhood in Nineteenth-Century France: Work, Health and Education among the 'Classes Populaires'*. Cambridge: Cambridge University Press, 1988.

Hoérée, Arthur. 'Les Mélodies et l'œuvre lyrique'. *La Revue musicale* 6/6 ('Maurice Ravel', April 1925), 46–64.

Hoffmann, Léon-François. *Romantique Espagne: l'image de l'Espagne en France entre 1800 et 1850*. Paris: Presses Universitaires de France, 1961.

Holloway, Robin. *Debussy and Wagner*. London: Eulenberg, 1979.

Horne, John, and Alan Kramer. *German Atrocities, 1914: A History of Denial*. New Haven and London: Yale University Press, 2001.

Howat, Roy. 'Ravel and the piano'. In Mawer (ed.), *The Cambridge Companion to Ravel*, 71–96.

The Art of French Piano Music: Debussy, Ravel, Fauré, Chabrier. London and New Haven: Yale University Press, 2009.

Howat, Roy, and Emily Kilpatrick (eds.). *Gabriel Fauré: Complete Songs*, vol. I. London and Leipzig: Edition Peters, 2014, EP11391.

Huebner, Steven. *French Opera at the Fin de Siècle: Wagnerism, Nationalism and Style*. Oxford: Oxford University Press, 1999.

'Laughter: In Ravel's time'. *Cambridge Opera Journal* 18/3 (November 2006), 225–46.

'*L'Heure espagnole*: la grivoiserie moderne de Ravel'. In Jean-Christophe Branger and Vincent Giroud (eds.), *Aspects de l'opéra français de Meyerbeer à Honegger*. Lyon: Symétrie, 2009, 192–213.

'Maurice Ravel: Private life, public works'. In Jolanta T. Pekacz (ed.), *Musical Biography: Towards New Paradigms*. Aldershot: Ashgate, 2006, 69–88.

'Ravel's Child: Magic and moral development'. In Susan Boynton and Roe-Min Kok (eds.), *Musical Childhoods and the Cultures of Youth*. Middletown, Ct.: Wesleyan University Press, 2006, 69–88.

'Ravel's perfection'. In Mawer (ed.), *Ravel Studies*, 9–30.

'Ravel's poetics: Literary currents, classical takes'. In Kaminsky (ed.), *Unmasking Ravel*, 9–40.

Hurd, James. 'From a peacock to apocope: An examination of Maurice Ravel's text setting in the *Histoires naturelles, L'Heure espagnole* and other pre-WWI vocal works'. DMA diss., University of Cincinnati, 2009.

Hymes, Dell H. 'Phonological aspects of style'. In Thomas A. Sebeok (ed.), *Style in Language*. Cambridge, Mass.: MIT Press, 1960, 109–31.

Jacobshagen, Arnold. 'Staging at the Opéra-Comique in nineteenth-century Paris: Auber's *Fra Diavolo* and the "livrets de mise-en-scène"'. *Cambridge Opera Journal* 13/3 (November 2001), 239–60.

Jambou, Louis (ed.). *La Musique entre France et Espagne: interactions stylistiques*. Paris: Presses de l'Université de Paris-Sorbonne, 2003.

Jankélévitch, Vladimir. *Ravel*. Paris: Seuil, 1956/1995. English edition, trans. Margaret Crosland: *Ravel*. New York and London: John Calder, 1959.

Jourdan-Morhange, Hélène. 'Ravel à Montfort l'Amaury'. In Émile Vuillermoz, Hélène Jourdan-Morhange, Roland-Manuel *et al.*, *Maurice Ravel par quelques-uns de ses familiers*, 163–70.

Ravel et nous. Geneva: Milieu du monde, 1945.

Jung, Carl, and Carl Kerényi. *Introduction to a Science of Mythology: The Myth of the Divine Child and the Mysteries of Eleusis*, trans. R. F. C. Hull. London: Routledge & Kegan Paul, 1970.

Kaminsky, Peter. 'Of children, princesses, dreams and isomorphisms: Text–music transformation in Ravel's vocal works'. *Music Analysis* 19/1 (2000), 29–68.

'Ravel's late music and the problem of "polytonality"'. *Music Theory Spectrum* 26/2 (2004), 237–64.

'The Child on the couch'. In Kaminsky (ed.), *Unmasking Ravel*, 306–30.

'Vocal music and the lures of exoticism and irony'. In Mawer (ed.), *The Cambridge Companion to Ravel*, 162–87.

(ed.), *Unmasking Ravel: New Perspectives on the Music*. University of Rochester Press, 2011, 306–30.

Kelly, Barbara. 'History and homage'. In Mawer (ed.), *The Cambridge Companion to Ravel*, 7–26.

Music and Ultra-Modernism in France: A Fragile Consensus, 1913–1939. Woodbridge: Boydell and Brewer, 2013.

'Raoul Gunsbourg'. *Grove Music Online*, accessed 18 March 2011, www.oxford musiconline.com.

'Ravel after Debussy: Inheritance, influence and style'. In Kelly and Murphy (eds.), *Berlioz and Debussy*, 167–80.

Kelly, Barbara, and Kerry Murphy (eds.). *Berlioz and Debussy: Sources, Contexts, Legacies*. Aldershot: Ashgate, 2007.

Kilpatrick, Emily. 'Enchantments and illusions: Recasting the creation of *L'Enfant et les sortilèges*'. In Mawer (ed.), *Ravel Studies*, 31–55.

'"Into the woods": Retelling the wartime fairytales of Maurice Ravel'. *Musical Times* 149/1902 (Spring 2008), 57–66.

'"Jangling in symmetrical sounds": Maurice Ravel as storyteller and poet'. *Journal of Music Research Online* 1 (April 2009), 1–19, http://journal.mca.org.au.

'The Carbonne copy: Tracing the première of *L'Heure espagnole*'. *Revue de musicologie* 95/1 (2009), 97–135.

'The language of enchantment: Childhood and fairytale in the music of Maurice Ravel'. Ph.D. diss., University of Adelaide, 2008.

'Therein lies a tale: Musical and literary structure in Ravel's *Ma mère l'Oye*'. *Context* 34 (2009), 45–62.

See also under Howat.

Kisselgoff, Anna. 'Ballet: *Parade*'s dances made into curtain-raiser'. *New York Times*, 22 February 1981.

Klein, Melanie. 'Infantile anxiety-situations reflected in a work of art and in the creative impulse'. *International Journal of Psychoanalysis* 10 (1929), 436–43.

Klingsor, Tristan. 'L'Époque Ravel'. In Émile Vuillermoz, Hélène Jourdan-Morhange, Roland-Manuel *et al.*, *Maurice Ravel par quelques-uns de ses familiers*, 125–40.

Koechlin, Charles. '*Le Mariage*, comédie musicale de Moussorgski'. *La Revue musicale* 4/7 (1 May 1923), 73–7.

Kristeva, Julia. *Le Génie féminin: la vie, la folie, les mots*. Vol. III, *Colette*. Paris: Fayard, 2002.

'L., P.' 'L'Académie Française a décerné hier ses deux grands prix annuels'. *Comœdia*, 11 November 1932.

Lacombe, Hervé. 'L'Espagne à l'Opéra-Comique avant *Carmen*: du *Guitarrero de Halévy* (1841) à *Don César de Bazan* de Massenet (1872)'. In Lesure (ed.), *Echanges musicaux franco-espagnols*, 161–94.

'L'Espagne à Paris au milieu de XIXe siècle (1847–1857): l'influence d'artistes espagnols sur l'imaginaire parisien et la construction d'une "hispanicité"'. *Revue de musicologie* 88/2 (2002), 289–431.

'The writing of exoticism in the libretti of the Opéra-Comique, 1825–1862', trans. Peter Glidden. *Cambridge Opera Journal* 11/2 (July 1999), 135–58.

Langham Smith, Richard. 'Colette as critic'. *Music and Musicians* 25 (1977), 26–8.

'French operatic spectacle in the twentieth century'. In Richard Langham Smith and Caroline Potter (eds.), *French Music since Berlioz*. Aldershot: Ashgate, 2006, 117–59.

'Ravel's operatic spectacles: *L'Heure* and *L'Enfant*'. In Mawer (ed.), *The Cambridge Companion to Ravel*, 188–210.

'Taming two Spanish women: Reflections on editing opera'. In Kelly and Murphy (eds.), *Berlioz and Debussy*, 83–102.

(ed.) *Carmen: A Performance Urtext*. London: Edition Peters, 2013.

See also under Debussy and under Nichols.

Laparra, Raoul. *Bizet et l'Espagne*. Paris: Delagrave, 1935.

'La Musique et la danse populaires en Espagne' [1914]. *Encyclopédie de la musique et dictionnaire du Conservatoire*. Paris: Delagrave, 1920, 2353–400.

Larner, Gerald. *Maurice Ravel*. London: Phaidon, 1996.

Lassus, Marie-Pierre. 'Ravel, l'enchanteur: structure poétique et structure musicale dans *L'Enfant et les sortilèges*'. *Analyse musicale* 26 (1992), 40–7.

Laurent, Linda. 'Jane Bathori, interprète de Ravel'. *CMR* 2 (1986), 63–9.

Lavelli, Jorge. 'Le Cauchemar de l'initiation'. Theatre programme: *L'Enfant et les sortilèges*. Opéra Garnier, May 1979.

Lesure, François (ed.). *Echanges musicaux franco-espagnols, XVIIIe–XIXe siècles. Actes des Rencontres de Villecroze*. Paris: Klincksieck, 2000.

See also under Debussy.

Little, Elden Stewart. 'Discrepancies and consistencies among autograph manuscripts and Durand editions of Maurice Ravel's songs'. DMA diss., University of Texas at Austin, 1999.

Llano, Samuel. 'España en la vitrina: Maurice Ravel, el mito de la autenticidad y el neoimperialismo español'. *Journal of Spanish Cultural Studies* 11/1 (June 2010), 1–15.

'Spanish traditions in a cross-cultural perspective: Raoul Laparra's *La Habanera* (1908) and French critics'. *Journal of the Royal Musical Association* 136/1 (May 2011), 97–140.

Whose Spain? Negotiating 'Spanish Music' in Paris, 1908–1929. Foreword by Michael Christoforidis. New York: Oxford University Press, 2013.

Locke, Ralph. 'A broader view of musical exoticism'. *Journal of Musicology* 24/4 (Fall 2007), 477–521.

Musical Exoticism: Images and Reflections. Cambridge: Cambridge University Press, 2009.

Lüthi, Max. *Once Upon a Time: On the Nature of Fairy Tales*, trans. Lee Chadeayne and Paul Gottwald. New York: Ungar, 1970.

Macdonald, Hugh. 'Carmen'. *Grove Music Online (New Grove Dictionary of Opera)*, accessed 15 June 2013, www.oxfordmusiconline.com.

'The prose libretto'. *Cambridge Opera Journal* 1/2 (1989), 155–66.

de Maré, Rolf, Michel Fokine, Alexandre Tansman *et al*. *Les Ballets suédois dans l'art contemporain*. Paris: Trianon, 1931.

Marnat, Marcel. *Maurice Ravel*. Paris: Fayard, 1986.

'Ravel en représentation'. *L'Avant-scène opéra* 127 (January 1990), 10–17.

(ed.) *Ravel: Souvenirs de Manuel Rosenthal*. Paris: Hazan, 1995.

Martin, George. *A Companion to Twentieth-Century Opera*. London: Gollancz, 1980.

Mason, Francis (ed.). *I Remember Balanchine: Recollections of the Ballet Master by Those Who Knew Him*. New York: Doubleday, 1991.

Mavor, Carol. 'Introduction: The unmaking of childhood'. In Marilyn Brown (ed.), *Picturing Children: Constructions of Childhood between Rousseau and Freud*. Aldershot: Ashgate, 2002, 27–41.

Mawer, Deborah. 'Musical objects and machines'. In Mawer (ed.), *The Cambridge Companion to Ravel*, 47–67.

The Ballets of Maurice Ravel. Aldershot: Ashgate, 2006.

(ed.) *Ravel Studies*. Cambridge: Cambridge University Press, 2010.

(ed.) *The Cambridge Companion to Ravel*. Cambridge: Cambridge University Press, 2000.

Max-Harry. 'M. Maurice Ravel écrit à son tour un "Don Quichotte"'. Unidentified periodical [BnF AdS, Dossier Maurice Ravel], 12 January 1912.

McCarty, Mari Ward. 'The theatre as literary model: Role-playing in *Chéri* and *The Last of Chéri*'. In Eisinger and McCarty (eds.), *Colette: The Woman, the Writer*, 125–34.

Mercier, Michel. '*L'Enfant et les sortilèges*: Analyses / Genèse / Prolongements / Autres prolongements'. *Cahiers Colette* 29 ('Sido et les sortilèges', 2007), 69–86.

Milner, Christine. 'Le Corps de Sido'. *Revue littéraire mensuelle* 631 (1981), 71–84.

'Notice' and 'Note sur le texte' to *L'Enfant et les sortilèges*. In Colette, *Œuvres*, vol. III.

Milnes, Rodney. '*L'Heure espagnole* and *L'Enfant et les sortilèges*'. *Opera Magazine*, accessed 5 March 2013, www.opera.co.uk/view-review.php?reviewID=130.

Mirambel, André. 'L'Inspiration grecque dans l'œuvre de Ravel'. *La Revue musicale* 19/187 ('Hommage à Maurice Ravel', December 1938), 112–18.

Moore, Burness E., and Bernard D. Fine. *Psychoanalytic Terms and Concepts*. New Haven: American Psychoanalytic Association and Yale University Press, 1990.

Mordier, Jean-Pierre. *Les Débuts de la psychanalyse en France, 1895–1926*. Paris: Maspero, 1981.

Morrison, Simon. 'The origins of *Daphnis et Chloé* (1912)'. *19th-Century Music* 28/1 (Summer 2004), 50–76.

Murphy, Kerry. '*Carmen*: *Couleur locale* or the real thing'. In Fauser and Everist (eds.), *Music, Theater, and Cultural Transfer*, 509–48.

Narbaitz, Pierre. *Maurice Ravel: un orfèvre basque*. Anglet (Côte basque): L'Académie internationale Maurice Ravel, 1975.

Newbould, Brian. 'Ravel's *Pantoum*'. *Musical Times* 116/1585 (March 1975), 228–31.

Nichols, Roger. *Ravel*. New Haven and London: Yale University Press, 2011.

Ravel Remembered. London: Faber, 1987.

The Harlequin Years: Music in Paris 1917–1929. London: Thames and Hudson, 2002.

Nichols, Roger, and Richard Langham Smith. *Claude Debussy: Pelléas et Mélisande*. Cambridge: Cambridge University Press, 1989.

Nohain, Jean. 'Quand j'avais onze ans j'ai entendu siffler et huer *L'Heure espagnole*'. Unidentified periodical [BnF Mus., Fonds Montpensier (Ravel)], 10 August 1941.

Nozière. [Hommage à Franc-Nohain], *Gringoire*, 6 March 1931.

Oldani, Robert W. 'Musorgsky'. *Grove Music Online*, accessed 10 July 2011, www.oxfordmusiconline.com.

Olénine d'Alheim, Marie. *Concerts de 1912*. Moscow: Maison du Lied, 1912.

Orenstein, Arbie. '*L'Enfant et les sortilèges*: correspondance inédite de Ravel et Colette'. *Revue de musicologie* 52/2 (1966), 215–20.

    Maurice Ravel: lettres, écrits, entretiens. Paris: Flammarion, 1989. English edition: *A Ravel Reader: Correspondence, Articles, Interviews*. New York: Columbia University Press, 1990.

    Ravel, Man and Musician. New York: Dover, 1975 (rev. 1991).

    'Some unpublished music and letters by Maurice Ravel'. *The Music Forum* 3 (1973), 291–334.

    (ed.) 'La Correspondance de Maurice Ravel à Lucien Garban'. Part 1: 1901–1918; part 2: 1919–1934. *CMR* 7–8 (2000 & 2004), 19–68 & 9–89.

    (ed.). *Maurice Ravel: Songs, 1896–1914*. New York: Dover, 1990.

Orledge, Robert. *Debussy and the Theatre*. Cambridge: Cambridge University Press, 1982.

Palmer, Christopher. 'Debussy, Ravel and Alain-Fournier', *Music and Letters* 50/2 (April 1969), 267–72.

Parakilas, James. 'How Spain got a soul'. In Bellman (ed.), *The Exotic in Western Music*, 137–93.

Pasler, Jann. 'A sociology of the Apaches: Sacred battalion for *Pelléas*'. In Kelly and Murphy (eds.), *Berlioz and Debussy*, 149–66.

    Composing the Citizen: Music as Public Utility in Third Republic France. Berkeley: University of California Press, 2009.

Pellissier, Georges. *Traité théorique et historique de la versification française*. Paris: Garnier, 1894.

Petersen, Cornelia. *Die Lieder von Maurice Ravel*. Frankfurt: Peter Lang, 1995.

Phillips, Edward. *Gabriel Fauré: A Guide to Research*. New York: Garland, 2000.

Piasa. *Lettres et manuscrits autographes*, no. 286. Catalogue of sale, December 2011 (Salle Drouot). Paris: Piasa.

Pichois, Claude. *Colette*. Paris: Fallois, 1998.

    See also under Colette.

Poulenc, Francis. *Moi et mes amis*. Paris and Geneva: La Palatine, 1963.

de Pourtalès, Guy. 'Petit hommage à Ravel'. *La Revue musicale* 19/187 ('Hommage à Maurice Ravel', December 1938), 34–5.

Priest, Deborah. *Louis Laloy (1874–1944) on Debussy, Ravel and Stravinsky*. Aldershot: Ashgate, 1999.

Prost, Christine. '*L'Enfant et les sortilèges*: l'infidélité aux modèles'. *Analyse musicale* 26/6 (February 1992), 59–63.

'Maurice Ravel: *L'Enfant et les sortilèges*, "Cacher l'art pour l'art meme"'. *Analyse musicale* 21 (November 1990), 65–81.

Prunières, Henry. 'Trois silhouettes de musiciens: César Franck, Saint-Saëns, Maurice Ravel'. *La Revue musicale* 7/11 (October 1926), 225–40.

Puri, Michael. *Ravel the Decadent: Memory, Sublimation and Desire*. New York: Oxford University Press, 2012.

Ravel, Maurice. *Édition (la plus complète possible) des correspondances, articles et entretiens de Maurice Ravel*, ed. Manuel Cornejo. Paris: Le Passeur, in preparation for 2016.

Ravel, Maurice *et al*. 'Sous la musique que faut-il mettre?' *Musica* 101/102 (February/March 1911), 38–40 & 58–60.

Renard, Jules. *Journal: 1887–1910*, ed. Henry Bouillier. Paris: Laffont, 1990.

Reuillard, Gabriel. 'Franc-Nohain'. *Paris-Soir*, 29 December 1925.

Richardson, Joanna. *Colette*. London: Methuen, 1983.

Roberts, W. Wright. 'Child Studies in Music'. *Music & Letters* 9/1–2 (January & April 1928), 9–17 & 152–60.

Rodriguez, Philippe. '*L'Heure espagnole*: chronologie critique des sources autour des "auditions privées" entre 1907 et 1911'. *CMR* 15 (2012), 7–25.

'Mme Jean Cruppi: un prénom, un visage, une vie'. *CMR* 13 (2010), 126–48.

[Roland-Manuel]. *Archives Roland-Manuel*. Catalogue of sale, 24 March 2000. Paris: Thierry Bodin.

Roland-Manuel [Roland Alexis Manuel Lévy]. 'Des Valses à *La Valse* (1911–1921)'. In Émile Vuillermoz, Hélène Jourdan-Morhange, Roland-Manuel *et al.*, *Maurice Ravel par quelques-uns de ses familiers*, 141–52.

Maurice Ravel et son œuvre dramatique. Paris: Les Editions Musicales de la Librairie de France, 1928.

Ravel. Paris: Nouvelle Revue Critique, 1938. English edition, trans. Cynthia Jolly: *Maurice Ravel*. London: Dobson, 1947.

Rousseaux, André. 'Un quart d'heure avec M. Franc-Nohain'. *Comoedia*, 23 May 1924.

Roy, Jean (ed.). *Maurice Ravel: Lettres à Roland-Manuel et à sa famille*. Quimper: Calligrammes, 1986.

'Soixante-deux lettres de Maurice Ravel à Hélène et Alfredo Casella'. *CMR* 1 (1985), 59–111.

'Vingt-cinq lettres de Maurice Ravel à Maurice et Nelly Delage'. *CMR* 2 (1986), 13–40.

Russell, John. 'David Hockney's designs for Met Opera's *Parade*'. *New York Times*, 20 February 1981.

Saint-André, Pascale. 'Commentaire musical et littéraire [de *L'Enfant et les sortilèges*]'. *L'Avant-scène opéra* 127 (January 1990), 28–57.

Saint-Marceaux, Marguerite. *Journal, 1894–1927*, edited under the direction of Myriam Chimènes, preface by Michelle Perrot. Paris: Fayard, 2007.

Saint-Saëns, Camille. 'La Question de l'*E* muet, au double point de vue littéraire et musical'. *Le Figaro*, 19 August 1904.

Sanson, David. *Maurice Ravel*. Arles: Actes Sud, 2005.

Savage, Catherine H. 'Nostalgia in Alain-Fournier and Proust'. *French Review* 38/2 (1964), 167–72.

Schillmöller, Mathias. *Maurice Ravels Schlüsselwerk* L'Enfant et les sortilèges: *Eine ästhetisch-analytische Studie*. Frankfurt: Peter Lang, 1999.

Schwartz, Joseph. *Cassandra's Daughter: A History of Psychoanalysis in Europe and America*. London: Allen Lane, 1999.

Schwarz, Manuela. *Wagner-Rezeption und französische Oper des Fin de siècle*. Berlin: Technische Universität, 1999.

Sérieyx, Auguste. 'Salle Érard, Société Nationale' [*Histoires naturelles*]. *Le Courrier musical* 10/3 (1 February 1907), 77–8.

Shakespeare, William. *The Norton Shakespeare*, ed. Stephen Greenblatt, Walter Cohen, Jean E. Howard, Katharine Eisaman Maus, Gordon McMullan and Suzanne Gossett. London and New York: Norton, 1997.

Siegler, Robert, and Martha Alibali. *Children's Thinking*. Englewood Cliffs, NJ: Prentice Hall, 1986 (rev. 2005).

Souillard, Christine. 'Commentaire littéraire et musical [de *L'Heure espagnole*]'. *L'Avant-scène opéra* 127 (January 1990), 84–113.

Steedman, Caroline. *Strange Dislocations: Childhood and the Idea of Human Interiority, 1780–1930*. Cambridge, Mass.: Harvard University Press, 1995.

Stoullig, Edmond. *Les Annales du théâtre et de la musique* 37–39. Paris: Ollendorff, 1912–14.

Strauss, Richard, and Romain Rolland. *Richard Strauss et Romain Rolland: Correspondance, Fragments de journal*. Cahiers Romain Rolland 3. Paris: Albin Michel, 1950.

Suschitzky, Anya. '*Fervaal, Parsifal*, and French national identity'. *19th-Century Music* 25/2–3 (November 2001), 237–65.

Taruskin, Richard. *Musorgsky: Eight Essays and an Epilogue*. Princeton: Princeton University Press, 1993.

Thibaudet, Albert. 'Réflexions sur la littérature: psychanalyse et critique'. *Nouvelle Revue française* 91 (April 1921), 467–81.

Thurman, Judith. *Secrets of the Flesh: A Life of Colette*. New York: Knopf, 1999.

Tiersot, Julien. *Promenades musicales à l'Exposition*. Paris: Fischbacher, 1889.

Tisseur, Clair. *Modestes observations sur l'art de versifier*. Lyon: Bernoux et Cumin, 1893.

Tumanov, Alexander. *The Life and Artistry of Maria Olenina-d'Alheim*, trans. Christopher Barnes. Edmonton: University of Alberta Press, 2000.

Turkle, Sherry. *Psychoanalytic Politics: Freud's French Revolution*. New York: Basic Books, 1978.

Vuillermoz, Emile. 'L'Œuvre de Maurice Ravel'. In Émile Vuillermoz, Hélène Jourdan-Morhange, Roland-Manuel *et al.*, *Maurice Ravel par quelques-uns de ses familiers*, 1–96.

Vuillermoz, Émile, Hélène Jourdan-Morhange, Roland-Manuel *et al. Maurice Ravel par quelques-uns de ses familiers*. Paris: Tambourinaire, 1939.

Walrond-Skinner, Sue. *A Dictionary of Psychotherapy*. London and Boston: Routledge & Kegan Paul, 1986.

Wenk, Arthur. *Debussy and Twentieth-Century Music*. Boston: Twayne, 1983.

Wolff, Stéphane. *Un demi-siècle d'Opéra-Comique*. Paris: Bonne, 1953.

Wright, Lesley (ed.). *Dossier de presse: Carmen (1875)*. Heilbronn: Musik-Edition Lucie Galland, 2001.

Zachmann, Gayle. *Frameworks for Mallarmé: The Photo and the Graphic of an Interdisciplinary Aesthetic*. Albany: State University of New York Press, 2008.

Zank, Stephen. *Irony and Sound: The Music of Maurice Ravel*. Rochester: University of Rochester Press, 2009.

Maurice Ravel: A Guide to Research. New York: Routledge, 2005.

Index

Alain-Fournier, 198, 225
   Le grand Meaulnes, 217, 225
Alheim, Marie Olénine d', 94–5
Alheim, Pierre d', 94–5, 96
'Apaches, Les', 4, 170
Apollinaire, Guillaume, 76, 218n
Aragon, Louis, 76
Auberge du Clou, 238
Auric, Georges, 69

Bailly, Edmond, 237n
Bakst, Léon, 56
Balanchine, George, 45
Ballets russes, 9, 23, 45, 56, 58
   See also Diaghilev
Banville, Théodore de, 76, 90, 90n
Bathori, Jane, 18, 92, 93, 115
Baudelaire, Charles, 72, 75, 112, 199, 234,
     238, 241
   Morale du joujou, 199
Belhomme (bass), 24
Bellaigue, Camille, 27
Bellini, Vincenzo, 215
Bergson, Henri, 148n, 166, 231
Bériot, Charles de, 186
Berlioz, Hector, 29, 41
Bertrand, Aloysius, 75
Bizet, Georges, 145, 172, 174
   Carmen, xi, 3, 18, 23, 47, 172–5, 176, 179,
     189–90, 191n
     'L'amour est un oiseau rebelle'
      (Habanera), 186–8, 195
     'Chanson Bohème', 178
     See also L'Heure espagnole
   Jeux d'enfants, 198, 218
Boccaccio, 192
Boschot, Adolphe, 13, 60
Bruneau, Alfred, 118, 198n

Calvé, Emma, 189, 190
Calvocoressi, Michel-Dimitri, 4, 56, 58, 91,
     92n, 94, 95n
Cangiullo, Francesco, 9, 46

Caplet, André, 198
Carbonne, Ernest, 30, 31, 58
Carré, Albert, 8, 24, 25, 48, 59, 175
   and *L'Heure espagnole*, 16–23, 30–1
Casella, Hélène. *See* Kahn-Casella, Hélène
Cassatt, Mary, 198
Cazeneuve, Maurice, 23, 24, 26, 30
Chabrier, Emmanuel, 3, 28, 29n
   Une éducation manquée, 11
   Gwendoline, 47
   'Mélancolie', 242
   'Menuet pompeux', 46
   See also Ravel
Chadeigne, Marcel, 4
Chalupt, René, 22, 32n, 75
Charpentier, Gustave, 19
   Louise, 8, 12n, 19, 23
Chat noir, Le, 60, 195
childhood
   early 20th-century conceptions, 217,
     218–19, 231–2, 234
   late 19th-century conceptions, 197–9
   musical depictions, 198–9, 218
   operatic depictions, 215–16
Chopin, Fryderyk, 3, 5, 154n
   Étude op. 25 no. 1, 171
   'Marche funèbre' (Sonata op. 35), 163
Colette, Sidonie ('Sido'), 227–8
Colette, Sidonie-Gabrielle, 13, 36n, 48, 121,
     126n, 141–2, 197, 227–8, 241
   La Chambre éclairée, 228
   Claudine à Paris, 3n
   Dialogues de bêtes, 127
   L'Enfant et les sortilèges
     authorship (disputed), 126–8
     onomatopoeia and poetic affect, 130–6
     poetic structure, 121–3, 128–30, 136–8, 241
   L'Étoile vesper, 70
   L'Ingénue libertine, 140, 228
   Journal à rebours, 73
   La Maison de Claudine, 227–8
   Mes apprentissages, 141
   Œuvres complètes, 73

Colette, Sidonie-Gabrielle (cont.)
  La Paix chez les bêtes, 127–8
  'Un salon en 1900', 35–6, 65–6, 69–70, 71
  La Vagabonde, 39
commedia dell'arte, 185
Cornet, Charles (a.k.a. Tenroc), 21, 22, 51
Coulomb (ten.), 24, 26, 30
Courteault, Jane, 6, 17
Couzinou (bar.), 31
Cruppi, Jean, 18
Cruppi, Louise, 18, 19, 22
Cui, César, 94
Curzon, Henri de, 21

Danilova, Alexandra, 45
Debussy, Claude, 17, 19, 29, 31, 60, 75, 84, 89,
    92, 93, 96, 97, 145, 177
  Apparition, 237n
  'La Belle au bois dormant', 83n
  La Boîte à joujoux, 198
  Children's Corner, 198, 218
  'Clair de lune' (*Suite bergamasque*), 7
  Estampes, 83n
  Images (orch.), 83n
  Images (oubliées), 83n
  *Noël des enfants qui n'ont plus de
    maison*, 219
  Pelléas et Mélisande, 3, 5, 8, 10, 12n, 19, 22,
    23, 24, 27n, 84–6, 89, 90, 91, 93, 114,
    146, 168–71, 215n *See also L'Heure
    espagnole*
  Pour le piano, 5
  relations with Ravel. *See* Ravel
  Trois ballades de François Villon, 77
Delage, Maurice, 4, 170
Delvoye (bass), 23, 24, 26, 30
dépouillé (style), 49–50, 51
Dexter, John, 218, 220
Diaghilev, Sergei, 9, 45n, 56, 57, 58, 142
  and *L'Enfant et les sortilèges*, 45–7
  See also Ballets russes
Donval (ten.), 24
Doucet, Henri-Lucien, 189
Drésa, Jacques, 56
Droz, Alfred, 18, 19
Dubois (ten.), 31
Dukas, Paul, 17, 19, 36, 66, 77, 78
  L'Apprenti sorcier, 36
  Ariane et Barbe bleue, 8, 19
  La Péri, 36
Dumesnil, René, 81
Dumoutier (ten.), 30
Durand (publishing house), 4, 37, 44, 123

Durand, Hippolyte, 197
Durand, Jacques, 17, 20, 22, 44, 57, 63n

'*e muet*', 88–92, 114–17
Einstein, Albert, 166
Elsner, Joseph, 3
Éluard, Paul, 76
L'Enfant et les sortilèges.
  childhood (depictions of), 14, 198, 199,
    209–11, 216, 224–6, 233–4, 240
  composition, 9, 34–40, 42–4
  critical reception, 47–51, 63–4, 72, 198
  early titles, 11, 12, 35, 38, 39, 65, 67, 67n,
    228, 235
  episodes
    Animals' rising, 81, 123, 129, 136, 200–1
    Arithmetic scene, 39, 48, 81–2, 123, 127,
      128, 129, 130, 138, 200–1, 206,
      213, 220
    Bat's waltz, 127, 128, 132, 138, 207, 208,
      213, 227
    Cats' duet, 39, 48, 127, 138, 207, 208
    Child's monologue, 98, 129, 130, 132–4,
      137, 138, 201, 202, 211
    Child's rage, 136, 138, 202, 213, 233
    Clock, 128, 129, 130, 136, 138, 203,
      213–14, 220
    Cup and Teapot, 38, 39, 43, 123, 124–6,
      127, 130, 196, 203, 209–11
    'Danse des rainettes', 207, 208, 213, 219,
      221, 223
    Dragonfly's waltz, 127, 129, 131–3, 136,
      207, 208, 211, 212
    Fauteuil and Bergère, 121, 123, 129, 130,
      136, 202, 203, 213–15
    final chorus, 50, 137, 138, 139–41, 213
    Fire, 128, 130, 131–3, 136, 138, 203–4, 233
    Frog's dialogue, 126, 127, 128
    Garden scene, 131, 136, 138, 207–8, 211,
      212, 213, 221–2, 225, 233
    Maman's dialogue, 121, 132, 136, 137,
      139, 202
    Princess, 51, 83, 98, 121, 124, 130, 131,
      136, 138, 200, 204–6, 211, 213, 220,
      222, 227, 231, 232, 233
    Shepherds and Shepherdesses, 82–3, 123,
      129, 136, 201, 203, 204, 213, 220
    Squirrel, 38, 39, 98, 122–3, 127n, 128, 136,
      138, 200, 207–9, 211–13, 222, 224
    'Toi, le cœur de la rose', 44, 129, 130, 135,
      206, 220–1
    Trees, 136, 213–15
  fairytale elements, 122–3, 224, 226, 232, 240

falling fourths, 138, 227, 229
grotesque elements, 212–15
'Maman cadence', 138–9, 202, 213, 222, 227
Maman (character and meaning), 226–9
modifications to libretto, 123–7, 139–41
musical structure, 200–12, 216
nostalgia, 11, 217, 220–4
orchestration, 49–50, 132–6, 204, 212–15,
     216, 241
pastiche, 11, 200, 224, 240, 241
pentatonic gestures, 209–12, 216
press interviews, 14, 39, 40, 41, 44, 226, 239
production history, 217–18, 220, 224–5,
     230, 235
   Monte Carlo (1925), 44–7, 51
   Opéra-Comique (1926), 47–51, 200
   Brussels (1926), 47, 69
   Vienna (1929), 51, 137, 199, 225, 230
   Opéra Garnier (1939), 52, 217
psychoanalytical interpretations, 11, 124,
     229–33
socio-political interpretations, 219–20
text-setting, 97–8, 132–6
wartime elements, 218–20, 235
See also Colette; Diaghilev; Gunsbourg;
     Rouché
Engel, Émile, 18
espagnolade, xi, 8, 173–5, 177, 178, 184, 188,
     193, 194, 196, 240

Fabert, Henri, 22, 31
fairytale, ix, 11, 14, 61, 83, 122–3, 131, 137, 219,
     222, 229, 232, 241
Falla, Manuel de, 176, 177, 186
Fargue, Léon-Paul, 4, 76
Fauré, Gabriel, 17, 29, 65, 76, 77, 84n, 89, 145,
     175
   Dolly, 198, 218
   Pénélope, 3, 8, 41
   review of *L'Heure espagnole*, 26, 28–9
Fokine, Michel, 56–7, 58, 68
Franc-Nohain (Maurice Étienne Legrand), 12,
     13, 59–61, 195
   Le Chapeau chinois, 63n
   L'Heure espagnole
      as opera (engagement with), 23, 26, 58,
         60–3
      as play, 12–13, 55, 99, 166, 173, 183–5,
         193–4, 241
      poetic structure, 99–102, 107–14, 120,
         147, 182
   Jaboune, 13
   poetry, 60, 99, 241
Freud, Sigmund, 217, 231, 232

Galli-Marié, Célestine, 189, 190
Garban, Lucien, 9, 37, 40, 43, 44, 63n, 67
Garden, Mary, 93n
Gaubert, Philippe, 31
Gauley, Marie-Thérèse, 51
Gautier, Théophile, 76, 193
Gedalge, André, 9
Gerar, Marcelle, 42, 43
Gide, André, 60, 231
Gilles (bass), 30
Glyndebourne, 225
Godebska, Ida, 7, 10, 17, 18, 20, 23, 127
Godebska, Mimie, 234
Godebski, Cipa, 4, 19, 20, 22, 24
Gogol, Nicolai, 94, 96
Goudeket, Maurice, 69, 71, 72, 73, 74, 121n, 141
Gounod, Charles, 3, 116, 145, 189
   Faust, 3, 78, 118
Gourmont, Rémy de, 90
Goya, Francisco, 189, 190
Grammont, Maurice, 108, 111, 132
Grétry, Modeste, 89
Gunsbourg, Raoul, 33, 40–1, 47, 58
   and *L'Enfant et les sortilèges*, 40, 41–2,
      43–4

habanera, 186–7
Hahn, Reynaldo, 27, 77, 246
Harcourt, Raoul d', 95
Hasselmans, Louis, 22, 23, 24
Hauptmann, Gerhardt, 9, 10
Heldy, Fanny, 31
Hellé, André, 199
Hérold, Ferdinand, 9, 10
L'Heure espagnole
   'Adieu, cellule. . .', 22, 154, 179
   Carmen (relative to), 172, 178–9, 185–93,
      194–6
   'clock' motif, 148, 158, 159, 162–8
   composition, 6–8, 16
   Concepcion (characterisation), 112–14,
      185–92, 193, 194, 195
   Concepcion (musical material), 148, 157–9,
      169, 185–9
   critical reception, 21, 26–9, 31–2, 96–7,
      117–18, 195
   descending chromatic motif, 151–56, 159,
      160, 163, 167, 170
   'Enfin revient le jour si doux', 117, 179, 181,
      182, 183, 184
   falling fourths, 158–62, 165–6, 169
   final quintet, 59, 93, 107, 160, 170, 177, 178,
      185, 187
   Gonzalve (characterisation), 112, 180–5, 193

L'Heure espagnole (cont.)
  Gonzalve (musical material), 148, 151–4,
    156, 160, 178, 179–80, 181, 184
  habanera rhythms, 106, 149, 160, 177, 178,
    185–8
  Inigo (characterisation), 108–9
  Inigo (musical material), 109, 151–52, 156
  Introduction, 148, 151, 158, 163, 165, 165n,
    167, 178
  jota rhythms, 159, 177, 193
  modifications to libretto, 103–7, 183
  motivic structure, 146, 147–62, 168–71
  'O, la pitoyable aventure', 168, 180, 189
  operatic parody, 146, 171, 178, 180–1
  orchestration, 22, 169–70, 178, 181
  Pelléas et Mélisande (relative to), 97, 146,
    168–71
  press interviews, 62, 94, 103, 107, 110, 118,
    147, 194, 195, 239
  production history
    Opéra-Comique (1911), 23–31
      casting, 23–4
      costume designs, 189–92, 195
      rehearsal period, 23–6
      staging, 62–3, 173, 181–3, 189–91,
        194–6
    Brussels (1921), 31, 40, 195
    Opéra Garnier (1921), 26, 31–3, 40, 62,
      242
    Monte Carlo (1924), 33, 40, 40n, 41
  Ramiro (characterisation), 110–12, 164,
    192–3, 194
  Ramiro (musical material), 110, 111–12, 148,
    149, 156–60, 165–6, 169, 177, 186n
  self-parody, 179–80, 181
  text-setting, 92, 93, 96–7, 102–3, 107–19, 229
  Torquemada (characterisation), 107–8
  Torquemada (musical material), 148
  'Tristan' chords, 155–7, 170
  Wagner (relative to), 146, 168–71
  See also Carré; Franc-Nohain
Hockney, David, 218, 224, 225
Hoérée, Arthur, 98, 118
Honegger, Arthur, 47
Huberty, Albert, 31
Hugard, Jane, 58
Hugo, Victor, 76, 77, 198, 234

Inghelbrecht, Désiré-Émile, 22, 198
Isola, Émile and Vincent, 48

Jankélévitch, Vladimir, 119, 199
Jaques-Dalcroze, Émile, 12

Jarry, Alfred, 60
Jean-Aubry, Georges, 4, 6, 16
Jourdan-Morhange, Hélène, 43, 69, 70–2,
    73, 81
Jouvenel, Colette de, 40, 48, 67, 68, 228
Jouvenel, Henry de, 34, 126n
Jung, Carl, xii, 231, 232–3

Kahn-Casella, Hélène, 8, 43
Klein, Melanie, xii, 230–1, 232
Klingsor, Tristan (Léon Leclère), 4, 76, 84
Koechlin, Charles, 43

La Fontaine, Jean de, 61, 192
Lacroix, Eugène, 237n
Ladmirault, Paul, 4
Lalo, Pierre, 6, 7, 8, 10, 32, 98
  criticism of Ravel, 5–6, 21, 27, 32, 97
Laloy, Louis, 4, 26, 28, 32, 62, 84, 89n, 96, 100,
    108, 168n
Landormy, Paul, 49, 50
Laparra, Raoul, 26, 174–5, 181n, 195
  La Habanera, 174, 175, 195
  La Jota, 16, 25, 26, 174, 194, 195
Laure (bar.), 30n
Lavelli, Jorge, 220, 229, 230
Leconte de Lisle, Charles Marie René, 76, 79, 90
Lemaître, Jules, 90
Léon, René, 45, 46
Liszt, Franz, 5
Louÿs, Pierre, 60
Luquiens, Hélène, 5

Malibran, Maria, 186
Mallarmé, Stéphane, 76, 112, 130, 139, 181n,
    236–9, 242
  'Sainte', 79, 236–9, 241, 242
  See also Ravel
Manet, Édouard, 242
Maré, Rolf de, 58
Markova, Alicia, 45
Marnold, Georgette, 39
Marnold, Jean, 4, 17, 20, 21, 27, 28, 50
Martyl, Nelly, 30
Massé, Victor, 90
Massenet, Jules, 3, 12n, 26, 41, 77, 145, 198n,
    200, 220, 224
  Manon, 3, 18, 24, 60n, 220–1
  Thaïs, 47
  Thérèse, 16, 25, 26, 41
Masson, Fernand, 23, 25
Masson, Louis, 48
Matisse, Henri, 218, 235

Merentié, Marguerite, 189, 190
Messager, André, 50, 65
Metropolitan Opera House (New York), 21,
    218, 220, 225, 235
Molière (Jean-Baptiste Poquelin), 101, 194
Morisot, Berthe, 198
music hall, 195, 235
Musorgsky, Modest, 93–7, 199
    Boris Godunov, 93, 94, 215n
    Khovanshchina, 45
    The Marriage, 94–6, 97
    The Nursery, 93, 96, 198n

Nerval, Gérard de, 198
Nijinsky, Vaslav, 56
Nohain, Jean, 60, 61, 63
'Nous n'irons plus au bois', 82–3

Offenbach, Jacques, 19
Olénine, Marie. *See* Alheim
Opéra-Comique de Paris, 3, 7, 8, 13, 16–17, 21,
    22, 30, 44, 48, 51, 58, 62–3, 95n, 146,
    171, 172, 174, 177, 179n, 180,
    189–92, 194, 195, 196, 225
    registres (*livres de bord*), 23, 24–6, 61
Opéra de Monte-Carlo, 40, 41, 44, 45
Opéra Garnier (Académie nationale de
    musique), 8, 16, 33, 35, 37n, 44,
    146, 220

Pasquier (ten.), 30
Périer, Jean, 23, 24, 26, 30, 93, 110,
    171, 195
Piaget, Jean, 209–11
Poe, Edgar Allan, 72, 75, 238
Polignac, Prince Edmond de, 65
Pons, Charles
    Le Voile du bonheur, 16, 24, 25
Poulenc, Francis, 69, 198n
    Les Mamelles de Tirésias, 218, 220
Proust, Marcel, 198, 217, 234
Prunières, Henry, 29, 42, 47, 48, 50–1, 61, 127n
Psichari, Jean, 90
psychoanalysis, 231–2
Puccini, Giacomo, 23, 200, 215
    La bohème, 24, 30

Ravel, Édouard, 4, 228
Ravel, Marie (Delouart), 8, 37, 176, 186, 228–9
Ravel, Maurice
    Chabrier (opinion of), 12
    Colette (relations with), 35, 37–40, 42, 43,
        44, 55, 59, 63–70, 72, 73–4, 127

composition (thoughts on), 72, 73, 171, 235,
    240–1, 242
compositional aesthetic, 238–42
death, 52
Debussy (relations with), 5–6
Franc-Nohain (relations with), 55, 59–62, 63
Mallarmé (opinion of), 76
other works
    Adélaïde (*Valses nobles et sentimentales*),
        37n, 56, 59, 63
    Alborada del gracioso (orch.), 46
    Ballade de la Reine morte d'aimer, 79,
        84, 236
    Une barque sur l'océan (orch.), 5
    Berceuse sur le nom de Fauré, 198
    Boléro, 176
    Chanson du rouet, 76n, 79
    'Chanson espagnole', 175, 176
    Chansons madécasses, 77, 98
    Concerto for the Left Hand, 176
    Concerto in G, 165, 176, 201n, 229
    Daphnis et Chloé, 4, 23, 31, 45, 56–7, 58,
        66, 68, 165, 171, 229, 240
    Deux épigrammes de Clément Marot,
        79–80, 236n
    Don Quichotte à Dulcinée, 176
    Gaspard de la nuit, 4, 10, 22, 171, 241
        'Scarbo', 154n
    Un grand sommeil noir, 76n, 80, 236
    Les grands vents venus d'outremer, 5, 7, 86
    Histoires naturelles, 4, 5, 18, 28, 75, 77, 78,
        81, 86–9, 91–2, 93, 96, 97, 114, 115,
        116, 117, 119–20, 229
    Introduction et Allegro, 4, 5
    Jeux d'eau, 5
    Ma mère l'Oye (duet), 14, 39, 51n, 165,
        198, 218, 221–2, 229, 240, 241
        'Petit Poucet', 222, 223
        'Les Entretiens de la Belle et de la Bête',
            154n, 221, 222, 223
        'Le Jardin féerique', 222
    Ma mère l'Oye (ballet), 56, 58, 59, 68,
        221, 222
    Manteau de fleurs, 79
    Miroirs, 4, 5, 95n, 240
        'Noctuelles', 229
        'Alborada del gracioso', 154n, 176, 179,
            180, 181
        'La Vallée des cloches', 229
    Noël des jouets, 14, 77, 81, 198, 222
    Pavane pour une Infante défunte, 176
    Piano Trio, 177, 201n, 241
    Prix de Rome cantatas, 3, 4, 145

Ravel, Maurice (cont.)
  Rapsodie espagnole, 4, 8, 176, 177, 186
    'Malagueña', 180
    'Habanera', 154n, 176, 188
    'Feria', 179–80
  Sainte, 5, 79, 236–9, 242
  Sérénade grotesque, 176
  Shéhérazade (songs), 4, 75, 77, 84–6
  Si morne!, 80
  Sites auriculaires, 154n, 176, 188
  Sonata for Violin and Cello, 9, 40, 50
  Sonatine, 4, 229
  Sur l'herbe, 7, 76, 86, 93
  Le Tombeau de Couperin, 9, 58, 165, 241
  Trois chansons pour chœur mixte sans accompagnement, 14, 75, 77, 81–3, 127, 219
  Trois poèmes de Stéphane Mallarmé, 76, 97, 242
  Tzigane, 9
  La Valse, 9, 40, 46, 142, 219, 221
  Valses nobles et sentimentales, 171, 219n, 221, 241
  Violin Sonata, 201n
  Vocalise-Étude en forme de Habanera, 7, 154n, 176
  songs
    alliteration and onomatopoeia, 79–82
    choices of text, 75–8, 79
    poetic rhythm, 87–8
    text-setting, 84–8, 97–8, 115
    to his own texts, 77, 81–3
    See also 'e muet'
  Spain (heritage and musical inspiration), 14, 175–7, 180
  unrealised projects
    'Le ciel est, par-dessus le toit', 236
    La Cloche engloutie, 9–11, 75, 85, 86, 127n
    Le grand Meaulnes, 217n
    Jeanne d'Arc, 11
    Morgiane, 11
    Zazpiak Bat, 177
  Wagner (opinion of), 145, 146
  war service, 34, 37
  writings, 76
    'Esquisse autobiographique', 12, 51n, 84, 87, 122, 239, 240, 242
    'Mes souvenirs d'enfant paresseux', 29n, 240, 242
    'Sur la musique que faut-il mettre?', 77, 78, 87
Ravel, Pierre-Joseph, 6–7, 8, 10
Régnier, Henri de, 76

Renard, Jules, 57, 78, 80, 87, 88, 89, 242
  Histoires naturelles, 78, 87–8
Richter, Jean-Paul, 234
Ricou, Georges, 48
Rimsky-Korsakov, Nicolai, 95, 171
Roland-Manuel (Roland Alexis Manuel Lévy), 10, 21n, 29n, 40, 43, 48, 49n, 50, 51, 59, 65, 68, 73, 76
Rolland, Romain, 4, 6, 89, 90
Ronsard, Pierre de, 101
Rosenthal, Manuel, 52, 126, 181, 193, 218, 219n
Rostand, Edmond, 101
Rouché, Jacques, 8, 11, 26, 31, 32–3, 34–5, 37n, 55, 56, 57, 58, 66, 68, 123
  and *L'Enfant et les sortilèges*, 34–8, 41–2, 52
  See also Théâtre des Arts
Rousseau, Jean-Jacques, 234
Ruhlmann, François, 24, 26

Sabata, Victor de, 44
Saint-Exupéry, Antoine de, 225
Saint-Marceaux, Marguerite de, 20, 56, 65
Saint-Saëns, Camille, 41, 91
  Samson et Dalila, 47, 91
Satie, Erik, 198n
  Parade, 218, 220
Schmitt, Florent, 4
Schubert, Franz, 171
Schumann, Robert, 5, 154n, 234
  Kinderszenen, 198
Sendak, Maurice, 225
Sérieyx, Auguste, 89, 98, 146
Sert, Misia, 57
Séverac, Déodat de, 4, 198n
  Le Cœur du moulin, 17, 20
Shakespeare, William, 184, 226, 240
Silvestre, Armand, 76
'Six, Les', 31, 49
Société musicale indépendante, 22, 23
Société nationale de musique, 88, 89, 98
Sordes, Paul, 4
Steinhof, Eugène, 225
Strauss, Richard, 89, 90, 114
  Feuersnot, 20
  Die Frau ohne Schatten, 216
  Salomé, 89
Stravinsky, Igor, 36, 45, 66, 127, 162, 229
  L'Oiseau de feu, 23
  Le Rossignol, 36
Sullivan, Arthur, and W. S. Gilbert, 184
Symbolism, 8, 10, 76, 183, 184, 185
Szántó, Theodor, 10, 42

Tenroc, Charles. *See* Cornet, Charles
Terrasse, Claude, 12, 60
   Les Transatlantiques, 61
Terrasse, Michel, 225
Théâtre de l'Odéon, 13, 103
Théâtre des Arts, 30n, 34, 56
Théâtre du Châtelet, 56
Tirmont, Edmond, 23, 24
Trouhanova, Natalia, 56
Turina, Joaquín, 176

Valéry, Paul, 76
Valois, Ninette de, 45
Verdi, Giuseppe, 215
Verlaine, Paul, 76, 77, 80, 83, 99, 236
Viardot, Pauline, 186
Villiers de l'Isle Adam, Auguste, 76
Viñes, Ricardo, 4, 17, 75, 170, 176, 238, 239

Vix, Geneviève, 23, 24, 26, 30, 172, 189,
   190, 194
Voltaire, 89
Vuillermoz, Émile, 3, 4, 89, 111, 117–18,
   217, 229

Wagner, Richard, 10, 65, 145–6, 155, 168–71,
   239, 242
   Lettre sur la musique, 239n, 242
   Ring cycle, 41
   Tristan und Isolde, 145, 170, 239
   See also L'Heure espagnole
Weber, Carl Maria von
   Der Freischütz, 9
Wolff, Albert, 51
World War I, ix, 8, 34, 122, 218–19, 231

Zogheb, Jacques de, 69, 71